WHEN YOUR NUMBER'S UP

WHEN YOUR NUMBER'S UP

DESMOND MORTON

THE CANADIAN SOLDIER IN THE FIRST WORLD WAR

RANDOM HOUSE OF CANADA

Copyright © 1993 by Desmond Morton

All rights reserved under International and Pan-American
Copyright Conventions.
Published in Canada in 1993 by Random House of Canada Ltd., Toronto

Canadian Cataloguing in Publication Data

Morton, Desmond, 1937 –
When your number's up : the canadian soldier in the First World War

ISBN 0-394-22288-1

1. World War, 1914–1918 – Canada.   2. Soldiers – Canada – History.
I. Title.

D547.C2M67 1993   940.53'71   c93-094014-8

Printed and bound in the United States of America.

10 9 8 7 6 5 4 3 2 1

CONTENTS

INTRODUCTION

Wars are made by masses of people—mothers bear infants; voters vote; workers labour to feed, clothe, and arm populations; armies move across landscapes. And masses are made up of individuals, with their own motives and experiences, joys, terrors, and tragedies. I have written about masses; I have always wanted to write about the people I got to know on the way.

Between 1914 and 1918, Canadians helped create one of the best little armies in the world. Its skill and spirit helped end a terrible war a year early. Some years ago, Jack Granatstein and I wrote about that army in *Marching to Armageddon*. Now I am writing about the individuals who formed that army, and the factors that shaped their lives and hastened their deaths. Why did they join? What did they learn that transformed them into soldiers? Who were their officers? How did they fight, and how, in the end, did they overcome? What happened to them when they were wounded or captured or killed? What helped them to endure their revolting and terrifying ordeal? And what became of those who came home when the war was over?

Often we accept a static image of the First World War. Canadians know about poison gas at Ypres and the conscription crisis of 1917. Observing Remembrance Day has lodged in the mind the poppy and the washbasin-style steel helmet. The slaughter on the Somme and in the mud of Passchendaele sums up all that needs to be remembered about bloody-minded generals and their suffering subordinates. Soldiers themselves contributed to the unchanging image because, for so many, a year was their life span at the front. Only a small minority of the "Old Originals" at Ypres survived to see the Canadian Corps's first real victory at Vimy Ridge in 1917 and their perspective was transformed by brutal experience and promotion. Wilfred Kerr, a gunner and future historian, noted how the British accents of the Canadian Expeditionary Force's non-commissioned officers in 1916 were slowly supplanted by flat Canadian tones in 1917. In turn, the battles of 1917 brought a new generation to the Corps in 1918. Men remembered the war as they had experienced it, unaware that each year's war was different.

The fifty months from August 1914 to November 1918 witnessed a remarkable transformation in almost everything that affected the soldiers. Few of the men who served for weeks in the shallow, flooded ditches at Ypres in 1915, with their battered parapets and partially buried bodies, lived to see the complex trench systems of 1917 where men slept in dugouts and were relieved after only a few days' service. The tools of war changed too. In 1915, shells were rationed, gunners being issued three or four a day; a year later, huge stacks of shells were available, but many—British and Canadian made—were duds. In 1916, Canadians were given replacements for their Ross rifles and Colt machine-guns and acquired their shrapnel helmets. In 1917, gunners finally had shells that exploded on impact, blasting the tangles of barbed wire that had trapped the infantry and channelled them to their death. Now, as soldiers sweated at their tasks, the enemy dosed them with mustard gas, giving them the choice of burning, suffocating in respirators and heavy clothing, or quitting. In 1918, Canadians finally worked with tanks and even a few wireless sets.

Tactics changed as well—the crude formations of semi-trained battalions in 1915 gave way to the sophisticated teamwork of fire and movement that troops practised in the winter of 1917. Between the grand strategies of politicians and generals and the intense experiences of front-line soldiers was the reflective wisdom of staff officers. They lived in enviable comfort, but most were chosen from the best and brightest of fighting soldiers, and from them would come the solution to the problem of trench warfare: how attackers could get through the thickening band of barbed wire, trenches, and trackless mire to the green fields beyond before an

enemy could gather the forces to destroy them. Silly answers prolif-
erated; really good answers were beyond the technologies of 1918.
No one could make war painless or victory easy. Still, 1918 did not
end as 1916 had: infantrymen fought beyond the range of the guns
and far past the point where the last tank had wallowed to a halt.
The Great War became a gunner's war—60 per cent of casualties
were from artillery or mortar shells—but it was a war only the
infantry could win. Ultimately they did so, with tactics that fitted
Canadians like their well-worn tunics.

This book has been on my mind for thirty years. It began in 1963
when the old Historical Section in Army Headquarters invited me
to find out why, in 1916, three Canadian generals each believed
himself to be in command of all Canadians in England. My fasci-
nation with the Canadian experience of war has continued almost
unabated. It revived in 1972 when I discovered why twenty-five
Canadians died in front of firing squads and why a sad battalion
ensured that there would never be more than one French-Canadian unit in the Canadian Corps. Curiosity about Canada's early
welfare state, shared with Glenn Wright, then of the National
Archives of Canada, led us to its first beneficiaries, the veterans of
the First World War. An able graduate student with a technological
bent, Bill Rawling, persuaded me that tactics had been more
important than technology in winning the war, and led me firmly
back to the trenches. This book often reflects our dialogue.

Diaries, letters, and memoirs tell us much about the war. They
often leave out what participants took for granted—the smell of
wet serge, the obscenity of shattered bodies—or what they never
knew—the rationale for futile hours of instruction in "bayonet
fighting" or why Aubrey Griffiths's platoon carried four different
types of weapons. I wanted answers to questions that had always
troubled me. Old and new ideas fought in my head, and the turmoil may sometimes be visible in these pages. At times I changed
my mind, rejecting what I once believed about Canadians and the
war. Evidence has a way of dissolving theories.

This book, like any other, is the result of partnership—with

Jack Granatstein, co-author of *Marching to Armageddon* and *Forged in Fire* (our book on the Second World War); with Alec Douglas and his colleagues in the Directorate of History; and, above all, with the incomparable Barbara Wilson of the National Archives of Canada—no one knows more about the public and private history of the CEF; no one could be more generous in sharing her knowledge with or more patient in enlarging the research of others. A vast array of partners—some still alive, most now dead—did their utmost to let me know what their war was like. Two of them—William B. Woods of Ridgeway, Ontario, late of the 1st Battalion, and R.E. Henley of Sidney, B.C., a veteran of the 42nd Battalion—have been constant companions and inspirations during the many years of work on this book. I hope they feel that their patient instruction had some effect. Finally, no one did more to give me access to veterans of the Great War than Bill MacNeil, a good friend of so many Canadians.

By their hospitality, Sandra and Glenn Wright have allowed me the leisurely enjoyment of the resources of an archives they both serve with spirit and dedication. Roderick Suddaby kindly gave me access to the rich collection of CEF material in the Imperial War Museum in London, and the late and lamented Social Science and Humanities Research Council gave me the means to complete many years of research and to bring the book to publication. Other patient friends struggled to improve the manuscript. Cheryl Smith checked notes and references with inspired ingenuity. Susan Glover, a brilliant writer, sustained my sense of wonder at the redoubtable forebears who created the CEF. Her inspiration gave fresh meaning to this book and my life. Only my editor and I know how much better this book is for her care, and she won't tell.

None of them, of course, can overcome that "invincible ignorance" which the Book of Common Prayer discovered and which this author possesses in abundance. Survivors who remember how little staff officers knew of battles a few miles away will perhaps sympathize with the errors of a book written two or three lifetimes from the event.

Mississauga, 5 August 1992

LIST OF ABBREVIATIONS

ADS	advanced dressing station
AIF	Australian Imperial Force
ANV	Army and Navy Veterans
ANZAC	Australian and New Zealand Army Corps
ASC	Army Service Corps
BEF	British Expeditionary Force
BESL	British Empire Service League
BPC	Board of Pension Commissioners
CADC	Canadian Army Dental Corps
CAMC	Canadian Army Medical Corps
CASC	Canadian Army Service Corps
CB	counter-bombardment
CCB	Canadian Cavalry Brigade
CCF	Co-operative Commonwealth Federation
CCS	casualty clearing station
CEF	Canadian Expeditionary Force
CFA	Canadian Field Artillery
CMR	Canadian Mounted Rifles
CO	commanding officer
CPF	Canadian Patriotic Fund
CQMS	company quartermaster sergeant
CWRO	Canadian War Record Office
DAV	Disabled American Veterans
DCM	Distinguished Conduct Medal

DCM	District Court Martial
DSCR	Department of Soldiers' Civil Re-establishment
DSO	Distinguished Service Order
F.P.	Field Punishment No. 1
FGCM	Field General Court Martial
FOO	forward observation officer
GAR	Grand Army of the Republic
GAUV	Grand Army of United Veterans
GHQ	general headquarters
GP	general practitioner
GWVA	Great War Veterans' Association
IODE	Imperial Order Daughters of the Empire
IWM	Imperial War Museum
K in A	killed in action
LOB	left out of battle
M&V	Machonochie's Meat and Vegetable
MC	Military Cross
MD	Military District
MHC	Military Hospitals Commission
MLA	member of the Legislative Assembly
MO	medical officer
MP	member of Parliament
MSA	Military Service Act
NAC	National Archives of Canada
NCO	non-commissioned officer
NWMP	North-West Mounted Police
NYD(N)	not yet diagnosed (nervous)
OIC	Officer-in-Command
OMFC	Overseas Military Forces of Canada
OTC	Officer Training Corps
PF	Permanent Force
PPCLI	Princess Patricia's Canadian Light Infantry

PT	physical training
PUO	pyrexia of unknown origin
QAIMNS	Queen Alexandria's Imperial Military Nursing Service
RAMC	Royal Army Medical Corps
RAP	regimental aid post
RSM	regimental sergeant-major
SBR	special box respirator
SIW	self-inflicted wound
TB	tuberculosis
VAD	Voluntary Aid Detachment
VC	Victoria Cross
VD	venereal disease
YMCA	Young Men's Christian Association

CHAPTER ONE

BUSINESS AS USUAL

GOING TO WAR

Not for a century had Europe gone to war as it did in 1914. And never had Canadians even remotely shared such an experience. Still, memories matter more than the imagination in human affairs. In Britain, the slogan "Business as usual" sought to allay panic and restore a shaken sense of proportion. In Canada, it also helped to guide leaders and private citizens through the unexpected.

ACROSS CANADA, August 1914 began hot. Many towns celebrated a midsummer civic holiday, but, despite the heat, a strange excitement kept people from the beaches and parks. Militia sweating in new drab serge uniforms stood guard self-consciously at bridges and railway stations. Newspaper offices held crowds entranced by issuing huge bulletins about events taking place thousands of miles away. By nightfall on Sunday, August 2, it seemed possible that the European war would involve Britain. In Halifax, Quebec City, Victoria, and cities in between, crowds burst into cheers and raucous renderings of "God Save the King." On Monday, August 3, people returned for more news of armies marching, fleets sailing. Finally, on Tuesday, August 4, at 8:55 p.m. Ottawa time, Whitehall's ultimatum to Berlin expired. Great Britain was at war. So was Canada.[1]

It had happened with an awful suddenness. Only days earlier, war had seemed unthinkable. The Canadian Defence League, formed in 1910 to promote universal military training, had expired in March. In a year when Canadians were celebrating one hundred years of peace with the United States, militarism had seemed not so much wrong as irrelevant. Indeed, in the winter and spring of 1914, most Canadians were too preoccupied with the disastrous depression that followed the railway construction boom of the 1900s and with a widespread prairie crop failure to theorize about peace or war. Once a centre of military enthusiasm, the University of Toronto announced that it had no plans to imitate Laval and McGill by creating an officers' training corps. Maurice Hutton, the principal of University College and at one time a militarist, explained that students would be too busy for such activities.[2]

Now, because a Habsburg archduke and his wife had fallen victim to a Serb terrorist in Sarajevo, the European alliances had clicked into place. Because the Austro-Hungarian Empire would avenge itself on tiny Serbia, the Russian Empire mobilized its forces. Germany's Kaiser Wilhelm II prepared to back his Habsburg ally, but his General Staff knew that it must first knock out Russia's ally, France. According to a pre-war plan, most German armies moved west, sweeping across Belgium to envelop the French forces. Despite an increasingly bitter naval rivalry with Germany, the British government hesitated. Allied to France by no more than a vague "entente," Britain could remain neutral. The invasion of Belgium was another matter.

From June 28, when Franz Ferdinand was murdered at Sarajevo, Canadians followed the development of the annual Balkan crisis in their newspapers. Not until the end of July could anyone have imagined that Canadians would be affected. "Business as usual during alterations to the map of Europe" was the sign William Woods's employer put in the window of his Brantford bookshop. He removed it hurriedly after the Canadians became involved.[3]

War, for most Canadians, was a remote, romantic adventure. Even a vociferous peace movement, strong among the Protestant churches, knew war only as an abstract evil.[4] Others saw it as the test of manhood and valour a few thousand Canadians had experienced in South Africa more than a decade earlier. But, in August 1914, few thought Canadians would see much action: military and civilian experts almost unanimously agreed that modern wars would last no more than a few months. Without a quick victory, the thinking went, complex economies would collapse and nations would be compelled to make peace. At midnight on August 4, the British ultimatum to Berlin expired. The British Empire was at war.[5]

Among those most delighted with the news was a former athlete, editor, railway promoter, and member of Parliament from Lindsay, Ontario. Colonel Sam Hughes had won glory enough in South Africa fourteen years earlier to deserve (in his own mind, at least) a Victoria Cross. Now age sixty-one, Hughes, who had become Minister of Militia in Sir Robert Borden's Conservative government in 1911, again lusted for battle. In the days before the outbreak, his fear that the British would "skunk it" put him into a rage and he ordered the Union Jack hauled down from its post atop Militia Headquarters.[6] Fortunately, Great Britain did its duty by Sam Hughes. As crowds sang, chanted, and cheered the coming of war, the minister was busy making plans. He had an army to create.

The skeleton of a Canadian army existed already. Unlike its neighbouring dominion, Newfoundland, which had nothing more military than the Boys' Brigade, an Anglican youth organization, Canada maintained 77,000 peacetime militia and had a long military tradition. Outsiders scoffed at the pretensions of the Canadian Militia, and the Duke of Connaught, Canada's governor general, dismissed it as the worst military organization in the Empire. Sam Hughes disagreed. He thought it was easily the finest, and he was not alone.[7] During the Fenian Raids forty-five years earlier, he had joined his county battalion and, during his career as schoolteacher and publisher, he had risen to command the 45th Victoria County Regiment. An expert marksman, he had gloried in what was then a popular sport. He had revelled in the summer camps, the sham battles, and the church parades; he had led the cheers for the red-coated volunteers, resplendent in the new white helmets purchased by the county council; he had raged at the condescending criticisms from the few "regulahs."

As defence minister since 1911, Sam Hughes had publicly scolded the full-time staff officers and the 3,000 members of the Permanent Force.[8] Henceforth, he insisted, they would be humble servants of Canada's real defenders, the Volunteers. Hughes did more. In a few years as minister, he doubled militia spending, expanded the force in western Canada, made boots available to militiamen at a subsidized rate, and met other long-standing demands from colonels and privates alike.

In only one respect was Hughes at odds with his easygoing, bibulous fellow officers: he was a strict teetotaller. Over a babble of dissent from fellow colonels, he insisted that militia camps would henceforth be dry.[9] When regular officers defended their messes, the press overheard Hughes call them "bar-room loafers."

The minister was not embarrassed: he never was. Like members of the defunct Canadian Defence League, Hughes was an unashamed militarist. It ran in the family. His brother James, superintendent of Toronto's schools, had required every boy in the school system to drill and to salute his betters. As an early feminist, he would gladly have extended the training to girls.[10] Sam's Liberal predecessor, Sir Fred Borden, spread the cadet movement across Canada. But if mothers were to allow their sons to go to camp or even to the local armouries, someone had to dry out the militia and their notorious summer camps. Hughes did it. By 1914, 44,680 youngsters had drilled with the various cadet corps. So had 60,000 of the 74,000 men borne on the rolls of militia units ranging from 28 cavalry regiments and 99 infantry regiments to 35 batteries of field artillery and 5 companies of engineers.[11] At camp, militiamen sang a song about Hughes to the tune of "John Peel":

> D'ye ken Sam Hughes, he's the foe of booze;
> He's the real champeen of the dry canteen;
> For the camp is dead, and we're sent to bed,
> So we won't have a head in the morning.

Hughes's convictions mattered, not just because he had a domineering personality but because Canadian ministers of the day were all-powerful in their departments. In 1874, Ottawa had been so eager to preserve the British commitment to defend Canada that the Militia Act was amended to ensure that a British officer would still command the militia. These good intentions were superseded by a higher principle—the supremacy of civil over military authority—and subverted by an irrepressible habit of using the militia for political patronage. In battles with the militia commander, ministers could rely on a solid Canadian distaste for British interference. From 1874 to 1904, a series of disputes showed that the minister would prevail over the general, however sordid or petty the issue. After reforms in 1904 created a militia council and replaced the position of General Officer Commanding with that of Chief of the General Staff, British officers continued to hold the top posts in the militia. The Minister of Militia continued to give the orders.[12]

Canada's militia had a stout national pride. Some officers believed that they would have done better in the 1885 Northwest Rebellion without a British officer, Major-General Fred Middleton, to lead them.[13] The South African War convinced many of them, including Hughes, that Canadians made better soldiers than did the British.[14] In fact, Canadian self-confidence was anchored in a lack of experience and of contact with serious armies—a weakness shared with the British army itself.

In many communities across Canada, a militia commission demonstrated social respectability, not military knowledge. A few militia officers devoted time and energy to studying their avocation; others were better at politics than soldiering. Many had earned their commissions after a three-month course at one of the schools run by the Permanent Force; more qualified after a few nights and weekends at the local armouries.[15]

City regiments became smart social clubs, offering members splendid dress uniforms and athletic and social activities, and providing their communities with colourful parades. Rural units came together only for summer camps. Rank-and-file members earned a little money and escaped for two weeks from family, farm, or work.

Life under canvas and a diet of ill-cooked camp food were no hardship to the veterans of lumber camps and harvest gangs, and boozy evenings in a nearby town were one of the rites of passage for many young Canadian males. Even military visitors were impressed by how much the militia learned in a two-week camp, but, despite higher pay for longer service, most men attended only a single camp, and the same training occurred every year. A few hours of drill and rifle practice, climaxed by a grand review or a mock battle, was hardly preparation for modern warfare.

The field artillery was generally considered the most efficient branch, since British gunners admired the ability to move guns with dash and there was no lack of young Canadians eager to show their skill in handling horses. The artillery trained longer than other branches and had more Permanent Force batteries to set them an example.[16]

All Canada's soldiers needed, insisted Hughes, were manliness, patriotism, a good rifle, and enough skill "to pink the enemy every time."[17] Even as opposition defence critic, Hughes had worked with Sir Fred Borden, then defence minister, to reform the Canadian Militia.[18] Hughes played a key role in persuading the Laurier government in 1902 to adopt Sir Charles Ross's new rifle instead of the British Lee-Enfield—and to build the Ross Rifle Company factory near Laurier's Quebec City constituency.

If the militia was expected to defend Canada from the Americans, as both Borden and Hughes believed, it had to become a self-contained army and not a scattering of cavalry, infantry, and artillery units. Starting with an Army Medical Corps in 1901, Borden added an Army Service Corps, an Ordnance Corps, and a Signal Corps, and began promoting colonels to take charge of the brigades and divisions that would be formed if the war came. When Canada took over the British Imperial fortress at Halifax in 1905, Borden expanded the Permanent Force to 3,000, including a handful of nursing sisters.[19] The old military districts were replaced by regional "divisions" that grouped infantry, cavalry, and artillery units in the formations they would join in the admittedly far-fetched possibility of war with the United States.[20] The new organization justified orders for modern artillery, machine-guns, and equipment that British and Canadian factories were languidly delivering in 1914. True, Canada's defence organization lagged far behind in terms of reforms instituted in Britain, or even in Australia, but what was the urgency? An American invasion was an improbable "worst case."[21]

"Imperial nationalists" like Hughes had reservations about the English, but embraced British military traditions.[22] Since creating the militia in the 1860s, the British had supplied the model, from drills to the customs of the officers' mess. Like the British themselves, Canadians clung to the traditional red coat long past common sense. Most militia units still wore it in 1914. In 1902, the British army adopted khaki serge for its active service uniform and approved the scientifically designed Webb equipment to carry a soldier's bayonet, ammunition, food, and spare clothing. In 1914, the British switched to a comfortable khaki service uniform. Canada slowly followed; having made a tight-fitting khaki uniform regulation in 1907, Ottawa reluctantly accepted the cost of providing its part-time soldiers with two uniforms, one for show and one for service. While Canada might have made official issue the distinctive felt hat its mounted troops wore in South Africa (and which the RCMP still wears), the truth was that it soon lost its shape, got dirty, and became a nuisance on active service. Besides, the Americans, the militia's likeliest enemy, were wearing the same style of hat. The alternative was a stiff-brimmed peaked cap with most of the same disadvantages.

At an Imperial Conference in 1907, agreement had been reached that Britain and her dominions would adopt the same organization, tactics, and training so that, in time of war, the armies could easily be integrated.[23] Canada's regular soldiers took their professional training in Britain; British officers filled staff positions in the expanded Canadian military organization. Since few Canadians wanted the low pay and harsh discipline of the Permanent Force, expansion after 1907 brought hundreds of time-expired British soldiers into its ranks. Thousands of other British veterans joined the huge pre-1914 wave of immigration from the British Isles. Men who had preferred the brutally hard life of a British soldier to unemployment in industrial slums or rural poverty also saw Canada as a chance for a fresh start when their time "with the colours" was up. Of course, as "reservists," they would have to go back to their regiments if war was declared.[24]

Within hours of the outbreak of war, Britain had accepted Canada's offer of an infantry division. In 1910, on orders from Sir Fred Borden, Colonel Willoughby Gwatkin, a British staff officer at Militia Headquarters, had prepared a plan to send an infantry division and a cavalry brigade "to a civilized country in a temperate climate." Promoted to Chief of the General Staff and major-general in 1913, Gwatkin saw his mobilization plan trashed a year later, just when it was needed.[25] The new minister had little use for plans. All his life, Sam Hughes had bent or broken any rule that impeded his genius, and he was sure that any staff work meant red tape and delay. He would create Canada's expeditionary force his way. On August 6, he sent 226 telegrams to as many militia colonels across Canada, summoning them and whatever men they could assemble to Valcartier, a camp he had yet to construct on a site outside Quebec City. It was, he later boasted, like the blazing bonfires on the hills that had once summoned the fighting hosts of Ireland and Scotland.[26] Fresh telegrams daily fleshed out the minister's orders, revising and usually repeating the same details Gwatkin had painstakingly worked out years earlier.

Hughes trusted his intuition. Five days before the outbreak, he had promised that "every Canadian would respond to the old flag."[27] On August 22, when Parliament met in special session, Hughes boasted that 100,000 men had already volunteered. No one was unpatriotic enough to challenge his figures.[28] Even before the 226 telegrams arrived, volunteers besieged militia armouries in the major cities. Local militia commanders knew how to recruit; they did it all the time. They also knew the physical qualifications well: minimum height 5 feet 3 inches, and a chest measuring 33 1/2 inches for the infantry, Army Service Corps, and Army Medical Corps. Men expected to do heavy work had to be bigger: gunners had to be 5 feet 7 inches tall with a 34 1/2–inch chest. The age limit was eighteen to forty-five. Unmarried men would be given preference over married men, particularly those with children.[29]

Recruiters were instructed to demand a high standard of marksmanship. Once men were enrolled and medically examined, units would send in the names and Ottawa would set quotas.

Most Canadians assumed that members of the peacetime militia would fill the contingent. At a weekend house party near Pembroke on the Ottawa River, guests excitedly debated the war and what they should do. One of the young men, Alf Bastedo, quieter than the rest, finally broke in: as a militia captain, he would be going home to join his regiment.[30] The others were struck dumb. Another youth, Roy Macfie, helped with the family farm at Dunchurch. Though he had last been to militia camp in 1910, none the less he collected his old red tunic and trousers from the local drill shed and set off for Parry Sound to join up.[31]

Most other militia members could not go. They had families, jobs, and commitments they could not drop for a war that would probably be over before the Canadians arrived. Crops had failed on the prairies, but good harvests were due in central Canada and the Maritimes.[32] Farmers and their sons knew their priorities.

For the most part, the crowds of men who jammed into the armouries were neither militia nor even Canadian-born. The emotional links to a suddenly embattled Britain tugged strongest at the British-born. Army reservists, of course, had no choice but to return to their units, though almost none tried to dodge his duty. Even those who had established themselves with families and jobs felt an obligation to stand by their homeland. For others less idealistically motivated, the Canadian dream had turned into a nightmare of unemployment and rejection. The economic depression, likely to be worsened by a war, had left thousands of men with plenty of leisure. Whether or not the war lasted past Christmas, some of them confessed, they would have an all-expenses-paid trip home.

Meanwhile, in Ottawa, government officials responded to the declaration of war by working overtime. Even a War Book, finished on the eve of the outbreak, could not prepare them fully for the predicted and mostly unpredicted problems of taking the country to war. Successive waves of telegrams informed local headquarters that volunteers must first be enrolled in the militia. Officers would have a $150 outfit allowance. When they joined, officers would get $1.50 a day subsistence; other ranks would have to be content to eat and sleep for 75 cents.[33] On August 18, after Parliament assembled and the politicians had unleashed their best patriotic rhetoric, the first business of the war included the re-establishing of the Canadian Patriotic Fund (CPF). Since 1812, Canada had looked to private generosity for the means to finance pensions, medical care, welfare for soldiers' families, and even medals. The fund created for the South African War reported a healthy balance, which was to be transferred to the new war. However, the new fund would fill a more limited role. Its architect and guiding spirit, Herbert Ames, a Montreal MP and amateur social scientist, insisted that the fund would only be used to look after the families of serving soldiers. Costs of pensions, rehabilitation, medals, and other essentials would have to be borne by government.[34]

By August 18, Ottawa reported that 1,435 officers and 24,815 other ranks had enrolled for overseas service; by mid-September, the rolls had grown to 33,000. In Regina, Garnet Durham, one of 600 applicants, found that the 95th Saskatchewan Rifles put him through three tests on the rifle, two medical exams, and a further test of his knowledge of drill. Only 170 of Durham's fellow applicants were deemed acceptable.[35] The 101st Edmonton Fusiliers, more broad-minded, marched to the station with 940 men, some in khaki, others in red tunics, and most in civilian clothes.[36] In Port Credit, a little town west of Toronto, the local football team finished a game and joined up en masse.[37] Ian Sinclair, a recent graduate of the University of Toronto, left his job on a construction gang after his father got the promise of a commission for him in the 48th Highlanders. He and ten other brand-new officers qualified after a few days of drill at Long Branch.[38] The 48th and its Montreal counterpart, the 5th Royal Highlanders, went their usual independent way, organizing whole battalions for Valcartier.

Other city regiments formed composite battalions. Toronto's 2nd Queen's Own Rifles and its old rival, the 10th Royal Grenadiers, united behind the Toronto Regiment. A company of the 65th Carabiniers Mont-Royal in the self-styled "Royal Montreal Regiment" turned out to be the only French-speaking element in the entire contingent.[39]

In previous wars, wealthy patriots had raised their own regiments for the sovereign. The corps of mounted rifles Lord Strathcona created for the South African War had survived as the only Permanent Force (PF) regiment on the Prairies. Now a wealthy Montreal militia officer, J. Hamilton Gault, offered $100,000 to raise a regiment with Canadian officers and British reservists in the ranks. Faced with the task of getting reservists back to England, the governor general's office cheerfully approved. The Duke of Connaught's daughter lent her name: Princess Patricia's Canadian Light Infantry (PPCLI) took shape in Ottawa, and later at Lévis under the governor general's military secretary, Lieutenant-Colonel F.D. Farquhar.[40] A.D. Mackenzie, a Scot, having come from Edmonton to join the regiment, reported "there were too many blokes for me to feel at home." He was not much better pleased by the artillery unit that accepted him: "This 2nd Battery is in poor shape. If they weren't they wouldn't have taken me."[41]

No one was sensible enough to mix the British reservists with the raw Canadian volunteers. Hughes would simply never have seen the need. Instead of sending Canada's only regular infantry to the new camp at Valcartier, he offered the Halifax-based Royal Canadian Regiment to the British to replace their garrison in Bermuda. Only 80 Permanent Force instructors were on hand to train an expected 25,000 men.[42]

One of the most pressing tasks for the time being remained. Hughes assigned the job of creating the camp on the sandy plain northwest of Quebec City to a local lumberman, William Price. He began work immediately. Men and machinery building the Connaught Ranges outside Ottawa were sent by train to build the new 1,500-target rifle range at Valcartier. Other workers were hired to harvest crops; clear the land; and lay out roads, sewers, water-pipes, and electrical lines. All the remaining PF troops unloaded and erected thousands of tents from militia stores.[43] In a breathless two weeks, the site was made ready. Canadians thought Valcartier a miracle: in fact, it grew, on a grand scale, out of half a century of militia experience in setting up summer camps.

When the first of hundreds of contingents arrived in mid-August, a familiar camp spirit prevailed. Any militia-camp veteran knew how to put up a tent, loosen guy-ropes for the nightly dew, and ditch it to drain off rainwater. Training was guided by the syllabus prepared for the June 1914 camps. Men from the militia's Army Service Corps companies took over baking, butchering, and issuing rations, as they had at camps since 1901; doctors and orderlies of the Canadian Army Medical Corps set up hospitals; an Engineer unit from Kingston took charge of the water supply.[44] Around the camp grounds, contractors erected prefabricated huts and sold "eatables," soft drinks, postcards, sweaters, and anything else a soldier might like. At nightfall, the "boys" started up an impromptu sing-song. Someone always knew where booze could be found—at a price. At least one recruit was pleasantly surprised to learn that soldiers were actually paid—a dollar a day for a private, plus ten cents "field allowance."[45]

If there was anything different about Valcartier, compared with the usual militia camp, it lay in the kinds of men who volunteered. A high proportion were British-born—too many for Roy Macfie: "there are so many Englishmen in the outfit and they are always running the Canadians and everything that is Canadian down; they think nobody knows anything but them. The Scotch are not so bad, but I hate the sight of an Englishman, the kind that are here, anyway."[46]

Nominally, the militia's adjutant-general, Colonel Victor Williams, was in command.[47] Sam Hughes, of course, was in charge. A huge Union Jack snapped in the breeze to mark the house just outside the camp where the minister made his headquarters. Uniformed as a staff colonel; mounted; and accompanied by a cloud of aides, petitioners, and admirers, Hughes was everywhere at once, welcoming arrivals, correcting errors in drill, scolding officers in front of their men, and enthusiastically extracting order out of the chaos he had created.[48] His efforts were rewarded. The contingent needed 22,000 men for the infantry division and cavalry brigade Canada had promised the mother country; a succession of trains disgorged more than 33,000 volunteers at the camp. Arriving officers looked for their orders and renewed old friendships while their men waited. Eventually, they all shouldered their kits and marched—and then marched back again when orders were countermanded.

Understandably, as they milled about, the soldiers suspected general disorganization, even though some milling about must have been inevitable. Even under General Gwatkin's proposed decentralized mobilization plan, units would have had to be amalgamated. At Valcartier, the reorganization was effected on a much grander scale. An infantry division included twelve infantry battalions, each consisting of about a thousand men, organized in three brigades. In the original plan, most of the infantry would have been drawn from eastern Canada, taking care to ensure regional and French-Canadian representation, while most of the mounted units would come from the West.[49] In practice, the double factor of British immigration and unemployment in the western provinces ensured that more than a third of the infantry that arrived at Valcartier haled from western Canada.

Contingents proved far larger than even Sam Hughes had expected, and invariably contributed more officers than the official organization tables required. Lieutenant Ian Sinclair, for example, discovered that his colonel, the Conservative MP for Simcoe North, had invited so many influential constituents to join as officers that he himself was surplus. Fortunately, friends in Montreal's Royal Highlanders made Sinclair welcome. He would finish the war as their commanding officer.[50]

To satisfy legality, Ottawa authorized "overseas battalions" as temporary units of the militia serving in a Canadian Expeditionary Force (CEF), which, in turn, was an "Imperial" contingent raised by the authority of Britain's Army Act.[51] The units that shipped large numbers to Valcartier formed the core of most of the new CEF battalions. Winnipeg's 90th Rifles—"The Little Black Devils" of 1885 fame—passed on its badge and rifle-regiment tradition to the 8th Battalion; the 5th Royal Highlanders and 48th Highlanders became the 13th and 15th Battalion, respectively. The 101st from Edmonton, which arrived over a thousand strong, became the 9th Battalion. The composite units from Toronto and Montreal were designated the 3rd and 14th battalions. A year's "strike duty" at the coal mines around Nanaimo simplified the organization of the 1st British Columbia Regiment. Hughes called it the 7th Battalion. Mounted units from the Prairies became the 5th Western Cavalry, under the command of a tough Saskatchewan farmer, George Tuxford. Winnipeg's Fort Garry Horse emerged as the 6th Battalion, CEF. Other Winnipeggers and Calgarians joined together in the 10th Battalion. Ontario county militia units provided three battalions: the 1st Battalion from western and northern Ontario, the 2nd from the eastern counties, and the 4th from central Ontario.

As more and more units and men swelled the ranks, units were rearranged and more battalions set up. Eventually the First Canadian Contingent included seventeen infantry battalions. East of Ontario, enlistment was more sparse. Except for Montreal's 65th Carabiniers in the 14th "Royal Montreal Regiment," French-Canadian units sent tiny contingents, which were merged with New Brunswickers and Prince Edward Islanders in the 12th Battalion. The 17th Battalion was assigned to Nova Scotia, with some help from other provinces. Its two most senior officers were bitter rivals and made life difficult for their men. Some other battalions were not much happier.[52]

Hughes insisted on picking the commanders for the brigades and battalions himself. Colonel Richard Turner was an obvious choice. A militia cavalry officer and wholesale merchant from Quebec City, he was physically slight, chinless, and seemingly unimpressive, but he was a good Conservative, popular, and, above all, he had won a Victoria Cross in South Africa. He was an obvious choice for the 3rd Brigade, with its two Montreal regiments; Toronto's 15th Battalion; and another kilted regiment, the 16th, with contingents from British Columbia, Winnipeg, and

Hamilton. The 1st Brigade, with the 1st, 2nd, 3rd, and 4th battalions, all from Ontario, went to Lieutenant-Colonel Malcolm S. Mercer, a quiet bachelor lawyer from Toronto who had devoted his life to the Queen's Own Rifles.

Garnet Hughes, the minister's only son, solved the problem of finding a commander for the 2nd, or Western, Brigade. Lieutenant-Colonel Arthur Currie, a Victoria real estate and insurance dealer, had commanded a coastal artillery regiment before being asked by local enthusiasts to organize the brand-new 50th Gordon Highlanders. As Currie's second-in-command, Garnet admired his colonel's cool dedication and recommended him to his father. Besides, as a known Liberal, Currie added a little balance to offset the Conservative tone of the Contingent's officer. Hughes allowed Lieutenant-Colonel Harry Burstall, a PF officer but the son of a solid Quebec Tory, to command the artillery, but Lieutenant Colonel E.W.B. "Dinky" Morrison, a popular South African War veteran who edited the then Tory Ottawa *Citizen*, took the 1st Field Brigade.[53]

Favouritism is not necessarily bad. The brigadiers and colonels Sam Hughes selected at Valcartier would lead the Canadian Corps for the rest of the 1914–18 war. Some of them proved less than brilliant, and a few later broke under the strain, but it is not obvious that better officers were available.[54]

While Hughes organized the infantry at Valcartier, other branches followed Gwatkin's original mobilization plan more closely. Designated units of the peacetime militia put together the ten field-artillery batteries, four ammunition columns, and three field companies of engineers needed for the division. The officers were generally chosen for their proven efficiency at pre-war camps.

The Canadian Army Medical Corps justified its historian's boast that it was readier for war than were other branches.[55] In peacetime, it had attracted many of Canada's best practitioners. Now they hurriedly organized the field ambulances and the general, stationary, and clearing hospitals the British medical system required to support a division in the field. Other doctors, attached to units as medical officers, checked the physical condition of recruits, advised on camp hygiene, and soon learned to sort out the collection of "sick, lame, and lazy" at early morning "sick parade."

As he raced about Valcartier, promoting, demoting, scolding, and delivering inspirational messages, Hughes believed that his young army was undergoing vigorous training. By the relaxed standards of a normal summer camp, it probably was. Nervous that the minister could descend on them at any moment, officers assembled their troops and tried out their word of command.[56] Old-timers explained drill movements to enthusiastic recruits. Groups of soldiers went off to the ranges with their new Ross rifles to fire a few rounds. Despite Hughes's demands for good marksmen, most had never fired a rifle before.[57] Late delivery of the rifles limited training in another of the minister's passions, bayonet fighting. At Valcartier and later, nothing pleased Hughes more than seeing sweating soldiers going through the motions of "thrust," "parry," and "withdraw." Given half a chance, the veteran athlete took a hand in the instruction himself.[58]

For the most part, despite the busyness of their daily routine, the raw recruits learned how to be soldiers by osmosis. W.S. Lighthall, an educated young Montrealer, had bought a ticket for Valcartier and was waiting at the siding when a train carrying the Royal Canadian Dragoons, a Permanent Force unit, pulled in. As its men set up their tents, Lighthall was allowed to enlist. The seasoned veterans of peacetime soldiering soon showed him how to lay out his kit; salute; and stand to attention, heels together, feet at forty-five degrees, and arms pressed tightly at his sides.[59] It was as much or as little instruction as many of the men received.

Three times in September, Hughes cancelled all training so that the entire Contingent could march past in grand reviews for the governor general and admiring politicians. Other days were devoted to sham battles, when senior officers made and lost their reputations in the eyes of the minister or their men. "Colonel Loomis lost his head as usual & mucked things up completely," recorded Stanley Brittain of the 13th Battalion. "The Colonel was *quite* excelling himself in giving wrong orders & generally messing things up, & the general opinion throughout the whole regiment is that the sooner we get rid of him the better."[60]

Valcartier taught the soldiers an important lesson about their new way of life. From then on they would spend much of their time waiting. They waited for medical examinations. They lined up for vaccinations—which were compulsory—and typhoid inoculations—which Hughes insisted were voluntary. They paraded to sign new attestation forms that made them members of the British army as well as the Canadian Militia.[61] Men who had never been subjected to more official paperwork than that required to obtain a birth certificate discovered with some surprise that the army was full of paperwork and "red tape." Men attested in the CEF became members of the British army under the authority of Britain's Army Act, and subject to its harsh disciplinary code.[62] CEF officers received an "Imperial" or British as well as a Canadian commission. Since 70 per cent of the Contingent's other ranks were British-born, it would hardly have troubled them to belong to the British army—especially at the vastly more generous Canadian rates of pay.

Much of the waiting at Valcartier was for issues of kit and equipment that trickled in from contractors. "I was never so well fixed for good clothes before," reported Roy Macfie. "I have a dandy suit and a nice warm overcoat and shoes."[63] Most thought the uniform smart, especially after weeks spent living in rumpled, sweat-soaked civilian clothes. The outfit included a peaked cap with a bronzed maple-leaf cap badge, a tight-fitting khaki serge tunic with stand-up collar and seven brass buttons, matching serge trousers, brown boots, and puttees—long woollen strips bound around the ankle and up the calf almost to the knee, or from the knee down, as the mounted units rolled them. Underneath, the soldier wore a collarless grey flannel shirt, or "greyback"; heavy woollen socks; woollen drawers; and a sleeved undershirt. A long greatcoat served as raincoat, winter warmth, and a supplement to the two coarse grey army blankets. Army issue included a razor, shaving brush, hair brush, boot brush, and toothbrush; a mess tin; two hand towels; woollen gloves; and a "cap comforter" that resembled a toque and could be rolled down over the face, with a hole for the eyes and nose.[64] The Oliver equipment, which a British army surgeon in Halifax had persuaded Ottawa to adopt in the 1890s as a means of carrying ammunition, food, water, and clothing, arrived as a mysterious tangle of leather straps, pouches, and packs. The ammunition pouch, worn over the stomach, guaranteed that its wearers would not crawl into battle.[65] Each man received his Ross rifle, with a sling, a bayonet, and a scabbard, an oil bottle, and a pull-through—a length of cord with a weight at one end and a loop at the other so that pieces of flannel ("four by twos") could be hauled through the barrel to clean it.

The freshly uniformed volunteers did their best to look like soldiers. Tailor shops that sprang up on the edge of the camp did good business fitting uniforms. Veteran soldiers showed the novices how to polish their boots and brass buttons and to roll their puttees so they did not collapse around their ankles as an inspecting officer approached.

Paid, attested, and finally fitted out in a uniform, Gunner John Sutton set out for Quebec to learn another lesson of soldiering. At the entrance to the Château Frontenac, a military policeman stopped him—"Officers only." Sutton sneaked in the back way and was spotted and caught. "Get out and I mean stay out," roared the military policeman. Even in Sam Hughes's politically managed army, common soldiers were no longer equal citizens with their commissioned superiors.[66]

Weapons for the fledgling force varied in practicality and availability. Since Canada possessed only a handful of old machine-guns, Hughes placed an order in Hartford, Connecticut, for fifty of the best Colt air-cooled "automatic guns." Salesmen convinced him that the Canadians would have the best machine-gun in the world.[67] To carry its baggage, supplies, and artillery ammunition, the Contingent needed 853 Bain wagons, known to farmers across Canada. An enthusiastic fan of the newfangled automobile, Hughes had already forced his staff officers to use Model-T Fords, not horses. How better to show off Canadian motor manufacturing to the world, he claimed, than by allowing 5 different manufacturers to supply the 133 trucks needed for the Artillery's ammunition parks, the Army Service Corps's supply column, and the Medical Corps's ambulances? Private donors financed a uniquely Canadian unit, the 1st Canadian Automobile Machine Gun Brigade. Its transport, however, including eight armour-plated machine-gun carriers, was purchased in the United States.

Despite the value of motorized vehicles, a more traditional form of motive power mattered even more. The Contingent's horses—8,150 of them—cost an average of $172.45 a head. By the end of September, 291 had been rejected as unfit, including one venerable nag turned down for the South African War fifteen years earlier. By the time the camp broke up, almost 500 of the horses had so deteriorated in camp conditions that they were left behind for disposal.[68]

To the new volunteers, Valcartier was pleasant. Despite a few heavy rains and a cold snap, the weather held sunny and crisp. The setting was framed in distant blue hills, and the maples turned with the season. The camp was never silent. Night and day, teams and wagons rattled through, hauling tents, supplies, and rations.

Soldiers in a holiday mood added to the din: "men singing, yelling, playing all kinds of music and making enough noise to waken the dead," one man reported, as he tried to explain why letter writing was difficult.[69] "The boys," as Hughes called them, demonstrated a will of their own. When a contractor showed the serial movie *The Perils of Pauline* once too often, the troops pulled down his tent. In the ensuing confusion, it caught fire and the cashbox disappeared.[70]

Life in camp continued to improve. By mid-September, the camp boasted electric lights, enough water to offer daily showers, free movies, a host of private "canteens," and even a store that sold used typewriters.[71] Garnet Durham preferred a scarcer luxury of army life—solitude. One idyllic afternoon, he and a friend went hiking. They climbed a hill, squeezed through dense firs, and crossed a big muskeg: "Afterwards we came to the Jacques Cartier river, clear, cold and sandy. We stripped and swam across, then climbing a small hill in our birthday suits we had a nice view of the St. Lawrence twelve miles away."[72]

Having created and, in his eyes, trained an army, Hughes wished next to get it to the war. Even when the most obviously unsuitable would-be volunteers had been sent home, more than thirty thousand men remained. The Cabinet had authorized him to send, at most, 25,000. Impressed by the "miracle" wrought at Valcartier, the prime minister paused, pondered, and then announced that all the men could go. Hughes burst into tears.[73]

Five more ships had to be added to the twenty-five vessels already chartered. Staff officers had already prepared embarkation plans based on ample British experience of embarking troops and equipment. Instead, Hughes turned again to William Price, the Quebec City lumberman, in hopes that he could repeat the Valcartier organizational miracle. Applying his talent to filling ships with troops and cargo proved difficult. Some of the ships' holds were given over completely to the 135,425 bags of flour that Canada would present as a wartime gift to Britain. Shipping firms haggled over the right number of officers per cabin and horses per handler. Guns and wagons were loaded with their wheels attached, taking up far more than the space allotted them on paper. Cargo hatches proved to be too narrow to accommodate the Contingent's motor vehicles. The 8th Battalion, 1,161 strong, boarded the *Bermudian* only to discover that the ship could carry half that number. In some battalions, the officers showed more interest in getting their own baggage aboard than in what was happening to their men. At the same time, traffic jams at the Quebec docks kept the troops waiting for hours, giving the men plenty of opportunities to make up for the dry spell at Valcartier. "Chaos reigned supreme," wrote one of Price's harried assistants. Price persevered with his Herculean task, managing with his few helpers to load all 30,617 men; 7,697 horses; 127 guns; hundreds of wagons; and tons of kit, equipment, and supplies on the ships within one week.[74] In the process, any connection between units and their equipment and horses tended to be coincidental.

One by one, the big liners, already painted a wartime grey,

slipped their moorings and slid down the St. Lawrence. Bands and pipers played; troops sent echoing cheers against the rocky face of Cape Diamond. As they waved to each other, the crowds on shore and the men on board felt the drama and pathos of soldiers going to war.

Far downstream, at Pointe-aux-Pères, the ships dropped anchor again to wait for the whole convoy to collect. Despite attempts at security and warnings to the press, Ottawa maintained its reputation for leaking secrets. Even the governor general told a public meeting on September 28 that he had recently been present at "what is perhaps no longer a secret, the embarkation of the Canadian troops."[75] The German Admiralty duly expected the Canadians at Le Havre on October 8.

The convoy moved into the Gulf on October 3, a day after Hughes had sailed around the fleet, distributing bundles of printed flyers entitled "Where Duty Leads," the motto of his old militia regiment. "You have been perfected in rifle shooting," he assured them, "and today are as fine a body of men—Officers and Men—as ever faced a foe." His message closed on a sober note:

> Some may not return—and pray God they be few—For such, not only will their memory be ever cherished by loved ones near and dear, and by a grateful country, but throughout the ages freemen of all lands will revere the heroes who sacrificed themselves in preserving unimpaired the Priceless Gem of Liberty. But the soldier who goes down in the cause of freedom never dies—Immortality is his. What recks he whether his resting place may be bedecked with the gold lilies of France or amid the vine-clad hills of the Rhine. The principles for which you strive are eternal.[76]

As the message passed from hand to hand, recalled Captain Fortescue Duguid, "soldiers received it with mixed feelings."[77] Many, already cynics, consigned the minister's message to the sea.

CHAPTER TWO

THE OLD ORIGINALS

CREATING AN ARMY

Later, they called themselves the "Old Originals." Mostly British-born, they had gathered in the holiday-camp atmosphere of Val-cartier; shivered through the icy rain and mud of Salisbury Plain; and finally fought and died at Ypres, Givenchy, and Festubert. From its generals to its sergeant-majors, the Canadian Corps was run by survivors. The lists of dead, wounded, and gassed told Canadians that war was not a brief, gallant adventure.

CROSSING the Atlantic took ten days. On the second day out, October 4, the *Florizel* joined the convoy with five hundred men from Newfoundland. The early-October weather remained warm, the sea smooth, and 20,000 doses of a secret seasickness remedy untried. Altogether, most troops travelled in a comfort that later drafts of Canadians would never know.[1] They could be grateful for the uncertainty of the experts who had yet to figure with mathematical precision how to cram troops into every dank corner of a ship. Officers took the first-class cabins; lower-ranking soldiers filled the rest. Troops dined in unaccustomed style, though they grumbled when they found that officers could order beer and whisky while they could not.[2]

Routines on board varied by ship. On the *Ivernia*, Lieutenant-Colonel John Creelman insisted on regular drill, physical training (PT), and Sunday church parades, and sentenced troublemakers to terms in the ship's stokehold; on other liners, the men lounged, played cards, and shared rumours. One soldier fell overboard and was rescued by the *Franconia*, providing its contingent of nurses with a patient. Gossip in the convoy rapidly identified him as an overly zealous provost sergeant who had offended some of "the boys." On the *Alaunia*, Stanley Brittain of the 13th Battalion reported that a Scottish soldier had been arrested as a German spy.[3] Another rumour tripled the number of spies and declared that two of them were promptly shot on arrival in England. A ship's engineer, Lou Elliott, insisted he could see their graves from his ship.[4]

A healthy new respect for German submarines diverted the Canadian convoy to the historic naval port of Plymouth.[5] Astonished to find Imperial history unfolding before them, welcoming civilian throngs crowded the shore and pleaded for Canadian badges and buttons as souvenirs. It took nine full days to get all the troops and their equipment ashore.

Discipline among the troops was fragile. Colonel Creelman noted stiffly that "moral conditions" between nurses and male officers on the nearby *Franconia* were what he would have predicted: "Last night we could see dozens of hugging couples and the ship's officers say that that was the chronic condition throughout."[6] After long, thirsty weeks on the ships, many of the new arrivals headed straight for Plymouth's pubs to discover the power of British beer.

On the *Grampian*, a mischievous signaller transformed a message that officers could go ashore into permission for everyone to go. The colonel accordingly let half his men disembark, learned of his mistake, and cancelled leave for the rest. They rebelled. A boatload of British marines stood by while peace and good feeling were restored.[7] Roy Macfie's major warned his company that any drunks would be sent home—and promptly went off and got drunk himself.[8] He was not the only one. Captain J.F.C. Fuller, sent by the War Office to oversee the disembarkation, confided to his mother that Canadians would make excellent soldiers if only all their officers were shot.[9] When Fuller asked for men to unload their gear, the Canadians retorted that they had not enlisted to be common labourers. Prudently, he did not press the issue, and summoned British army recruits to do the work.[10]

Loaded and now unloaded in utter confusion, boxes, baggage, equipment, and harness were dumped along English country lanes for the units to sort out their own property. It was a long, sometimes hopeless, task.[11]

Once he had said farewell at Pointe-aux-Pères, the Minister of Militia raced to New York and took a fast liner to Britain to greet his boys. Despite Hughes's desperate wish to take personal command of the Contingent, the prime minister; Canada's high commissioner in London, Sir George Perley; and the British agreed that it was out of the question. Instead, Hughes grudgingly accepted one of the three British generals he was offered to fill the position. Major-General Edwin Alderson had commanded Canadians in South Africa in 1900, and both sides remembered the experience favourably.[12]

The legend that Hughes pounded on Lord Kitchener's desk and defied him to break up the Canadian Contingent surfaced fifteen years after Hughes died. It must have been a myth because he would have enjoyed the tale too much to leave it a secret.[13] In their meetings, the two war ministers agreed that the war would last three more years. Kitchener insisted that Hughes's best contribution would be to recruit more men.[14] As solace for Hughes's disappointment, Borden finally yielded to Hughes's long campaign to become a major-general.[15] Just in case the Canadian minister tried to pull rank, the War Office promptly promoted Alderson to lieutenant-general. To keep a watchful eye on his interests and Canada's, Hughes left behind as his "special representative" his old friend Colonel John Wallace Carson, a wealthy Montreal mining promoter.[16]

The War Office had offered the Canadians space on Salisbury Plain, a stretch of rolling hills and scattered farms acquired as an army training area fifteen years earlier. Trains took Canadians from Plymouth to Cheriton, leaving them a nine-mile march in full kit to one of three tented camps. After weeks aboard ship and a monumental carouse in Plymouth, many found this stage a hard struggle, though a sturdy few had enough energy left over to explore the pubs in neighbouring villages. Lieutenant-Colonel Russ Boyle, the big Alberta rancher who commanded the 10th Battalion, celebrated his arrival by parading his men, removing his coat, and inviting any or all of the soldiers "who said they'd like to punch the hell out of me" to have a try. No one moved.[17]

The Canadians had plenty to do, from sorting out equipment to sightseeing. Garnet Durham described a chum—"a born Canadian"—who asked a keeper at nearby Stonehenge for a hammer to chip off a souvenir.[18] Many men went home to their families on a week's leave. A few negotiated commissions in the fast-growing British army. Most sampled the excitements of "the Big Smoke," London. Such adventures soon gave the medical officers the first of the more than a thousand cases of venereal disease they would treat over the next five months.[19] Publicity about the Canadians led to minor scandals. Men who had left families behind in England when they emigrated to Canada and had remarried across the Atlantic now returned to the "old country" and were charged with bigamy.[20]

A more pressing issue was the unending binge some of the well-paid Canadians had enjoyed since their landing at Plymouth. Little villages around Salisbury Plain were soon awash in drunken visitors. When Alderson visited the artillery lines, reported a shocked Colonel Morrison, the British general ordered men to break ranks and gather around his car "more like a crowd at a mass meeting than a body of formed troops." Alderson announced that "wet" canteens would henceforth be authorized in camps. Dismayed as Hughes and temperance enthusiasts were by this development, drunken Canadians became less of a public nuisance when they got drunk in their own camps.[21]

Within a week of the Canadians' arrival at Salisbury, cold, driving rain soaked the camps. Winds tore down the big marquees where troops gathered for messing and lectures. Chilled and soaked, the men struggled with the sodden canvas of their tents in the bleak light of dawn. The wettest winter in memory had begun. For 89 of the next 124 days, it rained, in between intermittent frosts and bit-ing winds.[22] The thin soil that covered the impermeable limestone under their feet became a shallow morass. Many officers fled the misery to join their wives in the nearby cathedral town of Salis-bury. Others departed for the comforts of London. Even bachelor officers could slip away for a bath, a dinner, and a visit to the the-atre.[23] The other ranks had no such relief. A few deserted; most stuck it out. "There was only one way to be reasonably comfort-able," recalled R.D. Haig, a Winnipegger. "That was never take your clothes off, because it was much easier to get up in the morn-ing damp-wet than to get up in the morning and try to put on cold, damp clothes."[24]

Troops lined up in the rain for meals—tea and porridge for breakfast; stew for dinner; bread, jam, and tea for supper, all slopped indiscriminately into their mess tins. Then they washed their mess tins and cooking pots in cold water and watched the grease congeal.[25] At the next meal it mixed with the tea. Quarter-masters issued extra blankets; these were soon as wet as the first ones. The horses, always at the mercy of weather and humankind, stood, day after day, up to their hocks in freezing mud. When Major Andrew McNaughton ordered scrubby trees chopped down to make hard standing for the horses of his artillery battery, he was almost court-martialled and sent home for ignoring regulations against environmental damage.[26]

After Colonel Carson visited the camp and saw the conditions, he complained directly to the War Office. The British were sur-prised to learn that the hardy Canadians even noticed the weather, None the less, they promised to put their own recruits into tents and hand over their billets. An embarrassed Alderson refused the offer, and a discomfited Carson promptly returned to Canada to complain to Hughes.[27] The Canadian government sent him back with a larger and even vaguer mandate as the "Minister's Represen-tative." By 1916, he had parlayed it into a major-generalship and an unauthorized mastery of Canadian affairs in England. Meanwhile, Lord Kitchener had promised the Canadians huts; contractors set to work, and more than a thousand soldiers were diverted from regular training to help with the construction. Lacking carpenters, most units sent the contractors their troublemakers. "Talk about rag-tag and bobtail," recalled R.L. Christopherson, a peacetime bank clerk and one of the "skilled construction workers."[28]

By New Year's 1915, most of the Contingent was housed in huts. An unexpected result was a dramatic increase in sickness. Despite the appalling conditions in the tents, the men had remained surprisingly healthy and cheerful. In the damp, ill-ventilated huts, infections spread fast. A fatal strain of meningitis, barely noticed at Valcartier, multiplied its victims at a frightening rate. By February, there were thirty-nine cases, of which twenty-eight proved fatal.[29]

Weather, leave, sickness, and a shortage of instructors limited serious training. Units continued to go through the motions of drill, physical training, and route marches. Officers lectured the troops on military law, tactics, hygiene, and other subjects they had studied the evening before. By now the troops knew that the war would not, in fact, be over by Christmas. While the fighting had bogged down in a kind of siege warfare, the battles of 1914 had little impact on training because Britain's small regular army had almost ceased to exist.

On August 23, the British Expeditionary Force (BEF) had reached the Belgian city of Mons only to be caught in the huge German phalanx bent on enveloping the French. With luck, hard marching, and occasional demonstrations of its terrific skill in rapid-fire shooting, the BEF saved itself—at a cost of almost half of its 80,000 men. The survivors even shared in the dramatic French counter-attack at the Marne. When German resistance stiffened, the exhausted survivors halted and dug in on the Aisne, unaware that they had established the line of trenches that would be the Western Front for the next four years.[30]

A last chance remained for a German victory before Christmas. As the trench lines thickened, a hole remained in the last corner of unconquered Belgium. Fresh divisions of German youngsters, ill-trained but utterly careless of their lives, hurled themselves into the gap. Waiting for them in front of the old city of Ypres were all that could still be mustered of the British regular army—about 80,000 men. After three terrible weeks of shelling and attacks, the Allied line barely held, but both sides had lost heavily: almost 60,000 British, 50,000 French, and 130,000 German casualties. The Germans, who had sent raw divisions of college and high school students, would remember the *Kindermord von Yperen.* By year's end, 90 per cent of the BEF were dead, wounded, or captured. British generals would remember where their old regiments, their friends, and often their own sons had died. Ypres had become sacred ground.[31]

The pre-war British army had some great virtues and some serious flaws. A brilliant Secretary of State for War, Richard Haldane, had shocked his generals by promising army reform based on "Hegelian principles," combined with the sharp cost-cutting his fellow Liberals demanded. This was not an easy task. Although the army had been reoriented to prepare for an increasingly probable European war and its arms, equipment, and training had been improved substantially, the army's main preoccupation before 1914 continued to be the maintenance of colonial garrisons concerned primarily with peacetime smartness and the minor tactics of small frontier wars. In Britain, the army's share of defence spending shrank steadily as the Liberal government struggled to finance naval expansion and badly needed health and social programs. Funds for ammunition to be used during training, moving troops to manoeuvres, and filling out the staff of wartime divisions and corps provided easy targets for budget cutters. When the generals requested six machine-guns per infantry battalion, not just two, the Chancellor of the Exchequer, David Lloyd George, refused. Four years later, he would condemn the same generals for refusing to take machine-guns seriously.

Politicians were easy scapegoats. The army's own conservative officers resented active-minded juniors, with their radical views on tactics, fire-power, and the significance of the lessons of the Russo-Japanese War. The army's historic regiments protected their traditional autonomy from meddling staffs. The cavalry, artillery, and infantry, as Shelford Bidwell and Dominick Graham have said, "dined at separate tables." The cavalry was better trained to fight with its rifles than were its European counterparts, but its officers still believed in their swords and lances. The field artillery boasted some excellent new guns, but its officers had little patience with the technicalities of hitting targets they could not see, and had no real idea of how they would support the infantry against well-armed enemies. As for the infantry, it was proud of its skill in rapid fire and confident that "pluck," discipline, and the "spirit of the bayonet" would always carry the day, as they usually did during the annual manoeuvres. The Royal Engineers sponsored experiments in signalling and gave birth to the new Royal Flying Corps, but its officers specialized as narrowly as any others. Staff College instructors and manuals insisted that war demanded teamwork from all four branches, but no one from Haldane's controversial new General Staff imposed any cooperation on the gunners, sappers, cavalry, and foot-sloggers, or developed a doctrine of how the British army would fight a modern war. Sadly, the army would learn its lessons the hard way.[32]

Even more sadly, by the end of 1914 the officers thrown into that terrible education were mostly dead, wounded, or captured. There was no adequate replacement for the army that died or for the experience that perished with it. Most of the wounded would ultimately rejoin. New regular divisions were formed from battalions called home from remote colonies. Divisions shattered at Ypres were rebuilt from reservists, raw recruits, and retired officers. Princess Patricia's Canadian Light Infantry (PPCLI), almost the equivalent of a regular battalion, joined the 27th Division and went to France on December 20, 1914. The Newfoundlanders left for Scotland, and ultimately for the Dardanelles and the Somme, as part of another regular division, the 29th.

Meanwhile, the exhausted, shell-shocked survivors of the BEF in France urgently needed help. Fourteen Territorial Army divisions—Britain's equivalent of the Canadian Militia—had mobilized for home defence. Now they began sending battalions, drafts, and eventually whole divisions to bolster the established British line. That left Kitchener's "New Army," hundreds of thousands of volunteers who had answered his call and who drilled with broomsticks through the winter of 1914–15, clad in civilian clothes and scraps of uniform. When Canadians refused to unload their ships at Plymouth, New Army men obediently did the job. Desperate for every trained soldier to hold its share of the Western Front, the army could spare only a handful of officers and non-commissioned officers (NCOs) to staff and instruct its new divisions. Some were lent to the Canadians.

By January 1915, Alderson had sent some of his worst men home to Canada.[33] Field batteries waited their turn to practise on the few artillery ranges a peacetime England had allowed its army. With enough huts built, the Canadian Engineers finally got a few weeks of field training. Infantry battalions marched out to fire 155 rounds per man and to practise the assault formations that would sweep a way to Berlin once the spring offensive began. After three weeks of practising on the obsolete Maxim, Bill Alldritt's machine-gun section got a glimpse of a new Colt gun in early February.[34] The cavalry regiments, a company of cyclists, and the Army Service Corps practised whatever the pre-war manuals taught. With neither a manual nor precedents to guide him, Major Raymond Brutinel, a former French army officer, could only dream up tactics for his Automobile Machine Gun Brigade.[35]

Even by February, any professional could see that the Canadian division was woefully unready. The Canadian lack of discipline, at least in the eyes of regulars, was notorious. Commanders and staff officers had little experience in peace or war. The artillery had fired about fifty shells per battery.

By now, too, the quality of the weapons themselves was becoming obvious. Hughes's faith in his men's marksmanship with the Ross was sadly misplaced. Unknown to the war minister, the pre-war British army had discovered that rapid fire was more effective than precise accuracy. Accordingly, its soldiers practised the "mad-minute," getting twelve to fifteen aimed shots a minute from their Lee-Enfields. However, rapid fire only exacerbated the most obvious defect of the Ross rifle—its tendency to seize up when overheated.[36] Except for the few men who became snipers, few soldiers believed that their rifle, with its weight, its powerful kick, and its constant need to be cleaned, would ever become their "best friend."

Other troops, and even some Canadians, confessed Alex Sinclair of the 5th Battalion, referred to the CEF as the "Comedian Contingent."[37] Still, were they worse than the British Territorials? With their naïve self-confidence, would the Canadians ever learn anything until they actually met the brutal experts in the art of war, the Germans? It was time to go to France.

But first, the embarrassing matter of Canadian equipment had to be addressed. Hughes's scheme to turn the Contingent into a travelling exhibit of Canadian manufacturing prowess had backfired. The months on Salisbury Plain had revealed flaws in the Contingent's costly outfit. The tightly fitted khaki tunics split at the seams, and the greatcoats, cheaply made of cotton and wool, resisted neither rain nor cold. Canadian boots, hurriedly produced, had literally dissolved in the Salisbury mud. Troops claimed the soles were made from cardboard and dubbed the minister himself "Sham Shoes." Herbert Ames, whose company had been the main contractor, was a better philanthropist than a manufacturer.[38] Condemned fifteen years earlier, during the South African War, as uncomfortable, awkward, and unable to carry a soldier's basic needs, the Oliver equipment was finally replaced by Webb equipment, manufactured from woven string.[39] Struggling to clothe its own troops, Britain's War Office somehow managed to find a pair of its heavy hobnailed boots and one of its loose-fitting, comfortable tunics for each Canadian—though not until the eve of embarkation for France.

A few months' actual use revealed further problems with the Contingent's major equipment. The Bain wagons could not be adapted to a military harness, which allowed a dead or wounded horse to be cut free at one stroke—an enormous advantage under fire. Worse still, the wood used in the hurriedly built wagons and tool-carts was green, warped, and splintered; some of the wheels were rotten; and the driver's seat regularly broke loose. When loaded with the usual stock of artillery ammunition, the whole wagon threated to collapse. Canadian-made water-carts could be neither drained nor cleaned.[40] Those few months on Salisbury Plain had also worn out the varied fleet of Canadian-made trucks, cars, and ambulances. Some had serious mechanical defects; others simply had no spare parts.[41] Again, the British did their best to help out a division that had been promised as fully equipped. Trucks, wagons, and even new field telephones gradually appeared. Many of the sturdy General Service wagons arrived with the paint still wet, and the Engineers got their new tool-carts at night, five hours before they left for France.[42]

Some problems could not be solved. Despite serious reservations about the American-made Colt machine-guns and the Ross rifle, British replacements were simply not available. Whether or not Canadian soldiers shared Hughes's enthusiasm for his chosen machine gun and rifle, they would have to fight with them.[43] As for the $1.35 MacAdam shield-shovel issued to each Canadian— awkward, heavy, and patently useless for digging—its fate was settled when Lieutenant-Colonel Fred Loomis picked up a rifle and peppered one of the tools at 200 yards; in 1917, 22,000 of the shovels fetched $1,400 as scrap iron.[44] Alderson's own appeal to Ottawa for effective wire-cutters went unanswered.[45]

While adjusting to new equipment, the Contingent also had to reshape itself as a British regular infantry division. In Canada, infantry battalions were organized in 8 companies of about 125 men each. In 1914, British battalions had switched to the European model of 4 companies, each with 250 men, split into 4 platoons. Three times on Salisbury Plain, Canadian battalions had switched—from eight to four, to eight, and back to four companies.[46] Each change disrupted training, spread confusion, and, since the Contingent had far more officers than it needed, heightened tensions. In the familiar Canadian way, disappointed officers blamed politics or regional favouritism for their own demotion or exclusion.

Total strength of the force changed only slightly. A battalion was still a unit of about a thousand men, under a lieutenant-colonel. Companies were commanded by a major, with a captain as second-in-command (often the winner and loser of the eight-into-four company merger). Four lieutenants each commanded a platoon, though, in many battalions, lack of experienced officers and NCOs made platoons notional. Each battalion had a machine-gun section with two pairs of Colt guns. Other soldiers served as signallers, runners, buglers, scouts, or clerks, or, like Roy Macfie, looked after the battalion's transport. Members of the brass or pipe band doubled as stretcher-bearers.

Since a division needed only three brigades and twelve infantry battalions, the tough choice Hughes had avoided at Valcartier fell to General Alderson. Which units would share the glory of battle? The selection was not all that difficult, though the units left behind obviously disagreed.[47] Garnet Durham of the 9th Battalion and Major Peter Anderson of the 11th were equally convinced that their battalions had been left behind because their colonels were Liberals. "You have to be in with the government to get anywhere in Canadian affairs," complained Durham.[48] French Canadians and New Brunswickers in the 12th Battalion and Nova Scotians in the 17th, both believed they were excluded because of regional and linguistic prejudice.

Four of the surplus battalions became the Canadian Training Depot and settled briefly at Tidworth. To fit into the latest British organization and to provide for their own replacements, Canadian artillery batteries dropped two of their six guns, leaving them and the extra gunners to form reserve batteries. The 6th Battalion, Winnipeg's Fort Garry Horse, became a depot for the cavalry. The Royal Canadian Dragoons, Lord Strathcona's Horse, and the Royal Canadian Horse Artillery, all from the Permanent Force, helped form the Canadian Cavalry Brigade (CCB). The third regiment, the 2nd King Edward's Horse, was a British unit formed from "colonials" who happened to be living and working in London.[49] Without consulting Ottawa, the War Office solved one of its own political problems by giving the brigade to Colonel J.E.B. Seely, a

British amateur soldier who had followed Richard Haldane as Secretary of State for War until the Curragh Mutiny only weeks before the outbreak of war.[50] The decision to hand Canadians over to a British political appointee infuriated Sir Robert Borden: "I shall see to it that the next Mounted Corps that goes from Canada is placed in command of one of our own men as Brigadier."[51]

On February 4, in the usual pouring rain, battalions turned out in the pre-dawn darkness and headed for a divisional rendezvous on Salisbury Plain. As is usual in the army, they then waited. Finally, the rain stopped, and both a pale, wintry sun and King George V appeared. The small, bearded monarch rode slowly down the massed ranks, doubtless noting, with his meticulous attention to uniform, the blue, red, yellow, and maroon shoulder straps that identified infantry, gunners, cavalry, medical corps, and other branches. Then he waited at the salute as more than 20,000 Canadians marched past.[52]

The royal visit meant that the Canadians were going to France. Advance parties left in late January. Last-minute gaps in the departing units were filled. Like other battalions, Ian Sinclair's 13th had dropped its "thugs and troublemakers" and replaced them with men from the 17th Battalion. "They're not a bad lot," he reported, "though utterly without discipline and untrained in every way."[53] For next four years, this would be the universal judgement passed on any "reinforcement" soldier.

Ten days after the king's inspection, the Canadians began moving to Avonmouth, where small coastal steamers loaded men and equipment for the voyage to the Atlantic port of St. Nazaire. Officers, Sinclair reported, were strictly limited to thirty-five pounds of baggage for the company cart, including a camp bed and sleeping-bag. He abandoned his sword in favour of a revolver.[54] Private Stanley Brittain staggered aboard the *Novian* under eighty pounds of clothing, equipment, rifle, and bayonet.[55] The tiny steamer sailed into a roaring Atlantic gale. "It is something terrible down below," he recorded in his illegal diary, "about 200 cramped into a very small space in the hold with no ventilators except what comes through the small space where the ladder is. Nearly everyone is

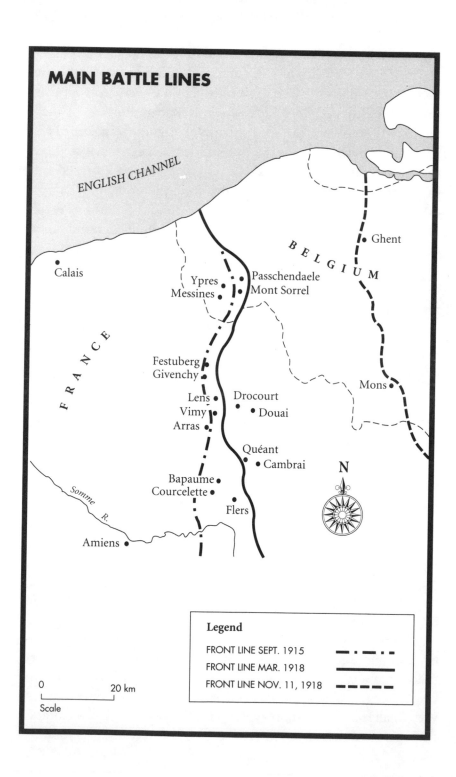

MAIN BATTLE LINES

ENGLISH CHANNEL

BELGIUM

Ghent

Calais

Ypres
Messines

Passchendaele
Mont Sorrel

FRANCE

Festuberg
Givenchy

Mons

Lens
Vimy
Arras

Drocourt
Douai

Quéant
Cambrai

N

Bapaume
Courcelette

Somme R.

Flers

Amiens

Legend

FRONT LINE SEPT. 1915   — · — · —

FRONT LINE MAR. 1918   ————

FRONT LINE NOV. 11, 1918   — — — —

0   20 km

Scale

very sick which makes it worse." He managed to spend his days on deck: "It is much better to be cold and wet through than to be in that filthy hold."[56]

After three miserable days, Brittain found himself at St. Nazaire at dawn on February 15. Another day and a half passed before dock space was found for the ship to unload its passengers and cargo. Almost immediately, Brittain loaded himself and his kit on one of the small French freight cars marked "40 hommes, 8 chevaux."[57]

The rail journey on the "side-door Pullman" took forty-eight sleepless hours. "You couldn't lie down in any comfortable position that somebody wasn't lying over your legs or something like that," reported Private Cuthbert Johnson of the 14th Battalion.[58] One comfort was the intermittent chance to buy a quart of wine for a franc—about 20 cents. A temporary misery was the goatskin waistcoat soldiers received at St. Nazaire. Most discreetly dumped them when they tired of the pungent goatish smell.[59]

By the time the Canadians landed in France, the preparation of a raw division for the front line was almost a ritual. In a quiet sector, individual Canadians were paired up with British troops for forty-eight hours to learn the routines of trench warfare. Then their platoon and company officers took charge while battalion commanders learned the details of administration under fire.[60] On March 3, the Canadian Division replaced the 7th British Division on 6,400 yards of front south of Armentieères.

A week later, the Canadians played a minor role in the first Allied offensive of 1915. On March 10, the French army launched a major assault on the Germans, aiming to capture Vimy Ridge. As the Canadians opened fire to divert German attention, on their right four British and Indian divisions rose from their trenches and advanced on Aubers Ridge. By the afternoon of March 12, the British had lost 12,892 men and gained only the German front line and the ruins of Neuve Chapelle.[61] The Canadians amassed a hundred casualties in the battle, slightly more than the usual weekly loss to intermittent shelling and the deadly German snipers.[62]

In late March, the BEF introduced the first Territorial divisions

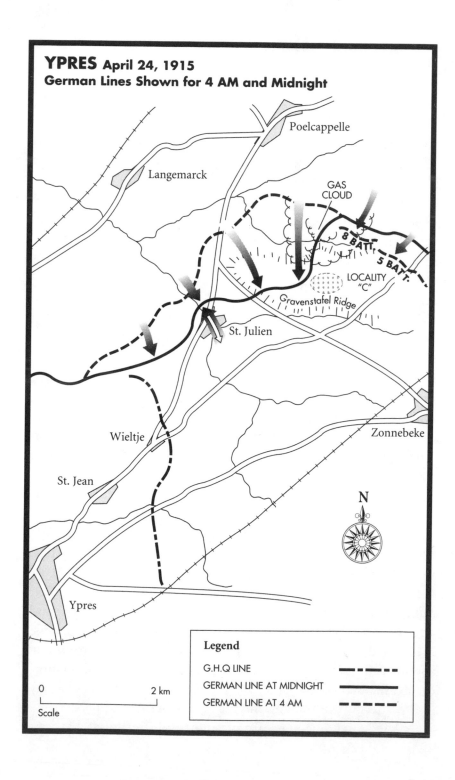

YPRES April 24, 1915
German Lines Shown for 4 AM and Midnight

Poelcappelle

Langemarck

GAS
CLOUD

8 BATT.

5 BATT.

LOCALITY
"C"

Gravenstafel Ridge

St. Julien

Wieltje

St. Jean

Zonnebeke

N

Ypres

Legend	
G.H.Q LINE	— ·· — ·· —
GERMAN LINE AT MIDNIGHT	——————
GERMAN LINE AT 4 AM	— — — —

0   2 km
Scale

to the front, and the British agreed to take over some of the French army's trenches near Ypres. Accordingly, the Canadians shifted from Sir Douglas Haig's First Army to the Second Army. They were pleased. Their new commander, Sir Horace Smith-Dorrien, had been popular with the Canadians in South Africa.[63]

Between April 14 and 17, Alderson's men replaced the French 11th Division. British regulars of the 28th Division were on the right; on the left were the 45th Algerian and 87th Territorial divisions of the French army. Canadians soon found out why troops cursed the historical accident that had made Ypres sacred ground. The last city in Belgian hands, Ypres sat in a shallow saucer of land, commanded from high ground on three sides by German artillery. Only sentiment—Belgian and British—made Ypres important.[64]

The Canadians also discovered that French and British defence tactics differed. Since superior German artillery blasted any objective before an attack, the French held their ground lightly with makeshift trenches, withdrew during the attack, and then expected to wipe out their enemies with their quick-firing 75-mm field guns.[65] The Canadians, therefore, inherited flimsy defences—"a mere breastwork," Raymond McIlree remembered. He also recalled unburied bodies and ripe faeces in every shell hole.[66]

British defensive style was utterly different. Alderson's orders were simply "to hold the front trenches at all costs."[67] That would have been easier if his men had dug deeper trenches, but any hole in the Flanders mud met water two feet down. "Trenches" were really mud and sandbagged walls that artillery could easily smash.

The late-April days were sunny with the promise of spring, but nights were chilly. That was when troops in the trenches worked hardest. With a novice's enthusiasm, the Canadians got busy improving the defences along Strombeek Ridge, with the 5th and 8th battalions of Currie's brigade on the right, Turner's 13th and 15th Highlanders on the left, and other battalions in support. In the rear, Mercer's 1st Brigade waited in reserve west of Ypres. One member of his brigade recalled races in full kit and equipment to keep the troops fit.[68]

In early April, for some veiled but devilish reason, Germans began to devastate the hitherto undamaged old city. A trail of pathetic refugees wended past Mercer's men. Surely that was not a soldier's concern.

At 3:00 p.m. on April 22, a message notified Turner's brigade that a hundred mouth-organs could be collected that night from division headquarters.[69] At 4:00 p.m., violent shelling began pulverizing the Algerian positions; at 5:00 p.m., a strange greenish cloud rose from the German lines and rolled forward, propelled by a light northwest breeze. Within minutes, hundreds of Algerians and Senegalese fled before a nameless horror that blinded them and left them suffocating and in agony. The French Territorials followed suit. Two entire French divisions had dissolved.

The Canadians escaped all but a whiff of Germany's latest secret weapon—150,000 kilograms of chlorine gas, released from cylinders in their forward trenches. For all their talk of German atrocities, the British had never believed that Germany would use a weapon specifically banned by the Hague Convention of 1907. The Germans eased their consciences by claiming that the French had already used tear gas.[70] Besides, as both sides knew, secret weapons seldom worked very well. Since the effects dissipated rapidly, the Germans issued their own only gauze face masks, purchased in Brussels a few days earlier.[71] Unaware that the French divisions had literally disappeared, the German assault troops advanced cautiously, suspecting a trap. At dusk, they stopped and dug in.[72]

Alderson and Brigadier-General Harry Burstall, visiting trenches near St. Julien, had watched the disaster helplessly. They had two miles to walk back to their horses before they could race to headquarters and give their orders.[73] In the meantime, German shells now rained on the Canadian trenches. Turner found that his telephone wires were cut. Although his brigade was closest to the gas attack, he had little idea what was happening to his men or the front. Later, critics at a safe distance wondered why a Victoria Cross winner or Garnet Hughes, Turner's brigade major, did not emerge amid the German shells to see for himself. As army commander, Smith-Dorrien was better informed: he knew what had befallen the French. His greenest division might be next. Reserve troops were soon on the move. By nightfall, Mercer's 1st Brigade and the first of an eventual thirty-three British battalions had come under Alderson's command.[74]

That night, as backing for a promised French counter-attack, Alderson sent two of his own battalions, the 10th and the 16th, to recapture Kitchener's Wood and the British heavy guns abandoned there. It was the first significant Canadian operation of the war, and it showed. Orders were sketchy; so was artillery support. Two excited and inexperienced colonels had too few questions. At 10:00 p.m., 1,500 men set out in six waves, marching shoulder to shoulder. They were 500 yards from the dark mass of their objective when the Germans opened fire. Guided by the flash of rifles and machine guns, the troops raced forward into the wood. Colonel Russ Boyle and most other officers lay dead or wounded, and none of the surviving officers had any plans for consolidation. The French had not moved. By morning, 500 survivors clung to a trench on the edge of the wood.[75]

At dawn, Lieutenant-Colonel David Watson's 2nd Battalion tried to take the nearby Oblong Farm. "Time spent in reconnaissance is seldom wasted" was an old Staff College saying, but, by the time officers had surveyed the ground and the attack got under way, it was fully daylight. The German gunners could hardly miss. A fresh attack, by the 1st and 4th battalions, suffered a similar fate. The 4th lost its colonel, and the two units lost 858 dead and wounded, altogether more than half their battle strength.[76]

Later that afternoon, after confusion led to postponement, a British brigade also attacked. British and Canadian gunners, unaware of the delay, had fired off almost all their shells, notifying the enemy of the coming assault and running out of ammunition once the doomed attack actually began. Still, the Germans had been stopped; units from Turner's and Mercer's brigades held a frail line, and seven of the twelve Canadian battalions remained relatively unscathed.

On April 23, a German bombardment soon wrecked the frail defences on Strombeek Ridge. At 4:00 a.m. on Saturday, April 24, shelling resumed with a new fury, crushing the mud walls where soldiers sought safety. Next, a "dense, greenish wall, ten or twelve feet high," emerged from the German trenches and a gentle breeze teased it up the slope. Lieutenant-Colonel Louis Lipsett, a British officer who had once instructed Arthur Currie, listened to the advice of the CEF's tiny chemist, Lieutenant-Colonel George Nasmith. Then Lipsett told the men of his 8th Battalion to soak their handkerchiefs or cotton bandoliers and hold them over their noses. Some of the men used their urine, hoping that it might help.

The wind carried most of the gas past all but a company of Lipsett's battalion. Then his Winnipeggers leaped up and kept shooting. The neighbouring 15th Battalion received the full brunt of the chemical. "Imagine Hell in its worst form," as a sergeant expressed it.[77] Between them, the gas and shelling destroyed the two forward companies. A witness recalled seeing survivors casting off rifles and kits as they ran, ripping open their tunics and shirts in their efforts to breathe. Dying men writhed in agony and then lay still. A greenish foam formed over their lips.[78] Later, the Germans described the 15th Battalion's forward trench as a mass grave.[79]

Relatively unaffected by the gas, the 13th Battalion beat off a first attack. The mass of Germans made an easy target; the constant jamming of the Ross rifles made them unbearably hard to shoot. Arthur Corker remembered: "There were some fellers crying in the trenches because they couldn't fire their damned rifles."[80] Renewed shelling and an open flank forced the battalion back to Gravenstafel Ridge, abandoning remnants of the 15th and a British company to surrender or die. Through inexperience, Morrison's artillery batteries were posted too far back to help the Canadians. British Columbians of the 7th Battalion covered the retreat to Gravenstafel Ridge and then to another line farther back. Members of two of the 7th's own companies were killed or captured in the retreat. As the Canadians fell back, companies of the 3rd and 13th battalions, guarding St. Julien, were cut off. Ordered to hold the village to the last, the tiny garrison was overwhelmed by 3:00 p.m.

Two British Territorial battalions recaptured the ruined village an hour too late to save them.[81]

At the apex of the Canadian position, most of the 8th Battalion remained, covered by fire from Colonel George Tuxford's 5th Western Cavalry. Gasping and in tears from the chlorine, the Winnipeggers felt as though their hands and feet were freezing. They remembered an overpowering urge to lie down and rest—a fatal urge, since the gas was densest at the bottom of trenches and in the few dugouts. Somehow, enough men stuck it out to repel a succession of attacks. Having lost his 10th Battalion and most of the 7th, and unaware of Turner's troubles at St. Julien, Currie pleaded in vain for help. Finally, he left Lipsett in charge and walked back himself to see what he could do, "it being thought that they might move for me when unlikely to move for officers of lesser rank."[82] He found the right man: Major-General T. D'O. Snow of the 27th Division had assumed command of all the reserves in the Ypres salient. Unfortunately what Snow, reputedly "the rudest man in the British Army," saw was a panicky colonial brigadier who had abandoned his men.[83] Exhausted and harshly rebuked, Currie returned to his headquarters with a handful of stragglers from the 7th Battalion. Later, he went back to collect all that remained of the 7th and 10th battalions—about 300 men.

Lipsett had more success getting help from the neighbouring 28th Division, but it was not enough. On Sunday, April 25, all that was left of the 2nd Brigade pulled back from the front line, leaving its wounded to become prisoners. It was a day of shelling and continuing losses, but no more gas. By dawn on Monday, April 26, British relief allowed the 1st and 3rd Canadian brigades to move back to rest; the 2nd Brigade followed on the 27th, after German artillery, machine-guns, and a renewed use of gas defeated a further counter-attack by the Indian Army's Lahore Division.[84]

The Second Battle of Ypres was far from over. Canadian gunners remained at their posts throughout the two-week battle, struggling with meagre stocks of ammunition to support British troops against increasingly desperate German attacks and in their own counter-attacks. As part of Snow's 27th Division, the PPCLI lost 80 men holding the line on April 24, while their general argued with Currie. On May 4, in shallow trenches near Hooge, German shelling cost the Patricias 122 more.

On May 8, the Germans launched more assaults on the Ypres salient. On the third attempt, the Germans drove British regulars from Frezenberg Ridge. The PPCLI found itself holding the shoulder of a mile-deep gap in the line. Whole sections of its trenches and their defenders vanished under German shells. Now in command of the battalion he had financed, Major Hamilton Gault ordered cooks, signallers, and orderlies into the line. Somehow the surviving Patricias hung on to most of their position and staved off the German attacks. The day cost the PPCLI 392 casualties. At midnight, when the unit was relieved, only 4 officers and 150 men walked out.[85]

For the Canadian Division the worst of the fighting and dying had ended on the night of April 24. The Canadians had lost St. Julien and the Strombeek and Gravenstafel ridges, ground they had pledged to defend. The battle had cost the raw division 3 of its best colonels and 6,036 men, half its infantry strength. Tens of thousands of homes across Canada felt the loss directly. In Pembroke, Ontario, Grace Craig did not have to look far down the casualty list for the man who might have become her husband: Captain Alfred Bastedo, 4th Battalion, killed in action. Many more would die. Thousands more would go on suffering. The Germans took 1,410 Canadian prisoners at Ypres: 627 of them wounded and 87 of them due to die of their wounds.

Wisely, the British commander-in-chief preferred to praise Alderson's men, not to blame them. The Canadians, claimed Sir John French, "had saved the situation." The phrase gave Canadians at home and overseas badly needed pride and comfort as the names of their fellows at Ypres filled columns of their newspapers for weeks after the battle. To contemporary Canadians, the names Ypres, St. Julien, Gravenstafel Ridge, and Frezenberg retained a weight that Vimy, Hill 60, or the Canal du Nord would never transcend.

Faced with the French collapse, the horror of poison gas, and their own inexperience, the Canadians might well have fled, as veteran troops had before and would in future. Hindsight suggested that the whole Ypres salient should have been abandoned as a useless death-trap. In fact, when Smith-Dorrien suggested this in mid-battle, his old enemy, Sir John French, fired him on the spot. General Headquarters referred to no other problems revealed by the heat of battle: Alderson's seeming lack of contact with his troops throughout April 24, General Turner's persistent ignorance about what was happening on his front and flanks, Currie's encounter with Major-General Snow, and the bad staff work all three problems reflected. Nor would much be done about Currie's namesake, the commanding officer of the 15th Battalion. Colonel Creelman had found the drunken, frightened Colonel J.A. Currie in his dugout, two miles from where his men were being slaughtered. Later, he was found safely in Boulogne, while the survivors of the 15th journeyed by cattle-car into captivity.[86] Currie went home to be promoted for his services.

Most of all, censors suppressed any comments about the survivors' bitterest memory. German attacks had succeeded in part because of the Ross rifle. Just as it had during its first trials in 1901 and ever since, it had seized up on rapid fire. Being equipped with a rifle that could be loaded only after a sharp kick or a blow from a shovel was a scandal only partly remedied when Canadian survivors helped themselves to the Lee-Enfields of the British dead. Nor had the heavy, awkward Colts fared much better.

By dawn on April 25, 263 days after the war began, a few days of battle had transformed the survivors of Second Ypres into soldiers. They had more to learn, as they would painfully discover at Festubert and Givenchy, and in the battles of 1916, but the veterans of Ypres would be ready. Some had reached their personal limits: that summer the division suffered its first self-inflicted wounds. Others would become the generals and colonels and sergeant-majors of the first Canadian army. They had learned what they could never grasp on Salisbury Plain, at Valcartier, or at countless militia camps from Gordon Head to McNab's Island: wars are ugly, merciless struggles, in which skill and ruthlessness alone determine the outcome. The battle had taught the survivors to overcome an enemy more deadly than the Germans: themselves. That alone entitled them to the coloured shoulder straps that identified them as the "Old Originals." Later, Harold Peat, who left part of his leg at Ypres, would remember that little piece of cloth as his proudest possession.[87]

CHAPTER THREE

DOING YOUR BIT

VOLUNTEERS AND CONSCRIPTS

An early wartime slogan promised victory if all "did their bit." The biggest "bit" anyone could do was to join the army. Why did men—and some women—enlist? How were they transformed from civilians into soldiers? Why did some of them have little choice in the matter?

W E COULD SEND enough men to add the finishing touches to Germany without assistance from England or France," Colonel Sam Hughes boasted to reporters in New York before he sailed to meet "his boys."[1] Three days after the first Canadian convoy dropped down the St. Lawrence, Ottawa announced a second contingent of 20,000 men. On December 1, after Britain had declared war on Turkey, Hughes offered the British four regiments of Canadian Mounted Rifles. Britain accepted them and asked for more. Ultimately, thirteen regiments were approved, each half the size of an infantry battalion. In January, Hughes announced a third contingent, adding, "I could raise three more contingents in three weeks."[2]

How would Canada raise its army? In 1917, when the U.S. Congress accepted President Wilson's war message, it enacted a system of selective service. Draft boards decided who could be spared to fight and die. The European powers operated under a different system, prudently training their young men in peacetime for rapid mobilization in time of war. Britain alone depended on volunteers.

However, the drastic pre-war reforms associated with Richard Haldane had prepared a small, reasonably efficient regular army and reorganized part-time volunteers into a Territorial Army, ostensibly for home defence. In practice, the Territorials were more likely to serve overseas and to expand under the oversight of county associations run by local magnates. Officer Training Corps (OTCS) in the universities and England's famous public schools guaranteed a generous supply of enthusiastic junior officers.

Haldane's reforms affected Canada. By integrating British and colonial forces, he ensured that overseas contingents would be more quickly useful. A handful of Canadian officers came to England before the war to absorb the new professionalism, and British officers like Gwatkin and Lipsett went to Canada. If Territorials could form divisions, so could Canada's militia. Of course, there were differences. The militia lagged behind the Territorials in training and organization, but believed themselves far superior. No Imperial scheme could make allowances for Imperialists like Sam Hughes, his passion for the Ross, and his hearty contempt for professionals.

Lord Roberts in Britain and the Canadian Defence League in Canada had led pre-war campaigns for universal military training, but peacetime conscription was anathema in both countries.[3] In 1911, *nationaliste* claims that Sir Wilfrid Laurier's new navy would lead to conscription cost the Liberals votes in Quebec and helped Robert Borden's Conservatives win. Farmers would also resent any government that took their cheapest labour, their sons, and an election was due in 1915. "There has not been, there will not be, compulsion or conscription," the prime minister assured his Halifax constituents in December.[4] To Hughes personally, conscription insulted Canada's manhood. And what was the need, when men everywhere clamoured to enlist?

After August 4, 1914, not Haldane but the great Imperial proconsul, Lord Kitchener, was at the War Office. He disliked his predecessor and he despised the Territorial Army. Rather than draw on the county associations to raise men, he had invented his own "New Army." Helped by posters featuring his stern countenance and the words "Your King and Country Need YOU," Kitchener raised 250,000 men in one month, and 1.3 million by Christmas. With astonishing patience and fortitude, New Army recruits had drilled without weapons or uniforms through that winter Canadians on Salisbury Plain had found so abominable. Thanks to the pre-war OTCs, the army could find lots of newly fledged officers. Senior officers were another matter. With so much of the regular army gone, regimental depots had to rely on superannuated "dugouts" whose service had sometimes ended before the Boer War. Seldom in the history of war had finer volunteers been saddled with more obsolete commanders.

After Valcartier, many Canadians thought Hughes a genius for getting a division overseas in two months. By comparison, Militia Headquarters had managed, by decentralization, to raise, equip, and despatch 1,100 men to South Africa in two weeks in October 1899. However, winter made a tented camp uninhabitable, and reports from Salisbury Plain persuaded Hughes that the battalions of the Second Contingent would be better housed in armouries, disused factories, and exhibition halls across Canada.

This time Gwatkin's plan was followed. Two of Ontario's four battalions were organized in Toronto, and one each at London and Kingston. Each western province had a battalion; so did Nova Scotia and New Brunswick. When a powerful Montreal delegation demanded a French-speaking battalion, it pushed at an open door. The 22nd (French-Canadian) Battalion was approved; so was the 24th, a battalion of English-speaking Quebeckers. Across Canada, Artillery, Engineer, Medical Corps, and Service Corps units took shape, with help from their peacetime counterparts. The contingent even boasted the first members of a newfangled Canadian Army Dental Corps. The 22nd Battalion needed French-speaking recruits from other units of the Contingent and was finally moved to Nova Scotia to slow a haemorrhage of deserters from its ranks. Otherwise, recruiting went so well that, between January and June 1915, Hughes invited thirty-five more colonels to raise battalions.

The wealthy contributed to the cause. Joe Boyle, a Yukon mining magnate, equipped and despatched a fifty-member Yukon Machine Gun Battery to Vancouver. Their cap badges included a small but genuine nugget of Klondike gold. Montreal mining promoters recruited Borden's Armoured Battery from miners at Cobalt and Haileybury. In Toronto, the Eaton family provided $206,807 for armoured cars and $30,340 for other vehicles for their Machine Gun Battery.

With no apparent policy in mind beyond offering encouragement, in June the government announced 150,000 as the authorized strength of the Canadian Expeditionary Force. That summer, Borden visited England and France, and found a dismaying lack of "earnestness" there. If only to prove his own commitment, he arbitrarily raised Canada's target to 250,000 men. At the end of 1915, angry that the British government was still not taking the war or Canada seriously enough, the prime minister announced in a New Year's message to the troops that Canada would raise 500,000 men. That, he felt, would demonstrate "an unflinchable resolve to crown the justice of our cause with victory and with an abiding peace."[5]

The question lingers: why did anyone enlist? Cynics claimed that a cold winter and unemployment drove men to the recruiting stations for "a dollar a day and all found." Veterans of the 22nd Battalion told their historian, Jean-Pierre Gagnon, that most of the recruits were unemployed or veterans who joined "tout simplement parce qu'ils n'avaient pas d'emploi, parfois parce qu'ils étaient épris de l'aventure."[6] Frank Maheux, an Ottawa Valley logger and South African War veteran who joined the 21st Battalion, qualified on both counts. As he explained to his Angeline, the best he could earn in the shanty was $22 a month; as a soldier's wife, she and their three children would get $20 separation allowance, $25 from the Patriotic Fund, and half his pay.[7] Understandably, since his wife could still refuse to allow him into the CEF, Maheux exaggerated a little. CPF benefits varied by community and province, and ignored inflation. By 1915, a soldier had to assign half his pay to receive separation allowance, and only then did Maheux keep his promise. Still, for many Canadian families in the 1914 depression, a soldier's pay could look very attractive.

A patriot like J.M. Macdonell, a Rhodes Scholar who left the presidency of National Trust at twenty-nine to become an artillery officer, understandably found such considerations a little base. "Men enlisted, not from the highest motives but because they thought they would like it, because they were out of work, because they were drunk, because they were militiamen and had to save their face," he reported to his father, though he graciously added, "being 'in' they have quit themselves like men."[8] Major Andrew Macphail of the Canadian Army Medical Corps would not give them even that credit. According to him, the army had swept up idlers and the chronically unemployed: "These men have a genius for discovering the easy place," he complained, "and hospital accommodation is so enormous that they have little difficult in gaining admission."[9]

The army attracted all kinds, but idealists were more common than idlers. Most of the men who joined in 1915 left good jobs behind them. They could have had few illusions about glory or easy victories. M.M. Hood was a theology student in 1915: "I was a Scot and my country was at war," he explained later, "and automatically Canada was also at war with my country's enemies."[10] Donald Fraser, another Scot, the son of a successful Edinburgh businessman, came to Canada in 1906, worked as a clerk in Calgary and Vancouver, and returned to Calgary early in 1915 to join the 31st Battalion, "Bell's Bulldogs." A quiet, reserved man, he took it for granted that anyone would know why he joined. George Pearkes had emigrated from England to a Saskatchewan homestead. He joined the Mounted Police when he realized there were too many brothers for the farm, and he was in the Yukon when war broke out. He resigned as soon as he could, and joined the 2nd Canadian Mounted Rifles as a roughrider, to break the unit's horses. "I can't say I ever thought much at that time about fighting for Canada or fighting for democracy," he told his biographer; "we were fighting for England."[11] Federal and provincial governments and many private employers promised to pay salaries and keep jobs open, though when the war entered a second year, they wished they had been more cautious. After years of drought and depression, prairie farmers had the best year they could remember in 1915, which made it a bad time for a homesteader's sons to join up. Many did anyway. No one reimbursed them for lost income.

Then and now, one can only guess why most men enlisted. Social pressure, unemployment, escape from a tiresome family or a dead-end job, self-respect, and proving one's manhood have motived soldiers through the ages. An English immigrant explained joining the CEF as a means of getting to England, securing a New Army commission, and raising his social standing. Others, like A.G. May, simply recalled that it was "the thing to do."[12] W.M. Foster enlisted at New Liskeard in northern Ontario: "I, being of age, thought it my duty to go to France and stand up for my country."[13] That consciousness of duty owed much to pre-war education and upbringing. In England and Canada, school readers excerpted the "gospel of manliness" and the unabashed patriotism of W.E. Henley, Henry Newbolt, and Rudyard Kipling. Maps, with their generous swatches of Imperial red, reminded students that they were co-proprietors of the world's greatest empire and inheritors of "The White Man's Burden."

"We felt that we were fighting for what was right," claimed Edgar Harold, successful on his third attempt to enlist. "We were brought up on the *Boy's Own Annual* and *Chums* and on novels like those of Henty and Ballantyne."[14] A young history professor, Frank Underhill, felt ashamed of just delivering patriotic speeches and enlisted. Like other CEF privates, he got a British commission in England.[15] Garnet Durham, who had joined the First Contingent, debated by mail whether his brother Dick would enlist. "Personally I hate the idea of fighting but as Conan Doyle says in one of his books, 'There are times when every one of us must make a stand for human right and justice or never feel clean again.' Personally I could not have seen others going and felt comfortable."[16] Dick joined up.

No sooner are soldiers enrolled in an army than they start to disappear. Thirty-six thousand men came to Valcartier, but more than five thousand went home again for health reasons, as discipline problems, or because a wife or parent had refused permission. In England, 68 died; 273 officers and other ranks accepted New Army commissions; and 802 of all ranks were sent home as unfit, unwanted, undesirable, or, in the case of 46 "aliens," untrusted.

In one day at Ypres, the Canadian Division lost almost half its infantry strength in dead, wounded, and prisoners. Bloody experience told the British that units needed not 10 but 60 per cent of their strength available as trained replacements. Even after the wounded returned to duty, an infantry division needed 12,000 to 20,000 new men a year. When the Second Contingent became the 2nd Canadian Division in September 1915, Canada had two such divisions in the field; a year later, it had four. To keep them there would take 80,000 soldiers a year, most of them infantry.

Organizing "reinforcements," as the army called them, is unglamorous but essential. Gwatkin had planned regional depots to recruit men and keep the local battalions up to strength. Hughes preferred an ever-expanding Canadian army, with new battalions constantly forming new divisions. In the fall of 1915, Gwatkin predicted that Canada would have trouble maintaining more than three divisions.

Hughes ignored him. In early 1916, he promised an army of twenty-one divisions, five of them from Toronto. How existing battalions would fill ranks emptied by sickness, desertion, and enemy action never fazed him. His biographer ventured to suggest that the minister's mind simply could not handle these sorts of details.[17]

Yet the battalions of the "Old Originals" could not be discarded like empty bottles. Five of the First Contingent battalions had been broken up for reinforcements, and three Second Contingent battalions left in January and February to meet the same fate. To preserve its élite image, the PPCLI filled its depleted ranks with special companies of university students. In the spring and summer of 1915, most battalions in Canada were ordered to send 250-man reinforcement drafts. Colonels faced a familiar military test of character: whether to send their best men or their worst.

In many cases, their choices made no difference. Of the thirty-eight units that sent drafts, twenty-seven would get no closer to Berlin than Bramshott in southern England. Besides the Royal Canadian Regiment in Bermuda, the PPCLI in France, and the Canadian Mounted Rifles (CMR) regiments, which, at the end of 1915, were reorganized as four infantry battalions, Canada had created ninety infantry battalions by October 1915. At its largest, with a fifth division in England, the CEF required only sixty-five infantry and pioneer battalions.

Hughes could have heeded Gwatkin, calculated Canada's realistic manpower potential, authorized depots, or at least undertaken the systematic management of recruiting. Being Hughes, he did nothing of the kind.

The shock of Ypres had aroused influential citizens. Sir John French's claim that the Canadians "had saved the situation" created a heroic legend. The horror of German gas and appalling casualty lists inspired pride, rage, sorrow, and a renewed patriotism. Canadians were not merely helping the mother country; they were battling Hunnish villainy. The news of Ypres was followed on May 7 by news that the huge steamer *Lusitania* had been torpedoed off Ireland, with a loss of 1,195 lives. A hundred of them were Canadians, mostly wives and children going to England to be closer to their husbands and fathers in the CEF. Mobs in Victoria, Montreal, and Vancouver demolished German businesses; next day, more "enemy aliens" were sent to join the thousands already held in Canadian internment camps.

Across Canada, the "better elements" found a new way to do their bit. Speakers' bureaus, patriotic associations, and recruiting leagues sprang up, encouraging younger men to give their all. Editors grew strident about lagging enlistment. Clergy preached on patriotic duty. Methodists, humiliated by statistics showing a mere 8 per cent Methodist share of the CEF's volunteers, pledged to do better.[18] Recruiting meetings, complete with military bands, amateur entertainers, and flickering films from the front, showcased patriotic orators and occasional "returned men" with gory tales from the trenches. *The Globe* reported a Toronto meeting at which, after "an eloquent address," men too old for service but who would volunteer if they were younger were asked to stand. Then the women present were asked to rise, and then the munition workers, until, finally, only eligible recruits were left seated under the stares of the crowd. Prudent young men quickly learned to avoid such public meetings; old-timers volunteered again and again. In 1916, men rejected from service on account of health or age could finally obtain a special badge so that the myrmidons of patriotism would not shame them as "slackers." For the same reason, returned soldiers received a discharge button from the Patriotic Fund.

Patriotic help was soon followed by criticism. Why wasn't there more snap and vigour in recruiting? In Britain, the Parliamentary Recruiting League had produced a hundred different posters and distributed two and a half million of them. Some Canadian associations bought copies and sold them. The Militia Department eventually issued two posters of its own, but when the French section of Montreal's Citizens' Recruiting Association asked for posters in its own language, Ottawa refused, "such expenditures not having been incurred by the department in the past."[19]

Indeed, the department had never played any direct role in recruiting. Its main intervention in 1916 was to order military district commanders to appoint a director of recruiting. In Montreal, Major-General E.W. Wilson, a local insurance executive in civilian life, proposed two directors, one French, one English. Thanks to a local organization that had thrived since the fall of 1914, it was easy to find Major C.A. Williams, a prominent Methodist minister. Although he had approached a long list of French-speaking notables, ranging from Senator Raoul Dandurand to the Archbishop of Montreal, Wilson had to report: "I regret to inform you that they had been unable to secure the name of a Priest who would undertake the duties." Months later, Liberals and *nationalistes* insisted recruiting had failed in French-speaking Quebec because Hughes had deliberately put a Methodist in charge.[20]

The militia regiments felt the criticisms too. Why did they not do more? Where were their posters and brochures? The answer was simple. Pre-war regulations helped protect taxpayers from recruiting costs. If a colonel wanted to print a poster or a brochure, he applied to his district officer commanding, who sought approval from Militia Headquarters, where the deputy minister's branch would seek consent and appropriate rates from the King's Printer. A sensible officer took the money from regimental funds or forgot about the whole business. Private or regimental funds financed band instruments, an unofficial battalion cap badge, and basic furnishings for the officers' and sergeants' messes.

By August 1915, a year's recruiting had worn out many regiments. Their best officers and NCOs had long since gone overseas. Funds were exhausted. In French Canada and the Maritimes, most militia units had never been very popular or strong. Neither was recruiting.

Finally, the Militia Department tried to make recruiting easier. In July 1915, it cut the standards for height and chest measurement. In August, men lost the right to buy themselves out, and wives lost the right to stop their husbands from joining. To soften rural resistance, soldiers could be released on harvest leave. This helped farmers to sacrifice their sons, but it disorganized training. So did Hughes's solution to the accommodation problem in the fall of 1915: recruits in towns and cities could live at home on a subsistence allowance of 60 cents a day. When rural battalions complained about discrimination, they were allowed to billet their men in platoon-sized detachments throughout their recruiting area— provided no liquor was sold on the premises.

In England, Hughes had been delighted by Kitchener's New Army, with its battalions of sportsmen, "chums," and some so elegant that men paid three guineas or more to join. Kilts, temperance, and a love of sports could attract many Canadians too. Soon Hughes turned to politicians, businessmen, and prominent local heroes to head battalions.[21] Any Ontario county could have its own unit. So would Prince Edward Island. If the Scots had battalions, so must the Irish. The protests from military district commanders and militia regiments were ignored: of course, they would protect their red tape.

During the fall of 1915, Hughes authorized eighty-six new CEF battalions; in the winter of 1916, he added fifty-eight more. Anyone with a bright idea and access to the minister had a chance to set up his own unit. Lieutenant-Colonel John Thompson, the son of a former prime minister, insisted he could recruit a battalion if the men were allowed to wear breeches and boots. Henri Bourassa's errant lieutenant Olivar Asselin, disgusted by the human dregs who enlisted after the 22nd Battalion left, offered to recruit. His 163th "Poil-aux-Pattes" would appeal only to Quebec's élite. Glenlyon Campbell, a former Tory MP and veteran of the 1885 campaign, promised to recruit cowboys and Indians for the 107th Battalion, and did.[22] Danish Canadians, eager to avenge the Prussian seizure of Schleswig-Holstein, also asked to raise a battalion. Hughes agreed.

Embarrassed by his province's weak showing, Borden lent his support to trying to raise an entire Highland brigade in Nova Scotia. A Winnipeg battalion filled its ranks by promising strict temperance. A New Brunswick battalion advertised only for Acadians; Lieutenant-Colonel Joseph Daigle had to explain: "the French Acadians are a distinct people from the French Canadians both in character and temperament."[23] Three Ontario battalions appealed for "Men of the North." At Moose Jaw, a renegade member of the Legion of Frontiersmen tried to raise a battalion in the Legion's name. Hughes's pal, Sam Sharpe, MP for Ontario, raised the 116th from his county. Officers and men of the 118th Battalion patriotically made life miserable for German-speaking citizens of Berlin (later Kitchener) and Waterloo County, Ontario.[24]

"Do something to give all a show," Hughes urged. In practice, by handing over recruiting to colonels, Hughes lost control. For all his brusque authority, the minister could not convince colonels to accept blacks. When black Canadians finally got their own unit, it turned out to be a labour battalion. Enthusiasm plummeted.[25] Denied their own battalion and rejected by recruiters in their native British Columbia, Japanese Canadians crossed the Rockies to Alberta, where the racial climate was a little more tolerant.[26] Short men were treated better: two battalions accepted "Bantams," men under the minimum height of 5 feet 2 inches.

Native Canadians were sought after in the CEF, and more than a third of the 11,500 eligible men enlisted. Of course, colonels who boasted that they could appeal to "dusky warriors" usually failed. Glen Campbell's 107th Battalion was an exception, perhaps because he did not patronize his Native recruits. After several of their men died at Ypres, the Six Nations tried to ban recruiting on their reserves.

A number of battalions across Canada recruited as "The American Legion" and actively encouraged men to cross the border to enlist. This offence against American law angered Washington and exasperated the British, who were doing their utmost to cultivate official American support. Caught in limbo, the American Legion battalions eventually distributed their turbulent recruits to other CEF units and disappeared from all but legend.

CEF BATTALIONS AUTHORIZED 1914-1918

Year	1914	1915	1916	1917	1918	Total
BC	2	16	2	–	–	20
ALTA	3	15	7			25
SASK	1	7	9			17
MAN	2	15	16			33
ONT	5	75	29			109
QUE						
(ENG.)	2	9	4			15
(FRE.)	½	7	5	1		13½
NB	½	7½	2			10
PEI	–	1½	–			1½
NS	1	6	5			12
MISC.					2	2
	17	158	69	1	2	258

Plus PPCLI *formed in Ottawa*
RCR *(permanent force, based in Halifax)*

Popular militia regiments like Montreal's Black Watch or Toronto's Queen's Own continued to sponsor their own battalions, but now they faced intense rivals. In early 1916, three battalions competed for Edmontonians; Winnipeg had six battalions; Toronto had eight. In the new, competitive era, "shaming" tactics resumed, though deplored by militia authorities. In Saskatchewan, the Citizens' Recruiting League persuaded prominent wives and mothers to sign a circular urging that slackers be boycotted socially. By entertaining "these wretched apologies," it warned, "you foully wrong their manhood by encouraging them to perform their parlour tricks while Europe is burning up."[27] A Dutch-born theology student, Pierre van Paassen, said that he was forced to enlist by a woman in Toronto. The watching crowd helped her pin a white feather on the "cowardly alien."[28] He spent the rest of the war in a Pioneer unit.

More common were the efforts expended by patriotic associations to persuade women that they were unpatriotic if they sheltered their menfolk from enlisting. Toronto's 123rd Battalion urged women to spurn any man who lacked the courage to join up. Its rival, the 124th, appealed to "pals," promising that the battalion would keep friends who enlisted together. Both units reached their quota and became the most junior of the "Overseas Battalions" to reach France.

Poaching was a contentious issue among recruiters. Battalions recruiting in rural areas were assigned to set districts, but recruiting parties and volunteers still strayed over the arbitrary borders. All three battalions assigned to Ontario's Peel County, for instance, found most of their men in nearby Toronto. One of them also accepted some stray "Russians" whom no one else seemed to want.[29] Around tiny Moosomin, in Saskatchewan, a pair of battalions competed fiercely for men. As recruiting progressed, it also grew costly: organizers needed money for posters, advertisements, meeting halls, and travel by recruiting teams. Toronto's *Daily Star* estimated that raising a battalion in that city cost $13,384, including $2,554 for advertising and $930 for telephones.[30] A more frugal unit might forgo $2,000 for brass and bugle bands, or $2,500 to buy a pair of field kitchens. The men who wanted the glory of being colonels had to dig in their own pockets, and sometimes deeper. Patriotic associations and county and municipal councils were expected to help out financially.

However, the sheer number of recruits seemed to confirm Hughes's genius. While volunteering petered out in Britain by the autumn of 1915, it appeared to take off in Canada. From 12,410 recruits who signed up in October 1915, the number shot up to 28,185 in January 1916, and to 33,960 in March. Between October 1915 and the following May, the CEF signed up 185,887 recruits.

As usual, amid all the organizational complications, Hughes ignored the tiresome details. The cost was high. In the scramble for men, many battalions had not been fussy about whom they accepted. Doctors ignored physical defects and passed men as fit because their colonel needed them. Ultimately, these same recruits saddled the country with huge medical and pension bills. By September 1916, the problem was big enough to force the Militia Department to bar attestation until a man was checked out by a medical board armed with X-rays and other diagnostic tools. Some men enlisted to get free treatment for old ailments. A three-dollar tuberculin test would have saved Canadian taxpayers on average $5,000, later spent to treat each case of tuberculosis.[31]

Men who were tricked or coerced into enlisting usually became deserters or discipline problems later. An order-in-council passed in late September permitted colonels to dock the pay of absentees and deserters to cover the cost of bringing them back to barracks. Underlying the glowing reports sent to Ottawa, total strengths concealed the fact that units routinely lost a quarter of the men they enrolled. The 217th Battalion, one of the two that hunted for volunteers around Moosomin, found 1,039 recruits, but only 809 of them appeared for the inspector general, and 634 eventually embarked for overseas. After terrorizing German Canadians in Berlin, Ontario, the 118th Battalion left Canada with a mere 246 men. The Viking image of the 223rd Battalion helped attract 925 men, but only 507 left for England.

Exhausted by their recruiting efforts, influential Canadians grumbled ominously about the eligible men who had ignored the national crusade. They might have criticized rural Ontario or the Maritimes; they preferred to complain about French Canada. With 61 per cent of the population, Ontario and the West provided 73.3 per cent of CEF enlistments; Quebec, with 27.3 per cent of the population, supplied only 14.2 per cent, and most of them came from the 18 per cent of Quebeckers who spoke English. Sixty-two per cent of Quebec's infantry volunteers had joined English-speaking battalions.

This reflected an old, uncomfortable weakness in the country's militia organizations. For years, ministers and generals had ignored the feeble state of the militia in French Canada and the lack of able French-speaking officers in the PF. Now they reaped the consequences. When the 22nd Battalion went overseas, most of French Canada's warlike spirit went with it. Its Third Contingent successor, the 41st, needed a company of "Russians" to meet its quota. In England, roving gangs from the 41st Battalion terrorized the camp and neighbouring towns. Claude Craig's unit inherited its quarters when it was dissolved: "There never was a rougher Battalion ever mobilized."[32]

Nine other battalions sought French-speaking recruits. Two of them, Asselin's Poil-aux-Pattes and Lieutenant-Colonel Philippe-Auguste Piuze's 189th from the Gaspé, performed as well as the best. In the rest, however, incompetent or corrupt colonels swept through the Montreal slums, promising recruits regular meals, a warm overcoat, and a pension. Lieutenant-Colonel Tancrède Pagnuelo grandly assured volunteers for his 206th Battalion that theirs would be "the last regiment to go; the first to profit from victory."[33] By the summer of 1916, recruiters in Montreal and outlying Quebec towns faced insults and small riots. Ottawa responded sharply: an order-in-council made it an offence to disrupt a recruiting meeting.

Embarrassed Quebeckers blamed Hughes's Orange bigotry, Methodist recruiting officers, and the minister's failure to distribute high commands to French-Canadian officers or to create a French-speaking brigade. Historians have explained that French

Canadians married young and stayed on the farm. Few French-speaking Quebeckers considered the war their crusade and few tried to change their minds. In three years, Sir Wilfrid Laurier delivered only two eloquent recruiting speeches. In Quebec City, Colonel A.O. Fages complained that prominent citizens declined to address recruiting rallies, lesser figures wanted to be paid for the job, and the French-speaking members of a Women's Recruiting League "did their best to put obstacles in the way to stop the movement."34 When Borden's Quebec ministers tried to help, crowds heckled them and reminded them of their *nationaliste* past. By the time the Militia Department finally acknowledged that Quebec could not be treated as a province like the others, it was too late. In mid-1916 it appointed Colonel Arthur Mignault as its chief recruiting officer in the province and gave him a budget and staff. Mignault, a prominent and patriotic manufacturer of quack remedies, applied himself to the hopeless task and then reproached the department bitterly when he failed.

By the fall of 1916, Mignault would have failed anywhere in Canada. Voluntary enlistment in the infantry had dried up. In western Canada, the CEF's best recruiting ground, 23 battalions raised 21,897 men in the last three months of 1915; 34 battalions needed the next six months to raise 22,593. From July to October 1916, three more battalions gathered only 896 men. In Ontario, between January and October 1915, 23 battalions sent an average of 1,535 men each overseas. Between November 1915 and February 1916, 62 newly authorized battalions eventually sent 60,980 men to England—an average of 983 per unit. Twenty-eight battalions, added later in 1916, despatched only 13,092 men. Even Hughes must have noticed that the 252nd Battalion, recruiting in his own riding of Victoria and Haliburton, found only 153 men fit for service.

After the summer of 1916, a few thousand men joined the CEF monthly, but they chose the Artillery, Engineers, or Army Medical Corps. Several CEF battalions, unable to enlist infantry, settled for becoming units of the Canadian Forestry Corps or the Canadian Railway Troops. Important as such troops were, they could not replace most of the 80,000 dead and permanently maimed that the Canadian Corps lost each year.

Because of faulty statistics, Hughes's blind optimism, and the proliferation of battalions and troops everywhere, hardly anyone in Ottawa noticed that recruiting was drying up. Only in November 1916, after Hughes's resignation, did the truth begin to emerge. Why did recruiting fail? When his beloved 157th Simcoe County Battalion was broken up, Leslie Frost suggested that potential recruits were disgusted by the official breach of a promise that men would serve together.[35] In English Canada, editors and politicians blamed Henri Bourassa and other *nationalistes* for subverting Quebec. Others blamed farmers and business for their selfishness, wives and mothers for their overprotectiveness, and the young for sheer pleasure-seeking.

Actually there was a limit to the number of Canadians willing to face the harsh life and cruel death of an infantry soldier. At a meeting of western Ontario colonels in early 1917, Lieutenant-Colonel H.T. Rance spoke for more than Huron County when he reported that "the men have been talked to death by the preachers and newspapers and magazine, and one half of the people of the county will recruit the other half.... They are gone who are willing to go as volunteers, the others must be pressed."[36]

By 1916, most men were carrying out some form of war service, even if they had not enlisted. At the same time that Borden announced his target of attracting 500,000 men to the army, farmers counted their best income in decades. And they needed more labour to meet government demands for still greater production. The new munitions industry enlisted 300,000 men by paying good wages. The boost to industry created thousands of new jobs.

Following the recruiting frenzy of 1915–16, more than a quarter of the military-age group had joined up; the majority had refused. Hughes's successor, Sir Edward Kemp, accepted the inevitable in January 1917: there would be no more "Overseas Battalions." Any further recruits would be sent over in drafts. Any CEF battalion with more than 700 men could embark as a unit.[37] Men still joined other branches and services, but, by mid-war, Canada had abandoned its voluntary system for recruiting infantry. If the ranks of the Canadian Corps were not to dwindle, some other way had to be found.

Conscription was not a new idea in Canada. Politicians had debated the subject in pre-war Britain and Canada. The patriotic and recruiting leagues had called for it as early as 1915. By 1917, Borden had done all he could to avoid it. He had encouraged recruiters for his Nova Scotia Highland Brigade and from New Brunswick to invade the New England states and bring back enough men to fill out the cloyingly named 236th "MacLean Kilties," the last full-strength CEF battalion.

In Quebec, Borden sent his postmaster general, P.E. Blondin, and an elderly Major-General François-Louis Lessard in a last attempt to recruit a battalion. They met with contempt and indifference and returned with ninety-two men, most of them deemed unfit. Over the furious objections of organized labour, a scheme of National Registration, managed by R.B. Bennett, tried to identify men who should volunteer. Almost no one came forward.

In April 1917, Borden was in London, finally sharing in Imperial strategy and learning how desperate the Allied cause had become. Then fate stepped in. That month, the Canadian Corps captured Vimy Ridge. Despite the stiff price of 10,602 men, 3,598 of them dead, Sir Robert and all Canada basked in the glory of the Allies' first major victory. That month 4,492 men volunteered, few of them choosing the infantry. In the British capital, Canada's prime minister faced an uncomfortable choice: he could allow the Canadian Corps to shrink, or he had to find a new way of supplying men for the Allied effort. Borden was a drab, dogged, decent man. He bravely ate his 1914 promises. He returned to Canada convinced of the need for conscription for overseas service. On May 18, MPS listened to the prime minister's report on the "extreme gravity" of the situation in Europe. Men, he insisted, must be found, and voluntary enlistment had reached its limits. "By compulsory military enlistment on a selective basis," the government proposed to provide "such reinforcements as may be necessary to maintain the

Canadian Army to-day in the field as one of the finest fighting units of the Empire. The number of men required will be not less than 50,000 and will probably be 100,000."[38]

The ensuing political struggle consumed the rest of 1917. To design the Military Service Act (MSA), Borden turned to Arthur Meighen, the brightest and toughest of his ministers. Mindful that the prime minister had pledged to respect religious beliefs and to disrupt farming, business, and family life as little as possible, Meighen studied the new American selective-service law. By following that model for the Canadian legislation, the federal government joined the Americans, making it easier for both sides to crack down on evaders.

Men aged between twenty and forty-three were divided into six classes, according to age and marital status, beginning with single men aged twenty to thirty-four, and ending with married men aged forty-one to forty-four. Those who married after July 6, 1917, were defined as single. Soldiers, the obviously disabled, men in essential jobs or with special skills, the clergy, and conscientious objectors could apply for exemption to one of 1,253 two-member local tribunals. The government and opposition each named a member. Appeal lay through 195 special courts to a single central appeal judge, Mr. Justice Lyman Duff, a British Columbian on the Supreme Court. Managing the MSA was mainly a job for the Department of Justice, with the Military Service Council, under E.L. Newcombe, Deputy Minister of Justice, to oversee the regulations, and Lieutenant-Colonel H.A.C. Machin, a Conservative MLA from Kenora, as director.

By the time the Military Service Act became law on August 29, patience, boldness, and luck helped Borden convert a political liability into a temporary asset. His Liberal opponents were more split than his own party, and the opposition was outflanked by legislation enfranchising soldiers and their female relatives. Aliens were denied the vote if naturalized since 1902 on the basis that they would not be conscripted and had no right to decide the outcome. When Borden announced an election for December 17, plans for a coalition fell in place.

The first meeting of the new Union government ordered members of Class I to report by November 10, and directed that they be called "drafted men," not "conscripts." Then Native people and Asians were exempted because of their limited political rights. Union ministers secured their flanks in the turbulent election campaign by promising to exempt farmers' sons and the brothers of serving soldiers from conscription. That promise and a vaguer pledge of a home furlough for surviving "Old Originals" consolidated the military vote. Unlike the Australian troops, who twice joined a home majority to defeat conscription, CEF members favoured the government. Military voters doubled Borden's majority of 200,000 and switched fourteen seats from the Liberals to Unionists. The losers cried foul, claiming that officers had told their men how to vote. They condemned a loophole in the Military Voters Act that allowed soldiers with no Canadian domicile to choose the riding where they wished to register their votes. As the Minister of Justice had sweetly observed during debate on the Military Voters Act, the opportunity to persuade soldiers to use their votes wisely existed for both parties.[39]

Even before the December 17 election, it appeared that the MSA's own rules might frustrate finding large numbers of men. A worried Militia Department modified its recruiting standards. Despite the problems a small man might have carrying eighty to ninety pounds of kit and equipment, a five-foot-tall recruit could be accepted for the infantry. Men for the Medical Corps, the Pioneers, and the Railway Troops could be 4 feet 11 inches. Provided they had bush experience, the Forestry Corps accepted men with defective eyesight and hearing.

Physical fitness was not, in fact, the main problem. Out of 405,395 Class I men who reported, 380,510 filed for exemption, and in 334,989 cases, tribunals found for the claimants. The decisions looked political. Every student at Quebec's Laval University was exempted. A Montreal tribunal heard 2,595 cases in two days, and exempted 2,021. In contrast, an officer who watched proceedings at a St. Catharines, Ontario, tribunal, wryly commented, "I believe even a dead man would have to show good reason."[40] Appeal courts heard 120,448 challenges and ordered 36,781 men to serve. As the final arbiter, Mr. Justice Duff dealt with 42,300 cases, and ruled against 20,240 men. Appeal judges decided that Doukhobors, Mennonites, and Canadian Hutterites were conscientious objectors, but not Plymouth Brethren, Jehovah's Witnesses, secular pacifists, or Hutterites who had fled the American draft. Over all, 50,299 conscripts were denied exemption.[41]

By April 1, 1918, only 20,025 MSA men had reported for service, 6,775 others had volunteered, and 4,495 evaders had been captured. In British Columbia, Ginger Goodwin, a prominent labour leader, was shot "trying to escape." In Quebec, most police refused to help MSA officials enforce conscription. The Dominion Police, a tiny federal force responsible for guarding federal buildings in Ottawa, was hurriedly expanded to help enforce the law in eastern Canada, while the Royal North-West Mounted Police did the same job in the West. An agreement with the United States made MSA conscripts subject to the U.S. draft if they tried to leave Canada.

On March 28, just before Easter, the Dominion Police in Quebec City sparked a riot when they tried to arrest draft dodgers. By the night of April 1, five soldiers were wounded and five civilians lay dead in the snow. Most had died when troops brought from Toronto panicked under a rain of stones and snowballs, and opened fire. An alarmed federal cabinet passed orders suspending *habeas corpus*, conscripting rioters, and putting the city under virtual martial law. An equally shocked clergy commanded the faithful to respect public order and obey a distasteful law—and to most people's surprise, they did.

It was just as well. On March 21, German offensives pulverized the British line. On April 11, Borden pleaded for accurate word from overseas: "we are all terribly disturbed and depressed by the continuing success of the German drive."[42] From London, Clifford Sifton, one of the most influential members of Borden's Union government, wired back: "Every available fighting man should be got over here at earliest possible moment." Warned by Kemp as Minister of Militia that, at current rates of conscription, there might be no men left by July 1, the government called a secret session of Parliament on April 17 to explain why it would cancel exemptions. It did so in open session on April 19 and warned that the draft age limit would also be dropped to nineteen. Discreet protests won concessions for religious conscientious objectors and soldiers' brothers. Furious farmers, who had saved their sons in 1917 and now lost them, got them back again briefly, but only for seeding and harvest leave. Otherwise, the government was firm. In Alberta, R.B. Bennett secured a writ of *habeas corpus* for an MSA man whose exemption had expired. The Cabinet promptly set aside any judicial decision interfering with conscription, and on July 18 the Supreme Court upheld the government by four to two.

MSA men got a mixed welcome to the ranks. "I pity the poor devils that are forced into it," Ernest Hamilton wrote to his wife, "as they will not get the treatment we get & that is not saying very much."[43] Frances Upton, a nursing sister, sewed on her overseas-service chevrons to make a point to those who had not volunteered. Headquarters warned that anyone who used the word *conscript* would be punished. "I think most of the chaps will take a chance on the punishment, and get a bit off their chests first," Captain Claude Williams suggested. "The draftees' path is not to be strewn with roses."[44] Neither, however, was it notably rough. Unlike the Australians, men of the CEF had supported conscription, and they absorbed the result. Brutality was reserved for those who still refused to come. Some 636 conscientious objectors denied exemption by the appeal system were enlisted, sent to England, court-martialled if they refused to serve, and sentenced to two or more years in military prisons. Two Jehovah's Witnesses and a Pentecostal told of being hosed down with icy water and forced to sit naked on an icy slab in a Winnipeg armouries until they physically collapsed. Like many others, they ended the war at the notorious British military prison at Wandsworth.[45]

For years Gwatkin had wanted a rationalization of the CEF's organization. With the MSA, his plan was finally implemented. In 1917, overseas battalions in France and the reserve battalions in England that fed them reinforcements were formally linked to a province or region. The MSA enabled Gwatkin to create provincial or regional regiments, with depot battalions to receive all recruits, drafted or volunteer. An infantry recruit from Saint John, for example, would join the 1st Battalion, New Brunswick Regiment; head straight to England for training; and eventually join one of his province's two battalions in the Canadian Corps.

Running a depot battalion was no picnic. Lieutenant-Colonel W.A.E. Baywater, commanding the 2nd Battalion of the Eastern Ontario Regiment, based at Ottawa, recalled that when 200 men were needed overseas, he warned 600 "who promptly wired home and brought down such an avalanche of Members, Clergmen [sic] Lawyers and their own family that on the day of departure the camp developed into a sort of madhouse." French Canadians, 40 per cent of the unit's intake, "were usually hostile to the Service, but after a few days settled down and became cheerful and quickly took up the work and became good soldiers."[46]

Reorganization underlined another problem: British Columbia, Manitoba, and English-speaking Quebec had more battalions with the Corps than their dwindling manpower could sustain. Ontario and the Maritimes, in particular, were underrepresented. In 1917, the Canadian authorities replaced two Quebec English battalions, the 60th and 73rd, with Nova Scotia's 85th Highlanders and Ontario's 116th Battalion. Substituting two veteran battalions with two raw units caused such ill-feeling that another option was tried: battalions were allocated to other regions. The 54th from the Kootenays became the 54th (Central Ontario) Battalion, and, in 1918, the 47th from New Westminster and the 102nd from northern B.C. were redesignated the "Western Ontario" and "Central Ontario" Battalion, respectively. Winnipeg's 44th Battalion moved to New Brunswick. Veteran soldiers deeply resented the changes and made life even more uncomfortable for the MSA men, who were often the first representatives of the new province or region to arrive. French-speaking conscripts were slated to displace the English in their province's battalions.[47]

Critics of conscription have simultaneously condemned the MSA as a needless act of oppression and a half-hearted failure. Defenders have insisted that conscription was necessary and successful. Statistics serve the government; the historical unforeseen satisfies their critics.

According to Colonel H.A.C. Machin, director of the conscription program, 129,569 of the men in Class I had reported by November 11, 1918; 105,016 were accepted for service; and 96,379 were actually on duty. The Militia Department reported a larger figure. Of the total of 99,651 MSA men accepted, 47,509 had gone overseas, and 24,132 were with the Canadian Corps in France.

Was their journey necessary? Because the 5th Division had finally been broken up in early 1918, the Corps had enough men for its August and September battles. Ironically, the MSA men filled the ranks only when the worst fighting was over and victory was just over the horizon. Earlier or more ruthless conscription could have brought the 5th Division to France, equalling the force a smaller Australia maintained on the Western Front. Most Canadians were not interested in that kind of competition.

Of course, the Allies expected victory in 1920, not at the end of 1918. By then, any Canadian Corps would have depended utterly on conscripts to fill its ranks. In September 1918, Major-General S.C. Mewburn, Minister of Militia in the Union government, estimated publicly that the CEF would require 120,000 more reinforcements. This time, married men aged twenty to thirty-four would be called up. The British were already conscripting fifty-year-olds. It was long past time for the war to end.

CHAPTER FOUR

SOLDIERING

TRAINING FOR WAR

The men who joined the CEF soon learned that there was "the right way, the wrong way and the army way." In assuming their new roles, they inherited many of the trappings of a despised underclass—its values, institutions, and language. "Soldiering" itself was a synonym for avoiding work.

I N 1915, the CEF's recruiting procedures were simple. An officer or sergeant sat at a folding table behind a stack of forms and copied down each man's personal details: date of birth, country of origin, trade, marital status, former service, and whether he was willing to be vaccinated for smallpox. The medical examination foretold much about army life. Sam Hughes brusquely told Norman Rawson to enlist in the ranks instead of seeking a chaplaincy. The young clergyman received his first shock when a medical orderly commanded him to strip. "I expected to have a jacket or something to put around me, but I had to cover myself as best I could with my hands."[1] Frank Worthington recalled sitting with other men on benches worn smooth by countless other bare buttocks until an orderly curtly summoned him for his turn.[2] The doctor—often a civilian, working for 50 cents a head—swiftly completed the few elementary tests of medical fitness.[3] Like countless other soldiers, Ernest Davis recalled feeling "like so much meat on the hoof."[4] A decrepit but patriotic seventy-four-year-old from Tofino, J.W. Thompson, exercised, massaged away his wrinkles, and dyed his hair—but was turned down by a doctor who noted his chest hair. Thompson tried again and, by the end of the war, he was a sergeant. Those hard of hearing feigned lack of English; the short-sighted memorized the standard eye chart. The chances of success depended on the need for men and the energy or patriotic sympathy of the practitioner on duty.

G.S. Strathy, a young Toronto doctor who inspected men for the First and Second contingents, recalled the poor eyesight of many. The CEF demanded 6/6 for the eye a man would favour in aiming a rifle, and many volunteers, unaware that they were short sighted, managed only 6/18. Bad teeth and flat feet were an even bigger factor: "The teeth of the Canadian born are seldom a cause of rejection, but those of the British born, especially ex–service men, are very bad, in most cases missing. About the feet, what I never appreciated before is the number of labourers who have flat feet, but seldom have pain in them. The feet are flat, but not weak."[5]

To be "attested," a volunteer agreed to serve in the "Canadian Over-Seas Expeditionary Force" for at least a year and at most the duration of the war, plus six months. They swore to "be faithful and bear true Allegiance to His Majesty KING GEORGE THE FIFTH, His Heirs and Successors" and to "observe and obey all orders of His Majesty, His Heirs and Successors and of all the Generals and Officers set over me." Lacking convenient photographic identification, another form recorded a soldier's height, chest measurements, eye and hair colour, complexion, distinctive marks, religious denomination, and "apparent age."

The new soldier received blankets and a palliasse cover, to be filled with straw. Then he bedded down in his unit's "barracks"— often the floor of the local armouries or the horse palace at the local fairground. By the spring of 1915, clothing contractors had overcome backlogs and the worst quality problems. The soldier was soon kitted out in cap, tunic, breeches, greatcoat, boots, and the notorious puttees. In Canada, during the summer, he wore a "cow's breakfast," a farmer's straw hat sometimes looped up with a regimental badge. CEF battalions found that kilts attracted recruits. When Thomas Dinesen joined the Black Watch, he "soon discovered that wearing pants beneath your kilt is considered a very serious breach of etiquette."[6] Transferred to the kilted 134th Battalion, Ernest Hamilton confessed to his wife: "I cut off the legs of my summer underwear to hide my nakedness as the wind sometimes plays tricks."[7] More conventionally uniformed soldiers complained that army underwear was "an inch thick." Pyjamas were considered effete: a soldier "slept in his shirt like a man."

A new soldier found that there was much else he should do "like a man." Old soldiers set the style. As was common with the bunkhouse life of mining, logging, and construction camps, his new comrades expected a man to drink, smoke, swear, and gamble. Whatever his pay, a good soldier spent it generously and wound up broke. William Lighthall marvelled at the old soldier's capacity to find liquor and avoid work. His squadron cook was rotten at his trade but so skilled at gambling with his Crown-and-Anchor board that his English wife owned two pubs. The man's Canadian wife presumably lived off the Patriotic Fund.[8] Thomas Dinesen heard soldiers describing women with a coarse explicitness and contempt that he found nauseating. Others, writing to mothers or wives, never mentioned it.

For a timid, retiring man, the regular fights, the endless swearing, and the constant noise made barrack-room life an ordeal. "Most of my companions in France were savages," wrote Harold Baldwin once he was safely back in civilian life; "common, common little people who proved a far greater trial than the real horror."[9] Andy Munro assured his father in a letter home that he would never drink or gamble: "I see enough of it on every hand to disgust one. It is too bad the way some of them go on."[10]

For others, the intensity of human comradeship was the best memory of their army life. E.W. Russell, an English professional surveyor, refused a commission: "I certainly felt I was among quite good ordinary men and firmly decided I would keep among them."[11] Writing home, Roy Macfie apologized for the state of the paper, "but I started a long time ago and we had a few wrestles and fights and eat a lot of candies and a big piece of dandy fruit cake all the way from Canada since I began this, and my hands are black as the ace of spades too."[12] Garnet Durham apologized for one of his distracted letters home: "The usual poker game is in blasphemous progress, and those not playing are mostly round the stove swapping yarns more vivid than truthful."[13]

A man joined the CEF to become a hero and patriot to his family and friends, but his first sacrifice was to plummet to the bottom of the social scale. His pay, separation allowance, and even his eventual pension depended on the wage scales of unskilled casual labour. Even in Canada, privates found that the better hotels and restaurants often barred them. This rankled, but the men seldom challenged the rules.

The CEF had only a little of the restless egalitarian "mateship" of the Australian Imperial Forces. Canadian-born officers and predominantly British-born other ranks helped maintain a deep social gulf. Once enlisted and equipped, private soldiers had to wear their uniforms at all times. When Lawrence Youell and his fellow officers condescended to attend a party at an NCO's house in Guelph, they conscientiously dressed in civilian clothes for the occasion "to avoid awkwardness."[14]

The government had succeeded in making recruiting a mass enterprise, involving men and women across Canada. Making soldiers out of recruits was a more specialized business, left to officers and NCOs who had little or no experience of war. By example and frequently profane description, a handful of British and PF veterans taught new soldiers how to roll their puttees and to use an array of specialized brushes that cleaned anything from teeth to boots. Whether as NCOs or as "characters," British army veterans shaped the culture of the CEF, introducing a British army vocabulary gleaned from Queen Victoria's Empire. *Breeches, cushy, chit,* and *dekko* ("look-see") came from India; *buckshee* ("cost-free") and *bundhook* ("rifle") from Arabic; and *bumf* and *bum fodder* ("paper") from plain English. The new war had already contributed *napoo* or "finished" (from the French *il n'y en a plus*).[15] Signallers, struggling with the crackling sounds of primitive wireless, practised several attempts at a phonetic alphabet. Times before noon, or a.m., were "Ack Emma"; afternoon, p.m., became "Pip Emma." By 1917, the staff was trying to establish the logic of the twenty-four-hour clock.

There was a serious limit to what veterans could teach. Armies exist for emergencies, but, unlike fire-fighters and police, soldiers can wait a whole career for active service. The ex-regulars in the CEF had last fought in South Africa, and very few had encountered the increased professionalism of the pre-1914 years. Instead, like the instructors of Kitchener's New Army, they knew mainly of peacetime garrison life: long hours of drill, guard-mounting, and polishing; even longer evenings in the canteen or the sergeants' mess; with a little old-fashioned tactical training in case a war interrupted "real soldiering."

As "regulars," British troops should have been the best trained in Europe. They were not. German conscripts were inducted each October from the most physically fit of their age group, and spent two years of intensive training with the units they would join in time of war. To the officers, and especially the NCOs who instructed recruits, training was a profession.

The British recruited volunteers from the rural and urban slums. They often needed months of adequate food and physical conditioning before they were fit enough to serve. British regimental depots provided basic training. They and battalions in England sent drafts of soldiers to keep overseas units in India or elsewhere in the Empire up to strength. Up to 70 per cent of the BEF in 1914 were reservists with rusty military skills and no physical conditioning at all. In light of their preparation, the "Old Contemptibles" performed better than anyone had a right to expect. If they were sometimes too exhausted to march or fight, it was because they had been civilians only days earlier.

The peacetime regular army produced two kinds of soldiers. There were steady dependable men, and there were those who made "soldiering" a synonym for avoiding work. A "regimental" minority thrived on discipline, order, and certainty, and emerged with the crowns and chevrons on their sleeves emblematic of the army's non-commissioned ranks: its corporals, sergeants, and sergeant-majors. At their head, the Regimental Sergeant-Major held a rank so lofty it entitled him to wear an officer's Sam Browne belt. Solid, reliable, and unimaginative, senior NCOs felt, justifiably, that they were the backbone of the regiment.

In the new 39th Battalion, A.G. May believed that the colonel and a few senior officers knew their business but that other officers had not even been to training courses. Everything depended on "a real fine sergeant major," May insisted. "He was hard-boiled and completely efficient when on duty but nevertheless helpful and father-like to us when off duty."[16] In the 5th Field Ambulance, Sergeant-Major "Bob" Franklin, a former Royal Marine, terrorized officers as much as lesser soldiers: "When I say 'Double', I don't just mean 'Double'—I mean for you to bloody well fly!"[17] By example and precept, the NCOs showed that the army wanted short hair, buttoned pockets, and crisp salutes. They could not teach their men to cope with machine-guns, poison gas, or barbed wire. Nor could their instinctive adversaries, those for whom "soldiering" meant "swinging the lead" or "dodging the column." Instead, they suggested the means of passive resistance by which most people preserve a little of themselves in almost any authoritarian system.

Whether good or bad, soldiers quickly bonded with their new units. The Canadian Militia had embraced the British regimental system from its early years; in 1914 and after, its regiments fought for a place in the CEF. Even at Valcartier, Hughes had respected the fundamentals of the system by giving most battalions a regional identity and such common traditions as a Scottish kilt or the black horn buttons of a rifleman. Accustomed, as a conservative people in a new country, to creating instant traditions, Canadians soon invested the raw CEF battalions with at least some of the identity British regiments had evolved over many centuries.

There were complaints that Hughes had robbed the CEF of *esprit de corps* by creating the new "Overseas Battalions" at Valcartier. Even so, the new units took surprisingly little time to develop an identity as the "Dirty Third," the "Mad Fourth," or, later, the 29th "Tobin's Tigers" or the 116th "Umpty Umps."

Ideally, a soldier wore the same badge, shared the same tradi-

tions, gained promotion, and suffered punishment within one regimental family throughout his service. In the vast anonymity of the
army, a battalion or battery was like a small town, full of remembered faces, shared experiences, and old friends and enemies.

"It is funny when you go to new Reg[iment] and place every
thing is strange," Frank Maheux explained; "you don't know no
body."[18] Wounded at Passchendaele, Roy Macfie was glad to get
back to his 1st Battalion, even if he had to forfeit convalescence in
England: "I have been here so long I am lonesome anywhere else. I
am part of the works and all the fellows are like brothers."[19] Battalions mattered more because a soldier's real family, the few dozen
men of his platoon or section whom he knew by name and character, could vanish with devastating speed in the course of a battle.

To fill his overseas battalions with men, Hughes had promised
distinct unit identities. In practice, he betrayed his promise. When
most overseas battalions reached England, their privately purchased cap and collar badges, their expensive band instruments,
and the "regimental colours"—banners neatly embroidered by the
officers' wives—became superfluous. Those battalions already in
France desperately needed junior officers and soldiers to preserve
their own identity and contribute to their growing history.

Most of the fresh soldiers were devastated. For a soldier, losing
his own battalion was almost as traumatic as any family break-up.
They blamed their own officers, generals, staff officers, political
prejudice, and (comparatively seldom) Hughes himself for sending
them, orphan-like, to a new unit. While the private funds of the
vanished battalion or battery remained to be audited and disputed,
the colours found their way to some British or hometown church.

Once over that blow, most soldiers soon made the transition to
their new battalion. In fact, after the war, they usually identified
themselves as part of their front-line unit. The numbers required
to keep up a battalion were impressive. For an average nominal
strength of 800 to 1,000, an average Canadian infantry battalion
absorbed 4,500 to 5,500 men. In only two years of fighting, 5,640
officers and other ranks helped the 44th earn its reputation as a
hard-luck battalion; 1,193 were killed or died of wounds. Ottawa's

38th Battalion, also in the 4th Division, was luckier. It needed only 3,512 men, of whom 691 were killed or fatally wounded. Men who returned after weeks or months in hospital might be appalled by the number of unfamiliar faces around them. Men who transferred out to accept "bomb-proof" jobs in the rear bore a stigma as well as a sense of isolation. No matter how extensive the changes in the battalion, a soldier had no better home in the army.

Some armies deliberately mixed soldiers from different faiths, regions, and cultures; the British tradition endorsed distinctively homogeneous units. The Colonial Office had been the first to suggest a "Royal Montcalm Regiment" for French Canadians in August 1914.[20] CEF battalions recruited companies of "Russians," Scandinavians, and, especially, Native Canadians. Eagerly sought for their warlike traditions and, in some regions, eager to join, First Nations volunteers found that the army had little tolerance for braids, buckskins, or sacred amulets. Frank Pegahmabow decorated his tent with his clan symbol, and he attributed his survival, three Military Medals, and 368 dead Germans to the medicine bag he managed to carry throughout the war. Like him, several Indians found their most congenial role as snipers, the task that involved the most initiative, the least supervision, and a very substantial risk of death. Johnny Norwest, a Cree with the 50th Battalion, killed 115 Germans before he died at Amiens in 1918. Patrick Riel, grandson of the Metis leader of 1885, and Philip McDonald of the 8th Battalion each claimed more than a hundred kills before he died.[21]

Recruits expected quick training and early service. Few had joined for the pleasures of army service. As at Valcartier, they learned to wait. Second Contingent battalions filled up quickly, and records showed that the senior NCOs and even many corporals had solid military experience. That made basic training easy.

That was not so for most of the infantry recruited in 1915 and 1916. By that time, few good NCOs were left, filling the ranks took months, and the senior officers were often too busy or too inexperienced to organize training. Some of the men were kept busy with recruiting.

Canada's climate made outdoor training hard in winter and in summer. When Hughes allowed battalions to billet men in local detachments, he delighted mayors and hotel keepers, but he eliminated any possibility of serious training for the season. When raw lieutenants and untrained corporals attempted to enforce orders, trouble followed. In 1915 and 1916, several military riots erupted as boisterous, underemployed soldiers rescued arrested comrades, smashed German-owned property, or brawled in the streets.

Once the warmer weather returned, Hughes ordered battalions to muster at Camp Hughes in Manitoba or Camp Sarcee outside Calgary, at Niagara-on-the-Lake, and at Valcartier for Quebec and Maritime battalions. At Camp Borden, on the sandy Angus Plain, a layer of ash from an earlier forest fire lay under the parched grass. It soon worked its way to the surface under soldiers' trudging feet. On July 11, 1916, 10,000 soldiers waited for hours under the blazing sun for the minister to arrive in his private railway car to open the camp. Militia generals and colonels ordered their men not to touch their water bottles. To sip from them, even when parched with thirst, would be "unsoldierly." When Hughes and his friends arrived, battalion after battalion marched past the minister as sand, dust, and black ash blew over them. Summoned to report the minister's triumphant reception by the soldiers, journalists wrote instead that one man had died, thirty-five more had collapsed from the heat, and troops had booed Hughes's railway car when it pulled out. Most editors suppressed the story. The few who printed it finally shattered the myth of a special rapport between Hughes and "his boys."[22]

Between the old army view that a soldier was a feckless automaton and Hughes's faith in a free-spirited but respectful marksman lay the official doctrine. The British infantry training manual of 1914, familiar to most Canadian instructors, stated:

The objects in view in developing a soldierly spirit are to help the soldier to bear fatigue, privation and danger cheerfully; to imbue him with a sense of honour; to give him confidence in his superiors and comrades; to increase his power of initiative, of self-confidence and of self-restraint; to train him to obey orders, or to act in the absence of orders for the advantage of his regiment under all conditions; to produce such a high degree of courage and disregard of self that in the stress of battle he will use his brains and his weapons coolly and to the best advantage; to impress upon him that, so long as he is physically capable of fighting, surrender to the enemy is a disgraceful act; and finally to teach him how to act in combination with his comrades to defeat the enemy.[23]

Unlike the authors, real instructors had to cope with real people and their own limited pre-war experience. Much later, when enough returned officers and NCOs were available, Militia Headquarters devised a realistic fourteen-week recruit-training program. That was in 1917, long after volunteering had ended. When MSA men joined in 1918, they were promptly sent to England.

For the previous two years, CEF instructors in Canada drew mainly on their memories. For half a century, the militia camps had pretended that untrained men could advance from squad drill to brigade tactics in ten days. They would have agreed that real war differed from training, but how? Until they learned, instructors filled time. Men spent hours fencing with sheathed bayonets or jabbing at straw-filled bags while sergeants shrieked at them, presumably to enable them someday to "finish off the Hun with cold steel." Otherwise a soldier's day was given over to the peacetime stand-bys—physical training, drill, and route marches. Like much of the polishing of boots, buttons, and mess tins, such activities filled abundant time cheaply. The soldiers, with an average of eight months from enlistment to departure from Canada, had plenty of time to spend.

The training seemed almost leisurely: reveille at 6:00 a.m., followed by physical training (PT), cleaning, and breakfast, might seem demanding, but the rest of the working day was only six and a half hours long, from 8:00 a.m. to 4.30 p.m., with at least an hour for dinner. Unless on guard or serving punishment, a soldier was free until lights-out, at 10:00 p.m. When ranges were available, troops moved from "dry practice" with their Ross rifles to firing fifty rounds—not enough to teach anyone to "pink the enemy every time." Shrewd or lucky soldiers found other ways to pass the time. At Trenton, Alf May and Howard Graham, a future Chief of the General Staff, found "cushy" jobs in the quartermaster stores, dishing out uniforms and delivering rations with a horse and cart.[24] A telegrapher from Sudbury and a skilled pitcher, Claude Craig became a popular member of the 37th Battalion baseball team. Training seldom interfered with games or practices.[25]

Whatever the syllabus, drill and marching predominated. The parade square was central to most camps, and to training in all of them. Drill was "a perfect embodiment of all the qualities of soldierly discipline," claimed a 1918 training pamphlet: "prompt and methodical obedience, skill at arms, confidence in commanders and pride in the unit to which the soldier belongs." More often the men remembered sweat, sore feet, aching limbs, and occasional pride when, sometimes, a thousand men moved as one. Soldiers learned to stand stiffly to attention, thumbs at the seams of their trousers, heels together and feet angled out at forty-five degrees. They learned to salute—until 1918—with whatever arm was farthest from the officer.[26] They invested considerable time "forming fours," moving from two ranks to four. Troops numbered from the right and, on the command, men with even numbers took a pace back and to the right—agony for those unfortunates who had forgotten their numbers or could not distinguish right from left. Once in fours, columns of men marched, circling the parade square, or turned, halted, and "quick marched" again as the sergeants barked commands and the corporals cursed and scribbled down names for future punishment.

Regular route marches were even more important because infantry in the 1914–18 war still moved on foot. Long before the war, staff officers had calculated the savings in road space when men marched in files of four. The NCOs set the pace, 120 steps to the minute, which moved a column 3 miles in 50 minutes, or 12–15 miles a day, with a 10-minute rest every hour. Marching at ease, men sang, whistled, and tried to forget the pain as sixty to eighty pounds of rifle and kit dug into their shoulders and the merciless ground pounded their aching feet at every step. Senior officers rode on horseback; juniors, who carried much less kit than their men, might good-heartedly carry an exhausted straggler's rifle. At rest for ten minutes before the hour, troops loosened equipment and gratefully collapsed by the roadside, feet elevated above their heads to drain away the pumping blood. Then, on the hour, they formed up again, switching ranks and sequence in the column so all could share the dust and the wearisome accordion effect when raw troops lost the pace and alternately hurried and halted. After the march, tradition dictated that the men present their bare, sweaty feet for their officer's inspection. Young subalterns, directed to show solicitude for their men, poked at suspected blisters and withheld comments on the smell.

Hughes insisted that "his boys" were fully trained when they reached England. Therefore, some men spent weeks at specialized courses in signalling, "bombing," bayonet fighting, or studying machine-guns. Lacking direct experience of any of the equipment actually used at the front, instructors managed as best they could, with scraps of information from the trenches mixed with anti-quated drill. Signallers spent hours practising semaphore, though its use in France would have been suicidal. At a course on making "bean-can bombs" at Hamilton in 1916, W.B. Woods's instructor solemnly warned the class to use pincers, not their teeth, to "crimp" the detonator to the fuse—and promptly opened his jaws, like any veteran miner, and clamped down on the brass cap.

As they entered a military world, CEF recruits discovered a universe of regulations and potential offences, ranging from drunkenness and absence without leave to insubordination and its silent ver-sion, "dumb insolence." An offender was marched to the guard-room, deprived of cap and belt, and lodged in a cell. Next morning, the prisoner stood stiff and bare-headed before his com-pany or battery commander. Depending on the gravity of the charge and the need to make an example of him, he could also face

New names in Canadian history.

More are coming— Will you be there?

ENLIST!

Make us as proud of you as we are of him!

LEARNING TO SOLDIER

1-A (left) One of the few officially sponsored Canadian recruiting posters offered a mixture of national and imperial patriotism and an appeal to self-esteem. (National Archives, C 42420)

1-B (below) A very young sergeant-major waits for the photographer to finish before taking charge of a draft of volunteers. Most of them would wear out their civilian clothes before their new army uniforms arrived. (National Archives, PA 74747)

THE OLD ORIGINALS

1-C (above) The First Contingent at Valcartier wait for the next issue of kit. A mixture of militia veterans and recent British immigrants, the "Old Originals" provided leadership and traditions for the Canadian Expeditionary Force. (National Archives, PA 22739)

1-D (below) Men of Toronto's 48th Highlanders on a bathing parade near Port Credit before going to Valcartier. In August, 1914, most Canadians went to war in a holiday spirit, and worried whether the fighting would be over and the glory distributed before they arrived. (National Archives, PA 61208)

1-E (above) Canadian gunners practise loading their 18 pounder field gun on Salisbury plain. The upper "barrel" was an oil-filled buffer which absorbed the recoil and made it easier to aim the gun accurately. (National Archives, C 3540)

1-F (below) Stalwart members of the 15th Battalion model their goatskin jerkins on board the ship that took them to France. Two months later, most of these men would be dead or German prisoners after the gas attack at Ypres. (J.A. Currie Collection, Erindale College)

DOING YOUR BIT 1-G (above) The Signal Section of the 71st Battalion, C.E.
Raised at Woodstock in south-western Ontario, the 7
was typical of the units that drew on the great recruiti

enthusiasm of 1915. The faces reflect the age and emotions of Canadians drawn into the crusade. Hours spent learning semaphore would not be useful in trench warfare. (Author's Collection courtesy of G.R. Thaler)

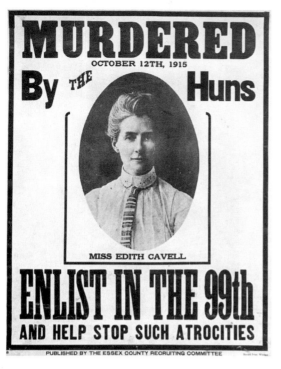

MURDERED
OCTOBER 12TH, 1915
By THE Huns

MISS EDITH CAVELL

ENLIST IN THE 99th
AND HELP STOP SUCH ATROCITIES

PUBLISHED BY THE ESSEX COUNTY RECRUITING COMMITTEE

The Happy Man Today is the Man at the Front

Royal Highlanders of Canada
Allied with the BLACK WATCH

Have Enlisted at their Armoury for Overseas Service
13th Bn. C.E.F. Now in France
42nd Bn. C.E.F. Now in England
AND THE
73rd Bn. C.E.F. is now Mobilizing

JOIN THE 73rd NOW

IF YOU WISH TO JOIN, WRITE TO
73rd ROYAL HIGHLANDERS OF CANADA
429 BLEURY ST., MONTREAL

ARRANGEMENTS WILL BE MADE FOR LOCAL MEDICAL EXAMINATION, AND TRANSPORTATION TO MONTREAL

1-H, 1-J (above) Recruiting appeals varied with the imagination of local committees. Windsor's 99th Battalion relied on horror at the execution of Edith Cavell, an English nurse in Brussels who was shot by the Germans for helping British soldiers escape to Holland. The 73rd Battalion went to France with the 4th Division but was eventually broken up because English-speaking Montrealers had as many battalions in action as Toronto and ran out of volunteers. (National Archives, C 95732, C 95748)

1-K (left) Winnipeggers were encouraged to enlist by this depiction of trench warfare on a vacant lot near Main Street. The soldiers in the foreground wear the awkward Oliver equipment. Other men, neatly silhouetted for the benefit of future German snipers, point their rifles over the parapet. (Manatoba Archives, Foote Collection, 1310)

1-L (above) A soldier, his very young wife, a chum and the next generation pose in the stands of the Canadian National Exhibition at Toronto. Members of a Peel county regiment, the soldiers wear the standard Canadian maple leaf cap badge and their tight-fitting Canadian serge tunics. Unit cap badges and the looser, better-made British uniforms would come later. (City of Toronto Archives, James Collection, 777F)

1 M (below) Billed as "Canada's Greatest Military Review," a score of CEF battalions marched past the Minister of Militia, Sir Sam Hughes, on July 11, 1916. Parched in the dust and sweltering heat, 39 soldiers collapsed and one died. Others jeered the Minister and shattered the myth of his mystic bond with "his boys." (National Archives, PA 66778)

Fighting Equipment

1-N (above) Under the eyes of Field Marshall Sir John French and a galaxy of generals and colonels, a Canadian sergeant goes through the ritual of instructing the latest draft of recruits from Canada, conspicuous in their stiff forage caps. (Ontario Archives Acc 11595 alb. 3 p.24)

1-O (left) An instructional illustration, to show the well-dressed soldier how to put on his kit and equipment. Despite efforts to reduce the soldier's load, the soldier's legs remained the only dependable means of conveying the growing array of weapons and equipment he needed in action. (Author's collection)

1-P (bottom) Instructors at the Brigade Entrenching School, Seaford, Kent. Among them, second from the left, is Sergeant Frank Maheux.

his colonel or a full court martial. A commanding officer, for example, could award twenty-eight days' field punishment or a week's detention.

For an offender on active service, a Field General Court Martial could go as far as to recommend death. Under section 74 of the Militia Act, members of the CEF were deemed to be on active service and subject to the Army Act as soon as they reached England. British soldiers, however, were considered on active service only when they went to France. Through such fine distinctions, lawyers grow rich. Other ranks could be tried by a District Court Martial (DCM) with three officers, or a Field General Court Martial (FGCM), which had five. An officer—often the accused's adjutant—prosecuted, and another officer could serve as the "prisoner's friend." By 1916, a legally trained officer of the Judge Advocate General's branch was often available to guide the court in serious cases. All proceedings were reviewed up the chain of command. Sentences of death—or dismissal and "cashiering" for officers—had to be confirmed by the commander-in-chief.

Most officers caught up in court-martial duty thumbed through their *Manual of Military Law* and wished they had stayed awake during the relevant lectures. Others, with the same self-confidence that had often earned them promotion, assumed that being "up on a charge" was *prima facie* evidence of guilt, and remembered that the aim of military law was not to seek justice but to uphold discipline. For a new soldier, claimed the 1908 edition of the *King's Regulations*, "admonition" was the most suitable punishment, and NCOs were enjoined against "intemperate language or an offensive manner."

Detention meant close confinement; forfeiture of pay; meals of bread and water for three days out of four; and as wearying a routine of drill, cleaning, and dirty jobs as the provost sergeant or his superiors could devise. Lesser punishments confined a soldier to barracks, and sometimes to his battalion's guardroom; compelled him to report in full kit for frequent inspections; and filled the rest of his spare time with "fatigues," army jargon for "chores."

In 1880, the British army had reluctantly replaced flogging with

Field Punishment No. 1.[27] Soldiers called it "crucifixion": "As I look out the door of my hut," wrote Colonel Creelman on the eve of the battle of the Somme, "I see my two servants tied up with their backs to the wheel of a telephone cart, both are doing F.P. No. 1 which includes being tied up for two hours each day. Their food is limited to bully, biscuits and unsweetened tea and if the unit is on the march, they accompany it on foot. The regulations governing this type of punishment are absolute and we cannot modify them in any way."[28] After the alleged use of "F.P. No. 1" at Camp Hughes in 1915, Militia Headquarters banned it in Canada, and the War Office forbade it in England, but it was part of "active service" overseas. Once tied up, the victim was prey to flies, cramps, and the embarrassed glances of fellow soldiers. Most CEF veterans remembered "F.P. No. 1" with a special loathing as a symbol of the humiliation a patriotic volunteer had to bear.

The mantle of authority and discipline cloaked the brutality and sadism of all military punishment. An unfair conviction for "impertinence" when he tried to answer a charge and a week of detention under "a rough-tongued red-faced bully called Simms" transformed Will Bird of the 193rd Battalion "from a soldier proud to be in uniform to one knowing there was no justice whatever in the army."[29]

Once the CEF's battalions had recruited as many men as they could—or whenever shipping and barrack space were available—drafts left for England. In the autumn of 1915, and again in 1916, Ottawa sent all the men it could to make room for fresh battalions.

Despite dire threats to the men and to journalists, troop trains never seemed to leave secretly. Lieutenant Lawrence Youell defied regulations and told his mother; Howard Graham was a good soldier, but his mother came to Barriefield to see him off anyway. At Guelph, Youell observed fewer tears than he expected "and most of our men at least seemed to be having the time of their lives by seeing how many girls they could get to kiss them goodbye."[30] The locomotive engineer pulled out, waited for the crowd to leave, and then backed up to await the preset departure time of 4:30 a.m.

Troop trains wended across Canada, often past small cheering crowds, though in Quebec this was seldom the case, soldiers noted sourly. At White River, Rivière-du-Loup, or Bathurst, soldiers piled out for exercise. Many men were seeing Canada for the first time. Bert Nelson thought farming in Quebec looked good, if old-fashioned, and judged Truro "a dandy station": "Numbers of coloured people here," he added.[31]

Depending on the season, ships waited for the trains at Montreal or Halifax. Few admired the Atlantic port. Nelson was confined to his train "as some of the boys came back pickled." In 1915, Belleville's Angus Mowat found Halifax "very old, very hilly and almost inconceivably dirty and ill-lighted."[32] Two years later, Ernest Hamilton considered it "a punk place" and "the more I see of it the better I like Toronto."[33]

At either port the men trooped up the gangplank and crowded aboard the increasingly battered troopships that plied between Canada and Britain. Some remembered Cunard and Allan Line steamers such as the *Megantic* and *Missanabie*; the former German immigrant ship the *Northland*; and, more rarely, a swift journey on the monster liner *Olympic*. Few found the comfort enjoyed by the First Contingent. Soldiers wedged themselves into bunks and hammocks in the holds or jammed into steerage, while their officers enjoyed relatively spacious cabins. Men of the 5th Field Ambulance, assigned to the upper deck, rejoiced too soon. Embarkation staff removed them in favour of a unit of medical students, described as "boys from good homes." The 5th soon found out why. "Can you ever forget the smell of the bilge in that awful place?" asked the unit diarist.[34] A.G. May remembered: "The food was insufficient and vile. The majority of the men were seasick half the time. This is hardly surprising for we were served tripe several times." He also recalled overcrowding and theft. He lost his money and his watch.[35]

There were other universal memories of the voyages—thieving stewards; storms that sent waves smashing over the bows; boxing matches and impromptu concerts on deck; furtive, but non-stop, gambling with playing-cards and Crown-and-Anchor boards down below; the fear of German u-boats heightened by armed sentries along the deck; and, finally, relief when British destroyers met them on the other side. Frank Maheux's ship passed close to where the *Lusitania* had gone down only days before. "I forgot to tell you," he wrote to his wife, "that some 80 nurses cross over with us. I am pretty certain some of them made something in their pants because one night I pretty near myself."[36] Although no U-boat sank a Canadian troopship, on June 27, 1918, the U-86 torpedoed the *Llandovery Castle*, a hospital ship returning empty from Canada, and machine-gunned survivors in the water.

In England, the Canadian-born found plenty of surprises, starting with the seemingly tiny railway trains that travelled "at a mile a minute without hardly any vibration," as Private Frank Hazlewood reported.[37] Noyes noted the lack of toilets: "Consequently the men were forced to take advantage of opened windows and with their natural modesty they chose times when they thought no town or village was near." Of course they regularly miscalculated.[38] Troops usually arrived at their camps after dark, sometimes in driving rain, and occasionally with sufficient spirit to make an impression on earlier arrivals. A disgusted Garnet Durham recalled a new cyclist company arriving at midnight, amid drums rolling and officers bellowing orders. "They were trying to demonstrate what real tin soldiers they were," he complained to his diary, "but will never live down their reputation as anything but boy scouts."[39]

New arrivals got a week's disembarkation leave and a railway warrant. Like the "Old Originals," those without English relatives headed for London to spend their pay. They would start at the Savoy or the Cecil, with filet mignon and lobster, drop down to Oxford Square and Lyons' Corner House, and wind up broke at the Union Jack Club or a Church Army hut. On the way, they would crowd into West End musicals, such as *Chu Chin Chow* or *The Maid of the Mountain*, or watch the Byng Boys at the Alhambra. Then they would straggle back to camp, always penniless, sometimes late, and usually with memories of St. Paul's Cathedral, the Houses of Parliament, and women who smoked and drank whisky in public view.

Maheux dutifully reported to his wife that his chaplain had warned that English women were "snakes from hell with fire in their mouth all over" and added, from direct observation, "you can see one in the street about a pound of powder in her face and rings they all covered with them."[40] A chum took Bert Nelson home to Sheffield in 1916: "All street car conductors in this city are girls," he reported. "Also girls driving delivery waggons, coal carts, taxi cabs, porters, ticket agents etc. etc."[41]

Troops soon encountered the more mundane features of English life in barracks—rain, badly heated quarters in the winter, and unexpected heat in midsummer. Men accustomed to easygoing militia discipline got a shock. "Believe me," Claude Craig recorded, "if anyone is foolish enough to overstay leave or get into trouble downtown or do a hundred things we used to do as a matter of course in Canada, they get soaked for it alright."[42]

Food, seldom a subject of complaint in Canada, became a major source of discontent. At Caesar's Camp, May remembered, "the food...was atrocious and after about a week there was a near-mutiny over this."[43] Canadians learned to know but seldom to love margarine, English sausages, suet pudding, and Pink's jam. They also complained that British army kitchens were dirty and old-fashioned. As early as 1915, anticipated food shortages led to cuts in the official ration. Army officers inspecting the mountain of rejected food had assumed that the troops were overfed. Members of the CEF were well-enough paid to fend for themselves, but local prices rose wherever the Canadians went, and by 1917, when the German blockade became effective, supplies were cut. "I manage to get enough to eat by visiting the canteen occassionally [sic]," Ernest Hamilton assured his wife, Sara, "but we cannot buy bread as it is prohibited to be sold."[44] Prohibition of liquor, already a powerful movement in Canada, found a few echoes in wartime Britain as public houses adjusted to tightly regulated afternoon and evening closing times.[45]

By Allied standards, Canadians were well paid. When heavy drinking, venereal disease, and resentment from British troops logically followed, Ottawa repented of some of its largesse and, in

early 1916, ordered paymasters overseas to hold back half the pay of
men in the ranks. A.M. Munro, freshly arrived in England,
assumed the pay cut was the result of a fiscal crisis: "Guess the con-
tinual drain on their finances is beginning to tell."[46] When he realized that English prices had not fallen to compensate, he expressed
the sense of general outrage: "The Canadians do not care a hang
now and they absolutely refuse to soldier properly." In practice,
grumbling worked itself out.

So did the fury, in late 1915, when "working pay" was abolished.
An allowance traditionally paid in the PF to those who practised
such civilian skills as cooking, harness making, or driving a
mechanical vehicle, working pay seemed unfair in an army where
such occupations were usually safer than service in the line. Still,
was it fair to change the rules after men had joined the game?
Almost five hundred soldiers, most of them Army Service Corps
drivers, cried foul and took their release. Fed up with early rising
and cranky feeders, hundreds of cooks also quit, though many
returned after they had sampled drill, fatigues, and other features
of a private soldier's life. After a few months, working pay was
restored for those who had received it before.

Mindful of the earlier complaints from the First Canadian Contingent, the British kicked a New Army division out of the historic
military camp at Shorncliffe near Folkestone, and offered Major-
General Sam Steele's Second Contingent some of the best military
accommodation in England. When the 2nd Canadian Division left
for France, Steele remained behind. The British generously gave
him command of the district and most Canadian units in England
congregated there, producing friction between Steele and the designated commander of the Canadian Training Division, Brigadier-
General J.C. MacDougall.

Back in London, with his links to the minister improved and his
authority vaguely enhanced, a newly promoted Brigadier-General
Carson alternately mediated and exacerbated the rivalry between
the two generals to enhance his own authority. By 1916, both Carson and MacDougall were also major-generals. Each of the three

Canadian generals firmly believed that he was in charge. As Hughes must have intended, each of the generals had to refer most decisions to the minister. With enough troubles of their own, the British kept their hands off.

Instead of bickering generals, the Canadian base in England needed a strong hand. Each contingent left behind its weakest units and officers. The Canadians in France depended on British supply lines, but they also needed trained CEF reinforcements. Caught between Hughes's insistence on having more Canadian divisions in France and the urgent need to replace their casualties, the divided Canadian command wavered. Hughes's recruiting policy left the onus for breaking up battalions on the generals in England. Once privates and subalterns had left, unemployed senior officers remained. Faced with furious and influential colonels and majors, it was tempting to buy off their anger with staff jobs. Later, Carson pioneered the "Cook's Tour": a few weeks with a battalion in France gave an unemployed senior officer a slim chance of nailing down a job, and certainly gave him something to talk about back home. Their hosts usually treated them with ill-natured disdain, and soldiers put under their command usually regarded them as a menace. The blame, appropriately enough, was put on the base.

Until mid-1916, few CEF battalions expected to be broken up. Once disembarkation leave ended and a battalion was ready to train, junior officers and NCOs disappeared for courses on bombing, digging, wiring, signalling, gas warfare, and machine-guns and musketry. Meanwhile, veteran instructors arrived to start again with basic training. Once the unit's officers and NCOs returned, they could take over the more advanced training. As usual, practice was less than perfect. Growing uncertainty about a unit's fate left men uneasy, while officers leveraged whatever influence that had got them their original commissions in the hope of improving their own fortunes. When drafts began to disappear, morale and training evaporated too. Both Winnipeg's 44th and Saskatchewan's 46th Battalion dissolved during June 1916, in the wake of the heavy

fighting at Mont-Sorrel. Later that summer, both were reconsti-
tuted for the 4th Division.

If training in Canada had been time-wasting and ineffective, it
did not always much improve in England. With some justice, the
British considered the new arrivals from Canada as little better
than raw recruits. In a familiar army refrain, the 44th Battalion
newcomers were told, "Forget everything they ever told you in
Canada."[47] Men gratefully traded their Canadian uniforms, boots,
and Oliver equipment for the British equivalent, but long after the
summer of 1916, when their rifle was replaced in France by the Lee-
Enfield, the Ross had to be used in England.[48]

Elderly, outdated instructors troubled the CEF as much as they
did the New Army. As a keen new corporal on manoeuvres, Frank
Worthington ordered his section to crawl forward to capture a
machine-gun post. A staff officer galloped up and denounced him
as a disgrace to his regiment: "No British soldier crawls into battle
on his belly!"[49] The British army's continued enthusiasm for
seeming frills was an added irritant. As a young machine-gun officer, Claude Williams went to London to learn the new "Chelsea
drill" from the Brigade of Guards. It was, he reported, "the last
word in smart movements" and "very much more difficult and
fancy than the foot drill we were taught in Canada."[50] Corporal
Nelson was a less grateful beneficiary of an eight-week NCO course
at the Guards Depot at Pirbright. "Imperial officers treat men like
dogs" was one of his sour conclusions.[51] By the time he was finished, his battalion had ceased to exist.

There were occasional compensations. Gordon Beatty's cyclist
company, on an exercise ride along the coast, came streaming
down a hilly coastal road and spotted their first women in single-
piece bathing suits. The result was a monster pile-up. Another
cyclist, Garnet Durham, recalled spending a lazy morning on
manoeuvres, scouting for plums, pears, and damsons, and then
sampling hazelnuts. At the same time, he caught some of the
"enemy," a pair of South Africans who had no idea that they could
find anything edible on an English roadside. They all retired to the
local pub, where the Canadians had established their headquarters.

Front-line soldiers knew that formal training in England had little value at the front, particularly because, until 1917, most of the officers and instructors had been deliberately left behind, unwanted for front-line service. Until 1917, most Canadian instructors in England had never been to France or had returned too quickly to learn much. From Alderson on, senior officers with the Canadian Corps insisted that the men learned better on the job. They would also learn more when men with front-line experience conducted the training.

An entire Canadian division, the 5th, was held at Bramshott as a command for Sir Sam Hughes's son, Garnet, and because Ottawa legitimately feared that it could not find enough men to reinforce five full divisions at the front. Men of the "Forgotten Fifth" rejoiced that their battalions had avoided break-up and then worried that their courage was being questioned. Though he knew he would lose his stripes, Robert Correll insisted that he was ready to go to France: "There are enough cold-footed NCOs around in this district now and I don't want to be classed with that bunch."[52]

Until Canadians had absorbed the savage lessons of the Somme and cleaned up their administrative mess in England, improvements were unlikely. The prime minister, briefed by the acting high commissioner in London, Sir George Perley, was finally convinced that the Canadian administrative structure in England was hopeless. His opportunity to act arrived in the fall of 1916. Hughes had spent the summer in England, had established a council of cronies in London to preserve his power, and had ignored his promise to consult. With unusual but overdue firmness, Sir Robert Borden forced his war minister out of office. "The greatest soldier since Napoleon has gone to his gassy Elba," wrote Colonel John Creelman, "and the greatest block to the successful termination of the war has been removed. Joy, Oh Joy."[53]

Sir Robert also decided that, henceforth, Canada's overseas soldiers would no longer be "Imperials" but members of the Canadian army, under a new Ministry of Overseas Military Forces of Canada (OMFC) located in London. By November 1916, Hughes was gone; Carson, Steele, and MacDougall followed him, and the new OMFC gradually took charge of the CEF on the far side of the Atlantic. The new minister, none other than Sir George Perley, preferred his job as Canadian high commissioner and cheerfully left his chosen military commander, Major-General Richard Turner, to manage. Turner dutifully assumed his new position. He proved himself a better administrator than a field commander. Turner adopted the British staff system, brought the best available men back from France, and organized his end of Gwatkin's regional reinforcement system for the infantry. For the first time, "reserve battalions" would undertake systematic instruction of recruits. By 1918, the system easily absorbed the MSA men.

Training continued as it had been. Traditions and past practices were hard to change. Officers and NCOs who had war experience did not necessarily perform as expert instructors. Many were selected because of battle exhaustion rather than enthusiasm or instructional skill. Parade-square drill and "eyewash" were almost as conspicuous in 1918 training programs as they had been in 1915. Tom Dinesen, who remembered his training in the Danish reserve, wondered why so little of the time spent in England in 1917–18 prepared him for what he would face in the trenches. Never once did he practise any of the real jobs he would carry out at night, from loading and firing his rifle to putting up a wire entanglement. Gas training he found useful, "perhaps because it was not part of the Marlborough tradition."[54] In contrast, grenade training was useless. He and others were "taught exceedingly carefully how to stand in a strange, theoretical position, left foot forward, body curved backwards; right arm pretending to hold the grenade at backward stretch; right foot at right angles to the given direction; then raise left arm; aim just above the knuckle of forefinger; swing right arm, stretched, in circular motion across shoulder, stretch right knee, bend left knee etc. etc."[55]

With all its irrelevance, training was only a phase. Having taught its men more about "soldiering" and how to endure endless hours of waiting than about beating the Kaiser's army, the army itself could move rapidly when it chose to do so. Soldiers "warned for a draft" were immediately confined to barracks while the clerks worked feverishly to prepare their documents and the quartermaster stores brought their kit up to standard. In the earlier years, one of the last issues was a pair of heavy, hobnailed "Kitchener" boots, to be painfully broken in on the cobblestoned *pavé* of France. Most drafts departed at night or in the early morning, boarding trains that took them to Dover, Folkestone, or Southampton. In October 1916, Lieutenant Claude Williams left Southampton for Le Havre on a former Clyde ferry: "men and officers were packed in like sardines, there wasn't a square foot anywhere where somebody wasn't lying down trying to get a bit of sleep."[56]

As the little ship throbbed out of the harbour, a steady drizzle matured into an ocean storm, men who had gobbled down their fat ham sandwiches vomited them up again, and the stench drove Williams on deck to endure the rain and spray. It took five hours to reach Le Havre. For the usual inscrutable army reasons, they then had to wait four more hours to disembark. They had learned about soldiering; they would now learn about war.

CHAPTER FIVE

OFFICERS AND GENTLEMEN

PREPARING THE LEADERS

Armies reflected a rigid class system that the war itself would greatly erode. If men in the ranks lost most of their social status when they enlisted, others were transformed by a King's commission into almost another species. They became officers and gentlemen.

A T THEIR ATTESTATION, soldiers swore to obey the king, his heirs and successors, and such generals and officers as the king might place over them. Such officers ranged from a new lance corporal in the full glory of his single chevron to Field-Marshal Sir Douglas Haig, Commander-in-Chief of the British Expeditionary Force. Without leaders, an army was an armed mob. Non-commissioned officers (NCOs), promoted from the ranks, enforced discipline, managed routine administration, and socialized recruits—and sometimes their commissioned superiors—in military ways. By common consent, they formed the backbone of their unit. Yet, in a tradition the CEF in no way challenged, the newest-joined lieutenant earned more ($2.60 a day) than the most senior sergeant-major ($2.30). Why the twenty-year-old son of a banker or clergyman would be a better leader of men than a thirty-year-old sergeant with a decade of soldiering to his credit was a question a lieutenant might ask himself. Perhaps he was wise not to pause for an answer. Or perhaps the answer was implicit in the words on the parchment scroll an officer received and left rolled up with his less urgently needed belongings. It commanded him: "at all times to exercise and well discipline in Arms both the inferior Officers and Men serving under you and use your best endeavours to keep them in good Order and Discipline,... And We do hereby Command them to obey you as their superior Officer, and you to observe and follow such Orders and Directions as from time to time you shall receive from Us or your Superior Officer, according to the Rules and Disciplines of War."[1]

The archaic language reflected an age when the sovereign summoned his nobles and later contracted with them to provide regiments. War was deemed the proper vocation for a gentleman: his courage could be assumed as an attribute of his class, and warlike skills were part of his upbringing. To prevent another presumptuous despot like Oliver Cromwell, with his competent but ill-bred colonels, the MPS at Westminster had done their best to ensure that Britain's army would henceforth be officered by men of property, regardless of their military skills. Not until 1871, and after bitter debate, had Parliament finally abolished the purchase and sale of army commissions. The relative pittance paid to junior officers guaranteed that almost all of them still needed private means to serve.

In conscious imitation, the élite regiments of the Canadian Militia required their officers to forgo their pay and invest in elaborate full-dress uniforms. The governor general graciously let it be known that officers who might not otherwise be socially acceptable might be received at Rideau Hall in their uniforms.[2] Since would-be officers needed at least a month at an often remote military school to qualify for a commission, labourers and poor farmers were unlikely to apply, and even the sons of the better-off often found instruction in mess etiquette an ordeal.

Despite these impediments, the class barrier was permeable in both Britain and Canada. Sir William Otter, the venerable "father of the force," liked to remind militia officers that he had begun his career as a private. In rural districts and French Canada, wealthy and well-connected officers were scarce. After long and exemplary service, a British soldier might hope for a commission in the limited role of quartermaster. After all, someone competent and cunning was needed to guarantee a unit its share of rations and supplies, and it was hardly a task a gentleman could be expected to perform. Occasionally merit was enough. An example was Sir William Robertson, an outstanding cavalry regimental sergeant-major (RSM) at the early age of twenty-five who, thanks to admiring superiors, was transformed into one of the army's oldest lieutenants. His talent, a shrewd marriage, and considerable luck ultimately made "Wully" the Chief of the Imperial General Staff for several crucial years of the Great War in spite of the uncertain aspirates that revealed his working-class origins. The army remembered how Robertson had delivered word of Sir Horace Smith-Dorrien's dismissal in 1915: "'Orace, you're for 'Ome."

At Valcartier, Hughes had personally chosen the officers for the First Contingent, and he did so again for the Second Contingent.[3] Beyond the simple joy he found in exercising power, the minister had reasons. All his political life he had battled snobbish Toronto Tories, and most of his tumultuous militia campaigns had been waged against snobs in the staff or the Permanent Force. When he insisted that officers could qualify in a few days at a provisional school instead of in a few months at one of the PF's barracks, he believed he was striking at élitism, not efficiency. His boys would not be put at the mercy of "Staff College pets" or Permanent Force favourites. Of 44 senior appointments in the first two contingents, only 9 were held by permanent officers. Of 1,114 combatant officers, 204 had no formal qualifications, and 186 (including 27 lieutenant-colonels) were not qualified for their rank. Hughes was unrepentant: the men he picked would learn their jobs or he would be the first to throw them out. After all, in this war no one was an expert.[4]

Of course, the men who had pulled political strings to get their CEF commissions would go on pulling them to get promotions and favourable appointments for themselves or their families, and not all of them would be forever grateful. Harold Daly, a Vancouver lawyer who came to Ottawa to help handle Hughes's impossible workload, wryly confessed that, though he had been especially helpful to lawyers, "I had done a lot for them—fixed up their sons, brothers and brothers-in-law—none of them gave me any business."5

Even if Hughes's judgement had been excellent, the army's hierarchy of authority and trust was sorely strained. Why did Hughes's friends Brigadier-General Richard Turner and Lieutenant-Colonel David Watson defend the Ross rifle after Second Ypres, while Brigadier-General Currie, a Liberal, denounced it, and Brigadier-General Mercer of the 1st Brigade kept silence? All four soon commanded divisions. St. Pierre Hughes, the minister's younger brother, got a battalion in the Second Contingent, a brigade in the 4th Division, and the sack within weeks of Hughes's downfall. Was this politics?

To qualify as an officer in the CEF, a man needed a militia commission and his colonel's consent. From its officers, the militia required the oath of allegiance, a minimum height of 5 feet 4 inches, a minimum chest measurement of 33 inches, and a minimum age of 18—and, above all, that the candidate (or his father) win the approval of a militia commanding officer. An initial provisional commission was confirmed when the candidate had completed a qualifying course that ranged in duration from three months for the infantry to ten months for heavy or "garrison" artillery at Quebec. At infantry schools, an officer qualified as a lieutenant by passing the first month's exams, as a captain after the second month, and as a major after the third. However, Hughes's insistence on bringing military schools to the militia confused standards. The same certificate might represent three months' training or seven evenings at the local armouries.

What sort of officers did the colonels approve? One of two inspectors general, Hughes's elder brother, John, looked closely at officers of western Canadian battalions. Craig Brown has examined his reports on ten of the reinforcement battalions raised in the second year of the war. In a sample of 369 officers, Hughes found 100 with commercial backgrounds, 87 from the professions, and 72 from finance—mostly bank employees. Only 20 came from farms and 22 from trades, and 3 had military backgrounds; 26 were students. In the relatively newly settled region, only 43 officers had western birthplaces; 106 were born in Ontario and 158 in the British Isles. Lieutenant-colonels averaged 44 years of age, and majors 36.8 years, while subalterns were a rather mature 29.9. Most senior officers were prominent citizens with Canadian Militia or British Territorial Army experience, though a few represented the frauds and wasters any frontier region attracts.[6] Junior officers in the eastern battalions, about whom only scattered information is available, were generally a few years younger, more likely to be students or in the liberal professions, and more likely to be the sons of professionals or prosperous members of the community.

The system was open to favours and bigotry. When Mohawks failed to volunteer for a company of the 20th Battalion, General Lessard asked for advice about the unit's two Indian platoon commanders. One was "a very efficient officer, only objection being his breed and dangerous to have in command of white troops."[7] To his credit, Hughes refused to endorse such nonsense, and several Indians and Metis served as CEF officers. The colonel of Montreal's 42nd Highlanders complained when a draft of 16 new officers included "3 Frenchmen & 1 Jew of pronounced appearance."[8] Lieutenant Myron Cohen stuck it out, "cleaned everybody's clocks" when fellow officers jeered at the package of kosher food his mother sent him, and proved to be such a tough fighter that his brigadier called him "MacCohen."[9]

Militia Headquarters set ambitious standards for an officer. He had to be fit for active service "and of an age to make it likely that he will be able to bear the strain of war."[10] According to a 1915 training circular, he needed the self-confidence to command a platoon and knowledge of squad drill; extended order drill; platoon, company, and bayonet-fighting drill; musketry; care of arms; judging distances; reporting messages; how to post sentries; how to command an outpost or a picquet; and, "if possible," how to fire a machine-gun.

To meet the challenge of trench warfare, an officer had to know about types of trenches, dugouts, and wire entanglements; how to tell off working parties; and how to lead a party of grenadiers. Billeting and feeding a platoon and making sanitary arrangements were part of the curriculum. An officer needed training in military law and how to report sick, how to get a soldier a new kit, how to take over trench stores, and "a slight knowledge" of field telephones. He also needed instruction in field messages and "a thorough training in writing clear and concise reports of happenings in his vicinity."[11]

In the mounted corps, such as the artillery, riding was both a skill and a test of character. "You know one must ride just so," Donald McKinnon reported from the Army Service Corps school at Quebec. "The riding instructor has his eyes on everyone—knees well in and gripping the sides of the horse firmly, elbows well in against the body, feet must not dangle but be gracefully carried in the stirrups."[12]

To provide the training, pre-war military schools expanded their enrolment and shortened their courses—if only because any modern equipment had been sent overseas. PF officers who had lacked the luck or influence to get themselves sent overseas with the CEF faced the thankless task of instructing other men who would. PF officers learned to be discreet. Experience taught the career-threatening danger of "running against a snag." It was safer to assign a chapter from Otter's famous *Guide*, hand over the parade to knowledgeable sergeants and retire with dignity to the mess.

Lieutenant-Colonel George Murphy of the Army Service Corps adopted a different approach. He summoned the would-be officers of a new divisional transport unit and opened with a discussion of the most convenient hours for training. The officers agreed to an hour of drill in the morning, lectures in the evening, and the rest of the day for their own business. "This very democratic and common-sense procedure appealed at once to all and got the class off to a good start."[13]

Not that all who flocked to qualify had any intention of going overseas: a militia commission and a military title became useful in wartime Canada. When Gwatkin and his staff pleaded that the schools be reserved for serious candidates for the CEF, Hughes refused: "Every eligible man who presents himself for training, being recommended, must be provided for. Thousands of Sergeants and Officers are required and we must rise to meet the circumstances."[14] The result, complained the director of training, Colonel R.A. Helmer, was that "mere youths with sufficient family or political influence, but utterly unfitted for responsibility have been given commissions and permitted to qualify."[15]

As befitted the militia's élite branch, the artillery schools at Kingston, Quebec, and Halifax set a tougher standard than most. In November 1915, Lawrence Youell and his closest chum braved the Royal School of Artillery at Kingston and its notorious chief instructor, Captain T.F.B. Ringwood. The two men lived at a nearby hotel, showed up at 6:00 a.m. for PT or stable duties, and continued with drill, equitation (riding), and lectures after breakfast until 5:30, with an hour and a half for lunch. Lacking guns of more recent vintage than the South African War, officers spent much of their training riding bareback and afterwards grooming their horses. Youell's splendid new uniform began to show signs of wear. Ringwood was not ingratiating: "he supposed most of us were here by political pull—which needless to say wouldn't help us here."[16] Ringwood's sarcasm echoed painfully after one of Youell's classmates—"one of those slow thinking chaps who looks at you like an owl"—died in a riding accident. "He has been telling us if we didn't learn to ride properly, he hoped that some of us would get killed and teach us a lesson which, although the class understands his idea, will look badly to the public."[17] A court of inquiry exonerated Ringwood, but anonymous student complaints persuaded Militia Headquarters to inquire about overly harsh instructors. A former engineering student and an athlete, Youell kept up with Ringwood on ten-mile runs, studied at night, and enjoyed mess life when, in the last two weeks of his course, he moved from the hotel: "At the mess everything is served in only the correct manner. There is wine always, of course," he explained to his father. "But you need have not the slightest worry on that account as not a dozen out of the forty or more members usually take any and I can promise you I won't touch it."[18]

Though Youell found his examinations "very stiff," he passed; most of his classmates failed, as did his best friend. Youell senior had obtained commissions for both young men in the 43rd Battery, and they spent a few sociable months in Guelph, enjoying local hospitality and learning to give orders, and reported: "I don't mind in the least handing out a 'Call down' when it's needed, which is seldom."[19] Meanwhile, his friend wrestled with his options, and finally, to the cheers of the men, took his place in the ranks.

Donald McKinnon, who had qualified as an officer in the Army Service Corps, did the same. Hanging around Ottawa, trying to arrange an appointment, soon disgusted him, and he enlisted in a Signals unit of the Canadian Engineers at Ottawa's Lansdowne Park.[20] To his dismayed family he reported: "the ranks seem to contain more real gentlemen than do the lists of officers. I have just seen enough of both to know."[21] Such selfless patriotism among young Canadians so astonished General Gwatkin that he summoned McKinnon, talked with him at length, and promised any assistance he could offer.[22]

From the outset, the CEF had a second source of junior officers—its own ranks. Before it left Salisbury, the Canadian Contingent had contributed 232 officers to Kitchener's Army. After Ypres, 35 men were commissioned from the ranks, and others were sent to British cadet schools. "I don't suppose you agree with the idea of giving commissions to the ranks," Ian Sinclair explained to his fiancée, "but it is different in our case to that of the regulars, as lots of our privates are as capable and of as good family as any of the officers."[23]

D'Arcy Leonard was the kind of man Sinclair had in mind. A recent graduate of the University of Toronto, he went to England with a draft for the 3rd Battalion, served a couple of months in the trenches, and, in October 1915, was sent to a British officers' school at St. Omer. He survived the course, earned top marks for his

revolver shooting, and soon instructed his sister in military etiquette: a lieutenant was addressed not by rank but as "Esq."[24] After
spending a week in England to buy his kit, he reported to the 5th
Battalion. Within a couple of weeks, a serious wound in his shoulder knocked him out of the war.

By 1916, the two sources of officers overflowed. When Hughes
was finally forced out in November 1916, Canada had far more officers with paper qualifications than it could ever employ. Camps in
England were awash with colonels, majors, and captains from bro-
ken-up battalions. Carson's "Cook's Tours," brief tours of duty at
the front to give senior officers the chance to earn a medal, had
exasperated the Corps without disposing of the problem. Even ill-
trained, inexperienced subalterns were a liability, especially to the
soldiers who had to obey their foolish orders. "It is sickening to see
some of the chumps who get commissions," complained Angus
Mowat. "Very few people seem to realize how much depends on
the infantry subaltern."[25] Parents and friends persuaded Hughes
and General Carson to grant special favours for sons, nephews,
and friends in the ranks.

C.G. Power, the hockey-playing son of a Quebec City MP, was a
private in the Medical Corps when a cable from Hughes commanded "find Chubby Power and give him a commission."[26] After
the usual military-bureaucratic tangles, Power emerged as a lieutenant in the 3rd Battalion, won an MC, and was badly wounded
just before the Somme. He happened to be a good choice; others
were not. As Colonel Duguid complained, "many with very inadequate qualifications were often withdrawn from France and
granted commissions directly over the heads of men better qualified in the field."[27]

By the spring of 1917, the new OMFC Headquarters was in place.
The Canadian Corps finally had support in high places for a policy
of drawing virtually all its new officers from its own ranks. General
Turner appointed a military secretary and assigned him the sensitive task of getting rid of surplus senior officers. "Cook's Tours"
stopped. In a series of painful interviews, officers were urged to
drop their rank with a guarantee that their separation allowance

and pension would be untouched, and their families would not be affected by the demotion. After delay and second thoughts, the same concession was made to surplus senior NCOs in England.

Some officers accepted the terms; most didn't, and returned to Canada. One of them, Major A.T. Hunter, left a lively description of their feelings: "I travelled back on the *Missanabie* with 150 surplus officers fresh from their experience in callous insult. To say they were peeved would not express it. If the steamer had lost her coal, she could have put a few of these gentlemen below the boilers and come home on her own steam."[28]

In 1916, the Canadian Corps created its own officers' school and, in 1917, after the reorganization in Britain, the Canadian Training School for Infantry Officers opened at Bexhill-on-Sea. The Corps seemed happy with its products, and visitors admired "its precision in drill movements, its *esprit-de-corps* and general efficiency."[29] Officers of the Machine Gun Corps received further training at Seaford. Gunner officers took five-month courses at Witley, and later at Bordon. Ed Russenholt of the 44th Battalion, a Bexhill graduate, praised the school. He also remembered how much morale improved when junior NCOs and men had this greater chance of promotion—though no man would admit such ambition to his pals.

Direct commissions from the ranks created their own problems. Ex-rankers lacked at least some of the skills, knowledge, and social polish their superiors wanted in an officer. Even privates noted the rough edges and wanted more in an officer than an NCO with a Sam Browne belt.

The gulf between a private soldier and a commissioned officer was a sharp reminder of a ordinary soldier's fallen status. A commission entitled an officer to a formal salute, sometimes only perfunctorily acknowledged. Soldiers lined up to have tea, soup, and "mulligan stew" ladled into their mess tins; officers were served in their own mess, with the dignity and comfort of gentlemen. D'Arcy Leonard was a little shocked to find his new colonel at breakfast in his shirt-sleeves. Not all colonels were Saskatchewan dirt farmers, though not many were as good at their job as George Tuxford.[30]

Even in the field, a self-respecting regiment would somehow provide tablecloths, dishes, silver, and attentive mess waiters. Lieutenant J.W.G. Clark, billeted behind the lines in 1916, reported to his father "how the boy is eating": "Last night's menu: yellow melon, lettuce, pink celery and olives, vermicelli soup, salmon salad, broiled steak and onions, Lyonaise [sic] potatoes, green beans, peaches and cream (real cream), bread and butter &c and tea. All this was beautifully dished up and cooked."[31] In the trenches, Clark and his fellow officers could expect to sleep in a dugout while their troops remained huddled against the trench wall. When an officer was wounded, special efforts were usually made to evacuate him. He could expect treatment in an officers' ward and his own section of a hospital train. If he died, casualty reports often gave his name, while losses among "the men" were reported as anonymous numbers.

An officer was entitled to a soldier servant or "batman" (from the Hindi word for "baggage") and, if mounted, a groom. Whether or not an efficient officer had the time or energy to do his job as well as performing his personal chores, a gentleman could not be expected to lay out his sleeping-bag, polish his own boots, or curry-comb his own horse. In his new company, D'Arcy Leonard found that two of the five batmen looked after the cooking; one handled the money; and the remaining two cleaned boots, brushed off mud, and kept five officers clean. "As a general rule they don't pay batmen at the front because they have a soft job and they know it."[32]

An officer purchased his own uniform. It was tailored, elegant, and of finer cloth than a soldier's rough khaki serge. He could choose a waterproof trenchcoat in milder weather or a fleece-lined British Warm when the driving rain turned to snow. An officer might purchase his own sword, at four guineas; he certainly needed a pistol, binoculars, and other field equipment; and, like many gentlemen, he expected his tailor and outfitter to be patient about being paid for services rendered. Gambling debts, of course, were a matter of honour and promptly paid.

An officer might abandon his highly polished Sam Browne belt in action and even adopt a soldier's tunic, but he invariably confirmed his status with a collar and necktie. Other ranks buttoned up their tunic collars to the neck. The tendency of regimental sergeant-majors and other warrant officers first class to adopt more of an officer's uniform than the Sam Browne was firmly checked in 1917. The opposite tendency—officers enhancing their survival by wearing other ranks' uniforms in battle—was discouraged, not forbidden.

As a gentleman, an officer served almost as much at his own pleasure as his sovereign's. Until conscription imposed a common obligation, he was free to resign if he chose. Probably no grievance rankled more with men in the ranks than an officer's privilege of leave four times a year, when they were lucky to have one week each year. Some officers also secured special leave to attend to their business or family affairs in Canada, a privilege seldom granted to men in the ranks.

Officers certainly had to satisfy a gentlemanly code of conduct. There was only one penalty for anyone found guilty of "behaving in a scandalous manner unbecoming the character of an officer": "cashiering" or dismissal with ignominy from His Majesty's service. Such behaviour could range from sodomy or a self-inflicted wound to passing a rubber cheque. An officer charged with a serious military offence had even another advantage over the men in the ranks; he was judged by a court martial composed of fellow officers—his peers.

A student of human nature and social class might not be surprised that 25.4 per cent of the officers charged with military offences were acquitted by British courts martial in the First World War, but only 10.2 per cent of accused other ranks had their charges dismissed.[33] One reason, obvious from court-martial transcripts, was that the word of officer-witnesses was normally accepted as true whenever it contradicted the testimony of men in the ranks, even if the soldiers were senior NCOS.[34] Higher authorities quashed twice as many verdicts on other ranks as on officers because they were obviously improper or indefensible. While an officer might be shot; "cashiered," or dismissed with disgrace; merely dismissed from His Majesty's service; fined; or reduced in seniority, he was immune from the vulgar penalties of detention or field punishment. During the course of the war, several officers were convicted of cowardice, desertion in the face of the enemy, and other offences that led men in the ranks to a firing-squad. However, no Canadian officer was executed.

In return for their privileges, what did officers actually do? The simple answer, at least for regimental officers, is that they gave leadership, took responsibility, and set an example, if necessary, by dying. Officers were middle managers, transmitting the often inscrutable and sometimes absurd orders of their superiors; investing them with their own personalities; and convincing soldiers to obey, even at the near-certain cost of their own lives. Implicit was the assumption that the officer would be the first to die in battle. Officers were the first out of the trench in an assault or a night patrol, and the last out in a retreat.

In truth, the CEF's mentors had to think out how to fight a trench war. Until the final years, when a tactical key was discovered that enhanced the value of small-group leadership, battles were regulated from the rear, and officers could only implement rigid plans as they received them. As a historian of Canadian officer and staff training, Stephen Harris concluded that "the tactical shortcomings of Hughes's under-trained appointments was [sic] not crucial as long as they had some talent for seeing to the needs of their men."[35] Compared with their allies and enemies, the British army had a high ratio of officers to other ranks, and it accepted that most of them would be poorly trained amateurs. What officers required was sacrificial courage, a rare quality that was surprisingly common among the young men from Haldane's OTCs. A brutal test of the unit's performance was the relative officer and other rank loss-survivor ratios. In good units, officers tended to die. In bad units, they left that duty to their men.

In addition to relaying orders and setting an heroic example, officers filled a host of roles, from plotting counter-bombardment programs to censoring their men's mail. They alone could sit as members of courts martial. In an infantry battalion, they inspected their men's feet to ensure that they were fit to march. They examined rifle barrels for flakes of rust and checked haversacks for the necessary clean white towel. Periodically, they stood by, with initial embarrassment, while medical officers inspected their men's genitals for evidence that any soldier had been concealing symptoms of venereal disease.

In the trenches they "stood to" with their men for an hour at dawn and dusk, and intermittently during the night they donned their sodden trench coats, strapped on a revolver, and went out to inspect the soaked and shivering sentries. In the Artillery or the Engineers, officers applied whatever technical training they possessed to the task of delivering accurate fire, calculating the ballast needed under a light railway, or directing a tunnelling operation. Staff officers handled the masses of "returns" and "states" and other documents that seemed inevitable if armies were to be fed and their losses replaced. Some of them planned the operations and issued the orders that sent others to be killed or maimed.

How well did Canadian officers do? Since officers or members of their class became the historians who told us most of what we now know about the CEF, suspicions of bias are not limited to the court-martial statistics. Some judgements have been harsh, from Captain J.F.C. Fuller's angry reaction at Plymouth in 1914 to Steve Harris's more recent conclusion in *Canadian Brass* that officers were not a strong point of the CEF.[36]

From the moment he encountered the Canadians, General Alderson concluded that his officers were the weakest feature of the contingent. He could forgive them their ignorance and inexperience; he could not condone their lack of "a power or habit of command" and their preoccupation with their own comfort.[37] Angry at the state of his 1st Division at midsummer, 1918, Major-General Macdonell believed his platoon officers were the core of the problem: "I wish every step taken to elevate the tone and status of Officers. Manners must be improved and character developed, in fact he must be a leader and an example in every way and inculcate the spirit of discipline by precept and example, creating an atmosphere by his own soldierly bearing and method of doing his duty."[38]

Macdonell's instructions were not needed in the Canadian Cavalry Brigade. As a major in 1918, the former private Lighthall described how, after a bitter fight and heavy shelling, the officers' mess pack horse arrived and the waiter laid out a white tablecloth, polished glasses, silver, and a respectable lunch, not excluding a discreet bottle of whisky. If the cavalry were not very valuable in trench warfare, they did bring a little social tone to the battlefield.[39]

Drunkenness remained a problem among officers from the day the first troopship docked at Plymouth, leading to more courts martial than all other offences combined. It contributed to other escapades too. In his memoirs as a lieutenant in the 4th Battalion, James Pedley recalled a fellow subaltern, an "Original" promoted from the ranks, whose past courage saved him from dismissal at his first court martial for drunkenness. The court showed no mercy after a second offence. The man was cashiered, reappeared later as an artillery sergeant, served at Archangel, and might have been commissioned again—save for yet another court martial. Treatment for alcoholism was not even considered.

Another officer, with the 48th Highlanders since 1893, had troubled his regiment for a long time before he was finally court-martialled at the end of 1915. Considering it a first offence, the commander-in-chief overruled a sentence of dismissal until General Mercer compelled the commanding officer of the 15th Battalion to tell the whole truth. The officer had been more or less drunk throughout his time overseas: "His conduct had become so notorious that he had completely lost all confidence and respect of his men."[40]

Men in the ranks seem to have accepted officers, like much else in the army, as inevitable. They admired an officer's courage and unselfishness, resented his privileges, remembered injustices, and saluted only when it was unavoidable. Claude Craig's diary revealed some familiar prejudices about superiors: "We have another new officer, Lt. Hall is his name. Believe me if there ever was a 'nut' he's it. He knows nothing about drill and less than that about signalling. He also wears glasses and lisps. Nut with a capital N."[41] Frank Hazlewood noted that he had crossed a street to avoid saluting an officer "when I saw it was Earl Wilmott."[42] The pleasure of the reunion was marred by discovering that Wilmott had already been on leave after only a few months in France.

Robert Correll wished his first platoon officer well: "I hope he comes through safely…. He used all the Whitby boys white and he tried hard to keep us together."[43] Colonel Farmer of the 5th Field Ambulance was explosively ill-tempered and hated the English, but his men believed that he looked after them. Fred Noyes described a hot route march that ended, unexpectedly, in a shady lane where a farmer "just happened" to be broaching a huge cask of cold ale.[44]

Since soldiers saw "eyewash" as an officer's way of showing off at his men's expense, they usually preferred easygoing superiors. Colonel William Allen, who took the 20th Battalion to England in 1915, refused to make his men dig trenches or carry their kit. He had not brought his men over to be pack mules, explained Private Jimmy Farrell from Streetsville. When Allen was removed from the command, his cheering men surrounded his car and then rushed off in a mob for a swim. They refused to settle down until Sam Hughes gave them a colonel they wanted.[45]

Like anyone else, soldiers rejoiced when a self-important officer got his comeuppance. Fresh from England, Lieutenant Claude Williams wanted spit, polish, and cleanliness from his front-line machine-gunners. A sudden enemy barrage cured his parade-square fixation. "Mired up to his knees with shells exploding all around him quite unnerved him," recorded Donald Fraser.[46] Once humbled, Williams turned out to be tolerable, particularly after his father, a Methodist minister, shipped the troops "lovely pure wool socks" knitted by his congregation. When Lieutenant J.V. Ferguson arrived in the 44th Battalion in the full glory of his Sam Browne and became excessively "regimental," the acting RSM, a pre-war pal, audibly demanded: "Whatinell's eating you, Judy?" According to Russenholt, Ferguson became a fine leader of troops.[47]

An officer could have many faults in the eyes of his men but, for front-line soldiers, the standing of a regimental officer was defined by his courage or cowardice. Under fire for the first time, Private Fraser watched his captain run around in a panic and finally bury his face in his hands: "Our estimation of our officers sank to zero and it was a lesson to us that in future it is best to rely on your own wits and do not expect too much from those senior to you."[48] Fred Noyes of the 5th Field Ambulance claimed that Colonel Farmer's successor hid in the Thelus cave during the weeks before Vimy. Despite strict orders to his men to use outdoor latrines, he used an oil barrel as his personal toilet and sent his batman up a hundred steps to empty it daily under shellfire.[49]

Good officers were prized. A.M. Munro of the 50th (Calgary) Battalion described his colonel, Lionel Page, as the reason for his battalion's success: "He is a prince, and every one simply worships him.... He is still in his twenties, I believe, and sets an example to his Battn in his fearlessness of danger."[50] Major Graham, he later reported, "is quite an old boozer" but "absolutely fearless."[51] In his memoirs, Frank Baxter, of the 116th Battalion, remembered the imperturbable George Pearkes, VC, as his ideal:

Col. Pearkes was the bravest man I ever knew. He was a strict disciplinarian. He was held in the highest esteem by all his officers and other ranks. He would never ask anyone to do anything that he himself would not be willing to do. Several times when I was going up to the front line with Colonel Pearkes, a burst of machine gun fire or an artillery shell would land very close to us. I would duck my head or fall flat on the ground. I never ever saw Colonel Pearkes even jump. He would often laugh and remark to me that if I kept on ducking I would lose my head and he also said not to worry about the shell that made a loud shriek but the one that landed close and you did not hear, it was the one to worry about.[52]

Tom Dinesen of the 42nd Battalion was exceptional in demanding more than courage from his superiors. He found that his officers were considerate, kindly, and brave: "All the same, I cannot help wishing that, beside these fine virtues, there might have been some small amount of ability, of trained skill and responsibility."[53] He might have added that scarcest of virtues, common sense, to the list. Soldiers were not grateful for officers who exposed their men to needless danger, either to prove their own courage or out of ignorance. "One night our idiot of a captain lined up our battalion just behind the front line and called the roll, formed fours and marched off like soldiers," complained Garnet Durham. "If Heinie had happened to send up a flare just then we would have got plastered all over the countryside."[54] Donald Fraser was wounded and crippled for the rest of his life when a new officer did much the same to him at Passchendaele.[55]

Will Bird had much to say about the officers of his 42nd Battalion. He admired his colonel and his regimental sergeant-major, who was "one of the finest men I met."[56] However, he insisted that "the average officer did not see more than a third as much of raw, undiluted war as did the men under him." Men, on post six hours on, six hours off, knew officers did duty for only two hours in twenty-four. Once a week, officers were detailed to lead carrying parties up the line; their men went out to fetch supplies almost every night. "Officers were simply men in uniforms designed to make them look better than privates, and they had responsibilities that we did not realize."[57]

As in other armies, soldiers sometimes talked about shooting unpopular officers. There was almost certainly more rumour than truth to talk on the subject. Under training in England, Private Robert Correll hinted to Lill about rumours from France: "It seems a hard thing to say but from what we can learn the ones that used the men dirty over here sometimes get 'accidentally' shot during a charge...the way some of the officers use the men is enough to make a man take a chance on getting them if nobody is looking at them." W.B. Woods recalled stopping to bandage a chum during an attack when an officer shouted at him. "I felt like asking him who he had bandaged but let it go as a deadpan stare." To his surprise, the officer hurried away, looking scared: "he must have heard one of those yarns about men getting rid of unliked officers in the heat of battle."

Some myths are irresistible, but no Canadian soldier was actually convicted of killing an officer in any circumstances throughout the war. One officer was found guilty of murdering a sergeant, and one private was shot for killing his sergeant-major.

No front-line soldier of any rank thought well of the officers on the staff. Seldom seen at the front, staff officers were conspicuous in neat uniforms, glistening boots, and their characteristic red cap band and gorget patches. The ranks rarely saw them at all, except as heralds of some new "push" or as the source of new directives about smartness and saluting. As they raced over the muddy roads, their staff cars splashed marching troops while their self-important occupants plotted fresh misery for them. If soldiers had read Siegfried Sassoon's dismissal of the red-tabbed breed, they might have approved.[58]

In fact, staff officers shaped the course of the war in its grandeur, its misery, and its outcome. Their plans moved the millions of men and the mountains of shells around Europe to create the stalemate on the Western Front and, in the end, they devised the techniques and tactics that broke that stalemate in 1918. If Canadians suffered at the hands of the staff, it was not because staff officers were a nuisance but because they desperately needed to get better at the job of serving the troops, and because, as the future Lieutenant-General E.L.M Burns observed, too many colonels grabbed at the chance to relieve themselves of their worst officers rather than their best, when vacancies for "staff learners" were announced.[59] Few realized how much their short-sighted solution to an immediate problem would return to plague them many times over.

In 1914, a few PF officers attended at the British army's staff college at Camberley; more might have been there if Canadian educational levels had been higher. A few dozen other officers had completed the militia's staff course. The British, expanding their own staff training in wartime, offered vacancies to the Canadians.

Sam Hughes abruptly refused the offer and insisted on creating his own staff course. Perley, his successor, closed it down and took up the British offer. Meanwhile, promising officers had joined brigade and division staffs as "learners."

They had a tremendous amount to learn. In battle, brigade staff had to prepare, coordinate, and transmit orders; keep in touch with flanking units; check out supply routes; set timings; and coordinate battalion plans. They had to collate all the miscellaneous and often contradictory information about the enemy's side and their own, and send what was relevant and accurate to the next-higher headquarters. The five officers at a Canadian brigade headquarters had to stay in two-way touch with their units and division headquarters, using all-too-mortal runners and telephones that died when a wire was cut—usually whenever shelling was fiercest. The brigade staff fed information to the brigadier and relayed his orders; reported casualties; arranged for replacements; and indented for food, ammunition, equipment, and forage for its many horses.

Divisional staff assumed the additional responsibility of appreciating the needs and tactical potential of gunners, engineers, an eventual battalion of machine-gunners, and batteries of trench mortars. A good senior staff officer meant an efficient headquarters, and the British generously gave the Canadians some of their best. Brigadier-General Charles Harington moved from the chief staff appointment in the Canadian Corps after working for Alderson and Byng to become chief of staff of Sir Herbert Plumer's Second Army. He made it unique among Haig's five armies in the field: veteran divisions dreamed of serving under Plumer and Harington.

The staff worked for the generals. Canada had 109 generals during the war, 59 of them overseas. A postwar book by Charles Yale Harrison, an American journalist in the ranks of the CEF, reflected a soldier's prejudices in its title: *Generals Die in Bed.* Most probably did. So did most privates. Jack Hyatt discovered that, of the 59 Canadian generals in France and England, 17 were wounded, though only one, Major-General M.S. Mercer, was killed in action.

(His brilliant successor, Major-General Louis Lipsett, was killed by a sniper in 1918 only after he returned to command the British 4th Division.) Unlike their troops, 78.3 per cent of the CEF's generals had been born in Canada, but, like their troops, the great majority came from Ontario and the West. They were two years older, on average, than their British counterparts; most were married; almost all had been in the militia or the PF before the war. Forty per cent had served in South Africa. All of them had a lot to learn; most of them knew it.

Most Canadian generals began their careers as CEF brigadiers or colonels with the approval of Sir Sam Hughes, including Currie and eight other Canadian generals who commanded divisions in the Corps. As long as he was minister, Hughes guarded the right to select senior officers himself, despite the fact that, until late in 1916, the Canadians were part of the British army. In retrospect, it is not obvious that a better system existed.[60]

Not all Hughes's choices were a success. Hughes's favourite British aristocrat, Lord Brooke, son of the Earl of Warwick, was twice imposed on the troops as a brigadier until a wound removed him from the war. Sir Richard Turner fared better as military commander at the Overseas Ministry than as a field commander, though one of the Corps's most respected staff officers, Colonel J. Sutherland Brown, preferred to blame Turner's brigade major, Garnet Hughes, for Turner's problems.[61] Colonel John Creelman resented Hughes deeply, possibly because he was one of the few First Contingent colonels not promoted after Ypres, while the unscientific "Dinky" Morrison, whom he despised, eventually commanded the Canadian Corps artillery.[62] No selection system is perfect. To Hughes's credit, he also selected Louis J. Lipsett, Archibald Macdonell, and the brilliant if utterly uncharismatic Arthur Currie, who rose to the top.

Divisional pride, like a battalion's *esprit-de-corps*, persuaded soldiers that their own formation was outstanding. On the basis of performance in 1917 and 1918, two Canadian divisions, the 1st and the 3rd, were luckier and more successful than the others. Sir Archibald Macdonell, Currie's successor in command of "The Old

Red Patch," was one of the few First World War generals to establish his eccentric personality among his admiring and occasionally embarrassed subordinates. A fierce old ex-Mountie from Windsor, "Batty Mac" was a single-minded cheerleader for "The Old Red Patch." Lieutenant Pedley recalled Macdonell telling officer cadets that he would "jump down the throats with spurs on and gallop the guts out of any officer" who failed to measure up to "Red Patch" standards. At gatherings, he would call out: "Who are you?" "The Red Patch!" "Are you with me?" "Yes!"—repeating the questions until he heard the right pitch of enthusiasm.

Both Macdonell and the 3rd Division's Major-General Lipsett visited the front lines frequently, an admirable habit that led to Lipsett's death in the last month of the war. In contrast to the flamboyant Macdonell, Lipsett was a soft-spoken British regular who advanced from command of the 8th Battalion to the 3rd Canadian Division because of skill, efficiency, and professional calm. Will Bird, no respecter of superiors, never forgot the time that Lipsett had appeared beside him at a lonely front-line sentry post.[63]

Another soldier, Ernest Davis, recalled a derailment behind the lines. Lipsett's staff car was the first to stop at the scene: "This general got out of his car, organized everyone within reach into a rescue squad, all of us heaving at the derailed car, including the general himself. As I recall it too, his chauffeur gave visible evidence of having to put his spotless shoulder to the load, but he had to…. That one encounter told me that here was a general one could follow 'knowing he was not one of the remote kind, far above his men.'"[64]

Small acts of personal integrity inspire those who witness them. Enough of them can change the course of history.

CHAPTER SIX

UP THE LINE

TRENCH WARFARE

Sooner or later, most soldiers went "up the line" to join the war in the trenches. It was an environment of misery and anonymous death. With time and labour, armies learned how to mitigate the worst of the misery, but skill in using old weapons and ingenuity in devising new ones meant that trench warfare remained as deadly as ever.

AT THE END OF 1916, a Canadian Corps of four infantry divisions held the line opposite Vimy Ridge, near the old city of Arras.

Fifteen months earlier, Major-General Richard Turner had brought the 2nd Division to France. General Alderson became commander of a new Canadian Corps, and Major-General Arthur Currie took over the 1st Division. Since an army corps normally had three divisions, two in the line and a third in reserve, Major-General M.S. Mercer formed the 3rd Division at the end of December. Among the units in France or summoned from England were four battalions of Canadian Mounted Rifles; the PPCLI, which rejoined the Canadians; and the Royal Canadian Regiment, rescued from exile in Bermuda. In April 1916, Major-General David Watson began organizing the 4th Division, and took it to France at the end of August. Artillery took longer to organize, and the 4th Division did not have its own guns until June 1917. After spending part of 1915 as infantry with the 1st Division, the Canadian Cavalry

Brigade joined the 5th British Cavalry Division, part of the huge cavalry army Haig reserved in case the infantry ever really cracked the German line.

Most men arrived in France as reinforcements, part of a merging stream of convalescents and raw trainees destined to replace losses in the units of the Canadian Corps. They all braved seasickness, submarines, and the British base at Etaples.

Like most military bases, Etaples was managed by strutting incompetents no longer wanted at the front. In early 1917, Will Bird found three inches of mud; a filthy cookhouse; and the "Bull Ring," a vast arena of sand dunes where raw recruits and returning convalescents were tested in the skills of trench warfare. Foul-mouthed,

THE CANADIAN CORPS 1917

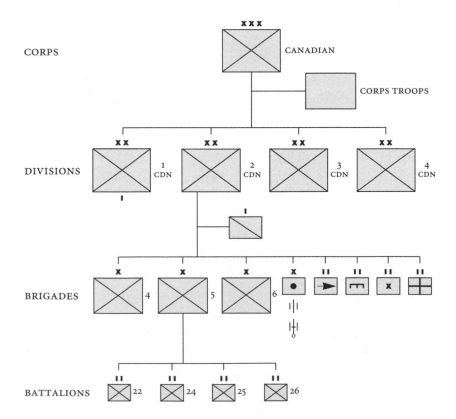

abusive NCOS, nicknamed "canaries" for their yellow armbands, cultivated the "offensive spirit." Apocryphal stories of German villainy abounded. Lieutenant C.V. Williams learned that a group of Germans had pretended to be wounded, slaughtered the Canadian stretcher-bearers who came to help them, and turned machine-guns on the Canadians' backs: "One of our Battalions was terribly cut to pieces by it but as soon as our boys found out who it was they let out one whoop, made for them and bayonetted them right and left even as they lay on the ground."[1]

More cynical soldiers suspected that make-believe ferocity kept the "canaries" in their "bomb-proof" jobs: "All the NCOS down here have to be very strict to hold their jobs as they don't want to go up the line any more," claimed Claude Craig, "and they just try and see how hard they can make the life of a poor buck."[2] The "spirit of the bayonet" reached a shrill crescendo. "Remember, boys, every prisoner means a day's less rations for you" was canary talk. "Carry a rusty fork in your puttees," a Bull Ring instructor told W.B. Woods, "and when you get close, jab him in the eye."[3] Later, Canadians bypassed the fatuity of the Bull Ring and trained at schools organized by the Canadian Corps.

At Étaples, or its Canadian successor near Rouen, reinforcements received all the kit and equipment the army judged necessary, and promptly jettisoned all that they could not carry: ragged French children, cadging cigarettes and bully beef by the roadside, were the main beneficiaries. To go "up the line," troops crammed themselves into tiny French boxcars, or "side-door Pullmans," while officers journeyed in dirty, unheated passenger coaches, equipped with hard wooden benches their men would have envied.

Most newcomers were sent to corps or divisional reinforcement units where they expended energy laying track, repairing roads, loading ammunition, or digging gun pits. The juxtaposition of danger, devastation, and continued civilian existence astonished them. Soldiers lived in tents or Nissen huts, or were billeted in French or Flemish barns. Behind the lines, troops frequented *estaminets*, or taverns, often run by refugees. They sold thin beer, cheap wine, and endless plates of fried eggs and chips. The local people were a revelation to the Canadians. Robert Correll echoed a common feeling: "we heard a great deal in Canada about little Belgium and her brave people, but since coming here we have changed our opinion of them. I suppose there are good and bad wherever you go, but the majority of Belgians seem to be bad." The irony of history had left part of pro-German Flanders under Allied occupation. Besides, the presence of hundreds of thousands of foreign troops would strain anyone's hospitality.

French and Flemish farmers often worked within German artillery range. Their farm buildings, arranged in a quadrangle around a large manure pit, served as quarters for troops at rest behind the lines.[4] At one such farm, Bird joined the 42nd, one of three battalions formed by Montreal's Black Watch. A "brick-hued bulging officer…told us we must realize what great privilege was ours to come and fight in the ranks of such a company as the Royal Highlanders. He hoped, he said, that we would always do our best—and his tone implied that he thought our best would be pitiful enough—and that implicit obedience to all orders would be very much to our advantage."[5]

The Canadian Corps fought its share of the war at the northern end of a trench system that stretched from the Swiss frontier to the sand dunes by the English Channel. Veterans would remember the yellowish mud of water-logged Flanders, the glue-like chalky soil of the Somme, and the brown dirt of the Arras plain. The power of modern artillery had forced both sides to dig in where they stood in 1914, and the "pushes" of 1915 and 1916 altered the line very little. The rival trench systems varied with the terrain and tactical doctrine, but they had much in common.

Any attacker faced a series of defended trenches, each protected by "aprons" of barbed wire. Stretched and stapled to stakes or laid out in coils, the wire was intended to funnel attackers into areas where they would be easy targets for machine-guns, set up in pairs in carefully sited and protected positions. When it was not firing at other targets, artillery was aimed at the likely approaches. "No man's land," from 30 yards to a mile or so wide, separated the lines.

At night, it was occupied by patrols and listening posts; by day it was left to rats and corpses.

Ideally, the forward trenches included three lines. The first was a fire trench that faced the enemy, sometimes with an "alternate" close behind, where men sheltered if their trench was receiving special attention from the enemy artillery. Second was a support trench, with dugouts for officers, and later for other ranks, and a greater aura of comfort and stability. Third was the reserve trench, where battalion headquarters, with its cooks and signallers, and specialist platoons sheltered. Behind the forward trenches, other defences were actually or tentatively sited, so that even the most

FRONT LINE TRENCHES

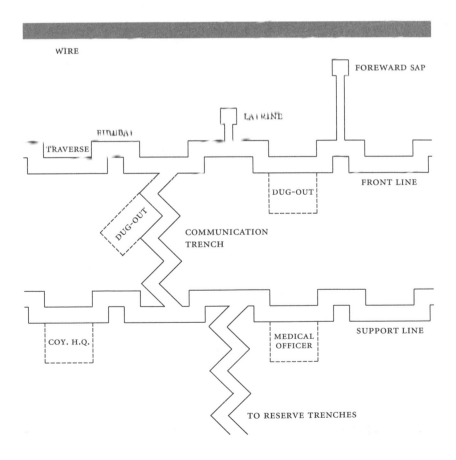

serious breakthrough could be harried, exhausted, and held until the railways could rush in reserve divisions to plug the gap and drive back the enemy.

That would never be necessary, of course, if Canadians followed Alderson's direction. His old regiment, he told new battalions, had never lost a trench. "I now belong to you and you belong to me and before long the Army will say 'The Canadians never budge'. Lads, it can be left there and there I leave it."[6]

At its simplest, a trench was a muddy and often watery ditch, reinforced with mud-filled sandbags. Sharply angled "bays" guaranteed that an enemy shell could devastate only a single traverse. A parapet in front and a parados behind protected soldiers while they fired their rifles; steel plates often "armoured" a sniper's loophole. Trench walls were "revetted," or reinforced, with any material at hand, from corrugated iron and chicken wire to the all-purpose sandbag. Shallower communications trenches connected the forward or "fire trench" to support and reserve trenches in the rear. Narrower trenches led to latrines. In the support and reserve trenches, dugouts—virtual caves in the ground—were excavated and covered with logs, corrugated iron, and dirt to make them safe from all but a direct hit. One small benefit of even a short advance was acquiring the deep, well-furnished, though vermin-infested, German dugouts. As Dinesen observed, on comparing the quality of German and Canadian construction, the Germans seemed to love hard work; Canadians paid the price for not emulating their enemy.[7]

Over time, conditions changed. In 1915, the few dugouts were reserved for officers' quarters, headquarters, or privileged specialists such as the battalion scouts, snipers, and bombers. Humbler soldiers carved themselves "funk holes" in the trench wall and huddled under their 3 foot–by–5 foot rubber sheets until driving rain sent viscous mud oozing out of the sandbags, and the walls gradually collapsed. By 1916, most trenches had enough dugouts to provide cramped, smelly shelter for everyone. At points, trenches looped around defended posts, with machine-guns, always in pairs, covering a vulnerable sector or taking advantage of higher ground. Duckboards or trench mats provided a floor for most fire and communication trenches.

Reliefs moved in at night. Weary soldiers heading out to rest met troops coming "up the line" with a ritual greeting: "Are you down-hearted?" "No!" "Well, you bloody soon will be." Relieving units marched 6 to 8 miles from their billets, burdened with a rifle and bayonet, 70 pounds of equipment, and between 120 and 150 rounds of ammunition (veteran units carried less). Often men rested a moment before they entered a mile or more of communication trenches. Sometimes they were directed to add ration bags, water cans, shovels, a bale of sandbags, or a sheet of revetting material to their loads. Then they peeled off in single file into the pitch-black trenches, struggling to keep up, tripping on a broken duckboard, or catching on overhead wires. On a quiet night, occasional shells lit the sky, and newcomers first heard the swish or sharp crack of enemy bullets passing overhead and ducked. Officers, lightly bur-dened but responsible for direction, lost their way in the maze of ditches, easily transformed by a recent shell burst. Exhausted sol-diers might stumble for hours in search of their destination.

Even after a year of training camp, a soldier had much to learn. Greenhorns, terrified by exploding shells or the sound of bullets above them, were mocked by young veterans with more trench wisdom. "When you hear the crack," Magnus Hood soon learned, "the bullet has gone past you. It's the one you don't hear that hits you."[8] Any relief was nerve-wracking: crowding two battalions into a single set of trenches offered the Germans an ideal artillery tar-get. Officers signed for "trench stores," ranging from periscopes to hipwaders. Sentries memorized passwords and warnings about dangerous enemy habits. New men raised snipers' scores when they forgot the first rule of trench survival: "keep your head down."

For an hour at dawn and again at dusk, everyone "stood to," fully equipped, armed, and ready for the two periods in the day when attacks were most common.[9] Once rifles were cleaned and inspected, daylight was the time of rest. After a cold, wet night, the men welcomed stand-down, the time when the rum ration was issued under an officer's supervision. Rumours persisted that the

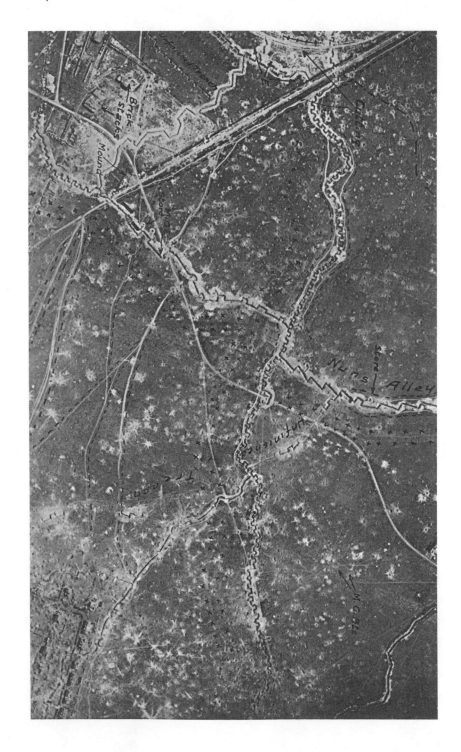

Army Service Corps and the sergeants had already helped themselves to the supply and diluted what remained in the brown, earthenware jugs marked "s.r.d." for "service rum, diluted."

Most found the rum fiery enough. After the bone-chilling cold of a winter night in the trenches, very few soldiers remembered their solemn pledges to mothers and sweethearts. "Rum's Up" was the easiest moment of the day, when soldiers joked, laughed, and produced greasy playing-cards for a quick game. "Tous les coeurs ont battu," remembered J.V. Lacasse of the 22nd Battalion, "les plus fatigués se cramponnent au rebord du talus. Les geignements se sont tus. Les figures emasciées deviennent tendues…. Le Rhum quoique dosé, est toujours le bienvenu."[10]

After stand-to, the daytime sentries—one man in twelve in the front line, fewer farther back—watched the enemy trenches through periscopes while their comrades smoked, cooked their meals, and demonstrated that exhausted men can sleep in impossible conditions. Officers, almost always better rested than their men, planned patrols, working parties, and reliefs for the coming night. Even in a quiet sector, a barrage from artillery or mortars might interrupt a brief peace. Retaliation invariably followed. The infantry on both sides served as victims. The day's damage added to the nightly list of repairs.

Trench warfare flourished at night. After dark, one in four men acted as sentry, giving his reliefs furtive two-hour naps. Meanwhile, patrols and wiring parties slipped into no man's land with orders to bring back information about the enemy and, ideally, a prisoner or two.[11] Staff officers were sceptical about reports, however straightforward, unless they included physical evidence—a German shoulder strap or a piece of the uniquely tough German wire. Two-man listening posts crawled out, conscious that they were prime targets for German patrols. Hundreds never came back. Meanwhile, ration parties went back to the reserve lines to collect the next day's food, water, and mail. Battalion stretcher-bearers—who often doubled as the battalion band out of action—evacuated any wounded who could not be removed during the day. Working parties busied themselves repairing damage, deepening a trench, digging a latrine, or building a new dugout. Sentries peered into the darkness, and sometimes into driving rain and snow. A nervous shot or a burst from a machine-gun could set the trench line blazing. Flares lit the sky, outlining the detritus of no man's land. Men caught in the open froze in the glare or lay prone in foul-smelling mud, cursing the deadly interruption. In the rear, guns added their fire to the orchestra. Then, as it had begun, the firing would slowly die away. Both sides checked for casualties.

Trench life was dangerous. Even in a quiet sector, a tour at the front seldom cost a battalion fewer than half a dozen dead and wounded. Signs warned soldiers about snipers, an important cause of death. Few Canadians were really skilled with their rifles, but crack shots from the battalion's platoon of scouts and snipers made up for them.

Raids were sudden hit-and-run attacks on enemy trenches, designed to seize prisoners and documents, destroy defences, and demolish the "live and let live" atmosphere that often developed on both sides. Despite a common myth, Canadians did not organize the first raids, but they garnered the credit—or the blame—for what Guy Chapman termed "the costly and depressing fashion of raiding the other side."[12] At Rivière Douve on the night of November 16–17, 1915, one of two raids launched by a couple of Currie's battalions scored a brilliant success. Through careful planning and rehearsal, artillery, snipers, bombers, even the handlers of a light bridge worked as a team and escaped with German prisoners, information, and a single fatality. Newly installed as British commander-in-chief, Sir Douglas Haig expressed delight about the Canadian success. He decided that this was how he would impose his will on the Germans and his mark on his own troops. Others soon learned that they must emulate the Canadian feat: generals and colonels found that holding their jobs thereafter depended on doing so. Certainly raiding gave Canadians and other raw soldiers in Haig's army the chance to hit back and, in their commander's view, to establish moral ascendancy on the battlefield.[13]

Canadian, Australian, and Scottish divisions seem to have taken to raiding with more relish than others. Clad in their oldest uniforms, stocking caps, and running shoes, their faces blackened, and armed with a wide assortment of weapons, the raiders brought some individuality and adventure to an otherwise "industrialized" war, but at a high price. Success in the dark, barbed wire–strewn morass of no man's land depended as much on luck as on skill and planning. The Germans were by no means helpless. They lit up the ground with superior pyrotechnics and used their plentiful stock of munitions to bathe it in shells if they suspected a raid was imminent. They also responded in kind. As might be expected, raids wore down front-line troops and exhausted any man's finite stock of courage. Between December 15, 1915, and May 15, 1916, a period of no significant battles, the BEF lost 83,000 men, most of them in actions associated with raids.[14] These heavy losses included the infantry's most enthusiastic officers and soldiers in operations that often seemed to lack any higher motive than a colonel's or a general's ambition. "That short and dry word 'raid'," Edmund Blunden recalled, "may be defined in the vocabulary of the war as the word which most instantly caused a sinking feeling in the stomach of ordinary mortals."[15] Soldiers prepared for them with a deep foreboding, grimly conscious that the efforts put into a raid were usually futile. Increasingly, senior officers demanded more evidence—a prisoner, or at least a fragment of German uniform, or the characteristic German barbed wire—to prove that the troops had not simply huddled on the friendly side of no man's land until it was time to crawl back to the comparative safety of their own trenches.

Haig could boast that a raid at Hooge in 1917 captured two German officers and some of their wine and cheese, without adding that, of the 650 men who set out, only 194 returned intact. When the 4th Canadian Division failed to meet all its objectives on Vimy Ridge on April 9, 1917, Lieutenant E.L.M. Burns, a future lieutenant-general, laid part of the blame on costly raiding, and a particularly disastrous attempted raid on March 1 that cost two good battalions their colonels and many of their best men.[16] Survivors of such tragedies had trouble trusting generals or their orders.

The Industrial Revolution had transformed the machinery of war.

While other industrial products had far greater impact on the battlefield, the most familiar symbol of change was the machine-gun.

In 1914, the BEF finally began replacing its Maxim machine-guns with the Vickers, a 58-pound, water-cooled gun that fired 500 rounds a minute with a range of 2,500 yards. Six men carried the gun, its tripod, and its water, and another sixteen carried the ammunition. Canadians were stuck with their air-cooled, undependable Colt guns until Vickers production speeded up.[17] By 1916, the British had created a separate Machine Gun Corps for the Vickers guns, and the Canadians followed suit. Infantry battalions also received the Lewis gun, a 26-pound, air-cooled weapon that fired 47 rounds per pan as fast as it was loaded—until it jammed. The Lewis worked better in aircraft, for which it was designed, but French-made alternatives, like the Hotchkiss, issued to British and Canadian cavalry, or the Chauchat, sold to the Americans in 1918, proved far worse. A strong man carried the Lewis gun; three to six more struggled under heavy canvas bags filled with loaded pans. By early 1916, an infantry battalion was entitled to eight Lewis guns; by early 1918, it had sixteen, one per platoon and four more for anti-aircraft protection.[18]

The machine-gun forced infantry to dig into the ground for protection. The resulting trench stalemate revived the archaic science of siegecraft, with its language of parapets and parados, traverses and revetments. Armies sought ideas and tools in museums. Grenades—hand-thrown bombs—had been an eighteenth-century weapon. At first soldiers improvised them with gun-cotton and scrap metal in recycled jam tins. As a newcomer, Lieutenant T.V. Anderson, a Canadian engineer officer, thought "jampot" was a French word.[19] Private W.S. Lighthall of the Royal Canadian Dragoons was taught to empty the jam tin, line it with burlap and an inner lining of mud. "Insert old nails and broken metal, centre a primer of gun cotton and make a small hole for the copper detonator and a short length of fuse. Cramp the copper with your teeth (dangerous). Apply more mud to hold the fuse in position, tie burlap around the fuse, light it with a cigarette, and wait five seconds for the explosion, preferably at a distance."[20]

Most soldiers preferred the Mills bomb. The thrower pulled a safety pin, held down the handle, and hurled the bomb. The handle flew off, a plunger ignited a fuse, and, three seconds later, the grenade exploded, hurling chunks of steel in all directions with deadly effect. Battalions formed platoons of bombers and sent would-be specialists for seventy-eight hours of training (including drill and bayonet fighting!) until the staff realized that almost anyone could learn to use them. By 1916, factories had made seventy-five million Mills bombs.

Mounted on a steel rod, fired from a rifle by the propulsive force of a blank, the No. 23 Mills bomb became a "rifle grenade." Opinions on its effectiveness varied widely. Staff officers concluded that it was a portable, if inaccurate, form of artillery for the infantry. Soldiers agreed about the inaccuracy: "We could not hit the broadside of a barn with it and besides it was dangerous as the extra pressure added by the rod in the barrel caused the rifle to split," recalled William Woods.[21]

Another eighteenth-century weapon, the mortar, was also brought out of retirement. Mortars were short tubes that used a bomb's built-in propellant to hurl it high in the air. Lucky shots landed in a trench; heavy ones could crush a dugout. Mortars had a psychological impact. Veterans admitted that it was profoundly demoralizing to watch bombs rise slowly in the air and head straight for them. Soldiers learned to survive in the trenches by watching mortar bombs and dodging out of a traverse instants before it was devastated. It was a nerve-wracking game.

British and German observers had watched the Japanese use bamboo mortars in their war with Russia, but only the Germans had taken note. As usual, there was catching-up to do. A German heavy *Minenwerfer* fired a devastating 200-pound bomb at three-minute intervals, wiping out whole platoons. Thanks to a $20,000 gift from a sympathetic Indian maharajah, an Englishman, Frederick Stokes, perfected his version of a mortar, a light tube that fired twenty-two bombs a minute. The "Stokes gun" was soon supplemented by the 60-pound "toffee apple" from the medium mortar and the 150-pound "flying pig" that a heavy mortar threw up to 1,000 yards.

As were machine-guns, trench mortars were soon served by specialized units. By July 1916, an infantry division included three light and three medium batteries and a heavy battery, each with four mortars.

Mortars were simply an adaptation of the decisive weapon of siege warfare—artillery. In peacetime, the power of gunnery had been underestimated. In 1870, the Germans had found that infantry weapons caused 91.6 per cent of casualties, and artillery 8.4 per cent. In the 1900s, European armies adopted modern quick-firing guns, with fixed ammunition, smokeless powder, and buffers to absorb recoil when they fired. They transformed the 1914–18 war far more than did machine-guns because they could deliver destruction with a speed, accuracy, and persistence impossible in earlier wars. In 1914–15, artillery caused 49.3 per cent of German losses. The proportion rose to 85 per cent in 1916–18. Using different statistical standards, the British blamed 39 per cent of their casualties on bullets, and 59 per cent on mortars and guns.

Guns dominated the war. Feeding them shells created huge industries in Britain, the United States, and Canada. Most of the 6,000 horses in each division hauled artillery ammunition. As in most aspects of war, the Germans were far ahead of the Allies. Their 7.7-cm high-velocity field gun fired "Whiz Bangs." It was mildly inadequate, but it was more than adequately supported by 10.5-cm field howitzers firing the deceptively named "Woolly Bear"; the 15-cm howitzer, with its "Crumps" or "Coal Boxes"; and the 12- or 16-inch very-heavy guns, which delivered stunning "Jack Johnsons," named after the first black heavyweight boxing champion. "First you hear it coming as a dull moan," explained Private T.L. Golden, "then it gradually develops into a weird whistle, then a shriek and the world rocks under you; you are covered with mud and earth and you are glad you are alive."[22] W.B. Woods, watching German artillery bombard Canadian guns, noted that he could see the explosion, hear it, and then hear the shriek of the trajectory, all in reverse order.[23]

The British 18-pounders were as good as any field gun in the war, but by 1915 shells for them were rationed to three a day; no high-explosive shells were available until mid-1916, and their shrapnel had little effect on German trenches or barbed wire. A shortage of guns, ammunition, and trained men by that time had forced the British to cut their field batteries from six to four guns, reducing divisional arms from seventy-six guns to fifty-two guns.

The Canadians had followed suit before they reached France. It took two years of war for the British to develop an artillery command system higher than a division, so that all the guns in range could be brought to bear on a single target. A jealous rivalry between the "bow-and-arrow gunners" of the Royal Field Artillery and their staidly scientific counterparts in the Royal Garrison Artillery did not help.

With improved production, artillery strength grew, particularly in heavy guns. In June 1915, the Garrison Artillery had only 105 heavy guns available. By the time of the Somme, in July 1916, the number had risen to 761, and, by early 1917, to 1,157. At that time, divisional artillery was reorganized from four into three brigades, with a divisional ammunition column. Within the brigade, a howitzer battery joined the three 18-pounder batteries. By 1917, battery strength had returned to six guns. The ammunition columns not only delivered shells but served as a reinforcement pool for the batteries. Supplies of other weapons also increased. Between the time Canadians fought at Ypres and their attack on Vimy Ridge in 1917, their front-line fire-power had quadrupled.

Soldiers remembered artillery bombardment as the most terrifying experience of the war. They sat helpless as the explosions came closer. "You hear the whine or shriek growing louder and louder," recalled Captain G.M. Davis at Ypres, "till at last it bursts with an ear-splitting explosion, digs a hole 3' deep in the ground and about 10' in diameter and throws dirt, stones etc. about 100' in the air."[24] "I had the wind up about a thousand times," recalled Private F.W. Powell of the Royal Canadian Dragoons. "About eight of us were crowded in one dugout. A deal of unnatural laughter was noticeable. Men attempted unconcern but failed. Conversation was forced and disconnected. Although their mouths shaped words, their minds were concentrated on the shells of the enemy."[25] At Mont-

Sorrel, George Bell had dragged a wounded comrade to safety: "Whang! Crash! I can't breath. A tremendous pressure seems to be squeezing me to death. My eyes feel that they are bursting from their sockets. My whole body feels like a lump of clay being force[d] into a shapeless mass."[26] He was dragged free and sent back, physically unharmed but unfit for more. Private Edward Foster, during an attack, saw his best chum "blown into a sieve" by a shell burst:

> The concussion made me sick and I sat there on my knees with a piece of meat between my teeth for possibly fifteen minutes while eight more shells cracked the trench all around and very near covered me with dust and dirt. A little dog came to the top of the trench to look at me while I was supposed to be having my dinner and the concussion of a shell hurled the dog right through the air on top of me (not saying how long I would have been in that position had the dog not aroused me) I threw the dog out and continued eating between bursts of shells (even if there was sand on my bread).[27]

Dominant and devastating though artillery proved to be, three other inventions—poison gas, the airplane, and wireless telegraphy—also carried science into war. Few Canadians had ever seen aircraft before the war. They became accustomed to them after their arrival in England. In France, men on the ground watched battles in the air with the detached passion of football fans. Edward Foster noticed little specks falling out of a flaming airplane. "These were men who would sooner fall through the air than burn," he explained.[28] Donald Fraser scanned the skies in 1917 and correctly observed, even at that stage of the war, that his side lacked the necessary skill and cunning, and adequate machines to defeat the enemy in the air. On April 2, 1917, he saw a German plane pounce on an Allied observation plane that, for its part, "made a poor attempt at flight and displayed a lack of wits."[29] A good many officers and some other ranks transferred to the Royal Flying Corps, though the great majority of the Canadians in the British flying services enlisted directly.[30]

Communications between troops on the ground and pilots in the air was a problem never really solved. In July 1916, the 2nd Division experimented with flares, shiny tin discs on soldiers' backs, mirrors, and black and white umbrellas. Pilots preferred the mirrors and umbrellas for clearer messages, adding further to the impedimenta troops had to carry during an attack. Sergeant Frank Maheux went flying to see how communications with the ground worked. "I went up about 3,000 feet," he told his wife; "it was lovely I enjoy my trip I was only afraid when we left the ground but it was all right after but I will never go in another aeroplane I had enough."[31]

At Passchendaele, in late 1917, when Canadians suffered their first serious strafing and bombing from the air, they considered the benefits of camouflage from the air and how to fight back. Battalions acquired more Lewis guns with special mounts to fire at hostile aircraft, and the Canadian Corps added an anti-aircraft battery to its artillery. By the end of the war, the Corps claimed to have downed sixteen German aircraft.[32]

Canadians had first experienced poison gas at Ypres in 1915. At Hooge, in 1916, they also faced German *Flammenwerfer* or flame-throwers. Once they had overcome their terror, soldiers learned that shooting at their highly visible storage tanks incinerated the *Flammenwerfer* carriers in a highly satisfying way. Later that year, the French introduced phosgene, far deadlier than chlorine. The worst chemical agent of the war, Yperite or mustard gas, appeared in July 1917. Originally developed to counteract blisters, mustard burned damp skin, particularly in the lungs, armpits, and crotch.

By the summer of 1915, troops had some protection, initially a heavy flannel hood with eyepieces, and later the SBR, or special box respirator, with rubber mask, glass eyepieces, and charcoal filter. Gas terrified everyone: one of the few popular experiences at the "Bull Ring" was to be fitted with a mask and then "proved" in an adjacent gas chamber.

Gas attacks were hard to detect without alert sentries. Chemical shells exploded with a dull *phut*, sounding exactly like duds. Once alarmed, gas sentries feverishly beat their shell casings or iron triangles. With a properly fitted mask, soldiers were half-blind and quite uncomfortable, but safe. A man who had forgotten his mask and inhaled mustard died a terrible death. Masks protected only the face and lungs. Stripped to the waist and sweating as they served their guns in the heat of summer, gunners were an obvious target for mustard gas. When chemical attacks forced them to work fully clothed and gas-masked during the Hill 70 battle in August 1917, some died of heat prostration.

Despite its fearsome reputation, poison gas remained an incidental horror of the war, not a decisive weapon. Like most risks, familiarity with it bred contempt, even among those who should have known better. Sir Julian Byng, Alderson's successor as Corps commander, remembered how he had spotted an officer sitting in the open without his respirator. He seized the obvious occasion for an impromptu lecture on gas protection. As Captain Walter Moorhouse remembered the story, Byng reminded the officer that it was important not only to carry a mask but also to be able to get it on in a hurry. To demonstrate, he tore open his own satchel and yanked out a pair of socks. And, the general added ruefully, "dirty ones at that."[33]

Communications was the most difficult and misunderstood problem of the war. In previous wars, commanders had controlled battles by delivering orders from a vantage point. In the Second World War and after, generals used the wireless to transmit their orders by voice. When they chose, they could speak directly to subordinates miles away. The 1914–18 war has been described by Sir Alan Bourne as the only conflict in history that generals could not control by their own voices. "Why didn't you and I and our generals go up and take charge—see for ourselves and give the necessary orders? What the hell use would we have been? The ONLY place where it was possible to know what was going on was at the end of a wire."[34]

In training, signallers practised with flags, heliographs, and carrier pigeons, but the field telephone and such variants as the earth-conducting "Fuller-phone," or "buzzer," became the basic means of passing messages. Initially, wireless radio was used almost as a toy; in 1915, a few Canadian signallers with time on their hands ordered parts from London, made their own set to receive news reports, which they then posted as bulletins. By 1917, the equipment had improved sufficiently to enable observers in airplanes and from Vimy Ridge to tell their artillery where their shells were falling. Before the Canadians moved on to Amiens in 1918, Sir Arthur Currie sent wireless detachments north to Ypres, successfully deceiving the Germans by pretending to broadcast Canadian traffic.

However, wireless sets remained heavy and fragile. After a ride in a signal cart, even resting on an inner-spring mattress, almost any set required a complete overhaul before it would operate. The heavy lead storage batteries needed to be recharged regularly at a back-breaking distance from the front. Like notions about the more famous "tanks," most of the right ideas about signals communication were alive and well by 1918; the technology to make them feasible had yet to be invented or developed.

Not that there was a dearth of ingenuity. Many inventions were thrust upon generals by the ingenious and the simple-minded, from a huge Ingersoll-Rand hydraulic boring machine to a large fish hook intended to haul away enemy barbed wire. Major-General Louis Lipsett of the 3rd Division was urged to try bear traps to catch German patrols. Various types of shields and body armour arrived regularly. The ill-conceived MacAdam shovels were resurrected as protection for snipers; even when the tools were doubled up, German bullets snarled through the blades. A Canadian inventor who promised "a noiseless gun, the secret of which would not be revealed without cash on the line," was not taken up on his offer.[35] Another demanded a million dollars a minute to explain "a mighty flying machine able to circle the earth in perfect safety in fifteen minutes."[36] More practical inventions included telescopic sights for snipers' rifles, and the steel trench helmet, which troops adopted with surprisingly little protest after they discovered that it really did reduce head wounds. Sadly, no one ever satisfied the constant front-line plea for wire-cutters good enough to slice through German barbed wire.

For all these new developments, technology did little to alleviate the daily misery of troops, in or out of the line. Arguably, the Canadian and British divisions were better fed and cared for than any major army in history. Even so, soldiers lived like tramps—filthy, lousy, sleeping rough in all weather, usually hungry, and almost always fearful of what lay ahead.

Aubrey Griffiths, a Welsh immigrant and Saskatchewan homesteader, more than anything else remembered the rain: "Our only protection against it was a waterproof sheet with grommets at each corner. It was about thirty-six inches wide and close to five feet long and was very useful because it kept our bodies fairly dry. We tied it around our shoulders but the rain falling from our caps would drip down our necks. Then the rain dripping from our sheets would gradually soak into our boots."[37] In the line, men lived with the stink of decaying garbage, carrion, and faeces overlaid with the sharp odour of chloride of lime. Colonel Joseph Chaballe of the 22nd remembered: "l'odeur écoeurante, indéfinissable, que tente en vaine de dissiper le chlorure de chaux généreusement répandu."[38]

By 1916, men routinely spent a week in the trenches, rotating between the three lines. In the fire trench, they sheltered from the rain in shallow "funk holes" carved in the trench wall. Farther back, dugouts provided dank, odorous shelter, sometimes with bunks made from scrap lumber and chicken wire, more often a bare mud floor covered with the men's waterproof sheets. There was seldom any system of ventilation to blow away the reek of unwashed bodies, wet serge, rotting food, and stale urine. Tom Dinesen described ten men crammed into a space 12 feet by 6 feet: "The dirt and the vermin, the thick, full-flavoured air—all this only serves to increase our feelings of comfort when we sit together here, warm and safe, chatting, singing and burning our fingers vainly endeavouring to make a basin of porridge boil over a sardine tin filled with bacon grease and with a wick made of rags from a piece of sandbag."[39]

A wealth of human and animal flesh produced a population explosion of rats. Rat legends spread like urban myths. Soldiers insisted that the rodents stopped work at midnight: "It was a different story after a certain gas attack, when blinded by the gas and unable to distinguish light from darkness the rats continued their activities during the hours of daylight."[40]

Officers, of course, lived different lives. Having escaped the overcrowded, stinking squalour of his men's dugout, Claude Williams described his own: "down 25 steps to two bunks, one for himself, the other for his sergeant or batman, walls of corrugated iron and a roof of heavy planks or steel girders. A table of rough lumber covered with sacking and a pantry with canned goods, pickles, crockery, a charcoal brazier and some jars of rum."[41] It was not paradise. As rain saturated the soil in the harsh winter of 1916–17, Williams's dugout turned into a cold, clammy shower· "It is like dodging the rain to try and dodge the drops in ours. The floor is one mass of mud with here and there a puddle, and everything one touches…is covered with mud, even our clothes. We creep between the blankets at night with a layer splattered all over our breeches (which we are not allowed to take off) crawl out the next morning, leaving the blankets stiff with mud. Nothing can be taken out to air—after the blankets are in the dugouts a few months they have a nice odor of their own."[42]

Over time, conditions in the trenches improved. Endless hours of digging and tons of lumber and corrugated iron lugged into the lines had to make a difference. So did systematic disposal of the dead. In 1915, Private W.S. Lighthall, of the Royal Canadian Dragoons, recalled moving up a shallow trench near Ypres where hundreds of corpses lay: "every step squelched as one stepped on one of the bodies that floored the trench."[43] Other soldiers recalled bodies buried in the trench walls, with a protruding foot or hand used to hang a haversack and shock a greenhorn. By 1917, grave registrations units and Pioneer companies removed the dead to official cemeteries. In quiet periods, corpses were removed within a day; clearing a major battlefield took much longer. An occasional body was overlooked. In 1918, Dinesen pursued a foul smell in his dugout and discovered the rotted corpse of a German. Otherwise, he insisted, all the talk of smells, like other alleged miseries of war, had been exaggerated.[44]

Through the endless labour of working parties delivering duck-boards or "bath mats," logs, and steel beams to roof dugouts and sheets of corrugated iron to line the trench walls, front-line condi-tions improved. Gasoline-powered pumps chugged patiently in a vain struggle against rain, snow, and seepage. Nothing made bad weather and mud a pleasure.

In the centuries of war that had swept across France and Flanders, armies had seldom faced the winter. As the season changed, sol-diers had retreated to their quarters, and their aristocratic officers had gone home to enjoy the social season. From 1914 to 1918, win-ter slowed the war, but never stopped it. Snow, rain, and frost destroyed roads, turned fields into swamps, and compelled the generals to postpone their offensives till the spring. For soldiers, the war went on against the enemy, and for their own survival. Staff officers turned to raids and aggressive patrolling to ensure that men kept their "fighting edge." Far from the comfortable châteaux where colonels and generals debated morale in the ranks, their troops struggled to keep warm. Winds sweeping out of Russia dropped temperatures in northern France ten or fifteen degrees below those in England. In the winter of 1916–17, Europe's coldest since 1881, German civilians starved, and occasional sentries froze to death at their posts. To men in the open, other winters seemed almost as bad. Robert Swan, a Nova Scotian, recalled tying up his legs in sandbags to keep warm when he slept. When he peeled them off in the morning, his legs were dry. "But they were all puck-ered—parboiled, you know,—and when you went out and you hit the cold air, and put your feet into cold water—boy, it was just like getting an electric shock."[45]

Influenza and pneumonia killed 4,000 Canadian soldiers in the war. While one might marvel that everyone did not succumb, a few found their war experiences exhilarating. With no apparent irony, Frank Powell remembered feeling splendid: "This soldiering game is a wonderful experience."[46] He was unusual. The miseries were real enough. Trench foot, an inflammation resembling frostbite and caused by prolonged exposure to cold and wet, almost crippled the BEF in 1914–15. Frequent changes of socks, enforced by daily foot inspections and holding commanding officers responsible for cases in their units, reduced but never eliminated the problem.

Kilts, the pride of battalions devoted to Highland tradition, caused acute misery. Not only were they drafty in winter, but mud hardened on the bottom edge, lacerating the backs of the men's knees as they marched. The pleats of the kilt were an ideal hatching place for lice. Finally, GHQ braved the wrath of traditionalists by ordering Highland battalions into trousers during the winter.[47]

GHQ aroused prohibitionists too by permitting half a gill of rum at the dawn stand-down. Colonel Tom Tremblay, of the 22nd Battalion, reflected a general judgement: "nous creverions tous si nous n'avions pas ce stimulant."[48] Sergeant Aubrey Griffiths recalled it as "the smoothest rum I have ever tasted because, after a chill cold night on duty it warmed our bodies all the way down to our boots."[49] Regulations allowed temperance enthusiasts like the 11th Brigade's General Victor Odlum to order extra rations of Oxo and pea soup in lieu of rum. After lengthy debate about costs and precedents, the War Office agreed to allow hot drinks for sentries on duty during the early-morning hours.[50]

Bitter weather slowed down the body lice that afflicted most soldiers—and warmer conditions revived them again. Within days of coming to France, most men, even officers, began what Gordon Beatty recalled as "a never-ending battle with cooties."[51] Soldiers remembered pictures of Napoleon and suggested that his hand, characteristically slipped under his lapel, was actually hunting "greybacks." "You know how much I hate mosquito bites," Lieutenant Claude Williams reminded his mother, "well these are about twice as bad and hardly a square inch of you is left untouched."[52] Body-lice or *pediculis corpori*, burrowed into the seams of shirts and underwear, in the folds of kilts, or under the knee of the tightly laced breeches worn by cavalry and gunners;

nits, or *phthirius pubis*, crowded under the patch of linen at the
crotch of army trousers. Head-lice became so annoying to some
men that they shaved themselves bald. Wherever they were, lice
caused a continuous and almost indescribable misery. Claudius
Corneloup, a sergeant-major, thought their torment was his worst
memory of a long war: "On voyait des pauvres diables en cassent le
tuyau de leur pipe avec leurs dents, tellement la douleur etait
forte." Desperate men stripped naked even in bitter weather to
attack their torturers. "Leurs corps labouré par les coups d'ongle
offrait de criantes et pénibles cicatrices bleuâtres."[53] Veterans recommended scores of solutions—Keating's Powder, creosote,
cheesecloth underwear, or, as Colonel Lionel Page recommended,
no underwear at all.

Will Bird favoured Zambuk, a liniment more commonly used
on stiff joints.[54] Soldiers spent their spare time half-naked, "chatting" or "crumbing"—burning lice by running a lighted candle
along a shirt seam and listening for the gratifying "pop."[55] Many
woke to find blood seeping from the gashes left by unconscious
scratching overnight. In the filthy conditions, infection soon followed.

With few other pleasures available, food and tobacco loomed large
in a soldier's mind. Cigarettes were part of the weekly rations;
YMCA huts and canteens sold them cheaply; families and friends
tucked them into parcels. Many soldiers routinely smoked fifty cigarettes a day, most of them "Oros"—"other ranks only." One non-
smoker kept his cigarette ration for men dying for a smoke: "I
saved a lot of lives."[56]

The BEF ate better than any other army on the Western Front,
though many Canadians thought the British ration boring,
unpleasant, and inadequate. Its staples were meat and bread. Officially, men at the front received 14 ounces of beef a day (which
included bone and gristle), or 12 ounces of canned bully beef, better known now as corned beef. An unwelcome substitute was
Machonochie's Meat and Vegetable, or M&V, which even the
authorities conceded was "too rich and sickly in flavour to form a

staple article of diet."[57] Pork and beans were popular, though the beans could seldom be digested and the pork served only as a flavouring. Bread arrived in three-pound loaves—"three men to a loaf." Some remembered it as the best bread they ever ate. No one liked the substitute, biscuit or hardtack, baked long before and doled out periodically to keep reserve stocks rotating. Men carried biscuit and a tiny of "bully" with them as "iron rations." "After several months," claimed John Sutton, the biscuits "had a nice muddy colour and were as hard as ever."[58]

At Boulogne, Chinese labourers loaded a train daily with each division's mail and its rations of food and fodder. Trucks from the division's CASC supply column met the train and delivered the bulk supplies to each brigade's refilling point. Army Service Corps men divided it into unit allotments, and battalion quartermasters sent wagons to collect their share. Each company quartermaster sergeant (CQMS) had a two-wheeled wagon with a compartment for each of his four platoons. At dusk, he took the wagon as far forward as he dared, to meet the ration parties. The NCO in charge carried the brown rum jar, fuelling the popular suspicion that the CQMS and his pals had already helped themselves to its precious contents. Food was delivered to platoons in jute sandbags, with the tea tied in one corner; sugar in the other; meat, vegetables, dried prunes, and canned food piled in the next; and mail and loaves of fresh bread on top.[59]

Aubrey Griffiths's memories were typical: "Our food consisted of one-third of a loaf of bread and a half dozen dried-up prunes which had the fibres of the gunny sack in which they came. We would try to clean them up a little but we ate them mostly fibers and all because our stomach could stand any amount of dirt. Occasionally we received a can of jam. But quite often our company cook would come up to the front line and serve us a thick rasher of bacon which would keep us warm for quite some time."[60] Firewood and charcoal were part of the official ration, though they grew scarce in the later years of the war. So did food and even rum, though whatever the front-liners' suspicions about the base, most ration reductions were officially limited to troops in the rear.

In the earlier years of the war, troops in the trenches cooked and ate their food alone or in small groups, on "Tommy cookers" fuelled by solidified alcohol. Others improvised coke and charcoal braziers by punching holes in an old bucket or oil drum. Fuel scarcity and greater skill and experience led company cooks to build kitchens in the reserve trenches and deliver hot soup and "mulligan" stew in insulated containers. A tin biscuit box, lined with hay and canvas, could keep stew warm for half a day. Canadians relied heavily on parcels from home and purchases just behind the line. Canned salmon, margarine, and tinned fruit were on sale at YMCA canteens behind the line—if the officers or their batmen had enough to spare. Closer than other war charities to knowing what men "living rough" needed, the Salvation Army won soldiers' hearts by serving free soup and stew and an absolute minimum of preaching, often dangerously close to the front lines. With effort, ingenuity, and a little expense, most soldiers could live comfortably. As cook for his section, Donald Fraser recorded rolled oats, bacon, bread, and tea for breakfast; mulligan stew, hardtack, rolled oats, and Oxo for dinner; and bully beef fried with bread, jam, lemon marmalade, and café au lait for supper.[61]

Officially, the ration supplied each man with 4,300 calories a day, compared with a civilian average of 3,859 calories. The English historian Denis Winter discovered that the official ration was nutritionally sufficient, though it left men constantly hungry and with such a tendency to flatulence that it might even have been dangerous for soldiers in the nervous quiet of no man's land.[62] Men in the ranks suspected that the ASC ("Ally Sloper's Cavalry") took the best, officers' servants picked over the rest, and privates got the leftovers.

Bully beef came in one-pound cans, mostly from the Argentine firm of Fray Bentos or from Swift, Armour, and other American packers. Fred Noyes recalled a shipment from the Toronto packer, William Davies. At first men rushed for "some good, wholesome Canadian meat" only to discover "a sort of jellified blob of gristle, fat and skin." Angry and humiliated, the troops used the cans to pave the entrance to their dugouts.[63]

George Bell, of the 1st Battalion, an "Old Original," remembered one of the more controversial rations:

The jam was one of the mysteries of the war. First it was "plum and apple" and then "apple and plum." But where were the apples and where were the plums? When the ration bags were opened a full-throated roar went up: "When in hell is it going to be strawberry?" But the corporal was calm as he answered. "Boys, there's a war on." And so we never found out when we'd have strawberry. As a matter of fact the stuff wasn't even apple or plum. The stuff was made of turnips with some sweet favouring. Out of this synthetic jam some one was making a fortune and probably was knighted for his services to his country.[64]

The Engineers supplied water. It reached the trenches in gasoline cans, sometimes tasting of gasoline. To ensure that all drinking-water was boiled, the army encouraged tea drinking and discouraged drinking from local sources. As part of wartime apocrypha, many soldiers recalled some version of George Bell's experience in 1916: "A little stream of water trickles under our front lines. It is slimy and covered with scum. Its odor is horrible. But it has been hours since we have had a drink. With our teeth we hold back the scum and gag as the water goes down our throats."[65] The next day, as they advanced, they found bloated German corpses lying in the trickle upstream.

Other soldiers recalled their terrible thirst when supplies were short. The well-salted bully beef and the biscuit of their rations only made their suffering worse. Arthur Lapointe recalled a small but desperate battle his unit experienced in the suffocating July heat of 1917. For two days the men had had no water. Some had died trying to refill their water bottles: "Je me penche machinalement vers la gourde et pour la dixième fois peut-être je la porte à mes lèvres sèches, espérant toujours extraire quelques goûtes mais vainement."[66]

Duty in the trenches dominated a soldier's life, but diaries demonstrate that it filled a only part of his time. Between September 20 and the end of 1915, when troops were scarce and overworked, Private Felix Cullen from Sault Ste. Marie served in the 19th Battalion during nine tours south of Ypres, for a total of fifty days. In twelve months, from November 1916, Captain Ian Sinclair survived eleven days of battle at Vimy Ridge, Lens, and Passchendaele and forty-seven days in the front lines. As an officer, of course, he had two extended periods of leave and a two-week convalescence, but even a private in his battalion could not have spent more than seventy days in the front-line trenches. For any soldier, these periods were quite long enough, though there were quiet sectors where the front may have seemed preferable to a "rest" devoted to "fatigues," drill, and senior officers' inspections.

Troops left the line as they had come—at night—this time with the weariness of too little sleep, too many calls on a limited stock of courage, and, after a bitter week of shelling and patrols, a memory of lost chums. Friends who "copped a Blighty," of course, would be envied the clean sheets and a nurse's care in England. Marching back to rest, soldiers were free of the extra burdens they had lugged into the trenches, but they often laboured under the extra pounds of mud that stuck to boots, puttees, and their rain-heavy woollen greatcoats. Authorities compelled those soldiers who hacked the long skirts off their overcoats to buy new ones, and occasionally sentenced them to field punishment for "damaging public property." At the rest camp, advanced parties from a good battalion had hot stew ready and huts clearly assigned.

On the first morning out, the army solicitously let its men sleep in, but soon they were back to the routines of "soldiering," cleaning weapons, and trying to beat the mud from their clothes in time for a 2:00 p.m. inspection.[67] A.M. Munro assured his father there were no complaints about fighting: "it is when we go back for a rest, and buttons have to be polished, boots shined, clothes cleaned etc. for inspection by some 'big guns', who hand out lots of Hot Air, of which the boys have long since gotten tired."[68] Soldiers took the word *rest* literally, and assumed they would be free to lounge, gossip, and hunt for something more potent than the sour wine or thin beer offered by the local *estaminet*. Saluting, however, never relaxed; division and brigade staff clearly judged it as the bench- mark of discipline and unit efficiency. A few ambitious colonels enforced saluting by charging offenders and inflicting extra drill and even Field Punishment No. 1 on the boldest of them. The Royal Canadian Regiment reinforced its PF traditions with an extra devotion to "spit and polish"; sneering rivals referred to its men as the "Shino Boys."

Part of any rest was a bath parade, ideally once a week, some- times only monthly. Facilities ranged from former breweries with open vats to the elegantly tiled minehead showers near Vimy Ridge where the men were crowded three to a stall. Many baths were housed in prefabricated metal huts where the winter wind whistled and water froze on the duckboards. Rusty nozzles emitted a few minutes of warm water, stopped for men to soap themselves, and gushed a few more minutes of cold water, leaving the shivering men to dry themselves with a dirty towel or a flannel shirttail. Medical officers insisted that hot showers would be "enervating."

"Imagine a watering can with all the holes but three blocked up, spraying tepid water for three minutes in a room without doors or windows, and a cold windy day," Garnet Durham explained.[69] A detail of men could be processed in thirty minutes. They were soon lousy again. Most baths included a laundry where Belgian refugee women washed, sorted, and sometimes repaired socks, shirts, and underwear. Attendants tossed "clean" clothes to shivering soldiers as they emerged. Sharp-eyed soldiers spotted the larvae that remained in the seams of flannel shirts and woollen drawers. In 1918, when lice were finally identified as the carriers of trench fever, a pair of Canadian medical officers finally had their ideas on effec- tive disinfection adopted, and both baths and disinfection improved.[70]

In the first few years of the war, "rest" usually included plenty of hard work. With trenches to dig, dugouts to build, and roads to repair, and no other source of labour to carry out such tasks, the staff turned to the p.b.i.—"the poor bloody infantry." Battalions out of the line were easy prey. To relieve exhausted troops from such work, the Canadian Corps created "entrenching battalions" from waiting reinforcement drafts. By early 1917, each division also included its own pioneer battalion—CEF units reprieved from break-up in return for doing constant labouring chores and, possibly, manning the line in a crisis. A year later, in a more drastic reorganization, the Corps commander, Sir Arthur Currie, transformed each division's pioneer battalion and its three companies of field engineers into a brigade of three engineer battalions. Meanwhile, thousands of African, West Indian, and Chinese labourers played a growing part in the army's maintenance, supplemented (with some strain on the Hague Convention) by companies of German prisoners of war.

There was a military reason for maintaining "soldiering" and reducing incidental labour, and it had little to do with the comfort or welfare of men in the ranks. The steady drain of casualties meant that infantry battalions in the field were perennially half-trained. Generals and their staffs also insisted that trench warfare was a temporary and unfortunate interlude. The war could never be won by sheltering in trenches or even by vigorous patrolling. Unless soldiers emerged to seize victory, defensive-mindedness would rot the will of politicians and perhaps even of soldiers themselves to continue the struggle. The official British manual on trench warfare was as emphatic as the official rhetorical style allowed: "It must...be clearly understood that trench fighting is only a phase of operations, and that instruction in this subject, essential as it is, is only one branch of the training of troops. To gain a decisive success the enemy must be driven out of his defences and his armies crushed in the open."[71]

Rest periods were needed to train for the form of warfare that had vanished so unexpectedly in 1914. Men had come "up the line." Now they must go "over the top."

UP THE LINE

2-A (above) From 1914-18, infantry soldiers still marched most of the way, 120 paces to the minute, five kilometres an hour, with 30–40 kilograms of steel helmet, rifle, bayonet, ammunition, gas mask, clothing, food and water clinging to every part of their body. Route marches were among the ordeals old soldiers preferred to forget. (National Archives, PA 1374)

2-B (above) Members of the 14th Battalion from Montreal's Canadian Grenadier Guards pose in a trench soon after reaching France in the winter of 1915. Compare trench conditions with later pictures of trenches. (National Archives, PA 107237)

2-C (left) A year later, two men of the 22nd Battalion share their breakfast, a slice of army bread and a cup of tea. Both men have primitive gasmasks in haversacks but steel helmets have not yet come into use. Trench walls have been shored up with sandbags. (National Archives, PA 157)

2-D (above) Later in 1916, steel helmets were regulation wear. After a night of digging, patrols and tand to, these soldiers spend part of the day trying to keep dry and get some sleep in shallow holes ug out of the parapet. (National Archives, PA 1326)

UP THE LINE

2-E (left) German trench mortar shells smashing barbed wire entanglements in May, 1917. Soldiers sometimes boasted that they could see mortar shells coming and dodge out of the way. For most, they were the most terrifying kind of shelling because of the long, slow trajectory and the violence of the explosion. (National Archives, PA 1907)

2-F (bottom) Vimy Ridge under bombardment prior to the Canadian attack on April 9, 1917. Hidden in this picture are hundreds of soldiers. Artillery shells, the greatest killer of soldiers in the 1914-18 war, are hunting them out. A modern battlefield can be a very lonely looking place. (National Archives, PA 1091)

2-G-A (above), 2-G-B (below) This famous picture of Canadians advancing on Vimy Ridge, taken by Captain H. E. Knobel, shows Vancouver's 29th Batallion with a Lewis Gun section in the foreground, moving up to take over the advance. The second, even more familiar version shows how a perfectly good photograph can be improved with a few artistic air bursts. Surely artistic license offers a little extra truth! (National Archives, PA 1086 (above) and PA 1020 (below)

2-H (above) There was no need to exaggerate the conditions at Passchendaele in October, 1917. Canadian pioneers try to manoeuvre duckboards into position to form a path between waterlogged shell holes while members of a stretcher party gratefully rest. The allied objective on the distant ridge seems very far away.

2-J (below) A sergeant leads the survivors of his platoon back from their ordeal in the mud. In addition to their regular load, rain-soaked, mud-caked clothing weighed down exhausted soldiers. Some men wear helmet covers made from sandbags to reduce the glare from the metal surface. By the end of 1917, soldiers have to think about concealment from enemy aircraft. (National Archives, PA 832)

2-K (left) A sentry in the spring of 1918 celebrates the return of warm weather by dressing for comfort and trying to spot birds. A home-made gas rattle near his right hand is the forebear of a more familiar holiday noise-maker. (National Archives PA 3254)

2-L (bottom) Two company cooks prepare hot meals just behind the front line in a collection of officially issued and "scrounged" materials. Soldiers lived like tramps, sleeping in the open and eating whatever cooks could concoct in a stew that was always called "Mulligan." (National Archives PA 834)

CHAPTER SEVEN

OVER THE TOP

CHANGING THE TACTICS OF ATTACK

The belief that tactics stagnated during the Great War is false. A ruthless and persistent process of trial and error transformed the way soldiers fought. In that process, Canadians were partners, and sometimes leaders. However, men had to go "over the top" to defeat an enemy that remained deadly to the end.

TRENCH WARFARE could easily become an end in itself. Some politicians and admirals, and even a few generals, urged the Allies to hold their seemingly impregnable lines and find the enemy's vulnerable flanks where the war might more easily be won. The trouble was that even ill-equipped Turks or Bulgarians promptly reproduced their own version of the trench stalemate at Gallipoli or in the mountains north of Salonika.

In 1897, in a book called *Is War Impossible?*, Ivan Bloch had answered his own question. He predicted that modern weapons would create a stalemate between rival trench lines. Victory would fall to the side that best staved off economic and social ruin. It was an amazingly accurate forecast of the Great War by the end of 1916, after the Germans had failed to capture Verdun, and the British and French had little to show for their bloodbath at the Somme. Bloch's own Russian Empire would be the first to collapse.

At the time, generals had dismissed Bloch's views as "trash"—in part because he was all the things aristocratic officers despised:

147

Polish, a Jew, and a banker. Bloch certainly seemed oblivious to how modern weapons might also assist attackers, but so were generals. Chiefly, Bloch had rudely fingered the generals' biggest problem: how to get attackers through the hail of fire they would face in the last 300 to 400 yards of an advance. Even if they succeeded once, how would troops endure a second slaughter when they charged the next line?

No general could admit defeat. The French insisted that a *rafale* or gust of fire, from their marvellous 75-mm quick-firers and the natural élan of masses of their patriotic, if ill-trained conscripts would carry the day, as it had in the age of the Revolution. The Germans drilled their troops to advance in open order, but preferably from the flanks. The British avoided theory entirely and assumed that pluck, common sense, and a local superiority of four or five men to one would carry the day.

Manoeuvres showed that troops who used their weapons in the attack tended to slow down and increase their vulnerability. Once troops had hit the ground to hide from enemy fire, it was never easy to get them up and going again. Canadians had learned that lesson in the Northwest campaign of 1885, and at Paardeberg in the South African War.[1] Instead, troops had to rely solely on their bayonets as they charged the last few hundred yards. "Victory is won actually by the bayonet, or by the fear of it, which amounts to the same thing as far as the actual conduct of the attack is concerned," claimed a youthful Lancelot Kiggell, Sir Douglas Haig's future chief of staff.[2] His professional colleagues agreed. No enemy would stay to face "cold steel." Once the infantry, with a little help from the artillery, had "broken through," the cavalry would race into the gap and destroy the fleeing enemy.

The late nineteenth century, when most German, French, and British generals of the 1914–18 war acquired their ideas, had been fascinated by notions of spirit and willpower. Victory belonged not to the strongest economy, as Bloch claimed, but to the side with the strongest will, as evinced by discipline, morale, and dedication. "A battle won," declared the influential French tactician Colonel Grandmaison, "is a battle in which one will not confess oneself beaten."[3] Haig insisted that, at Ypres, in 1914, he had prevailed when the Germans were on the verge of victory because he had refused to give up. Generals had to be confident, ruthless, and forceful; those who asked questions or criticized were obviously losing their will and likely to be "degummed," as Smith-Dorrien had been at Ypres.[4] Once discipline and morale broke, no tactics or weapons could save an army. To win, of course, there would be losses but, as the British military historian Michael Howard observed, "the casualty lists that a later generation was to find so horrifying were considered by contemporaries not as an indication of military incompetence but a measure of national resolve, of fitness to rank as a Great Power."[5]

Put to the test of actual war, most theories of the offensive failed. The French doctrine of attack *à l'outrance* cost them 110,000 dead and 175,000 wounded or captured, and hurled their armies into full retreat. The German search for flanks ended with the *Kindermorden* of Ypres. The British "muddle through" approach was drowned in their men's blood at Neuve Chapelle in March 1915, and again at Loos in October. The Canadians practised their own version of "the spirit of the bayonet" with disastrous results at Kitchener's Wood on the night of April 23, 1915, and again in assaults at Festubert and Givenchy a few weeks later.

Part of the Canadian problem was inexperience and military incompetence: vague orders, erroneous maps, no coordination between the infantry and the artillery. At Festubert, a month after Second Ypres, Brigadier-General Currie was told to take "K 5," an objective he himself could not locate. Nevertheless, he dutifully ordered his battalions to capture it, with predictable consequences. For his part, Turner bluntly called Alderson's directive murder, which made him no friends at divisional headquarters. After enough shelling to warn the Germans without actually hurting them, the Canadians attacked on five successive days, lost 2,468 killed and wounded, and gained a useless little corner of German trench. Twenty years later, Victor Odlum, then commanding the 7th Battalion, remembered Festubert as "the most unsatisfactory operation in which the Canadians took part."[6] Givenchy, where a British mine did more damage to the attacking Canadians than to the German defenders, was a comparable mess. The 1st Battalion lost 20 officers and 344 other ranks.

Changes were needed. The most drastic and the most difficult concerned the artillery. Shortages of guns and shells were a legitimate but insufficient alibi. It was true that neither France nor Britain had many heavy guns. Even with a war on, workers at the big Vickers's artillery factory had insisted on their usual Christmas and New Year's break, while the more patriotic of the workers had been allowed to enlist. Even so, the idea of depending on the scientific application of material force rather than human courage and determination was alien to most senior officers. Sir Douglas Haig was a former hussar; cavalry and infantry officers, not gunners, dominated the British high command. Eager to resume the "open warfare" they had studied in peacetime, and which alone promised early victory, generals were reluctant to admit that, to penetrate enemy trench systems, heavy artillery and engineers could accomplish more than infantry, and cavalry were virtually useless.

Even within the Royal Artillery, prestige and promotions had gone to field and horse artillery officers. These men prided themselves on dash and gallantry and despised the fussy precision of the Royal Garrison Artillery who served the siege guns. Each battery's forward observation officer (FOO) lived with the infantry, reporting targets, spotting the fall of shot, and signalling corrections with his field telephone until the shells hit the target. It was dangerous, exciting work, the kind any good army respects.

Siege gunners, working at longer ranges, had to calculate the effects of wind, temperature, propellant, and even the condition of the gun barrel. After a small army of surveyors had developed accurate maps and could locate guns and targets precisely, skilled gunners could come very close to a target with their first round. In 1915, such skills were almost as scarce as accurate maps and weather reports. Field artillery brigades and even batteries functioned as practically autonomous units. Even if tradition had allowed all of a division's or a corps's guns to fire as a unit, peacetime penny-pinching limited the issue of telephone wire for the necessary communications. No more than a brigade could be linked up.

During pre-war British manoeuvres, Colonel E.W.B. Morrison and other Canadian gunners had found nothing to criticize or to learn from their unscientific British counterparts. Until late 1916, the Canadians were too busy organizing new batteries and training officers to suggest better ideas. Those same years transformed gunnery. Heavy-artillery groups became part of the extra force that a corps, an army, or GHQ itself could add to a battle. With them came the possibility of counter-bombardment (CB) against enemy artillery. In 1914, at the Aisne, aircraft began their most important single role, guiding artillery fire. By 1916, a light wireless set connected the observer with the ground, and specialized fighter planes protected the slow, two-seater aircraft with the observer and his wireless set. The British never completely overcame their communications problems, but they learned to link scores of batteries with garlands of wire on poles, or stretched on the ground, or, ideally, buried four to six feet under ground. Once linked, a single fire plan was possible. At Festubert, in 1915, Canadian artillery signallers had learned to "ladder" their telephone lines, digging parallel trenches to bury two sets of wire and linking them at intervals. If one section were cut, the circuit might survive until the break could be found and repaired. Infantry, who did most of the pick-and-shovel work to bury cable, had another reason to grumble about the "long-range snipers."

In 1916, there were enough guns to restore field batteries to a full six guns. To strengthen coordination, separate howitzer brigades were broken up, and the batteries were added to the 18-pounder brigades. A division now had as many guns as in 1914, and there were lots more behind it. If only the shells had worked. Duds littered the battlefield at Loos; about a quarter of the shells fired never went off. "Shorts" fell on the infantry; "prematures" exploded in gun barrels, leading some batteries to call themselves "suicide clubs." When private business took over shell production from government-owned factories in Britain and Canada, output and prices soon soared; acceptable quality took a lot longer to achieve. Effective artillery support depended on more than technique. Guns, shells, and enough trained gunners mattered too. By 1917, the British—and the Canadians—were ready.

Comparable changes were necessary for the infantry, though the material problems were relatively minor and the real limits were training and imagination. Centralization of training and doctrine dangerously slowed the progress of innovation. So did dependence on hurriedly translated German manuals. Canadians, with less to unlearn and a yearning to win and go home, were more open to ideas than were many of their British mentors, but they seldom created innovations themselves.[7]

First World War generals were more responsive to new ideas than their critics have admitted. What critics ignore is that many new ideas were hare-brained. Even sensible ideas seldom worked very well at first. Digging under the enemy trenches to blow them up was both an old technique of siegecraft and a new idea backed by mining engineers. Experienced miners were organized in tunnelling companies to lay huge explosive charges or "mines" under the German trenches. Canadians organized three tunnelling companies. Warfare underground was cruel and terrifying, and occasionally it shattered the landscape. The spectacular explosions cost far more in manpower and resources than they were worth.

The tank was another disappointment. Excited by the concept, Haig asked for hundreds for his "Big Push" on the Somme on July 1, 1916. British manufacturing could deliver only forty-five by September 15, when the Canadians launched their phase of the battle. Most of the steel monsters broke down from mechanical defects before the attack. Sir Julian Byng, commanding the Canadian Corps, politely described tanks as a "useful accessory to the infantry, but nothing more." After initial panic, the Germans decided that tanks were another dead-end failure, though they developed field artillery shells to penetrate armour if the British foolishly persisted. But that was just what Haig did. He had the foresight to demand a thousand more tanks, and soon.[8]

After Second Ypres, it was more than a year before the 1st Canadian Division faced another major battle. The intervening months of trench warfare and unsuccessful attacks at Givenchy and Festubert helped transform the surviving "Old Originals," from staff officer to front-line private, into professionals. As they arrived, later Canadian divisions suffered their own bloody noses. At St. Eloi in April 1916, the 2nd Division lost the ground a British division had painfully captured. At Sanctuary Wood and Mont-Sorrel on June 2, the Germans killed or captured half a brigade of the 3rd Division. The intensive German bombardment was one foretaste of the future, but a more experienced division might have noted other evidence of German preparations. Brought up that night for a quick counter-attack to regain the lost ground, the same battle taught the 1st Division another brutal lesson. Almost everything went wrong. For the second try, Major-General Currie, as division commander, insisted on taking the time to prepare the second attempt. Haig allotted massive artillery support. Currie's chief gunner, Brigadier-General Burstall, devised an ingenious fire plan: repeatedly, the shooting stopped, Germans emerged to man their defences—and the gunfire resumed. By the time the infantry advanced, on the evening of June 12, there was a lot less resistance than on June 2. Later, the historian D.J. Goodspeed argued that Mont-Sorrel helped establish the Canadian fighting style: detailed planning and preparation, massive fire support, and a willingness to defy superiors to get the details right.[9]

The Canadian Corps was still in the line near Ypres on July 1, 1916, when, far to the south, near the river Somme, three weeks of bombardment ended and Kitchener's army climbed out of its trenches. In the next few hours, close to 60,000 British soldiers fell dead and wounded. Among them, near Beaumont Hamel, were 684 Newfoundlanders, mowed down by machine-guns when uncut German barbed wire channelled them into a human pen. By the time help came, 310 were dead. Newfoundlanders contributed about 1 per cent of the day-long human catastrophe that, in countless minds, still defines the Great War.[10]

Those trapped in the slaughter of the Somme, and most of

those who empathized with them, had little interest in the strategy, tactics, and technology that brought 60,000 men to such a fate, and only contempt for those who sent them. Their disdain has been transmitted to the rest of us by war poetry and memoirs, and by generations of derivative textbooks.[11]

To soldiers, too, the difference between a "good" and a "bad" show was the butcher's bill: the Somme was bad indeed. For once the generals could not claim to be short of men, guns, or shells because Haig had believed that he had all he needed for victory. Only when failure was self-evident did Haig insist—since he was never wrong—that his goal had always been attrition and that, in the end, the Germans had lost more than the Allies.

What failed? As they always did, staff officers compiled their post mortems and their judgements. Faced with the inevitable German counter-attacks, exhausted soldiers, despite eighty pounds of kit, weapons, and extra ammunition, had still been too ill-provided to protect the limited ground they had captured. As usual, communications had broken down, leaving the generals as helplessly out of touch with the battle as any subaltern cowering in a shell hole. Worst of all, days of British shelling and tons of shells had left German wire and dugouts virtually intact. Many shells had been "duds"; few of those that went off were powerful enough to crush the deep German dugouts. In theory, sprays of shrapnel balls should have shredded German barbed wire. As any pre-battle experiment would have shown, it was hardly damaged. Across the front, when the barrage moved on, assaulting troops had been trapped, like the Newfoundlanders, in deep wire entanglements and then slaughtered by German machine-gunners, emerging shaken but intact from the deep holes in the ground.

The British failure was not complete. On the right, Sir Ivor Maxse's XIII Corps had taken its objectives in an hour, admittedly with 30 per cent casualties. Unlike others, Maxse had taken German defences seriously. Elsewhere gunners ceased fire when the infantry emerged or, if they had enough range, shifted their fire to rear areas to discourage German counter-attackers. Maxse's artillery had kept a noisy, smoking line of shells just ahead of his infantry, lifting at intervals as troops approached. Surely a few casualties from shells falling short were acceptable if German machine-gunners stayed in their dugouts. On July 14, a night attack had swept its objectives, though German counter-attacks regained some of them. The experiment was not repeated: like many soldiers, Haig disliked night attacks.

Fighting on the Somme continued. When the Australians had endured their share at Pozières, three Canadian divisions marched south from Flanders, proudly bearing fresh insignia on their shoulders: red rectangles for the 1st Division, blue for the 2nd, French grey for the 3rd, and, later, green for the 4th.[12] Spirits were surprisingly high. The summer near Ypres had been quiet, and most units had time to fill their ranks, rest, and train. Most Canadians preferred France to Belgium. Their ultimate success at Mont-Sorrel had boosted their confidence.

Britain, France, Russia, and Italy had agreed on a common strategy. September 15 would mark the beginning of a coordinated series of assaults. Canadians would also benefit from a range of secret developments, from the new "tanks" to their own version of Maxse's "rolling barrages." Other tactics were unchanged. A 2nd Division training memo reminded battalions that companies were the basic unit in an attack. Increasingly, assaulting troops acted as specialists: bombers, riflemen, signallers, even "sandbagmen" to block off captured trenches. More and more men in an infantry company simply went along to carry extra bombs and ammunition. Some were even laden with steel loopholes, since captured German trenches were so deep that they could not be reversed without building firesteps and a new parados.

When the Canadians finally reached Albert, where they concentrated for their share of the latest Somme offensive, they had little chance to practise new roles or even to check out the ground. Conscientious and professional staff work managed to get thousands of men and their guns, ammunition, and supplies into position—and then left them almost no time to reconnoitre, rehearse, or understand their mission. Senior officers were briefed; hurried orders

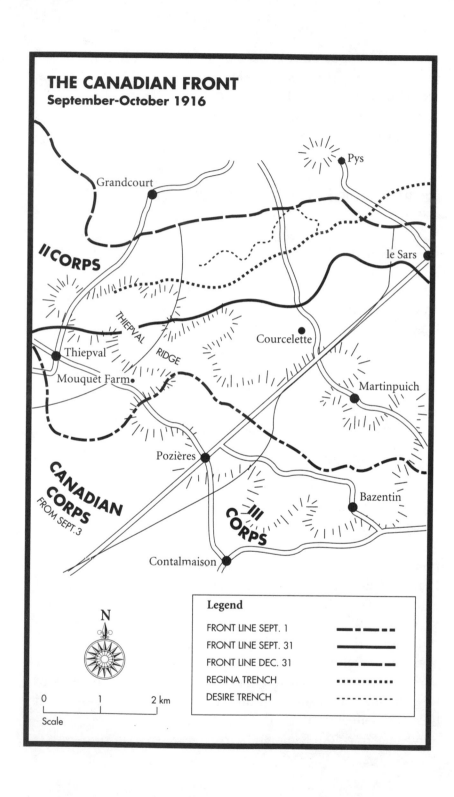

THE CANADIAN FRONT
September-October 1916

Pys

Grandcourt

le Sars

II CORPS

THIEPVAL RIDGE

Courcelette

Thiepval

Mouquet Farm

Martinpuich

Pozières

CANADIAN CORPS
FROM SEPT. 3

III CORPS

Bazentin

Contalmaison

N

Legend	
FRONT LINE SEPT. 1	— ·· — ·· —
FRONT LINE SEPT. 31	————
FRONT LINE DEC. 31	— — —
REGINA TRENCH	··········
DESIRE TRENCH	··········

0   1   2 km
Scale

passed down to officers and senior NCOs, and a colonel might have time to deliver a few inspiring words to the 600–700 men he would take into battle. That was all. Chaplains offered Holy Communion. Then the long khaki columns set off, laden like pack-animals, into unfamiliar trenches to an unknown destination. To many, that destination was death.

At the Somme, there was little systematic effort to silence the German artillery. During their approach and waiting, battalions suffered scores of casualties. By the time Zero Hour approached, some welcomed any release from helpless submission; others, grey-faced and quivering, had already lost control of their nerves. All remembered the endless, indescribable noise. At the Somme, as in other attacks, basic experiences and emotions were remarkably common. Maheux recalled that his battalion, the 21st, put out jars of rum for the men to help themselves. Other units followed regulations and formally issued a tot. General Odlum insisted that his men preferred hot soup or cocoa. One or two colonels followed the Australian practice of issuing rum only after the attack.

Officers checked their watches. At Zero Hour, they blew their whistles or, in the terrible din, simply set the example by climbing a wooden ladder into the open. Men followed. Sergeants urged on stragglers with cajolery and rough threats. Then, when a line had formed, officers ordered it forward with another whistle blast or a wave. Andrew Munro later recalled his mood as a member of an assault wave: "Everyone is a bundle of nerves, and excited, until the 'show' commences, then all at once everyone seems to get quite calm and over we go, without a qualm, some whistling, some singing etc. It is not the actual 'going over'—it is the suspense of waiting to go over. After that one would think it a picnic."[13]

Once in the open, though seldom spread at regulation two-yard intervals, twenty yards between lines, most men shared Munro's unexpected calm, even a sense of power and confidence as adrenaline pumped through them. Few paid heed or even noticed when comrades fell. Reality returned at the enemy trench, whether it was empty or bristled with fire. If leaders had fallen, the attack faltered, and men sought safety in shell holes or behind corpses.

If they got to the trench, a crippling exhaustion followed quickly: organs that had done a day's work in five minutes demanded rest. Men felt an overpowering urge to sleep. It took forceful, ruthless leadership to get men to defend themselves or to keep moving. Sometimes, the leaders in a crisis were men whom no one would ever have entrusted with a stripe. If the trench was taken, it had to be defended from the almost-automatic German counter-attacks.

Meanwhile, firesteps were frantically excavated, dugouts had to be cleared, and flanks protected by improvised walls. An unnoticed communication trench could bring a counter-attack into the midst of the new defenders. German guns, ranged to the yard on familiar ground, pounded the captured position. Terrified soldiers forgot how to use their rifles or to pull the pin from a grenade. Finding themselves alone in the terrible din, brave men panicked, fled, and then returned, weaker than ever, for a second try.

After his battalion captured a key objective at Courcelette at the cost of near-annihilation, Frank Maheux reported to his wife:

> I past the worse fighting here since the war started, we took all kinds of prisonners but God we lost heavy, all my camarades killed or wounded, we are only a few left but all the same we gain what we were after, we are in rest dear wife it is worse than hell, the ground is covered for miles with dead corpses all over and your Frank past all true that without a scratch pray for me dear wife I need it very bad I went true all the fights the same as if I was making logs I baynetted some killed others I was caught in one place with a chum of mine he was killed beside me when I saw he was killed I saw red we were the same like in a butchery, the Germans when they saw they were beaten they put up their hands up but dear wife it was to late as long as I leave I'll remember it.[14]

Canadians did as well or badly as anyone at the Somme. A single tank named *Crème de Menthe* survived to lead men of the 2nd Division through Courcelette. Beyond it, Nova Scotians and Quebeckers perished to capture a fortified sugar-beet factory. All three Canadian divisions struggled up Thiepval Ridge to be stymied on the reverse slope by the defences they called Regina Trench. Then, after a couple of weeks to refill their ranks with seemingly untrained recruits, the divisions tried again on the Ancre Heights, with huge losses and meagre gains. In October, the Germans turned their fire on Canadian artillery, and the gunners began sharing the infantry ordeal. On October 17, after little over a month, three shattered Canadian divisions withdrew to refit in a quiet sector in front of Vimy Ridge while the new 4th Division had its turn. Men paid the price of inexperience. Sam's younger brother St. Pierre Hughes sent Winnipeg's 44th Battalion to take Regina Trench. Ed Russenholt remembered rain-soaked mud-covered men struggling up the line, laden with 220 rounds of ammunition, 4 grenades, 5 sandbags, a shovel, and 2 days' rations, to crouch in the rain and wait for the attack.[15] When the time came, a pitiful dribble of artillery fire did no more than alert the Germans. In a few minutes, the raw battalion lost 200 men. Its neighbours fared as badly.

As the bitter winter of 1916–17 swept down on Europe, the 4th Division tried again. In snow and sleet and a wind that blasted straight from Siberia, the 10th Brigade finally took Regina Trench on November 11. A week later, Odlum's 11th Brigade took Desire Trench and beyond. Conditions were unbelievably awful. "With the snow and rain," reported General Watson, "the men's clothing becomes so coated with mud, great coat, trousers, puttees and boots sometimes weighing 120 pounds, that many could not carry out relief."[16] On November 21, Haig finally called a halt.

Canadians did not need poets or historians to tell them the Somme was a disaster; they knew it. The autumn campaign cost the Corps 24,029 men, virtually every second one of its infantrymen. Could they win with such tactics? Could they lose and go home? That was as unthinkable to most private soldiers as it was to their generals. Instead, in a couple of months in front of Vimy Ridge, a revolution in military technique took place.

The full Canadian Corps had never served together before. Except for the growing clusters of "specialists" in bombs, mortars,

HOW THE CANADIAN INFANTRY BATTALION CHANGED DURING THE FIRST WORLD WAR

1. Pre-War

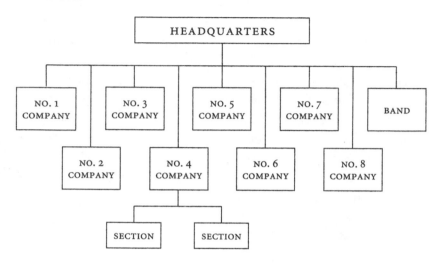

2. 1915-16

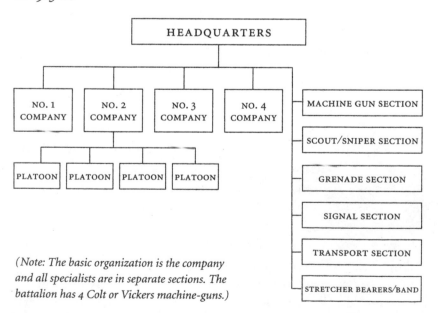

(Note: The basic organization is the company and all specialists are in separate sections. The battalion has 4 Colt or Vickers machine-guns.)

3. 1917

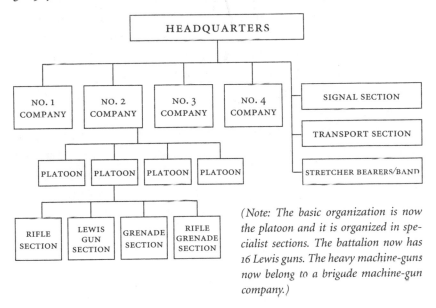

(Note: The basic organization is now the platoon and it is organized in specialist sections. The battalion now has 16 Lewis guns. The heavy machine-guns now belong to a brigade machine-gun company.)

4. 1918

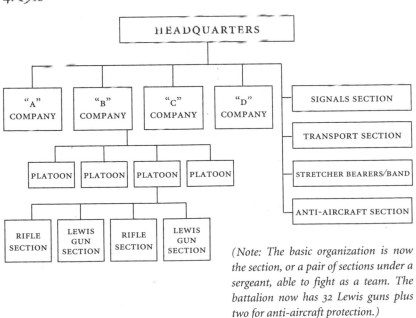

(Note: The basic organization is now the section, or a pair of sections under a sergeant, able to fight as a team. The battalion now has 32 Lewis guns plus two for anti-aircraft protection.)

wiring, gas, or sniping, there had been little chance for battalion, company, or platoon training, and few officers with much to teach. After the St. Eloi disaster, Alderson had recommended the removal of Turner and one of his brigadiers. Instead, it was Alderson who was fired.[17] If GHQ had not portrayed the Canadians as victors at Ypres, Festubert, and Givenchy, he might have gone long before. A decent man, eager to be of service, he had lacked tactical skill on the battlefield and in his periodic battles with Sir Sam Hughes. Alderson's successor, Sir Julian Byng, had suspicious credentials: he was a cavalryman in a gunner's war, he was widely considered stupid, and his nickname, "Bungo," promised very little. Appearances were deceiving. Within a year, his men had purloined the name of the London entertainers and proudly called themselves the "Byng Boys."

Normally a corps headquarters controlled a sector and planned battles for whatever divisions passed in and out of its control: under Byng, the four Canadian divisions fought as a unit. Since GHQ and its army headquarters offered little more than grand directives and windy principles, corps and divisions had to develop specific tactics for the tough problems the Germans regularly created. Byng was not shy and he was helped by a number of remarkable British staff officers who backed up the Canadian generals.

While their men floundered, froze, and died in the chalky Somme mud, cursing their generals and the red-tabbed staff, some of those same staff officers helped their generals turn the tragedy into lessons. Some of the lessons were brutal. Henceforth, in attacks, officers would dress "exactly the same as their men" to survive snipers.[18] Units would select twenty officers and eighty-eight men to be left out of battle (LOB) "to provide a nucleus to reorganize the battalion in the event of heavy casualties."[19] To hang on to captured trenches, back-up companies must carry shovels, picks, and wire-cutters.

Some problems seemed almost insoluble. Obviously soldiers in the Somme battles were hopelessly overloaded. Experts concluded that a healthy man could carry up to sixty-six pounds (modern thinking puts the maximum load at under a third of body weight). A post-Somme reform was "fighting order," but what did a soldier actually need to fight? The list had to include his uniform, a weapon and ammunition, a shovel, a respirator, a haversack with food, a waterproof sheet, a mess tin, a water bottle, and his share of the grenades, machine-gun belts, and aircraft flares. Despite imaginative efforts, the load never got close to sixty-six pounds. In 1917, a rifleman carried at least sixty-eight pounds of clothing, kit, and arms, a bomber or rifle grenadier seventy-eight pounds, and the Lewis-gunner ninety-two pounds. The tactics of the war were governed by a soldier's back and legs. After endless debate, the major reduction of a soldier's load was elimination of a second water bottle: "Men must be trained to drink sparingly."[20]

Tactical changes were far more radical. In the months after the Somme, Canadian infantry battalions rediscovered platoons. Officially they had always been there: thirty or forty men commanded by a lieutenant, with a couple of sergeants to assist him. In practice, pre-1917 tactics and the lack of reliable, experienced officers persuaded CEF battalions to rely on companies, with junior officers assigned duties at a company commander's convenience.

Now, instead of advancing as companies in line, as most troops had on the Somme, Byng insisted that his battalions organize four platoons per company on a permanent basis, each with four sections. Officers, sergeants, and even section commanders would be permanently assigned. Late in 1915, battalions had begun to give up their heavy Colt and Vickers machine-guns to a new Machine Gun Corps. Four machine-gun companies per division had sixteen guns each. Instead, battalions received more of the 42-pound Lewis guns. By 1917, most units had enough Lewis guns to give one to each platoon. One section would carry the gun and its awkward pans of ammunition. Another specialized in grenades, and a third chiefly carried rifle grenades. The fourth section relied on the rifle and bayonet.

A permanently constituted platoon with four specialized sections represented a fighting team that an officer might be able to control. Instead of companies advancing in line, halting until flanks were safe or the artillery had dealt with a problem, attacking infantry could manoeuvre against an enemy post that held them up. An infantry company would have four teams, each capable of fighting its own small battle. Leaders and men would know each other and, through briefings and rehearsals, all would know what to do. It had taken a long time, but Canadian infantry would be organized and trained to fight their own battles and not to be patriotic automata.

Byng's transformation of his corps's organization and tactics was hardly unique. By late 1914 the Germans were already feeling their way towards the all-arms teams they called *Stosstruppen*, or "stormtroopers." So were some French divisions. Unlike the German army, with its powerful tradition of decentralization and individual initiative, the British army believed in centralization of tactical doctrine, symbolized by the notorious Bull Ring. Haig's headquarters periodically reminded senior officers that the 1914 manuals were still in effect. Canadian officers had studied those manuals too, but they felt less obligation to live by them if that meant early and needless death. Divisions that moved from corps to corps needed standardized tactical responses. Because the Canadians, like the ANZACs, stayed together in their own formations, it was easier for them to innovate. Byng and his successor in June 1917, Sir Arthur Currie, had the brains and courage to experiment. Corps directives, reinforced by division and brigade commanders, imposed specific training programs and an accompanying insistence that the old military standbys, morale and discipline, could be improved by intelligence. For a start, officers had to be taught to teach. Practical instruction, insisted Brigadier-General W.A. Griesbach, had to be delivered in intense and practical sessions of thirty minutes at most, interspersed by short informal talks on unit history, military law, or how to avoid trench foot. "To stand in front of a squad of men for two hours giving them perfunctory instruction is an absolute waste of time."[21]

Griesbach's 1st Brigade was typical. In the winter of 1917, its four battalions each spent a week on individual training, a week on platoon attacks, and a third week on company-sized attacks—with a short burst of drill each morning. While officers attended evening lectures, concert parties and boxing matches would entertain the troops. Men were to practise throwing bombs and firing rifle grenades, and Lewis-gunners were to fire their weapon on the move, while slung from their shoulder. Someone at last had grasped that infantry might be more formidable if they kept shooting while they advanced.[22]

Of course, no changes work as well as promised. Veteran troops had to be persuaded that directives from the staff or new doctrines taught at the Corps schools made sense. Reinforcements thrown into units after battles missed the interludes of training, and even platoon tactics were a little complex for the "monkey see, monkey do" style of army instruction. Still, when it tackled its first common objective, Vimy Ridge, the infantry of the Canadian Corps shared a new style of organization and tactics. And, for the first time, the assaulting infantry had time to train instead of being worn out as cheap labour. Seldom had the training been better managed. Most of the men who attacked at Vimy Ridge remembered that, for once, they knew their job.[23]

The artillery was reshaped as much as the infantry. At the end of 1916, a new French hero, General Robert Nivelle, had emerged from the nine-month battle at Verdun. Handsome, soft-spoken, and fluently bilingual, Nivelle was the victorious exponent of devastating artillery bombardments. Once the guns had done their job, he insisted, the infantry could walk forward with near-impunity and take over. Paris and London, appalled by the wartime slaughter, welcomed any commander who offered a life-saving route to victory.

Canadians who visited the French army came back dismayed that the wisdom of senior officers bore no relation to the sloppy, inaccurate gunnery in the field. Still, if the need was stated, the solution could be found. Good British officers, frustrated by their own service, found Canadians to be eager pupils. The best of them was a peacetime professor of electrical engineering at McGill, Lieu-

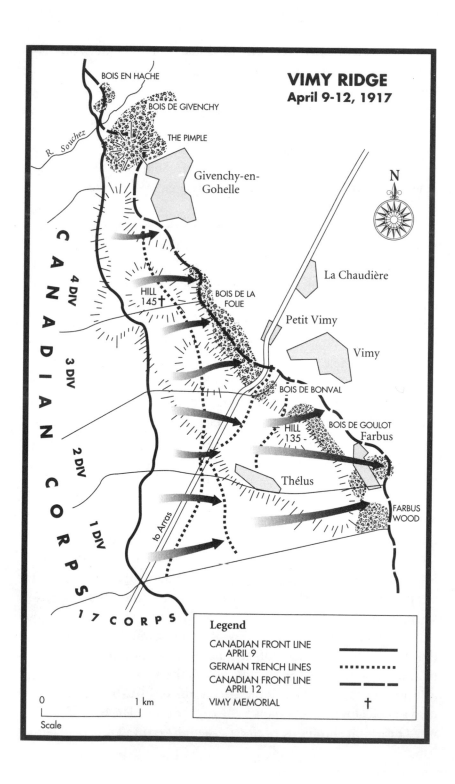

VIMY RIDGE
April 9-12, 1917

N

BOIS EN HACHE

BOIS DE GIVENCHY

R. Souchez

THE PIMPLE

Givenchy-en-Gohelle

La Chaudière

4 DIV

HILL 145 †

BOIS DE LA FOLIE

Petit Vimy

Vimy

3 DIV

BOIS DE BONVAL

HILL 135 -

BOIS DE GOULOT

Farbus

2 DIV

CANADIAN CORPS

Thélus

1 DIV

to Arras

FARBUS WOOD

17 CORPS

Legend

CANADIAN FRONT LINE APRIL 9 ———

GERMAN TRENCH LINES ············

CANADIAN FRONT LINE APRIL 12 – – –

VIMY MEMORIAL †

0   1 km

Scale

tenant-Colonel Andy McNaughton. Disillusioned with the French, he found a mentor in Lieutenant-Colonel A.G. Haig, a British mountain gunner with good ideas about how to locate German guns. Observers or microphones linked by telephone or wireless made it possible to locate enemy guns by their flash or the *thump* they made when they were fired. Once located, they could, in due course, be pounded into silence. Science and engineering skill helped McNaughton create a Canadian Corps counter-battery organization.[24]

By 1917, Canadian Corps artillery staff also insisted that calibration, meteorological reports, and surveying were no longer "siege gunner fandoodle" but possible, practical, and necessary. The Somme had taught that inflexible fire plans, set up because communications so often failed, usually left troops unprotected. Rolling barrages often rolled far ahead of troops caught in heavy shelling, unbroken wire, or even a stubborn machine-gun crew. Canadian gunners began to experiment in coordinated fire. To support a raid at Cité Calonne, Lieutenant-Colonel Keiller MacKay's 7th Brigade, CFA, organized twenty-four batteries to enclose the target in a box barrage. Raiders brought back a hundred prisoners. The Germans did not enjoy the experience. "Cut out your damned artillery fire" proclaimed a sign from one of the front trenches. "We are from the Somme too."[25]

Amid the bitter winter conditions of 1917, most Canadians realized that they would be attacking again, and the objective—a long low ridge that had been too much for the French in 1915—was no mystery. As part of getting ready to assault Vimy Ridge, Byng insisted on an even more important preparation: each of the four divisions had three weeks to reorganize and master the new tactics. Large-scale maps, a Plasticine model, and an area near Servins taped to represent the prospective battlefield allowed Byng's men to know what they would be doing along Vimy Ridge, from the Pimple on the north to Farbus Wood, where the ground sloped downward towards Bailleul.

At the northern flank of the imminent Arras offensive, Canadians at Vimy saw huge numbers of guns, heavy and field, positioned in the fields and forests behind their lines. Not that they had time to stare. To save men's lives, Byng was ruthless in demanding their energy. While infantry trained and raided to dominate no man's land and bring back information, ancillary troops, from cyclists to stretcher-bearers, took their turn digging tunnels, underground shelters, and deep ditches to protect cable. Soldiers laid track for light railways, stacked shells, and somehow kept roads from breaking down under heavy traffic and terrible winter weather.

Their reward came on Monday, April 9, 1917. McNaughton's preparations helped silence 83 per cent of German batteries. The new 106 fuse detonated high-explosive shells on impact, blasting at the thick belts of German wire. By Zero Hour, 50,000 tons of shells and days of freezing rain had turned the ridge into a sodden, pock-marked desert. Many remembered the deafening noise: "imagine the loudest clap of thunder you ever heard, multiplied by two and prolonged indefinitely," recalled E.L.M. Burns, the young signals officer. "The sky was a cupola of lead and the appalling uproar reflected down from it, pressed on one like deep water."[26] After a week of relentless bombardment, the Canadians left their trenches at 5:30 a.m., leaned into driving snow and sleet, and walked over the sodden, devastated battlefield, almost as Nivelle had promised. Except on the left, where part of the 4th Division was thrown back from the hill where the Canadian monument now stands, the battle was over by the afternoon.

Victory, of course, was not easy or cheap. German machine-gunners held out in the German second and third lines, beyond the artillery barrage, and exacted a heavy price from Canadian battalions. It took three days of bitter fighting and heavy losses before Brigadier-General Edward Hilliam of the 10th Brigade, an ex–British ranker, could telegraph "I am King of the Pimple." Vimy cost Canada 10,602 casualties, 3,598 of them dead.[27] For once there was something to show for the pain. The staff officers, with their perennial questions, would be improving on a success, not explaining another disaster. There were problems to solve—had the platoon worked?—could loads be reduced?—could attackers find a better response than going to ground when a machine-gun spattered the ground with bullets? But at least there was enough success to prove what worked. "The great lesson to be learned from these operations is this," boasted the 1st Division. "If the lessons of the war have been thoroughly mastered; if the artillery preparations and support is good; if our Intelligence is properly appreciated; there is no position that cannot be wrested from the enemy by well-disciplined, well-trained and well-led troops attacking on a sound plan."[28] The "ifs" were large and the arrogance was premature but the conclusions were fundamentally correct.

Vimy became a symbolic Canadian triumph, one of those "great things" that nations must do together to achieve identity. It made no difference that Byng and at least half the soldiers were British-born.

A solid, unequivocal victory also told Canadians—and their allies— that the secret of successful attacks had been unlocked, if not fully extracted. The futility of the Somme had been overcome. Even the hypercritical Private Fraser was pleased. Thanks to his briefing, "when the actual test came I had absolutely no difficulty in making for my objective without the least deviation. Everything loomed up as clear as crystal—the wire, the roads, the village, the cemetery."[29]

That was not the general result of the British and French offensive. Farther south, similar losses, without the compensating triumph, dissolved French divisions into sullen mutiny. Aware of Nivelle's widely published ideas, the Germans had dropped back to defences the Allies called the Hindenburg Line. They also thinned out their front lines, prepared powerful counter-attack forces, and waited for the French and British to struggle forward. When the exhausted, decimated attackers paused for breath, the Germans hit them mercilessly with shells and counter-attacks. One of them, at Monchy-le-Preux, almost wiped out the Newfoundland battalion for a second time. At Vimy, the new German system would have meant giving up the ridge without a fight. Local commanders had gambled that the old methods would work: they had failed. Success told the Canadians that their new infantry and artillery tactics worked, at least on the ridge and at no small cost. There would have to be more reforms.

Out on the Arras plain beyond Vimy, the tactics had to change. It took eight teams to haul a gun across the terrible mud on the ridge, down the forward slope, and out into the open. The only shelter for miles was a railway embankment—an obvious target for German howitzers. The 39th Field Battery lost eighteen guns— triple its strength—during three months in front of Vimy. After capturing Arleux and Fresnoy, Currie won promotion to Corps commander and a knighthood, but the price in dead and wounded was high for a country painfully negotiating conscription.

Ordered to take Lens in August, Sir Arthur Currie annoyed his British superiors by insisting on his own better plan. By capturing Hill 70, which dominated the battered mining town, he would force the enemy to try to take it back, making it a killing-ground for the German counter-attack divisions. With enough artillery in support and with machine-guns dug in on the forward slope, he could make the Germans pay a heavy price for the hill. Painstaking preparation for the attack included 400,000 shells; smoke screens; rolling, jumping, and box barrages; and the first significant use of wireless to help heavy guns register on targets visible from Vimy Ridge. Five German divisions successively tried to knock the Canadians off the hill, at a cost at least double the Canadian losses. When Canadians tried their own attack on Lens, they, too, were mauled, and the luckless 44th Battalion again lost almost half its men at the Green Crassier. No soldiers ever fought the Germans with impunity.

Currie was right about another battle too. He predicted that getting involved at Passchendaele, Haig's disastrous Flanders offensive, would cost Canada 16,000 men, and he did not want to go. Haig insisted: Currie, he promised, would learn why after the war.[30]

Soldiers, sent to the worst battlefield of the war, had no such promise. A summer of shelling and the heaviest rains in memory had allowed the British to recapture little more than the ground the 1st Canadian Division's "Old Originals" had lost in front of

Ypres in 1915. The horrors of "Pash" were legendary. Soldiers advanced across a featureless desert of yellow mud, pocked by flooded shell holes and bottomless morasses. Because it was so difficult to send up supplies and ammunition, troops were more heavy-laden than ever, and their rain-sodden uniforms and crushing loads transformed men into dazed, exhausted automata. Troops stumbled along the heaving duckboards and then waded through mud.

Horses and wounded men drowned in the foul-smelling yellow soup, though German shells and bombs also buried themselves uselessly. Reinforced concrete pillboxes, immune from almost any shell, sheltered machine-guns that sprayed the mud in interlocking fire. Only infantry ready to die could capture them, by getting close enough to lay explosives or smash in the doors.

All Currie could do for his men was to undertake the battle on his terms. He insisted on time to rebuild roads and tracks, repair and replace guns, and stockpile enough ammunition that Canadian gunners could deliver their "ultimate round." It was all done under steady German bombardment and, for the first time, sustained attack from German bombers and fighters. Clustered in two great clumps, the guns and gunners took a terrible beating. On November 6, 1917, Manitoba's 27th Battalion finally occupied the remnants of Passchendaele. The achievement had cost the Corps 15,634 soldiers, almost a quarter lost in the tough preparatory period. Few cared that Haig proclaimed a victory.

Three times Canadian divisions had done battle outside Ypres; they would not come back until 1944.

After Passchendaele, the Canadians returned to Vimy and Lens and to the old routines of trench warfare and raids. German offensives struck in March and again in April and June, wiping out every British gain in three years of fighting and almost eliminating Haig's Fifth Army. The Canadians were untouched. Despite Currie's insistence on keeping the Corps together, Canadian divisions moved where they were needed in March and April, and the 2nd Division did not return until July 1918, but they were not committed to battle. In the spare weeks, the Corps trained and rebuilt.

Currie kept Byng's Corps school, with courses for platoon commanders and instructors in drill, sniping, and bayonet fighting. The regime of the Bull Ring "canaries" ended when divisional schools took over the training of reinforcements. Training directives mixed old preoccupations and new ideas. "At all parades the men must be minutely inspected," warned the 2nd Division; "officers must see that equipment is properly put on and that articles of dress and equipment are spotlessly clean, except for mud splashes on the boots and putties [sic] caused by moving from billets to the parade ground."[31] There was also a persistent attempt to get soldiers to use their rifles as more than "a handle for the bayonet." Currie sponsored platoon competitions, with points for good battle procedure as well as success at the ranges. Falling plate targets were favoured over bull's-eyes: an enemy was knocked out whether he was hit in the heart or a shoulder.

Of course, parade-square values never quite vanished. A smart appearance, glistening brass, and well-scrubbed Webb equipment weighed heavily in the score, and platoon commanders lost points for ignoring any part of the official ritual.

On the whole, infantry tactics were probably about as good as they would get, given available technology, provided always that officers, sergeants, and the men themselves could be persuaded to take risks, use initiative, and push ahead. Canadians believed that these qualities were more natural to them than to the hide-bound British. Others might argue that the Prussian-disciplined Germans were even better, and that the British divisions were filled by now with boys, old men, and veterans who owed their longevity to the prudent avoidance of risk.

Cool, tough-minded veterans made a difference. When his platoon came under friendly fire near Cambrai, Bill Foster recalled how an experienced private grabbed a flare pistol from an indecisive officer and fired a "success" signal to stop the guns.[32] Another recalled how, after their platoon was pinned down, two privates coordinated an assault on the German machine-gun post. Their superiors seemed content to stay put. The two men got no medals; neither were they "crimed."

In 1918, gunners were still learning. For three years, attacks had literally bogged down in ground churned to a morass by long bombardments. Scientific gunners insisted that shells could hit targets if officers took technique seriously. By 1918, guns could be calibrated by shooting through a canvas screen. Six times a day "Meteor" reports gave wind direction and velocity and temperatures at set altitudes, data needed for ballistic science. Maps were good enough to plot a target, without even a preliminary registration. Brigadier-General Raymond Brutinel's machine-gunners made their own plans for the future. At Vimy, they had backed the artillery and the advancing infantry by firing sprays of bullets on "fixed lines," hoping to make German movement difficult. Now Brutinel schemed to lead his armoured machine-gun trucks though the German defences if they ever cracked. By the fall of 1917, that fantasy seemed possible.

While the Canadian Corps recuperated from Passchendaele and prepared to vote in the forthcoming Canadian election, its former commander was fifty miles to the south, opposite Cambrai, preparing to launch five divisions and almost three hundred tanks at the German line. On November 20, 1917, after General Byng's gunners had cleared a path through German defences without ploughing up the ground, the British struck. Tanks, infantry, and even cavalry poured through the German line and reached as far as the forest of Bourlon. Men of the Fort Garry Horse of the Canadian Cavalry Brigade charged an artillery battery and even slipped across the St. Quentin canal, near Masnières.

If only Haig and Byng had remembered that Cambrai was only a raid, not an offensive, the battle could have been an Allied triumph. Instead, railways brought up German reinforcements, a new line held, and Haig had no troops left to send. On November 30, the Germans gave a preview of their new offensive tactics: a shattering blast of artillery fire and gas shells on British strong points, stormtroops driving deep, hundreds of aircraft under the famous Baron von Richthofen strafing any enemy in sight. The

British reeled back, and both sides ended the battle after more than 40,000 casualties.

With winter came a chance to reflect, reorganize, and retrain. Thanks to Borden's election victory, the Canadians had guaranteed the Allies manpower; the British—and Australians who had twice rejected conscription—did not. In February, the British cut three battalions from each infantry division and waited for Currie to conform. By transferring the 5th Division to France, Canada could easily have six smaller divisions in the field, enough for a small army, with a few units left over.[33] Currie rejected any such change. The Corps, he insisted, was a balanced, experienced formation that needed more soldiers, not more generals. To the fury of its officers, and especially his one-time friend, Garnet Hughes, Currie insisted on breaking up the 5th Division and using its well-trained men to fill the front-line battalions. With some of the additional men, he tripled his strength. By April 1918, each of his four divisions had ninety-six Vickers guns, four times the number in 1915.

Currie's most drastic organizational change transformed his twelve field companies of engineers into battalions, with the ranks filled out by absorbing the Pioneer battalions. Traditionalists were outraged to see unskilled labour wearing Engineer badges, while infantry brigadiers were furious to see their authority over field companies supplanted by Currie's plump and resourceful Chief Engineer, Major-General W.B. Lindsay. What both men recognized was that the toughest problem in future advances would be mobility. That was the engineers' business. "I would rather do without infantry than without engineers," Currie insisted.[34] Thanks to conscription, Currie had few worries about either. By the summer of 1918, the Canadian Corps had been spared the devastating German spring offensives, and its units were retrained, rebuilt, and ready to fight as they never had been before. As a festival of pride in itself and its country, the Corps celebrated Dominion Day, July 1, 1918, at Tincques with interdivisional sports, a concert and tattoo by massed bands, and an outpouring of national pride that would have been impossible three years earlier.

The new Engineer battalions won some of the most hotly contested championships.

Retrained by Byng, reorganized by Currie, early in August, the Canadian Corps headed south. A printed note, pasted in soldiers' paybooks, brusquely ordered: "Keep your mouth shut."[35] The Canadians moved at night, in trucks, past their old Somme battlefields. A few moved north to Flanders where signallers used wireless to persuade German monitors of an impending offensive. Meanwhile, low-flying aircraft masked the sound of troops, guns, and tanks moving into forests west of Amiens. At precisely 4:20 a.m. on August 8, 900 guns opened fire. Men of four Canadian brigades walked forward into a thick dawn mist to attack. Tanks plunged across the landscape and, for the first time in strength, British aircraft supported a major offensive with ground attacks. Still, it was guns and infantry that shattered the German defences. By nightfall, the Canadians had smashed through the German front lines, captured 5,033 prisoners and 161 guns, and advanced 8 miles, for a loss of 1,036 dead. Australians had done as well. Less because of the breakthrough than because counter-attack forces moved with leaden reluctance, General Erich Ludendorff labelled August 8 as the black day of the German army. The tide was turning. Only the failure of raw or battle-weary French and British divisions on either flank limited the greatest single Allied victory of the war.

German resistance soon stiffened. As usual, railways allowed defenders to plug the gap faster than attackers could walk through them. Instead of continuing hopelessly, Currie insisted that the Allies settle for their gains and switch objectives. He would attack where Canadians knew the ground and had made their plans, on the extension of the Hindenburg Line called the Drocourt-Quéant Switch.

Critics could later argue that Amiens was an easy victory: the Germans were exhausted from their own offensive and they were fighting from captured positions. That was certainly not true of the Drocourt-Quéant Switch, the northern extension of the famous

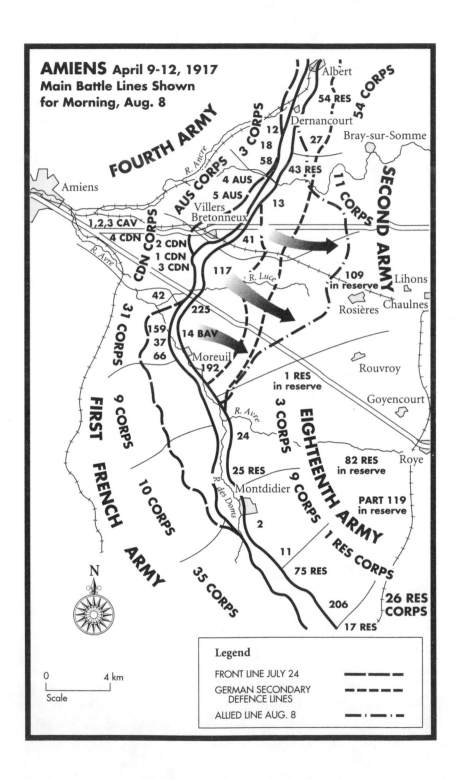

AMIENS April 9-12, 1917
Main Battle Lines Shown
for Morning, Aug. 8

FOURTH ARMY

54 CORPS

Albert

54 RES

Dernancourt

3 CORPS

12

18

58

27

Bray-sur-Somme

43 RES

11 CORPS

SECOND ARMY

AUS CORPS

4 AUS

5 AUS

Amiens

Villers
Bretonneux

13

1,2,3 CAV

4 CDN

CDN CORPS

2 CDN

1 CDN

3 CDN

41

R. Ancre

R. Avre

117

R. Luce

109
in reserve

Lihons

Chaulnes

Rosières

42

31 CORPS

225

159

37

66

14 BAV

Moreuil

192

Rouvroy

1 RES
in reserve

Goyencourt

FIRST FRENCH ARMY

9 CORPS

3 CORPS

R. Avre

24

Roye

82 RES
in reserve

25 RES

Montdidier

EIGHTEENTH ARMY

9 CORPS

PART 119
in reserve

10 CORPS

R. des Doms

2

11

1 RES CORPS

75 RES

N

35 CORPS

206

26 RES
CORPS

17 RES

Legend

FRONT LINE JULY 24

GERMAN SECONDARY
DEFENCE LINES

ALLIED LINE AUG. 8

0   4 km
Scale

Hindenburg Line. In three days, August 16 to 18, and at high cost, the 2nd and 3rd divisions cleared the approaches. The 22nd and 24th battalions, both from Montreal, were virtually wiped out at Chérisy. Lieutenant-Colonel W.H. Clark Kennedy put the remnants together and won a Victoria Cross for his leadership. Every combatant officer of the "Vandoos" was killed or wounded, and a sergeant-major led the 39 unwounded survivors out of action. By September 5, the 1st and 4th Canadian and 4th British divisions had broken the German line. The cost for a week of merciless fighting was 11,423 dead and wounded.

On September 27, 1918, the Corps forced the crossing of the Canal du Nord and took Bourlon Wood. Within two hours of the canal crossing, Lindsay's engineers had bridges in place, and within a day they had spanned the canal with two huge prefabricated bridges. Fighting on the flat terrain beyond Bourlon Wood, bogged down in a struggle for defended villages and railway embankments, decimated battalions, hurriedly rebuilt with ex-wounded and the first MSA men, were slowed by exhaustion, the erosion of their own combat skills, and stiff German resistance. Staffs which had excelled in short, "set-piece" operations, were less effective in impromptu battles. It took until October 11 to capture the ancient city of Cambrai, just before its German defenders reduced it to a smoking ruin.

The Canadian losses between August 22 and October 11—30,805 officers and men—far exceeded those of the Somme. Optimists took comfort: the losses paid for victories. "A large proportion of the wounded are slight bullet wounds," noted Colonel Lionel Page of the 50th Battalion. Capturing Sancourt virtually wiped out the 75th (Mississauga) Battalion: only 78 of 467 men survived unscathed—but only 25 of the 389 casualties were fatalities. That was small comfort.

After Cambrai, Currie himself was discouraged. Late in October he asked officers of the 42nd Battalion to tell him what had gone wrong. "I want to know exactly what you are thinking, whether you believe mistakes have been made by higher commanders or not. I want you to feel quite free to speak to me man to man and nothing you say will be held against you."[36] Men in the ranks, suddenly hopeful that they might out-live the war, also wondered whether they might also be the last to die. Albert West, with Winnipeg's 43rd Battalion, bitterly recorded in his diary: "We hear Gen. Currie has said he will have Cambrai 'tho he lose 75% of his corps. If so he is a fool and a murderer. Cambrai will be taken but we do not need to be slaughtered to capture it."[37]

That mood shaped the final Canadian battle. At Mont Houy, near Valenciennes, the Germans had thrown back the Canadians' best-loved rivals, the 51st Highland Division. Conscious that it was probably their last show, Canadian gunners collected 2,000 tons of shells to pound the hill with every kind of barrage their expertise could devise, including one that masqueraded realistically as misdirected German defensive fire. Two battalions of the 4th Division walked up the hill with virtual impunity. Then, on the far side, the Germans fought back. Sergeant Hugh Cairns from Saskatoon single-handedly took a machine-gun post and then another to earn the last Canadian Victoria Cross of the war. He was busy disarming prisoners in the industrial suburb of Marly when one of them killed him.

Cairns was brutally avenged. Valenciennes cost the Canadians 80 killed and 300 wounded, but the ancient French town was almost unscathed. Eight hundred Germans died too, but fewer enemies than surrendered survived to become prisoners. After the battle, Currie noted in his diary: "I know that it was not the intention of our fellows to take many German prisoners as, since they have lived amongst and talked to the French people here, they have become more bitter than ever against the Boche."[38]

The full story of the Hundred Days has been told elsewhere, but seldom as the fulfilment of a steady evolution in tactics and technology. This is understandable. The terrible casualty toll meant that most soldiers saw little of the final battles beyond their own brief, intense experience. Those who survived had no inclination to credit the staff for improvements in what remained, from start to finish, a hellish experience. Nothing lowered the cost of imposing defeat on the Germans at Amiens or breaking through the Hindenburg Line, or the murderous fighting in the fields and villages north of Cambrai. A fifth of Canada's casualties in the war occurred in its last few months.

Nor did every innovation succeed. Loading infantry in tanks to push through the enemy lines had seemed a good idea before the attack at Amiens, but those who passed the burned-out tanks late on August 8 never forgot the smell of roasting human flesh.[39] Brigadier-General Brutinel's plan to race his motorized machine-guns down the Arras-Cambrai road to the Canal du Nord may have seemed a stroke of genius to planners and his admiring biographer. To preserve the road surface for Brutinel's ill-considered scheme, artillery support for troops in the vicinity was cancelled. Cursing infantry, fighting their way across Mont Dury as comrades were slaughtered by chattering German machine-guns, paid the price. As for Brutinel's "Motors," a few fallen tree trunks stopped them.[40]

War is fought by two desperate adversaries. As in science, most experiments fail and, to the end, the Germans remained the best soldiers in Europe. Against them the Canadian Corps won victories impossible in 1916. There were reasons. Its four full-strength divisions and four-battalion brigades could sustain from two to four successive days of bitter fighting, while weaker British brigades fought a second day at little more than half-strength. Canadian infantry had learned that fire and movement could be standard tactics for competent, adequately equipped troops, and not, as the Germans believed, for élite specialists. Canadian gunners had mastered a practical science, delivering not just the "ultimate round" but the first one on target. Currie's engineers had bridges across the Canal du Nord within hours so that heavy tanks and guns could cross. Lindsay's men delivered 200 bridges, 773 miles of rebuilt motor road, and 290 miles of rails, with a million gallons of water a day for the 100,000 men and 25,000 horses.

Did men in the ranks, and even their officers, understand why disastrous failure at the Somme could become a costly victory at Amiens or the Canal du Nord? Censors ensured that soldiers never wrote home about new tactics and weapons. Neither did the subject fill their diaries and memoirs. Private William Woods of the 1st Battalion, who served from Vimy to the end, had no memory of learning about "fire and movement." He recalled the wisdom of sticking close to the artillery barrage and the temptation to curse the red-tabbed idiots who put him in such a dangerous place.[41]

Transforming the tactics of the Canadian Corps was a vast educational enterprise, and educators always know more about what should be taught than what is actually learned. In its manuals and directives, the army itself almost unconsciously mingled innovative ideas with endless preaching about saluting and cleanliness, and rigid directives about fostering initiative. Training was an endless cycle. Soldiers seldom lasted more than a year in action, and a quarter to half the men in any battalion always faced their first battle. How could they, in a few days, weeks, or months, absorb the intuitive expectations that real teamwork in sports or in battle requires?

Most soldiers, laden down with weapons, ammunition, and kit, were supporting players for the minority of desperate fighters, like Sergeant Hugh Cairns, who determined success or failure.

Back in Canada, poets, politicians, even veterans, preferred to dwell on military incompetence, not achievement. Even the British official historian, Brigadier-General James Edmonds, chose to deal first with the controversial battles of the Somme, Passchendaele, and the German offensives of 1918 a full decade before he turned to the final victories of 1918. By then, a second world war was in progress. Rather than grasp complex modern battles, British generals in the interwar years turned back to "real soldiering." By insisting that each of his decisions was right, not the result of difficult choices of uncertain options, Haig only encouraged those who saw him as a persistent and mindless butcher. What lay behind the unexpected victories of 1918 was easily forgotten. Now it has been recalled.

CHAPTER EIGHT

A BLIGHTY

THE SICK AND WOUNDED

Front-line soldiers allowed themselves one small dream: a "Blighty." This was the honourable wound that would release them from the squalor and terror of the trenches to a bed, sheets, regular meals, and the sight of a nursing sister. Considering the appalling plight of the sick and wounded in previous wars, the "Blighty" fantasy testified not merely to the horror of the trenches but to faith in the CEF's medical services.

WHEN THEY CREATED their first mass citizen army, Canadians wanted to know that their soldiers would not face what the suffering Florence Nightingale had seen at Scutari or that Canadians themselves had experienced in the typhoid hospitals of the South African War. The Canadian Army Medical Corps (CAMC), authorized in 1901, included half the country's physicians and surgeons by 1918. Even more important, the mothers and wives of Canada were represented by the 2,854 nursing sisters who watched over their sons and husbands. Medical science, mobilized in the CAMC, battled the traditional scourges of armies, from typhoid to trench fever. For the first time in a major war, disease killed fewer soldiers than did the enemy. Of 59,544 fatalities in the CEF, 39,488 died in action, 6,767 died of disease, and 13,289 died of wounds or accidents; 154,361 survived wounds. Despite the terrible injuries caused by modern war and the septic soils of France and Flanders, 93 per cent of those who reached treatment survived their wounds.

Even the Second World War could not match such a recovery rate.[1]

The CAMC was part of the self-contained militia army Canada had developed since 1900. Hughes's predecessor, Sir Frederick Borden, was a militia surgeon from Nova Scotia who was easily persuaded of the need. Dentists followed in 1902. Two years later, nurses joined the new medical corps. The militia was popular with health professionals eager for social status and an added source of patients at a time when Canada had more doctors than affluent fee-payers could support. The CAMC mobilized efficiently in 1914: the promise of a short war attracted many of the leaders of the profession. On Salisbury Plain, Canadian military medicine faced its first crisis when cerebrospinal meningitis struck. British doctors accused the Canadians of bringing a virulent strain of the disease to England; Canadian mothers wondered why their boys were dying.

The crisis and the recriminations faded when the Canadian Division moved to France. Amid the horror of the battlefield at Ypres, doctors and stretcher-bearers proved their heroism. Captain F.A.C. Scrimger won a Victoria Cross for tending wounded under shellfire. The CAMC has also demonstrated scientific prowess. Too short for the army at 4 foot 6 inches, George Nasmith, a colonel, was appointed by Sam Hughes to check the water supply. Having deliberately exposed himself to German gas, within days Nasmith devised at least partial protection, a pad soaked in hyposulphite of soda.[2] Ypres also inspired Colonel John McCrae, a gunner–turned–medical officer from Guelph, to send his short, scribbled poem to the editors of *Punch*.[3] Within a year, the CAMC had staked a claim in science, literature, and heroism.

In four years of war, the Canadian army's full-time medical staff mushroomed from the 13 officers and 5 nursing sisters of the pre-war Permanent Force to an establishment of 1,525 medical officers, 1,901 nursing sisters, and 15,624 other ranks. The Canadian Army Service Corps drove and maintained the CAMC's motor and horse-drawn ambulances. Hundreds of other Canadian doctors volunteered for the British army or cared for French, Belgian, Serbian, or Russian wounded.

The CAMC accepted any physician who met a province's standard for registration. Qualifications ranged from a few years at the Manitoba Medical College in the 1880s to recent graduates from McGill or Toronto with surgical fellowships in Edinburgh, London, or Leipzig. Problems of hierarchy arose inevitably, since prior military service, rather than medical standing, determined seniority. Ottawa tried to ease the problem by inviting university medical schools to organize their own hospital units, while older GPs, with fewer fellowships and more worldly experience, would perform as regimental medical officers. By 1916, with close to a third of the profession in uniform, a serious shortage of doctors persuaded the medical schools to accelerate training. At the same time, the CAMC encouraged medical students in its ranks to go home to complete their courses. Medical students and Canada's few women doctors were not considered for the CAMC. Nor were male nurses.

None the less, the CAMC was ahead of its time in gender equality. The British kept their nursing sisters in Queen Alexandria's Imperial Military Nursing Service (QAIMNS), a non-military organization; denied them rank; and classified them as other ranks. Since accepting nursing sisters in 1904, Canada's Army Medical Corps granted them the rank and pay of lieutenants, and matrons the status of captains. Precise professional standards for nursing remained highly contentious in Canada long after 1918, but the CAMC tried to avoid the controversy. It required a nursing sister to be single, a British subject aged twenty-one to thirty-eight, physically fit, and "a graduate of a three years' course at a recognized General Hospital," later adding the proviso that it must have "not less than 100 beds."

A steady flow of experienced volunteers and the assumption that Canadian nurses were better trained and socially superior to their British sisters satisfied official concerns about both rank and supply. Nursing in Canada, explained Colonel J.G. Adami, the CAMC's historian, "attracts in general, the daughters of professional men, and those from comfortable households. In a family of daughters, for example, it is quite the custom for the elder girls, when they have been 'out' for three or four seasons, to realize that they have had their opportunity, and rather than be in the way of their younger sisters, to elect to become a nurse."[4] While some Canadian women went to England to become untrained nurses in British-sponsored Voluntary Aid Detachments (VADS), the CAMC resisted dilution. In each hospital, nurses were commanded by a matron. The matron-in-chief, Margaret Clotilde MacDonald, a veteran of the South African War and the Permanent Force, ruled her large and sometimes quarrelsome flock with icy calm and the rank of major.[5]

The Royal Army Medical Corps and the pre-war CAMC regarded dentists, a despised subgroup of the healing professions, as auxiliaries. Indifferent to such prejudices, Hughes created the Canadian Army Dental Corps (CADC) in 1915, under his own Ottawa dentist, Lieutenant-Colonel J.A. Armstrong. A qualified dentist with the rank of captain, an orderly or assistant who was often a dental student, and a soldier-servant were attached to each hospital and field ambulance and to training camps, with authority to provide just enough free treatment to allow soldiers to "masticate their rations." That usually meant hurried and, to younger professionals, old-fashioned treatment—plenty of extractions, cheap amalgam fillings, vulcanite plates, and enough pain to entitle both patient and dentist to an occasional tooth glass of neat whisky.[6]

There was lots to do. Captain Bruce Kelly, a Nova Scotian who was so eager to get overseas that he volunteered as a private long before the dental corps appeared, reported in May 1916 that he had seen 330 patients; managed 550 fillings, 1,085 extractions, and 1,217 sundry treatments; and completed the documentation, all unaided. Another dentist, Captain B.L. Neilly, persuaded his superiors that a Canadian-run denture lab would save money and soldiers' time. He managed to produce plates within a week, no small benefit when patients were so mobile.[7] By the end of the war, Armstrong's original corps of 30 dentists had swelled to 223 officers, 221 NCOS, and 238 privates. About a quarter of Canada's dentists had served in uniform. The Corps reported 2,225,442 operations, including almost a million fillings and more than half a million extractions.[8]

The CAMC recruited rank and file as other CEF branches did, though there was an understandable tendency, in at least the first year of the war, to enlist junior medical students to share in what, after all, would be a brief adventure. Medical corps recruits spent their months of training in most of the same time-wasting activities as other soldiers. Intricate and repetitive "stretcher drill" replaced bayonet-fighting and rifle exercises. Like their officers, men in the ranks were officially non-combatants and beneficiaries of the Geneva Convention. Once the drudgery and humiliations of life in the ranks sank in, young men like "Chubby" Power and "Mike" Pearson felt little compunction about seeking a commission. Since they were leaving a non-combatant corps for the dangerous existence of an infantry subaltern or a flyer, no one could accuse them of cowardice.[9]

Major-General Guy Carleton Jones, one of the few Permanent Force medical officers, became surgeon-general for the CEF over seas. Jones was not an able practitioner or administrator: Andrew Macphail, former editor of the *University Magazine* and a hypercritical subordinate, described him as "a coarse stupid man" with a close physical resemblance to the German Kaiser.[10] Jones had trained with the Royal Army Medical Corps, with its long experience of keeping soldiers alive in the world's most inhospitable climates, and he did his best. A year's cruel experience indicated that a modern war produced masses of casualties, but in floods or trickles. Between 8,000 Canadian casualties at Mont-Sorrel in June 1916 and 24,000 during September and October on the Somme, only a few hundred a month were evacuated. Frugal like most peacetime regulars, Jones saw the wisdom of pooling British and Canadian resources. Others, like Lady Perley, wife of the Canadian high commissioner, saw Imperial bonds being strengthened by humanitarian collaboration.

The common cause persuaded Jones to send three of his hospitals to the Mediterranean where there were no Canadians but large numbers of British and Australian sick and wounded. At Lemnos and Salonika, doctors, nurses, and orderlies endured endless misery from heat, cold, malaria, dysentery, and desperate short-ages of food, bandages, and medicine. The Empire exacted a high price from its upholders.

According to the pre-war British medical system adopted by the CEF, a fighting unit had to evacuate its casualties to its regimental aid post (RAP). Four stretcher-bearers per company would deliver wounded to the medical officer at the RAP. Each division included three field ambulance units, organized to collect sick and wounded from the RAP and ferry them, by stages, to full medical care. Teams from the bearer section of the field ambulance collected casualties from the battalion and carried them to their advanced dressing sta-tion (ADS); there wounds were checked, dressings fixed, and mor-phia administered. The ADS had to be located where at least a horse-drawn ambulance could collect the sick or wounded and deliver them to the division's clearing hospital. Trucks and wagons returning from the delivery of ammunition and rations would carry wounded back to 600-bed general hospitals or smaller 200-bed stationary hospitals. Minor cases remained there for surgery, treatment and, in quiet times, full recovery.

Like other institutions and practices, the medical organization changed with the times. Evacuation from the front could be highly dangerous and utterly exhausting. Stretcher-bearers struggled along shallow, muddy communication trenches or across shell-swept mud with their heavy, pain-wracked burdens. Static warfare, massive and horrible wounds, a miserable climate, and rampant infection forced hospitals to expand and to move surgery closer to the front.

The clearing hospital was renamed a casualty clearing station (CCS) and then enlarged dramatically as the front stabilized. Soon the CCS was the centre for all urgent battlefield surgery, not merely head and stomach wounds, and nursing sisters were added to the staff, after official assurances that they would almost always be located beyond the range of shellfire. A sharp professional debate continued through the war about whether the ablest surgeons should be close to the battle or whether their skills were better used at general hospitals, repairing the damage done by inexperienced juniors and performing their own specialized operations. Motor ambulances gradually replaced horse-drawn wagons and trucks, though painfully wounded men, jolted over French or Belgian cobblestones, might not always have recognized the improvement.

Eighty per cent of the wounded moved rapidly through the ccs; serious cases and, in quiet times, cases that would recover in a week, stayed. Mass casualties meant "clearing" the battlefield with masses of manpower. Otherwise, assaulting units would disintegrate as soldiers ignored orders and stopped to care for wounded pals. In 1916, infantry battalions doubled their stretcher-bearer squads, from sixteen to thirty-two men, and assigned them to specific platoons, where they tended to act as first-aid men. Hundreds of men with stretchers followed the advancing infantry during major offensives from Vimy to Amiens. Battalion stretcher-bearers were ordered to bandage a wounded comrade, jab his bayoneted rifle into the ground to mark where he had fallen, and move on.[11]

As the Canadian Corps grew to four divisions, each of them required three field ambulances and a ccs. More and more hospitals were needed. Two of them, recruited in Quebec, served the French army in the Paris region. Eight others were scattered behind the British lines, and several more were located in England. Other special hospitals served orthopaedic, eye and ear, and mental cases. Two London hospitals, Hyde Park and the Petrograd Hotel, were reserved for Canadian officers. Two others, Etchinghill and Witley, treated venereal disease. Because of the presumed depravity of "venereals," nursing sisters did not serve at vD hospitals.

"The presence of a wounded officer, nco or man in the ranks who, though wounded, had the grit to continue fighting, is a fine example of courage and most inspiring to his comrades," advised a British training manual.[12] Such appeals had little weight. By common consent, any wound was considered excuse enough for a soldier to drop his rifle and kit and head back for treatment. Battle police were ordered to force walking wounded to bring back their rifle and equipment, but the orders were seldom enforced. Soldiers who faithfully did their duty over months and years of hardship and terror dreamed of a "Blighty," the wound that would rescue them from the trenches and give them a bed, sheets, and a chance to see England again. "I think I would rather come through with a good hide," Robert Correll assured his sister, Lil, "but a couple of months in a nice bed in a hospital looks pretty good, especially as the winter will soon be here."[13]

Of course, some men did more than their moral contract demanded. At Hill 70, a shell splinter left Tom Gosford with a huge gash in his cheek. He recalled that his captain checked over the wounded: "Gosford, if you leave the line, we will lose the war." "Well I was a trained soldier. I snapped my heels, gave a smart salute, saying 'in that case if you can have my wound attended to satisfactorily, I am willing to stay and fight.'" Later he explained to his colonel: "When I left my farm and came to Regina to volunteer myself to come to France to help fight a ruthless enemy, I did not come on a vacation."[14] Gosford needed thirty-five stitches to close the wound and a stiff drink of rum to endure the treatment.

Wounded soldiers recalled a feeling like a kick from a horse or a blow from a hard ball. Except for wounds in the hand, foot, or head, the pain came later. Unconscious wounded took moments or hours to revive. Each soldier carried a "first field dressing" sewn into the right front skirt of his tunic, complete with a bandage and little vial of iodine. Those who were lucky could crawl or limp to safety.

Near Arleux, in 1917, Sergeant Aubrey Griffiths of the 5th Western Cavalry was hit in the ankle during a counter-attack. He slowly dragged himself back to his own lines under fire: "I could see little splashes of mud where German bullets hit all around me" and he waited for the one that would enter his body. Once he could drop into the relative safety of a trench, he hopped along, using a rifle and the revetment to support himself. "By this time, my foot started to swell which tightened the bandage and the splints, and the pain started. I finally arrived at the evacuation dugout where an officer by the name of McAughie was in charge; his first name was Alex. I knew him in peacetime and was very surprised to find him even close to the fighting. He was small and not the leader type an officer should be; one couldn't look to him for leadership. I said 'Hello Alex,' unmindful of the fact that he was an officer and should be addressed as 'Sir.'" The regimental medical officer, "Doc" Brown, bandaged the leg but it was twelve hours before Griffiths could leave the dugout for hospital. "Our colonel, who was a very kindly man, was at "Doc's" side. His name was Dyer and he was affectionately called Daddy Dyer by all under his command. He gave me a cigarette, lit it and said 'Good boy, sergeant', and sent me on my way."[15]

Griffiths performed the most dangerous part of his evacuation himself. Others, wounded during an attack or a night patrol and unable to help themselves, sometimes had to wait for days before someone could rescue them. Ray LeBrun, a machine-gunner at Passchendaele with many macabre memories, heard someone in pain: "It was one of our infantrymen and he was sitting on the ground, propped up on his elbows, with his tunic open. I nearly vomited. His insides were spilling out of his stomach and he was holding himself and trying to push this awful stuff back in. When he saw me he said 'Finish it for me, mate. Put a bullet in me. Go on. I want you to. Finish it!' He had no gun himself. When I did nothing, he started to swear. He cursed and swore at me and kept on shouting even after I turned and ran."[16]

Much depended on the courage and the availability of the few bearers on hand. Pinned down by machine-gun fire at Drocourt-Quéant, stretcher-bearer Bill Foster of the 38th Battalion took his chances: "as I noticed any men I could help, I would run out and rescue them." He professed surprise at receiving a Military Medal: "I was under the impression that a hero was never frightened but they told me it didn't matter how I felt, for it was what I did that counted."[17]

Clearing the battlefield of wounded after an attack was a terrible task. Occasionally, after the disastrous Canadian raid on March 1, 1917, for example, the Germans allowed an impromptu truce. Usually, the battle went on. Passchendaele plumbed the depths of horror. Major G.S. Strathy, sent up from a field ambulance to relieve the medical officer of the 47th Battalion, found him hiding under a table in a German pillbox, his head covered in a ground sheet, oblivious to the desperately wounded men around him. His despair was understandable: shells fell steadily; the pillbox was jammed with huddled wounded—men with stomach, lung, and spinal injuries. One man with a broken femur lay out in the open under the freezing rain. Strathy did what he could, finding blankets, injecting morphia, and strapping a Liston splint to the broken leg. Before dawn he sent off his first stretcher. "The moon had gone down and it was not daylight." One of the bearers tripped. "The patient they were carrying—the fractured femur—fell from their shoulders into a shell hole full of mud and water."[18] At dawn, Strathy put up a Red Cross flag and the shelling stopped, but the Germans began a gas attack on the following night. After three sleepless days and nights, Strathy was relieved and reported back to his field ambulance with a painful cough from smoking during the gas attack, and a mild case of trench foot.

The fate of a wounded man was determined by arbitrary selection, discreetly camouflaged by the French word *triage*. Stretcher-bearers made the first choice: were the man's prospects of survival good enough to merit the long, heavy, and usually dangerous "carry" to the RAP or the ADS? Out of humanity, some chose desperate cases anyway; experience taught them to favour those who would survive. "What man who carried wounded…could ever forget the terrible groaning, cursing and pleading of the poor fellow, half rolling off a shoulder-high stretcher?" recalled Fred Noyes. "Who could ever forget the dark brown and purplish stain that seeped through the stretcher canvas and all too often dripped down our backs and arms?"[19]

The limits of contemporary surgical skill and medical knowledge made *triage* relatively easy. Two-thirds of stomach wounds and more than half of all chest wounds were likely to be fatal.[20] Eight per cent of British wounded died somewhere between their first documented admission to an RAP and their final discharge. British statistics, based on a large sample of wounded, showed that 7 per cent of those wounded died at the RAP or ADS and 16 per cent at the CCS, where *triage* formally segregated both minor and hopeless cases and left the latter to be sedated and nursed, if possible, until their inevitable deaths. In quiet times, everyone could be treated; when whole battalions fell, most wounded could wait days for treatment.

Little in their previous experience or training prepared doctors for the casualties of trench warfare. British medical manuals recalled South Africa, where shell casualties were few and the dry air healed most bullet wounds quickly. In Europe, between 1914 and 1919, high-velocity bullets shattered bones and pulped flesh. Machine-guns tore five or ten such wounds into a single body. Shell and grenade fragments sheared away flesh and bones. Shards of white-hot metal shattered faces, ripped off limbs, and left huge, gaping holes. A Canadian surgeon at Ypres remembered: "Legs, feet, hands missing; bleeding of stumps controlled by rough field tourniquets; large portions of the abdominal walls shot away; faces horribly mutilated; bones shattered to pieces; holes that you could put your clenched fist into, filled with dirt, mud, bits of equipment and clothing, until it all becomes a hideous nightmare."[21]

First World War doctors had no antibiotics. Without safe methods of storage and reliable blood-typing, blood transfusion was limited to available donors connected to the transfusee by glass pipes and rubber tubes. Efficient blood and plasma storage came only with the next world war. Doctors tried to stop a patient's slow slide to death by *réchauffement*, keeping him as warm as possible.[22] This could be difficult in field conditions and it was never a real solution. As suitable splints were not available until late in the war, the grating of bone-ends in a fractured femur always brought hideous pain, and often coma and death.

The wounded soldier's worst enemy was infection. Men fought amidst rotting corpses, rats, faeces, and Flemish mud. Fragments of cloth and kit mingled with local filth in any open wound. Infected wounds produced a bacteria-generated gas with a nauseating stench, monstrous swelling, and a dreadful death. French surgeons discovered that gas gangrene could be controlled only by cutting away every fragment of affected flesh and irrigating the wound with a solution of sodium hypochlorite. A typical operation enlarged a tiny infected shell-fragment wound into a hole two to three inches wide, six inches long, piercing deep into a soldier's thigh.

Managing the tubes and pumps required for irrigation took constant nursing. Sergeant Thomas Geggie recalled how a nurse led the twice-daily ceremony of "changing the plugs": "The withdrawal of the plug caused me to emit my first, and only, hospital yell. It was a good yell, though perhaps I say it who shouldn't. I was immediately told that it was a most ungentlemanly thing to do; that as an old soldier and a non-commissioned officer of some standing, I ought to show a better example. From that day I resorted to the time-honoured expedient of chewing holes in my leather belt during the plugging and unplugging."[23]

Despite attempts to maintain aseptic conditions and "radical debridement," as the chopping away of affected flesh was called, recurrent infection contributed to long periods of hospital care and convalescence. Patients had plenty of time to condemn hospital food, wear out their blue flannel hospital uniforms, and attract sympathetic visitors.[24] By 1916, with a manpower shortage looming, the CEF finally began to organize systematically to restore men to active service. Lieutenant-Colonel Tom Carter recognized the paragons he would need as convalescent instructors: "The work entails constant patience and superabundant energy, and unless the instructors come to each individual class day after day, full of energy and enthusiasm, as though they were attacking an interesting job for the first time, they will fail to get full benefit for that class. On them devolved the duty of making the men interested, in spite of themselves, of encouraging them to laughter and singing at nine o'clock in the morning, and leaving them at the end of the exercise invigorated, in good spirit, and looking forward to their next day's parade."[25]

Men deemed fit to return to France passed through an increasingly systematic program of physical retraining. Then they rejoined the reinforcement stream through their own reserve battalions. Others who convinced a medical board that they would likely be permanently disabled returned to Canada for discharge from the CEF or for treatment in a growing system of hospitals and convalescent homes managed by the civilian-run Military Hospitals Commission.

Novelists and dramatists have left an impression that the war wounded were predominantly amputees, blinded, or perhaps "gassed at Ypres." Of 95,160 arm or leg wounds, only 2,780 led to amputation, chiefly of legs, because those who could walk could usually reach help before infection set in. Surgeons also understood that there was no satisfactory prosthetic replacement for a missing arm. It was also true that many battlefield amputees did not survive their wounds.[26] The CEF discharged 178 members as blind, but fewer than half had lost their eyesight through wounds. Gas casualties were more common: 11,536 Canadians were treated in hospital for the effects of chemicals, though little could be done for them beyond giving them rest and oxygen. Doctors tried old-fashioned bleeding: it often improved a patient's appearance while accelerating death. Mustard gas stripped the bronchia and burned the skin. Its main effect was disablement and terror—precisely what an enemy wanted.

The CEF's doctors and nurses imagined themselves in heroic and sacrificial roles. Like many other soldiers, they found that the great adventure soon palled. Some found other compensations. For some, the army offered fresh professional opportunities and an escape from a small and uncertain income. How many general practitioners in rural or small-town Canada had had the chance to perform complex surgery? Many enjoyed the pleasures of officer status, with a soldier-servant, salutes, and an officers' mess. Yet their sacrifices were real. Successful doctors knew that their patients in Canada, however devoted, would not wait. Sick parades, VD lectures, and latrine inspections hardly served as relevant experience for a smart society practice. At times of crisis, during a major battle, front-line surgeons worked around the clock, exhausted, blood-soaked, and sometimes in danger. Like all soldiers, they had to accustom themselves to moments of acute, body-wrenching stress, alternated with long interludes of stultifying routine and discomfort. Older on average than combatant soldiers, doctors and nurses were acutely conscious of the cold, damp, and filth of their surroundings.

Women in particular remembered the heroic struggle to keep themselves and especially their hair free of lice. Anne Ross remembered the "sand, sand, sand" of Lemnos. Her matron, Jessie Jaggard, the wife of an American railroad president, died in 1916, worn out by the heat and the flies.[27] Marion Lavell from Calgary remembered the rats: "You would try to get to bed and to sleep before they came out."[28] During air raids, she had to share the floor with them.

The raids were real. At Etaples, on the night of May 19, bombing killed 66, 3 of them nurses. Other sisters courageously stayed with the 300 helpless men with femur fractures. At Doullens, 2 nurses died when a bomb landed on an operating theatre. On June 27, 1918, when the hospital ship *Llandovery Castle* was torpedoed, 234 staff and crew drowned. All 14 nurses in their lifeboat were sucked into the vortex of the sinking ship, even before the German submarine surfaced to machine-gun other survivors. In all, 61 Canadian medical officers, 21 nurses, and 528 other ranks of the CAMC died during the war, about half of them because of enemy action, the rest from sickness.[29]

Nurses also shared the constant strain of suffering and death. Once they completed their surgery or assigned a treatment, doctors could dismiss their patients; nurses carried on caring for men puffed to double their size with gas gangrene, stinking beyond a stomach's tolerance and suffering unspeakable agony. Elizabeth Paynter remembered a difficult night during the Somme offensive:

a haemorrhage, emergency operation, followed by an intravenous saline and constant watching and treatment until 3 a.m. when the fine looking New Zealand boy quietly breathed his last. The same night another patient died, and another still was very low, while there were at least four other delirious head cases, who seemed to take turns pulling off their dressings or getting out of bed. We also had a number of gas gangrene cases, and these are quite a worry, as the infection travels so fast, and last, but not least, the haemorrhages which so often occur in the dead of night when the lights are dim. Here is where my flashlight served me in good stead and I then blessed old Waldron for insisting on us buying them in Kingston, where we were outfitted.[30]

Soldiers had their own impressions of their medical benefactors. Their own battalion stretcher-bearers were heroes, chums in the same company or platoon, envied a little for their independence but not for the long, heavy tools of their trade. Most were profoundly admired for the sacrificial spirit that sent so many of them into no man's land or back across open ground pockmarked by bullets and shrapnel. They died as fast as other infantry, perhaps faster. CAMC men usually came forward only as far as the third line where the RAPs were situated, but no one who carried a stretcher, not even the German prisoners pressed into service, was despised.

Judgements were harsher on the medical staff farther back. Soldiers despised light-fingered medical orderlies and referred to their corps as "Rob All My Comrades," after the initials of the Royal Army Medical Corps. Some bearers insisted that they earned the right to go through a soldier's pockets as a traditional "perk" of their trade. If soldiers had little love for the orderlies or the CAMC or RAMC sergeants who kept order in the hospitals, wounded men idealized their nurses, the white-veiled "bluebirds" who had chosen to share their ordeal and alleviate their pain. When a nurse moved through the wards, any soldier tried to hide his pain and curb his customary language. There were exceptions. Evacuated to a hospital near Rouen with shrapnel in his spine, Garnet Durham found "the most disgraceful hospital I have seen yet. Dirty wards, indifferent sisters, and orderlies who had no idea of their work." Fortunately for him, the x-ray operator was cheerful and competent.[31]

Most soldiers encountered military medicine at sick parade. The army fulfilled its promise of "free medical attendance" when the unit's "sick, lame, and lazy" assembled before dawn to be inspected by the battalion orderly corporal and marched smartly to the medical inspection room. They got a frosty welcome. In civil life, a doctor's fees would have kept most such patients from his door. Medical colleagues warned any enthusiastic newcomer that malingerers and scrimshankers intended to prey on his good nature.

Sick parade was a battle of wits. Soldiers learned that swallowing a little cordite could produce "disordered action of the heart" or that a copper coin strapped to a well-scratched fleabite could ripen into an alarming-looking sore. Experienced medical officers murmured the time-honoured phrase "Old soldiers never die" and ordered "medicine and duty."[32] Frank Maheux, troubled by a painful ear, warned his wife, "I'll have to see the Doctor but the doctor anything wrong with you it makes no matter if it was sore eyes he always give Castor Oil we call him Castor Oil King."[33] A conscientious man felt humiliated to be treated as a deceitful hypochondriac. Months after his spine wound, Garnet Durham reported sick because of weakness and pain. When the medical officer, "Peevish Percival," told him to "run and play," Durham slipped away to a civilian doctor who gave him a glass of Scotch, explained the necessary operation to him, and refused a fee for performing it.

Medical officers resented their subordination to ill-qualified medical generals like Jones, but military discipline and proliferating health regulations also gave medical officers powers they might never have otherwise enjoyed. Medical officers examined a man's private parts, ordered punishment for trench foot, and advised on appropriate ration scales. Soldiers in the ranks felt like charity patients and hated it. Medical officers seldom let sick soldiers forget that, somehow, they had brought on their own misfortune by contravening one of the innumerable rules of sanitation or personal hygiene. Many medical officers seemed to believe that nasty medicine and gusts of freezing fresh air not only fought germs but strengthened character.

One of the more intrusive and controversial ways doctors exerted their authority over soldiers was the treatment of "shell shock" or what, in a later war, was more aptly described as "battle exhaustion." Psychiatry had little place in the CAMC when it went to war in 1914. Manly courage was taken for granted; cowardice was an offence under King's Regulations, punishable by death. Exhaustion could be cured by a day's rest or a good night's sleep.

Yet, early in the war, RAMC doctors had faced otherwise responsible but battle-weary soldiers displaying inexplicable paralysis, deafness, uncontrollable crying, or mutism.[34] Since doctors believed in physical causes for all behaviour, they named the problem "shell shock," by analogy with men found dead without a scratch after a nearby shell burst. Victims were evacuated; given food, rest, and sympathy; and often discharged. Cases returned to Canada were housed at a special hospital at Cobourg: insane heroes could not be mixed with common lunatics.[35]

Neither generals nor doctors could be satisfied by mere kindly treatment. The mission of the CAMC, after all, was not to be therapeutic or humanitarian, but "to conserve manpower." Its officers played a crucial role in identifying and punishing soldiers guilty of a "self-inflicted wound." Surely, doctors assumed, real or feigned "shell shock" was just another way of escaping from a grim but necessary duty. If men continued to succumb, who would defend the trenches or attack the enemy? In late 1916, British authorities went so far as to ban the term "shell shock" and insisted on "NYD(N)," "not yet diagnosed (nervous)": men so labelled were neither sick nor wounded. The medical profession searched for further analogies. Neurasthenia—exhaustion of the nervous system—seemed a plausible, alternative diagnosis, particularly in the case of officers, and its cure was rest and recreation, perhaps golfing in the north of Scotland or sun-bathing on the Riviera. An alternative was "hysteria," often manifested by mutism or paralysis and commonly reported in civilian life among women confined to charity wards. That diagnosis was obviously relevant to common soldiers but, oddly enough, was seldom encountered among officers. Shell shock, insisted Andrew Macphail, was "a manifestation of childishness and femininity."[36]

The diagnosis suggested the cure: a systematic application of pain. "The sting of a whip, no matter how vigorously applied," claimed Dr. Lewis Yealland, was "almost nothing compared with the sudden severe shock of a faridic current." Yealland had returned from Canada in 1914 to take up an appointment at London's famous Queen's Square mental hospital. His "Black Chamber," with its electric brushes, soon set the standard for treatment. Lengthy chats and apparent sympathy, Yealland insisted, only aggravated the problem. He strapped his patients to a table and subjected them to high-voltage electricity. A stubbornly mute veteran of Mons, Gallipoli, and Salonika yielded a single "ah" after one hour of treatment. Six other cases of mutism were cured in half an hour, two of them by the mere sight of the instruments. Yealland took pains to get a complete cure. "You have not recovered yet," he warned a patient; "your laugh is most offensive to me. I dislike it very much indeed." When Yealland returned after leaving the room for five minutes, he reported that the patient was "sober and rational."[37] Yealland's methods were not unique: the French claimed even greater success with their version of *torpillage*.

Still, there were questions. Were doctors entitled to cause such pain for such a purpose? Yes, answered the prominent psychiatrist William Bailey, "in the special circumstances of a war for civilization." Patients, Yealland insisted, had turned their will to private and selfish purposes; they had to be persuaded to yield their private will to the service of the nation. Pain had a purpose. "It gives the man an excuse to tell his comrades he has received some powerful treatment," explained Lieutenant-Colonel Colin Russell, who commanded the Canadian Special Hospital at Ramsgate. "He can thus save his face."[38] The CAMC kept few records of its "shell shock" and NYD(N) cases, though about 10,000 soldiers were treated or discharged for psychiatric reasons, about half of them labelled "nervous." The war did little to raise psychiatry's dismal reputation, and its victims were denied pensions on the argument that men who had purposely avoided danger must have no financial excuse to avoid hard work.

Saving battlefield casualties was the obvious and heroic side of military medicine. The real triumphs lay not in treatment but in prevention. Medical advice strongly influenced the adoption of steel "shrapnel helmets" in 1916. If doctors could do little to help gas casualties, they could prevent some of the effects. Within days of the chlorine-gas attack at Ypres, soldiers were issued primitive flannel helmets. By 1916, anyone not wearing a respirator when he was gassed was charged with a "self-inflicted wound."

Over all, army doctors tended to regard most sicknesses as self-induced. Medical officers condemned soldiers with trench foot and their officers for failing to carry out preventive measures— rubbing the feet with grease or whale oil and changing their socks regularly. Strict oral hygiene and regular dental inspections also curbed an acute gum infection called trench mouth. Men who had never before used a toothbrush learned the habit in the army. Neither doctors nor soldiers paid much attention to "trench cough," a chronic condition associated with constant damp and heavy smoking. "The MOS [medical officers] ... say there is very little harm in it," reported Claude Williams. "Their advice is to do without smoking for a while. Nobody does that, they had better take away our food rations first."[39]

Other miseries of trench life were less tractable. In 1916, scabies, or "seven-year itch," accounted for a quarter of hospital admissions in the Canadian Corps. Trench fever (discreetly titled PUO, or "pyrexia of unknown origin") induced short bouts of diarrhea, vomiting, and aching, and remained endemic through most of the war. In 1918, a Canadian, Captain A.C. Rankin, traced it to the soldier's most unwanted companion, the common flea. In contrast to the British, the American army responded promptly to infestations of fleas by taking steps to disinfect their men. Only in 1918 did the British finally follow suit. Two CAMC officers, Colonel John Amyot of the University of Toronto, and Major Harold Orr, had already developed suitable equipment and techniques, but the American example was what finally moved the War Office and the RAMC to act.

No wartime infection brought more controversy and less sympathy within and beyond the army than venereal disease (VD). By the end of the war, the CEF had accumulated 66,346 cases (compared with 45,460 cases of influenza). Nearly one in nine Canadians overseas was infected, a rate that exceeded even the Australian record. The epidemic began almost as soon as Canadians disembarked England, and continued until they went home. Idealists insisted that innocent young Canadians had been corrupted by England's army of industrious harlots; the more worldly wise argued that Canadian soldiers had brought their habits and some of their infection from home. High pay and long absence from their families fuelled the epidemic.

The CEF considered VD a moral and disciplinary problem as well as a disease, docking the pay of men under treatment. In 1914, CAMC doctors, who had enlisted for more heroic challenges, found only one junior colleague who admitted any expertise in the disease. He was assigned the task of treating the CEF's largest caseload. Before the 1st Division left for France in February 1915, most Canadian soldiers in hospital suffered from venereal disease, and it remained by far the largest single cause of hospitalization throughout the war.[40] "Salvarsan," an arsenical with alarming side-effects—cramps, vomiting, and acute pain—was the major treatment for syphilis. Beyond frequent irrigation of affected areas with disinfectants, there was no acknowledged cure for gonorrhoea. The fact that both treatments hurt the sufferer seemed somehow appropriate for patients widely regarded as moral pariahs.

Until November 1915, "venereals" were kept behind barbed wire at Shorncliffe—"moral lepers," as the hospital war diary termed them. When a hurricane demolished their leaky, unheated tents, authorities moved them to a former workhouse at Etchinghill, locally, if inaccurately, believed to be the model for Dickens's Bleak House. The Canadian Red Cross refused to provide VD patients with comforts, or even books to read. The British Red Cross was not quite so censorious. Under a more senior and aggressive commanding officer, Etchinghill later became less a prison, more a conscientious if austere therapeutic institution.[41] As the VD problem increased, a second hospital opened at Witley in 1917. Its commander acknowledged that his patients were depressed in appearance and attitude: "Those who have not dealt with Venereal patients in large numbers find it difficult to understand their mental attitude. They feel that they are repulsive to themselves and to others. Where confined in an enclosure they suffer from great depression and become exceedingly sensitive. This leads easily to disorderly outbreaks, which tend to relieve the monotony and to satisfy the grudge the soldier always feels towards the authorities when his pay is restricted and his normal liberty interfered with."[42]

Prevention made more sense than cure. Since men on leave could not be controlled, surely Britain's oldest profession could be constrained by regular medical examinations of its practitioners. The British refused to participate. Politicians still remembered an attempt, thirty years earlier, to regulate prostitution in garrison towns and seaports, and the righteous indignation of clergy and editors at the idea of trying to "license sin." The Canadians and other colonial contingents, insisted the War Office, were on their own. Overseas ministry leaflets and lecturers described the horrible consequences of syphilis and gonorrhoea and pleaded with soldiers to "play the game" for the sake of "the wife and kiddies at home," for Canada, for God, and for comrades in the trenches. The chaplains' service successfully resisted a CAMC plan to produce an educational film to be shown to troops going on leave. By 1917, a few London centres offered post-coital prophylaxes, and in 1918, Australians, Canadians, and New Zealanders joined in running "Blue Light Depots" where, after exposure, soldiers could wash their genitals with potassium permanganate, squirt calomel ointment into their penises, and get a "visa" card stamped. Such precautions became their alibi if they contracted the disease after all. Otherwise, they faced punishment. Some doctors doubted the value: of 2,728 patients admitted to Etchinghill after the Blue Light Depots opened, 2,132 claimed to have used the calomel tubes.[43]

To ensure that no one concealed the disease from comrades or superiors, medical officers were directed to conduct a weekly "short-arm" inspection of their men's genitals. An army that, in

1914, would not even enforce typhoid inoculations, now stripped men of their last vestige of privacy in the name, as ever, of an even higher good. Condoms were never contemplated. Instead, rumours spread that London's enterprising prostitutes were happy to infect frightened soldiers for a fee. "This practice was hard to check," explained Macphail, "as venereal disease is the least difficult of all self-inflicted wounds to inflict."[44]

At the 1917 Imperial Conference, the VD crisis prompted Sir Robert Borden to warn that if he were still Canada's prime minister and another war were declared, he would refuse to allow Canadian soldiers to leave Canada until the British cleaned up the problem of sexually transmitted diseases. When Americans arrived, they apparently wielded more clout with British officials than did colonial politicians. Whitehall briskly adopted regulations that threatened with prison any woman who infected a soldier. Experienced prostitutes had the sense not to give clients their real names or addresses, so the new regulations penalized only the innocent and the amateurs. These luckless women were arrested, medically examined, and, if infected, jailed without treatment. Canada imitated the British regulations, with much the same cruel consequences for women.

Venereal disease was the largest public-health issue facing the CEF, but not the only one. The army held commanding officers ultimately responsible for their men's health. Medical officers were supposed to be only expert advisers. CAMC doctors had to give themselves a crash course on the public-hygiene problems most contemporary medical schools ignored. British army manuals taught them how to inspect kitchens, design latrines, and control the inevitable fly population that accompanied such facilities. The battle to control trench mouth led to strict orders that mugs in canteens and YMCA coffee bars should henceforth be washed after each use, not just once daily as part of the evening clean-up. Soldiers were ordered to use their toothbrushes, and the CADC hunted for an appropriate dentifrice. After rejecting powder and paste, experts settled on a form of soap tightly sealed in a screw-top tin. "In the words of a far-flung advertisement," claimed the CADC's

Major A.D. Wells, "we can imagine that the Tommies are 'crying for it.'"[45]

In 1916, Hughes launched critical reviews of medical arrangements in Canada and England. His emissary to England, Colonel Herbert A. Bruce, was a brilliant surgeon and founder of Toronto's highly efficient Wellesley Hospital. As Hughes must have known, Bruce also had a score to settle with Major-General G.C. Jones. The CAMC hierarchy had rudely tried to enforce regulations when the ambitious and self-important Bruce had made up his mind to visit France a year earlier. Accordingly, his review of the overseas organization was devastating. After a ritual assertion that doctors and nurses were performing "beyond all praise," Bruce alleged that Major-General Jones had allowed incompetents, alcoholics, and "drug fiends" to practise medicine, and that unqualified surgeons had honed their skills on the bodies of young Canadians. The British hospitals where Jones sent Canadians served as little more than "marriage bureaus" for untrained VADS. Instead of leaving Canadians to endure misery in the Mediterranean, Canadian hospitals should have cared for them in France.[46] On receiving Bruce's report, Hughes promptly fired Jones, put Bruce in his place, and ignored the ensuing explosion from CAMC doctors.

Hardly had he done the deed than Hughes himself was fired. Sir George Perley inherited the mess. Later Perley confessed that he would never have accepted the job if he had known about all the problems that came with it.[47] In short measure he fired Bruce, brought Jones back for a face-saving interlude, and summoned Major-General G.L. Foster, director general of medical services for the Canadian Corps, to take over as surgeon general. An investigation of Bruce's charges found little hard evidence to support them, but the Canadian hospitals were recalled from Salonika, and many of Bruce's other recommendations were eventually adopted. Once the CAMC had been reorganized, and the Corps was suffering a steady stream of casualties, many of Bruce's ideas made sense.

The underlying dispute was not resolved. With lots of help

from the deposed Hughes, Bruce and his partisans continued a vendetta that soon extended to Perley and Foster. OMFC files swelled with reports of the conflicts and grievances of medical officers, occasionally spurred by the interventions of their underemployed wives. Foster's department fought back, recruiting the acid-penned Major Andrew Macphail to fight its battles. Macphail and the aged Canadian medical eminence, Sir William Osler, whom Bruce had annoyed, helped publicize CAMC achievements and convinced medical associations in Canada that Bruce's charges were unfounded, unprofessional, and, in time of war, unpatriotic. Though Bruce's struggle continued for forty years, the honours belonged to his enemies.

For all its conflicts and failures, the CAMC earned respect from its professional counterparts and from most Canadians. Like other branches of the CEF, the medical services faced unprecedented problems, from coping with huge volumes of casualties and horrifying new weapons to setting appropriate standards for treating its non-paying patients. A board of consultants, appointed by the Militia Department to reconcile the problems of military rank and medical expertise, ultimately found a way to describe the CAMC's medical standards: "The policy and object kept steadily in view has been to secure and provide economically, but not parsimoniously, for the invalid soldier the best possible care and treatment upon the most modern lines, and so as to fit him in the speediest way for return to duty or, where that is impossible, for his discharge at the earliest possible moment after treatment has attained finality, and the highest possible fitness secured."[48]

Was the war a catalyst for medical innovation or a tremendous distraction from medical progress? Had military medicine's disciplined team effort produced a sharing of advances or stultified initiative? Had the North American invasion done no more than introduce hookworm to Europe and import athlete's foot to Canada and the United States? "The great, outstanding feature of the War," wrote McGill's Dr. George Adami in 1920, "has been the triumph of preventive medicine."[49] Admittedly, inoculation, vaccination, and germ theory were all established long before 1914, but wartime experience in controlling contagion gave doctors and the public a faith in prevention they had never had before. Vaccination was 125 years old, but in 1914 it had seemed a bold measure to impose it on the CEF.

Compared with advances in medicine, surgical improvements hardly seemed as relevant. Gas gangrene was unlikely in a peace-time setting. Returning doctors, skilled in operating on facial mutilations or fractured femurs, were hardly prepared at all for the normal experiences of peacetime practice. At the same time, only wartime needs could have forced the pace in reconstructive surgery or could have allowed practitioners of blood transfusion to improve their primitive techniques. Within a couple of years after the war, Captain Bruce L. Richardson applied his wartime skill to saving severely burned infants at Toronto's Hospital for Sick Children.

In a far different realm, returning medical officers applied their experience to the brand-new field of industrial medicine, tackling occupational diseases, industrial hazards, and the unhygienic conditions of workplace life. Captain Bernard Wyatt, an apostle for the new specialty, reminded employers that "our great Canadian industries cannot maintain their place in the world's competition unless their employees are in good physical condition."[50] Whether or not employers believed such a claim, many doctors would. Post-war addresses to medical associations bristled with military metaphors as Canadian doctors inspired each other to believe that discipline, organization, and what generals had called "the offensive spirit" could put to flight the traditional enemies of human health. Whether or not doctors were prepared to alter the individualism of their practice of curative medicine, army experience had taught them that prevention could succeed only as a collective effort in which the state would play an increasingly important and wholly legitimate role. The public, too, came to appreciate that the war had had humanitarian as well as military victories.

Ordinary soldiers, of course, were not consulted. They might have complained that some of their treatment was old-fashioned, even barbaric. The wounded remembered the agonizing jolting of ambulance wagons, the hours spent waiting at clearing stations, and the petty rituals of hospital wards. Like most blessings, a "Blighty" was never as much of a relief as it had seemed in prospect. It was only better than the alternatives.

CHAPTER NINE

FANNIGANS

PRISONERS OF WAR

No group in the CEF has been more completely forgotten than its prisoners of war. They had lived when others died, undermining a myth of suicidal heroism, and their treatment was linked to the complex truth and falsehood of wartime-atrocity stories. The "fannigans," as they called themselves, faced helplessness and despair, and fought back in their own private ways.

A MONG 3.67 million Allied prisoners in German hands were 3,842 Canadian soldiers. How were they captured? Some 377 Canadians in the British flying services, including Conn Smythe, of Maple Leaf Gardens fame, survived crashes behind German lines. Two airmen endured Turkish prisons, and another was a guest of the Bulgarians.[1] In trench warfare, both sides grabbed prisoners for the information they shared; others got lost on night patrols. At Vimy and Lens, and in the battles of the Last Hundred Days, intrepid attackers fell victim to German counter-attacks. A Canadian soldier who became a prisoner was charged with desertion to the enemy. Others were suspected.[2]

Most Canadian prisoners surrendered on April 24, 1915, during the German assault on Ypres. Given their inexperience, defective weapons, and baffled commanders, most Canadians fought with impressive courage, but many were left behind as units fell back. At the apex of the Canadian position, the 15th Battalion dissolved in the face of a devastating artillery barrage and the worst of the chlorine gas. Four officers and 216 men died; 10 officers and 247 other ranks were captured. The forward companies of British Columbia's 7th Battalion lost 267 as prisoners. Survivors of the garrison of St. Julien, mostly from the 3rd Battalion, also surrendered. By day's end, the division had lost 6,036 men, half its infantry strength; 1,410 of them were German prisoners, 627 of them wounded and 87 due to die of their wounds. Most, as it happened, came from Toronto.

A year later, on June 2, 1916 at Mont-Sorrel, the Germans unleashed a devastating assault on another raw formation, Major-General M.S. Mercer's 3rd Division. Two battalions of Canadian Mounted Rifles (CMR) virtually ceased to exist. Trapped in the forward trenches, the division commander was killed, and Brigadier-General Victor Williams was badly wounded. He and more than a hundred men took shelter in a tunnel. "We were entirely surrounded by the enemy," explained Lieutenant-Colonel John Ussher of the 4th CMR; "Gen. Williams was not fit to consult and a decision devolved on me. There was nothing for it but to surrender. We were like rats in a trap: one German with a bomb could have finished the lot of us."[3] Ussher surrendered. So did 29 other officers, among them 2 medical officers, the brigade chaplain, Captain Gillie Wilken, and 506 other ranks.

There were other bad days. The 75th Mississaugas suffered the only major setback at the battle of Vimy Ridge in April 1917, and Toronto's 19th Battalion was overrun at Fresnoy a month later. At Lens, on August 23, Manitoba's bad-luck battalion, the 44th, lost 258 men in a hopeless attack on the Green Crassier; 87 became prisoners. Though not Canadian, the Newfoundland Battalion suffered a second annihilation at Monchy-le-Preux on April 14, 1917. Among the survivors, 150 officers and men became prisoners of war.

Being captured is the most dangerous experience in a soldier's life, more dangerous than a heavy bombardment or even an advance across no man's land. Blinded by bloodlust or bent on avenging a comrade, a soldier might not accept an enemy's surrender. Captors and captured alike are still under fire. Canadian prisoners recalled the cold-blooded killing of comrades. At Mont-Sorrel on June 2, 1916, wounded in the chest and right leg, with his jaw smashed, Corporal Peter Thornton of the 4th Canadian Mounted Rifles could march no farther. An impatient German officer shot him in the back and shoulder. Later, German stretcher-bearers collected him, and he survived.[4] Jack Finnemore of the 7th Battalion, wounded in the leg at Ypres, was saved by a German who hoisted him into a wheelbarrow under fire.

In their own letter and diaries, Canadians commonly boasted that they did not take prisoners—boasts the Germans soon discovered. Taken at the Canal du Nord in 1918, Fred Hamilton claimed that he was beaten by a German colonel and threatened with death. "I don't care for the English, Scotch, French, Australians or Belgians," shouted the colonel, "but damn you Canadians you take no prisoners and you kill our wounded."[5]

In the past, prisoners of war had routinely been slaughtered, enslaved or, in some of the camps of the American Civil War, simply left to die of hunger or disease. One of the claims of nineteenth-century humanitarians was that they had put away that aspect of their barbaric past. Like her enemies and most of her allies, Germany was a signatory to the Hague Conventions of 1898 and 1907, a set of principles that promised to make prisoners, in the view of one jurist, "the spoilt children" of international law.[6] Wounded and exhausted Canadians who complained that they were force-marched to the rear benefited from a Convention requirement to remove prisoners from the battlefield as quickly as possible. Beyond rifle range, German cavalry took over escort duties, using their lances to prod laggards and to fend off sympathetic French or Belgian civilians.

Despite the importance of prisoners as a source of information, few of the Canadians seized by the Germans claimed that threats or violence were used in interrogation. Most seem to have told their captors all they knew quite willingly. Corporal Edwards of the Patricias discovered that the Germans knew more than he did of recent changes of command in his battalion. When General Williams recovered sufficiently to talk, his interrogation report indicates that he denounced British generalship and military competence: "If the Germans want to punish me," he allegedly told his interrogator, "all they have to do is to put me together with English officers."[7] Williams hinted at an imminent British offensive and insisted that most Canadians had warm, friendly feelings for Germans.

In 1915, at least, the feeling was not reciprocated. Canadians taken at Ypres recalled beatings, harangues, and threats because they were *Geldsoldaten,* or mercenaries, with no business fighting Germany. Lieutenant Edward Bellew was sentenced to death for firing his machine-gun after a white flag had gone up. He was later reprieved, but the British suppressed news of his Victoria Cross until the end of the war. Asked why he had come so far to kill Germans, Bellew's fellow British Columbian Captain Tom Scudamore summoned up his half-forgotten German to answer, "it was for fun." He was promptly thrashed with the interrogator's riding whip.[8] When trainloads of Canadian captives passed through Germany, guards opened the doors to display their prisoners to angry German crowds. At Giessen, the destination for most of the other ranks, George Pearson of the PPCLI recalled "one man was hit full in the face by all the spit a well-dressed woman could collect."[9] A year later, Mont-Sorrel prisoners recalled fewer such hostile experiences.

Although German war plans called for the envelopment of enemy armies and masses of prisoners, the Germans neglected serious preparations to receive and care for them. Many of their prisoners spent the bitter winter of 1914–15 in tents and sheds, shivering in their summer uniforms. A German policy of mixing prisoners of different nationalities spread typhus from Russian prisoners to their reluctant French and British neighbours. At Wittenberg and Gardelegen, German guards simply fled the epidemic, leaving the prisoners and a few Allied doctors to cope as well as they could.

Reports of maltreatment and neglect added to Allied propaganda. The Germans responded with their own charges of Allied mistreatment of their prisoners. One beneficial result was that the American ambassador, James Gerard, used both sets of allegations

BEHIND THE LINES

3-A (above) British and Canadian soldiers enjoy "char and a wad," elsewhere known as tea and a bun, from a canteen established by an unnamed voluntary organization. Soldiers appreciated anyone who helped but their deepest gratitude was for organizations like the Salvation Army which did not charge. (National Archives, PA 926)

3-B (left) An ammunition box becomes a personal bathtub in the field. Living and sleeping close to the ground meant that men were seldom clean and frequently infested with lice. Not until 1918 were effective methods of disinfection introduced, largely because Canadian doctors proved that lice carried the infection of Trench Fever. (National Archives, PA 1804)

3-C (bottom) Men of the 2nd Division line up for a bath during the bitter winter of 1917. Stripping in an unheated corrugated iron barn, standing under a few dribbles of lukewarm water and drying oneself on a small hand towel were memorable ordeals experienced at least monthly. (National Archives, PA 2236)

3-D (above) The baseball team of the 85th Nova Scotia Highlanders strides out to defend the honour of the regiment. Sports were among the officially approved and generally enjoyed recreations of the Canadian Corps and enthusiasm for the most North American of games grew with the sense of national identity. (National Archives, PA 2464)

3-E (below) Dipping water out of a muddy ditch in the summer of 1918. While soldiers complained about the cold, wet weather of wartime winters, France and Belgium could be hot in summer and water was never plentiful. (National Archives, PA 2970)

3-F (above) A platoon commander briefs his men on a training exercise. Their rifles lie on the ground a few metres away. The most important factor in changing the failure at the Somme to the

successes of 1918 was the reorganization and retraining of the infantry platoon. (National Archives, PA 877)

3-G (left) A member of the Canadian Army Service Corps struggles to be charming with a French level-crossing guard. While Canadians, like their British allies, lived among their French and Belgian allies, cordial relations were exceptional and barriers of language and custom persisted. (National Archives, PA 1449)

3-H (below) The 22nd Battalion camps out in a field. A bivouac tent was made by clipping together two rubber sheets and supporting them on bayoneted rifles, with the low end held down by the handles from entrenching tools. Like much of army life, a "bivvy" worked better with a chum. (National Archives, PA 2955)

3-J (above) Officers and a contestant watch as a rifle grenade soars toward its target and other contestants get ready for their turn. Much of the time out of the line was spent learning new tactics and weapons for the time when the Great Offensive began. For these soldiers in the summer of 1918, it was not far off. (National Archives, PA 4745)

3-K (below) Men of the Fort Garry Horse, fresh from the mingled triumph and disaster at Cambrai, wait to vote in the 1917 election. On the right, a couple of soldiers hunt for their electoral district. Unlike Australians, Canadian soldiers had no trouble supporting conscription and a fairer share of their sacrifice. (National Archives, PA 2238)

3-L (left) Tom Dinesen (lower left) and four of his comrades from the 42nd Battalion pose for a French photographer. Only Dinesen would survive the war intact. Groups of pals were more important fighting units than platoons and battalions. (From Dinesen, *Merry Hell*)

3-M (bottom) Soldiers of the Grenade Section of Winnipeg's 8th Battalion pose for the camera during a summer rest before the Battle of the Somme in 1916. Others remain intent on what really mattered, the turn of the cards. Afterwards, men would remember the bonds of comradeship as the strongest force they had ever experienced in their lives. The bond of comradeship far more than patriotism or unit esprit de corps persuaded men to risk their lives in battle. (National Archives PA 151)

to justify a system of neutral inspection of camps. Since inspectors had to give notice of their coming and they saw only what was permitted, prisoners often criticized their neutral visitors, but the system seemed to curb the worst abuses and the wildest exaggerations on both sides. By the time the Canadians taken at Ypres reached Germany, the appalling conditions in the early months of the war had been corrected.

German military administration affected how prisoners were treated. Berlin issued vague guidelines to seven kingdoms and principalities, and twenty-two army corps districts, but German military tradition was based on the doctrine of *Alles haengt vom Kommandeur ab*, "all depends on the commander." Some districts left discipline to the prisoners' own NCOs; others reserved all authority for German guards, normally elderly reservists from the *Landwehr*. Most Canadian *Kriegsgefangener*, or prisoners of war, found themselves in the Tenth Army Corps district, composed of Hanover and parts of Westphalia.

Camps ranged in size from 20,000 to 40,000 men. Some occupied old German barracks; most were barbed-wire enclosures, set in open field and scrub land. At Giessen, a board fence, ten to twelve feet high, set the prisoners' horizon. Camps were subdivided into "battalions" of 2,000 Russian, French, Belgian, and British prisoners, usually housed in ten or a dozen low wooden barracks, with a few lean-tos housing latrines, wash stands, and a kitchen where the prison staples of soup and acorn coffee were boiled. Huts were crammed with double-tiered bunks and prisoners' belongings. A first source of friction among the Allies was ventilation: the tiny minority of British prisoners demanded fresh air; Russians were content with a malodorous fug; the French hated the smells but feared a draft. Latrine buckets in the corner, usually overflowing by morning, affected air quality.

An American observer described the hut where prisoners were destined to spend much the rest of the war:

Low long rows of double-tier bunks take up the central floor space of the barrack. Long tables for serving food are placed next to the walls. Bags filled with straw, sea grass or paper serve as mattresses. Each prisoner is supplied with two blankets and these are thrown over the mattresses. Every available space is used for food packages and clothes. The place has a dim, confused, unkempt appearance on account of the crowding of men, the arrangement of the bunks, food packages, clothes etc. At one end of the barrack a small room is usually walled off for the non-commissioned officers. This is furnished with cots instead of the usual bunk arrangement.[10]

Food soon became a constant preoccupation. The Germans insisted that their ration offered 2,700 calories of nourishment, more than enough to fuel prisoners for light manual work. Prisoners, they claimed, received plenty of soup, meat, fish, bread, and vegetables. Prisoners' recollections are consistent and unflattering. Breakfast was acorn coffee and a chunk of black bread issued the night before. Dinner consisted of soup. Supper, at 5:00 p.m., was a thin gruel with an occasional sausage or raw herring. Because the morning bread ration was issued at night, most men ate it at once for fear someone else would steal it while they slept. Few Canadians ever acknowledged that the German army's rations were fit for human consumption. They also accused French prisoners of monopolizing kitchen duties, serving their compatriots from the bottom of the pot while the British and Russians were given greasy liquid scooped from the top.[11]

So far as they possibly could, British and Canadian prisoners subsisted on parcels sent from home and from the Red Cross. Thanks to the neutral nations, postal services connected the belligerents. In 1914, the first public reports of suffering in the German camps initiated a flow of food parcels that continued throughout the war. Begun as a typically private response to need, by 1916 it had developed into an official Red Cross function. At the end of 1916, to strengthen censorship and prevent contraband reaching Germany, the British authorities banned all private parcels to other-rank prisoners, and Canadians were forced by their own Red Cross to conform. The discrimination in favour of officers obviously rankled, and within six months they also had been subjected to the ban, though the Red Cross discreetly undertook to fill parcels for officers in a way that would reflect their gentlemanly needs and tastes. British medical authorities designed four standard, nutritionally balanced packages, and the Red Cross undertook to deliver three ten-pound parcels to each prisoner every two weeks.[12] Each month, a prisoner received a half-pound tin of tobacco and 250 cigarettes; every six months he got a supply of clothing, and annually a new overcoat. A British woman, Lady Evelyn Duff, organized bakeries in Switzerland and later in Denmark to deliver loaves of white bread to British and Canadian prisoners. "Swiss dodgers" might be rock-hard or green with mould when they arrived, but hungry prisoners ate all they could.

Almost every prisoner recognized that the parcels were lifesavers. Just seeing the starving Russian prisoners or enduring periods when parcels were cut off demonstrated what difference the Red Cross made. Gratitude did not mean that prisoners were well fed: most of the food in the parcels was canned. While it is amazing that the starving Germans seldom stole prisoners' food parcels, the supplies could never more than supplement an inadequate basic diet. Moreover, prisoners on the move or under punishment received no parcels for long periods, nor did men whose capture the Germans delayed announcing. Back in England, where food shortages worsened in 1917, reductions in the number and contents of parcels and of the bread supply were often considered but never implemented. Whatever their state on arrival, Lady Duff's loaves represented useful propaganda: hungry Germans could see that their enemies still enjoyed the peacetime luxury of white bread.

As the Hague Convention dictated, wounded prisoners were generally treated like their captors' own casualties. A soldier could never enjoy lying in pain among his country's enemies, at the mercy of medical personnel whose own feelings might overcome Geneva principles. Added to these sentiments, Germany desperately needed drugs and cotton. Operations on prisoners and German soldiers alike were often performed without anaesthetic, and wounds were covered with paper bandages. The skill of a German surgeon was undone when a prisoner moved on to a camp where medical services were minimal. Wounded prisoners suffered brutality, incompetence, and neglect, but so did many German soldiers.

In camps, captured Allied medical personnel provided much of the medical attention. Captain F.S. Park, captured at Mont-Sorrel, spent most of his captivity working in the *Lazarett* at Minden and arguing with the German medical students in charge.

The Hague Convention was eloquent about the privileges owed to officer prisoners. The Germans, on the whole, observed the rules. They housed officers in schools, barracks, fortresses, and lower-quality hotels, sleeping several to a room, but always with orderlies from their own armies to attend to their needs. The German regulations promised officers "a sufficient and nutritious fare." At Bischofswerda, in 1915, Major Peter Anderson reported that daily meals included a small white roll and dishwater coffee for breakfast; soup, meat, sausage, fish, potatoes, and bread for dinner; and a pickled herring for tea.[13] To Canadian other ranks at Giessen, such rations would have seemed a treat.

Prison, of course, was prison. Several Canadian officers experienced two of the worst officers' camps, Clausthals and Holzminden. Each camp was commanded by a brother. Karl and Heinrich Niemeyer had lived in the United States, absorbed an easily caricatured variety of English, and tyrannized over their captives with lengthy roll-calls, surprise searches, and enough petty rules to keep the solitary-confinement cells filled. Whatever their rank, most prisoners suffered from their captivity.

As the war dragged on, observers began to talk about the neurotic symptoms they termed "barbed wire disease." Walter Haight, one of the medical officers captured at Mont-Sorrel, emerged from Holzminden with acne and rotten teeth and was so mentally disoriented that he could barely continue a hitherto brilliant medical career.[14] "Trifles, which in ordinary life one would absolutely ignore, assumed mammoth proportions when one was herded up in a small space for an indefinite period with three hundred men drawn from every walk of life," recalled Lieutenant Frederick

Walthew. "It was incredible the intensity of dislike one could work up in a very short time for a man's face, the way he did his hair and his habits and hobbies generally."[15]

For other-rank prisoners, the Germans had a cure for "barbed wire disease." The Hague Convention allowed them to put all but officers to work. The advantages were obvious. With millions of men in uniform, Germany needed labour for a thousand tasks, from making munitions to clearing land for food production to combat the effects of the Allied blockade. Admittedly, the Convention insisted that "the work shall not be excessive and shall have no connection with the operations of war," but that was a matter for the Germans to judge.[16] Beginning in 1915, prison camps became depots supplying men for hundreds and soon thousands of working parties or *Arbeitkommandos*. Employers in the Tenth Army Corps ranged from Krupp foundries and a huge Babcock and Wilcocks factory, to farmers in need of a few extra hands. Contracts required that prisoners be paid, but almost all the money was diverted to meet the cost of their food, shelter, and guards. By the end of 1916, Germany reported that 1.1 million prisoners were happily at work. Thanks to the food parcels, some of them were being fed at French and British expense.

Canadian prisoners chopped weeds, dug ditches, and, at Bohmte, dug a canal. At Vehnemoor, they worked up to their knees in brown, fetid water, cutting peat. Others toiled in steel mills and chemical factories. Still others laboured in coal and salt mines, or swept streets and collected garbage in German cities. On the North Sea coast, they built dikes. Wherever unskilled labour could be organized and guarded, prisoners could be employed. While some might argue that the Hague Convention was permissive, leaving it to prisoners to decide whether or not to work, neither the Germans nor the protecting power accepted that interpretation. As a good American, Ambassador Gerard expressed more concern about the effects of idleness on prisoners than about the legalistic claims of the work-shy. When British prisoners asked their government whether they must work, the Foreign Office answered vaguely: "His Majesty's Government did not wish them to work in the manner referred to."[17]

Many British prisoners chose to take that advice as an order to resist any work related to Germany's war effort. Many Canadians taken at Ypres identified with them. The patriotism that had made them enlist, the humiliation of capture, and the British roots of the great majority made it easy to make common cause with British prisoners who decided to defy their captors. The Germans responded with a repertoire of punishments. When Charles Taylor, a thirty-one-year-old Torontonian, refused to work, he "was taken out of the line before the squad and beaten with rifle butts." Fifteen years later, he could still feel the blows. Horace Pickering was also beaten and sentenced to thirty days in punishment barracks, spending his nights in a tiny cell and his days sitting in silence on a low stool. The commonest punishment was *Stillstande*, two or more hours of standing rigidly at attention, preferably facing the sun. Spencer Symonds, a McGill student captured with the Patricias in 1916, endured eight hours in wet, cold weather. Exasperated guards threatened to shoot him. Instead, he almost died of bronchial pneumonia.[18]

The Geisweid iron foundry, which obviously contributed to munitions production, employed a Giessen *Arbeitkommando*. Resisters there faced confinement in the steam room, a box-like cell where exhaust from foundry boilers made life miserable and breathing almost impossible. Colin Earle, a nineteen-year-old who had endured repeated savage beatings, gave up after a few hours in the box. One tough prisoner lasted five days. Another Geisweid punishment was *Stillstande* close to the molten ore. Guards kept their bayonets on prisoners' backs. Some Canadians at Giessen formed the "Iron Twenty" and challenged each other to endure whatever punishment the Germans could hand out without buckling. Under the Hague Convention, prisoners were subject to their captors' military law, and Germans considered refusal to work as mutiny. The Giessen resisters were court-martialled and sentenced to long terms at military prisons in Butzbach and Cologne.

Non-commissioned officers, who insisted that, as officers, they could not be obliged to work, were an ambiguous category. The Germans drilled NCO work-resisters for hours a day, in the awkward wooden clogs the Germans provided instead of boots. Other "nix arbeiters," as fellow-prisoners christened them, were sent to hard-labour camps like Vehnemoor or Mettingen, where prisoners lived in dugouts and laboured to drain swampland. Prisoners learned the German word *langsam,* or "slow," and practised it. Guards and overseers had the power to beat shirkers with rifle butts, bayonet scabbards, and rubber hoses.

The most notorious episode of work-camp discipline occurred at Bokelah. The arrival of a group of uncooperative Canadians in the spring of 1916 led to incidents of sabotage, lengthened working hours, bad tempers, and a noontime confrontation that ended with a bayonet assault and one British prisoner dead and nineteen prisoners, mostly Canadian, facing a German court martial. American observers accepted the German view that the Canadians had undermined camp discipline. The Germans seized on Private Fred Armstrong of the 13th Battalion as ringleader. A McGill University student big enough to be nicknamed "Tiny," he seemed a logical choice. His death sentence was ultimately commuted to thirteen years' solitary; six other Canadians got twelve-year sentences to serve at Cologne military prison. One of them, an Ottawa man named Billy Brooke, died in the punishment cells. His offence was a letter home with a flattering description of prison conditions and the ironic comment: "Mother, you know I'm not George Washington." Armstrong himself died within weeks of his release in 1919.[19]

Not all Canadian prisoners were brutalized. Many found relatively congenial work, living with farm families or working in factories where the pace was slow and supervisors were tolerant. Allan Beddoes, a future artist and heraldry expert, perfected his sketching technique by drawing his German guards; Alex Yetman played in a camp orchestra. A few remembered that decent treatment from guards and overseers made them work harder and more cheerfully.

Others found themselves in harsh punitive situations in which prisoners were deemed expendable. Sent to a chemical factory at

Mannheim, Percy Goseltine spent most of the war carrying heavy trays of burnt copper ore. One day he fell and injured his spine. Barely able to walk, he was locked in a basement cell without food or sanitary facilities. The fumes left him permanently disabled.[20] Working in a fertilizer plant left Walter Hayes with chronic eczema on his thighs and legs.[21] Daniel Merry blamed fumes and chemicals at the creosote plant where he worked for peeling the skin from his neck and face. At an oil sands refinery at Wietze, Andrew Fernie slaved alongside fellow prisoners and civilian convicts shovelling oil sand through a grate into a hot furnace. The fumes often overpowered him to the point of fainting. At the end of the war, he was evacuated as a stretcher case.[22]

Goggles, protective clothing, and even rudimentary safety equipment were available for civilian workers, but rarely for prisoners. During sixteen months at a foundry in Osnabrück, Frank Tilley, a twenty-year-old Torontonian, worked twelve-hour days. Unlike German workers, who had goggles, he was given a piece of iron mesh to protect his face. By the end of his time as a prisoner, he was "a mass of small burns on his body, feet and face" and his eyesight was permanently damaged.[23]

The worst labour conditions for Allied prisoners were in German mines.[24] Malnourished prisoners filled ore cars and dragged them back to the lifts, or they cooled red-hot coke and loaded it on to trucks. John O'Brien, captured with the 28th Battalion, spent a year at the Augusta-Victoria mine. After any working day when a shift fell short of its quota, he recalled, the prisoners had to run a gauntlet of German miners armed with knotted ropes.[25] In other mines, prisoners were forced to stay below until they had met their target.

Prisoners sent to Göttingen, mostly men of the 15th Battalion, endured the notorious Beienrode salt mine. Prisoners worked eight-hour shifts, seven days a week, loading the sharp crystals into ore-cars with their bare hands. A ten-man shift had to fill fifteen cars and, after September 1917, thirty cars. Salt-sores, boil-like eruptions, were the curse of salt-mining. The camp doctor enjoyed lancing them, leaving them to bleed and absorb fresh salt. Another guard used a club to break the sores. Broken sores invited further infection. Cruelty fed on itself. Guards and civilian miners casually beat prisoners. Lance-Corporal Andrew Haley-Jones described a fellow victim as "one mass of weals and blood ... coming through the skin."[26] Sergeant Bill Alldritt, a YMCA secretary from Winnipeg, was sent to a salt mine at Schende after a severe beating for interceding with a German officer who was punishing another prisoner:

> I worked at this salt mine till December 1917—about 18 British prisoners here—the work was very hard—Practically everyone suffered a great deal from boils—I have been forced to work when I was covered with masses of them—up to a 100 or more at once on legs, thighs, under the arms. I have worked when I couldn't lower either of my arms and when I got working, matter would be running from boils in both armpits.... In October I escaped from here by making a duplicate key to a door—was at large 10 days—was captured at Munster—was taken back to salt mines—beaten into insensibility with rifles by the soldiers. Given extra work at the mines—put in prison on Sundays. In December I was sent back to Hameln, completed my imprisonment (one week I think) and stayed in Hameln till I was exchanged.[27]

Haley-Jones of the 15th Battalion described the routine at Beienrode: wake-up at 4:00 a.m. for ersatz coffee, *Appell* at 4:45 a.m. and down the shaft at 5:30 to begin work from 6:00 a.m. to 1:45 p.m., with a breakfast break for cold soup. The afternoon shift worked from 2:00 to 9:30 at night, seven days a week. Salt was blasted into large heaps of sharp, jagged crystals, which prisoners loaded into carts with their bare hands. Ten men in a shift had fifteen cars to load and, from September 1917, thirty. If they failed, they stayed down until the work was done. Canadians found the sanitary conditions disgusting. Haley-Jones described a two-bucket latrine for 600 prisoners at one end of the hut, and a brick-channel urinal that drained outside. "The smell both from the wash house and latrine is unbearable in the building and even if you stand at the far end of the building the smell is perfectly disgusting. The cook house is also in the same building but partitioned off and the smell of the sour cabbage and turnips is perfectly revolting."[28]

Perhaps the saddest victim at Beienrode was Bill Lickers, a full-blooded Mohawk. From the moment of his capture in 1915, he seems to have been picked out for beatings, as the Germans, many of them raised on Karl May's pulp novels about the Wild West, tried to find out for themselves whether an Indian felt pain. At Celle-Lager, a German officer had beaten him for refusing to give his allegiance to the Kaiser. At Beienrode, guards routinely locked him in a cell and visited him after hours to "administer discipline." A blow with a heavy lump of salt left Lickers paralyzed for the rest of his life.[29]

Assigning contingents of prisoners to civilian overseers and leaving discipline in the hands of junior NCOs almost guaranteed abuses. Neutral inspectors could not possibly visit the thousands of work sites. Prisoners who chose to complain had to use German channels and then face punishment for spreading lies.

A larger abuse, in direct defiance of the Hague Convention, was holding and working prisoners behind the German lines. Because they were captured in 1915 and 1916, most Canadian prisoners escaped an experience that became routine for those men taken in the last stages of the Battle of the Somme until the end of the war. Initially in the name of reprisal, and later out of a desperate need for labour, the Germans kept prisoners working in France on military tasks. Prisoner-of-war labour built the trenches, pillboxes, and dugouts of the Hindenburg Line; repaired roads and railways under shell fire; loaded supplies and ammunition; and performed tasks that no interpretation of the Hague Convention could condone. Furthermore, prisoners were kept in dugouts and open fields, often without boots or overcoats during the coldest winter in European memory. They were "harshed about" by guards, fed starvation rations, and transferred to Germany only when their health and strength broke down. Until they reached Germany, the existence of "behind-the-lines" prisoners was never acknowledged or, if it was, their location was given as Limburg, one of the largest camps in Germany.

As "prisoners of reprisal," Canadians taken at Vimy and the Newfoundlanders captured at Monchy-le-Preux were crowded into the dank, unventilated casemates of Fort McDonald at Lille. An overflowing latrine bucket occupied the centre of the floor. Private J.C. Thompson of the 19th Battalion recalled prisoners using their helmets and boots to hold the thin cabbage soup they were given.[30] German guards issued postcards to the prisoners to report their conditions to friends and "persons of influence in England" so that German prisoners would be treated better. Only in July were the Newfoundlanders' names released, and by September none had yet received parcels. The names of Canadian cavalrymen captured at Cambrai in November 1917 were not released until the following April.

In Germany, Canadians recorded the arrival of behind-the-line prisoners. At Minden, on a bitter February day in 1917, Chaplain Wilken met the several hundred Somme prisoners who survived— "living skeletons, frozen, hollow-cheeked human wrecks."[31] Captain F.S. Park, as a Canadian medical officer at the same camp, tried to persuade the Germans to transfer the worst cases to Switzerland.[32] The Germans refused. On October 8, 1918, Private C.A. Beesley reported that 346 emaciated prisoners arrived. Within two months, 127 of them had died.[33]

All prisoners live for the end of their captivity. Some Canadians— ninety-nine other ranks and a single officer, Major Peter Anderson from Edmonton—managed to escape. A Canadian infantry officer designed the impressive tunnel that enabled a number of British officers to escape Captain Niemeyer's clutches at Holzminden. Men in the *Arbeitkommandos* had an easier time getting away than did prisoners in camps. Most successful Canadian escapes were made from working parties, particularly from a bridge-building project at Engers, near Bonn. Travelling through the hostile and well-patrolled German countryside without language and navigational skills was difficult, and escaping to neutral Denmark, Switzerland, and Holland meant first crossing the heavily guarded German frontier. Many more tried than succeeded: the Canadian record-holder, Private Arthur Corker of the 7th Battalion, made seven attempts before he succeeded.[34]

Punishment on recapture was almost routine: a savage beating, followed by two weeks to a month of "strength arrest": solitary confinement on bread and water—a psychological ordeal that affected some prisoners for the rest of their lives. Helped a little by his skilful amanuensis, the novelist Nellie McClung, Private Mervyn Simmons of the 7th Battalion recalled the first of his pangs of starvation in the blackness of his steel-walled cell: "I was beginning to feel the weariness which is not exactly a pain but is worse than any pain. I did not want to walk—it tired me—and my limbs ached as if I had *la grippe.*" On one of the soup days, the guard apparently forgot him: "It may have been the expectation of food, together with the hot coffee, which stimulated my stomach, for that day I experienced what starving men dread most of all—the hunger-pain. It is like a famished rat that gnaws and tears. I writhed on the floor and cried aloud in my agony while the cold sweat dripped from my face and hands. I do not remember what I said....I do not want to remember."[35] That night, Simmons recalled, he expected to die but he survived to try again—successfully.

Lieutenant John Thorn, an officer, decided after suffering for his third attempt that he would simply wait for internment in Switzerland. That was a more common option for officers than for privates. As a humanitarian intervention in the European tragedy, the Swiss in 1914 organized a clearing-house for prisoners' names and locations. Then Switzerland helped set up an exchange of the most seriously wounded prisoners. Finally, hoping to fill some of their empty tourist hotels, the Swiss agreed to hold less seriously sick and wounded prisoners in their own territory and in better conditions. In 1917, when the Netherlands replaced the United States as protecting power for British interests, the Dutch also offered to take in prisoners from both sides. Since officers and NCOs could not work and merely absorbed scarce food and guards, Germany was willing to oblige, releasing those who had spent two years in captivity if they were ineligible or unfit for labour. Canadians made up part of the British quotas. By the end of the war, the officers and most of the NCOs captured at Ypres and Mont-Sorrel had been released or interned.[36]

Until 1917, Ottawa had been content to leave prisoner-of-war concerns to the British. The furore over private parcels helped raise Canadian interest in getting involved. The creation of the Overseas Ministry in 1916 gave Ottawa a better means to intervene on behalf of its prisoners, though not before the OMFC tackled more urgent problems.[37] By the end of 1917, two Canadian missions had visited prisoners in Switzerland and, a year later, Canada began to exert itself on behalf of its bored, resentful, and underfed internees in Holland. Of course, the news of internment led to a flood of letters from worried parents and their political representatives, demanding the Borden government's prompt intervention to release a son or nephew.[38] A YMCA visitor to the Netherlands noted that, even in captivity, Canadians had begun to assert themselves as different, insisting on their own facilities, apart from the British. "Life in the colonies has developed our men along sufficiently different lines from life in the Old Country," reported the YMCA representative, "that they call for special treatment."[39] Whether that included a special $3,000 YMCA hut was another matter. The Armistice of November 11 interfered with more active intervention.

At the end of October 1918, there were 78 Canadian officers and 2,248 other ranks remained in Germany, 106 internees in Switzerland, and 42 officers and 286 soldiers in the Netherlands. In all, 28 officers and 255 other ranks had died in German hands, and 100 had escaped. The November 11 Armistice required "immediate repatriation without reciprocity" of all Allied prisoners. In the chaos of postwar Germany, with the red flags of workers' and soldiers' committees popping up, that was easier promised than delivered. In a few camps, prisoners complained that they were beaten when they refused to continue working after the Armistice. One undersized prisoner was locked in a cupboard by a farmer when he announced he was going home. Repatriation, however, was virtually complete by January 1919.

Prisoners of war were processed through camps at Calais, and at Ripon in Yorkshire. The Overseas Ministry had arranged for a comprehensive debriefing of each man, with special attention paid to incidents of maltreatment. Medical teams waited to examine former prisoners for ill-effects. In practice, the promise of twenty-eight days' leave, large sums of back pay, and the prospect of visiting postwar London made these constraints almost unbearable. If prisoners had looked into the future, fewer would have reported "treatment good" and fewer medical boards would have scribbled "all systems normal." That would have required a superhuman submission to the needs of bureaucracy.

Allied wartime propaganda had focused on German maltreatment of prisoners. A postwar exhibit of Canadian war art gave pride of place to one of the most notorious wartime atrocities. When crowds poured off the Strand into Burlington House, they were transfixed by the sight that greeted them: a bronze frieze of a soldier, arms outstretched on a great door, hands nailed to the wood by bayonets. Below, a cluster of German soldiers drank, threw dice, and mocked the soldier's agony. It was, said the *Daily Express*, "the ghastliest thing in these rooms."[40] London crowds would have heard of Canada's Golgotha as one of the recent war's worst atrocities: a Canadian sergeant had been found crucified after the heroic battle at Ypres in 1915. A British sculptor, Derwent Wood, had preserved for all time the evidence that countless witnesses had seen with their own eyes.

Or had they seen it? Well, not exactly. Certainly many had claimed to be witnesses, but they had done so at different places and at different times. In France, Sir Arthur Currie had devoted time and energy tracing the fate of a man who might well have come from his own 2nd Brigade. He finally concluded that the story was a fabrication. Posterity has agreed. Canada's most famous prisoner of war was a fake.[41] A sculpture designed to strengthen resolve against the hideous Hun served, instead, to symbolize the lying warmongers who had blackened Germany's name and who, by the 1930s, would resume with their talk of German militarism, Nazi concentration camps, and Jewish pogroms.[42]

The postwar world soon had other concerns than the treatment of prisoners. In November 1918, British voters wanted the Kaiser hanged and the German lemon squeezed till the pips squeaked—but not for long. When the Germans, under duress, held war-crimes trials at Leipzig in 1920, three of the six British cases addressed prison-camp brutality. Sergeant Karl Heyen had beaten and tortured prisoners at a Westphalian mine, but he had had orders to enforce discipline. His sentence was ten months. The commander of a camp behind the lines received six months. He had gone on sick leave just before the death rate soared. A camp guard guilty of twelve of seventeen assault charges was sentenced to six months in prison.[43]

When Canadian prisoners of war came home at last, public interest in their suffering faded quickly. Most other Canadians knew that the Red Cross food parcels had allowed them to eat better than their German captors. They had survived when nearly 60,000 other young Canadians died. Most people had been told that their brave boys fought to the death: who were these slackers who had lived under the protection of the Hague Convention? Official war histories by A. Fortescue Duguid in 1937 and G.W.L. Nicholson in 1962 spared no space for prisoners, and their reminiscences were buried with other wartime ephemera. The scars of beatings and salt sores, the ordeal at Beienrode and K-47, the vestiges of starvation, and the psycho-neuroses of solitary confinement and "barbed wire disease" were left for time to heal.

With one exception: under sections 21 and 232 of the Versailles Treaty, Germany agreed to pay reparations. One of the grounds for payment was "maltreatment of prisoners of war." There were other grounds too. Any civilian who had suffered from the war had a claim, and the Canadian Reparations Commission turned first to shipowners, people who had lost baggage on the *Lusitania* and other torpedoed liners, and Canadian civilians interned at Ruhleben, near

Berlin. The first Canadian reparations commissioner, William Pugsley, died in office; his successor, James Friel, was challenged when he tried to reduce some of Pugsley's more extravagant awards. Reparations was one of many unfinished businesses inherited in 1931 by R.B. Bennett. He gave the task to Errol McDougall, a tough-minded Montreal lawyer who took a year to dispose of a couple of hundred civilian cases before he turned to the prisoners of war.

In interpreting the treaty, McDougall took a narrow view. Given conditions in wartime Germany, malnutrition was not mal-treatment; nor was punishment, however brutal, for escaping and disobedience. The Hague Convention had clearly established the jurisdiction of Germany military law over prisoners of war. McDougall also compared statements and medical records from Ripon and Calais to prisoners' claims of lasting injury from German brutality. The commissioner was as sensitive to signs of impu-dence as any German guard. Harry Howland, one of the leaders of the Bokelah "mutiny," annoyed McDougall almost as much as his German guards: "Claimant's demeanour before this Commission was truculent and defiant and not such as to rouse sympathy but rather created the impression that he was not only capable of incit-ing hostility but did arouse the active enmity of his captors."[44] McDougall reserved special praise for ex-prisoners who admitted that anyone could avoid punishment by keeping his mouth shut and doing as he was told.

McDougall, in short, was a tough judge. His tests were severe and his awards were small. The highest to any prisoner of war went to Bill Lickers, the semi-paralyzed Mohawk: $3,000.[45] Major Clyde Scott, the army's Director of Records, was rewarded for an anky-losed knee and a smoothly prepared brief. Those who had suffered at Beienrode and behind the lines got $1,000 or smaller awards; so did the few survivors of the "Iron Twenty" from Giessen. McDougall's final report in 1933 closed the government's books on Canadian prisoners of war in the First World War. Most Canadians had scarcely realized that such men existed.

CHAPTER TEN

SOLDIER'S HEART

MORALE AND DISCIPLINE

Much about the war is inscrutable. The toughest question is how men endured so much. The army had its institutional answers—*esprit de corps*, "comforts," discipline. The full truth was as simple or as complex as the human spirit: all men had limited heart, stomach, and stamina for battle. Among the many labels for the symptoms of strain were "disordered action of the heart" or, more commonly, "soldier's heart."

No ONE WHO JOINED the Canadian Expeditionary Force could have foreseen the ordeal of "going up the line," the terror of bombardment, the fear of going "over the top," the agony of a "Blighty," or the deadening brutality of becoming a "fannigan." Front-line soldiers of the 1914–18 war endured more continuous danger than soldiers of most previous wars in which major battles might occur once or twice in a campaigning season. A quarter-century later, the American army estimated that one of its soldiers could endure 200 to 240 combat days; the British army expected its men to put up with 400 days of front-line service, with more frequent rests; the CEF required its men to fight until the war was over, with a week's leave each year.

A.M. Munro explained to his father that his chums called him "bomb-proof Andy" because he had survived for months without a scratch, but, he confessed, "my nerves are in a pretty shakey state now, just the same as the rest."[1] Joseph Clark, a newly arrived subaltern on the Somme, insisted to his sister: "I'm having a whale of a time out here, kid. We are so much superior to the Huns on this blooming front that we don't know what a fit of the blues is like."[2] Two months later, after surviving the campaign, he apologized to his father for concealing his true feelings: "as a man undergoing at times terrific hardships and perils I should let you know how I feel about it all because you are my father and should know these things."[3]

Front-line soldiers lived with horrors that seared their souls: a close chum torn to bleeding fragments by a shell or a mortar bomb; the rotted trunk of a corpse dissolving when a burial party lifted it by its arms and legs. "At one point I stepped on something that yielded," wrote Lieutenant E.L.M. Burns, "and there rose up before me the rear end of a dead German. His clothes had been torn off and his flesh, visible in places, through the mud, was green." When he was a lieutenant-general years later, Burns's memory of the horror had not faded.[4] Bill Foster, a stretcher-bearer, never forgot the two men caught by a phosphorous shell during the Drocourt-Quéant advance: "It burned their hair and heads causing them to scream and I could do little for them for if I touched them it would burn my hands so they soon died."[5] At the St. Eloi craters, Frank Maheux recalled for his wife, "We were walking on dead soldiers and the worse was they was about 3 feet of mud and water. I saw poor fellows trying to bandage their wounds, bombs, heavy shells falling all over them.... it is the worst sight that a man ever wants to see."[6]

Soldiers coped as best they could. Fatalism helped: "Whether it be shell or machine gun bullet," explained Clark, "if your number is on it, no matter how you avoid it, your time's up."[7] Maheux, an ex-logger, explained: "It is the same as on the drives, when your time is up you have to jump."[8] "In France," Robert Correll told his sister, "they say that those guys that go over there expecting to get 'put under' nearly always are the ones to get it first, but we are not in that class.... I think I was born under a lucky star."[9] He died two months later in the horrible agony of gas gangrene, after a minor wound became infected. Others had premonitions of death. Frank

Baxter's chum, Percy Scott, carefully prepared three letters for his mother, his girl friend, and "Whosoever findest my body" before the attack at Amiens. All three reached his parents in Orillia.[10] Will Bird insisted that his brother, killed two years earlier, appeared repeatedly to lead him out of danger. When a couple of fresh reinforcements refused to leave the dugout during a bombardment, George Bell and his chum went out to fill their water bottles. When they got back, the dugout had vanished. "Had the recruits been less timorous they would have gone after the water and I would have been in the dugout when the shell landed."[11] He lived until 1973. Some, like Donald Fraser, improved their chances by prudent survival skills—keeping their head down, never taking the same route twice, never volunteering. On leave in 1917, his Scottish brother-in-law shuddered when Fraser mentioned that he was returning to Ypres. "His premonition turned out to be too true, for within a fortnight, I was smashed up and out of the Great Adventure for good, disabled for life. But everyone gets it at Ypres."[12]

Survivors were those who learned quickly. They never put their heads over the parapet twice in the same place; never dallied near crossroads or trench intersections; and they hit the ground, whatever its condition, whenever a bullet smacked dangerously close. Fraser, a cautious Scot, calmly noted the fate of more aggressive colleagues. Seeing a body, he learned that it was a man he knew. "The news did not surprise me for Douglas was an active man with his rifle, ever on the lookout to get a pot at something and this class of man usually gets it sooner or later."[13]

Death was infinitely cunning and unpredictable. On a December night, Colonel Creelman had his battery commanders to dinner. One of them, his designated successor, left to return to his post. "He never reached there and this morning his body was found in a big pond just behind this house. He had to pass it on his way in the pitch black night with a wind blowing nearly sixty miles an hour. He evidently stumbled into the pond and started swimming until his feet got tangled in weeds and held him to the bottom in deep water."[14]

Death came suddenly or slowly, inevitably to those who defied the rules of survival and capriciously to those who observed them. E.W. Russell worked in a tunnel next to a young former teacher, anxious to "do his bit" but full of plans for his next classroom. A little later, Russell was sent for as a stretcher-bearer and discovered that he was to remove the teacher's body.[15] Soldiers had their own word for finality: rations, ammunition, or a chum were "napoo."[16]

Most men arrived at the front fearful of the unknown, mastered it if they survived, and then, in days, months or years, wore out their courage. Finally, even outstanding soldiers felt crippled by terror. Death, even of a close chum, had to be forgotten. "The mind is averted as well as the eyes," wrote the Australian soldier-author Frederick Manning; "and one moves on, leaving the mauled and bloody thing behind, gambling, in fact, on the implicit assurance each one of us has in his own immortality."[17]

The truth about death was best hidden from civilians. Bishop P.K. Fyson believed that his son Oliver "gave his life willingly for king and country and could not die a nobler death."[18] Perhaps. Whether or not they were believers, soldiers found comfort in the religious teaching of their childhood and shared that comfort with their families. "Remember that I am in God's keeping," Gibson Skelton, a bank clerk from Vermilion, reminded his mother, "and in what better way could I die than in fighting for Him and his country." He died of wounds on September 12, 1916. His brother had died three months earlier.[19]

Death was almost always ugly and often painful. A tiny shell splinter in a vulnerable place could be both fatal and almost invisible. More normally, bullets and shell fragments tore flesh, shattered bones, sheered skulls, and left human remains lying in a stink of excrement. A machine-gunner at Passchendaele, Ray LeBrun, remembered his chum's death: "His blood and brain, pieces of skull and lumps of hair spattered all over the front of my greatcoat and gas mask."[20] Others died more slowly at a CCS, "triaged" as a hopeless case, or sent back to England to die of complications.

Without humour, soldiers joked about the contrasting value the army put on a horse, a vehicle, or a piece of equipment, and on a human life. The loss of "His Majesty's property" led to a small mound of paperwork, a court of inquiry, and "there was hell to pay if any negligence was suspected," Fred Noyes remembered, but men were simply marked "K in A." "It was easy to get men, but horses and equipment cost money." [21] A circular to Canadian units at the end of the battle of the Somme complained that men were still being buried in their full equipment, and rifles were being used as grave markers: "In view of the great difficulties which exist in keeping up the supply of arms and equipment, wastage in this manner must cease." [22]

Morale demanded that the remains be respected, even if, in the case of Gunner Angus MacLeish, all his comrades ever found was his paybook and a boot with his ankle protruding. [23] Soldiers sometimes took great risks to haul back the corpse of a pal or a respected officer; in quiet periods, men volunteered to bury their comrades. Fraser helped carry the body of an admired sergeant to a grave, only to find it was a double burial and the other man had already been deposited under several inches of blood-reddened water: "Kemp was buried in this mess. As soon as the body stirred the liquid, it just about made us vomit, the effluvium being terrible." [24]

The scale of the war forced the army to supersede the old rule that units buried their own men. What happened when a unit itself, like the Newfoundlanders at Beaumont Hamel or the 44th Battalion at the Somme, was virtually wiped out? [25] Making burials the job of units, or even comrades, left bodies scattered everywhere in the broad swath of battlefield, and thousands of grave sites were lost. By 1916, the Canadian Corps Graves Registration Unit oversaw divisional graves detachments.

Graves registration was hard and sometimes dangerous work. At Passchendaele, a registration officer and several other ranks were killed collecting the bodies of 1,900 Canadians and 800 dead from other contingents. For the Engineers' workshops, a preliminary for any offensive was the manufacture of white wooden crosses and, later, of skewer-like grave markers, each with a hook to hold an identification tag. A dead soldier's personal possessions and one of two identity discs were put in a white cotton ration bag; the other disc remained with the corpse. Military kit, equipment, and the rifle were laid beside the grave, to be collected for recycling by the Corps salvage troops. Until October 1917, bodies were wrapped in blankets and tied up with rope or wire, producing a home-front fuss that the price of the blanket was deducted from a dead soldier's pay account. Regulations thereafter required that bodies be wrapped in hessian, a coarse sackcloth normally used for sandbags. Medical units were each directed to stock 100 yards of the material.

The Imperial War Graves Commission, a by-product of the 1917 Imperial Conference, was chartered in May 1917 "to make fit provision for the graves of all Officers and men of the Empire." The commission fought the pressure to bring home the dead, as the Americans would. In the face of passionate pressure from those who demanded private markers and memorials, it also enforced equality of treatment for officers and other ranks by establishing a simple, standard headstone. Colonel Fabian Ware, in charge of graves registration for the BEF, rose to the rank of major-general in charge of burials. He also became the logical person to head the commission after the war.[26]

A wife or mother read the dreaded news from a drab official telegram from the "OIC Records" at Militia Headquarters. The official notice read: "Deeply regret to inform you [*number, rank, name, branch*] officially reported killed in action [or *died of wounds*] on [*date*]." A "Circumstance of Death Report," a Death Certificate, and, finally (when it was possible), a Burial Report followed.[27] Also when possible, families received a specially printed card with a photograph of the grave site.

Surviving officers customarily wrote to assure "next of kin" that a son or husband had served faithfully and had died suddenly, gallantly, and painlessly. Donald McKinnon's battery commander was franker than most: he "went out gritting his teeth and smiling, gallant and fearless as a man could be."[28] For men evacuated to a medical unit, letter writing became an obligation for chaplains or nurses. Nursing Sister Eva Plewman reported to Mrs. Correll that her son's last request to her was: "Tell Mom not to worry."[29] Between official and unofficial messages, errors happened. The senior chaplain of his division wrote to Joss Strong's parents on May 5, 1918, with his deepest sympathy. On May 9, the Strongs learned that their son was in hospital at Rouen. In fact, he had been killed on April 25.[30]

Once an officer was dead, his kit and equipment were inventoried and despatched to Cox & Co, the traditional military agent in London, for shipment to relatives. Personal and sentimental items from a lower-rank soldier's kit were sent to London or on to Ottawa to be mailed to next of kin in the British Isles or Canada. Pay stopped on the day of death. Most soldiers had little enough to leave their families, though a home or a farm could pose a problem. Each soldier's paybook included a simple will form—unfortunately too simple, under most provincial statutes, to transfer real property.

After three years, George Bell of the 1st Battalion confessed that his "human machine was getting to be in bad shape."[31] Apart from the emotional strain of fear and horror encountered at the front, most soldiers were perennially hungry, dirty, short of sleep, and physically worn. Until mid-1917 and the advent of pioneers, entrenching battalions, and other forms of uniformed labour, "rest" for the infantry was often a euphemism for hours of digging, unloading, and stacking artillery ammunition. Staffs insisted on vigorous training and exhausting route marches in full equipment to "harden" troops for the days of "open warfare" that always lay beyond the next big "push." Even at its least demanding, soldiering in France imposed a brutal physical strain on anyone who had not found a "cushy" or "bomb-proof" job as a cook, clerk, or rear-area "detail."

The army recognized that leave was a legitimate release from the emotional tension and physical exhaustion of the front, but it distributed the blessing parsimoniously. After all, leave took men from the front, where manpower was always in short supply; it overstrained the battered French railway system and cross-Channel shipping; and it unleashed hordes of muddy, potentially turbulent men on London and other British cities. Too many of men on leave got drunk or infected with VD.

Leave allocations for the Canadian Corps ranged from a hundred men a day during midsummer campaigning to double that number during the quieter winter season. In November 1916, GHQ allocated the Canadians 108 leaves a day for men with nine or more months in France. A month later, with the battle on the Somme fully wound up, the allocation rose to 254. After Vimy, the Canadian Corps was granted 174 leave vacancies a day, with 21 officers and 138 other ranks allowed ordinary leave and 2 officers and 12 other ranks eligible for "special leave." A Canadian soldier could hope for ten days of leave a year. Two of the days vanished in travelling time to and from England. Officers could expect their ten days every quarter. No favour was more bitterly resented by men in the ranks.

Like other long-sought pleasures, leave often fell short of expectations. With only a few minutes' notice, a soldier collected his kit and walked or hitched a ride back to the divisional railhead, his cherished pass folded into his paybook. In winter, unheated windowless carriages worsened the ordeal of the slow, halting railway journey to Le Havre or Boulogne. A leave camp at Boulogne specialized in hot baths, fumigation, and better-than-average food. Usually soldiers arrived in the evening, spent the night at the camp, and departed by channel steamer in the morning, reaching London's Victoria station by late afternoon.

The thrill of the fabled "Big Smoke," reported by freshly arrived CEF volunteers, had usually vanished by the time the same men returned, weary and bedraggled, from a year in the trenches. George Bell, emerging from London's Victoria station in his torn, mud-caked greatcoat, laden with his full pack and rifle, felt like an alien. "No one notices me and I am unspeakably lonely, a solitary figure in that city of millions."[32] Like most other soldiers, he found a cheap hotel; budgeted his money for meals, a few shows, and souvenirs; and soon found his thoughts drifting back to his comrades in France. Andrew Munro was more cheerful: "When I landed in England, I was mud from head to foot, unashamed and dirty, some sight believe me." He found the Maple Leaf Club, opened by Lady Julia Drummond for Canadians on leave, got a bath and clean underwear, "and soon felt like a new man."[33]

Some officers moved their families to England, and British-born soldiers usually stayed with relatives. For Canadians with no family in England, leave could be a forlorn experience. Civil and military police hunted vigorously for drunks, deserters, and illegal absentees. Innumerable smartly dressed officers expected salutes. "I am getting sick of this place," confessed Maheux after only a couple of days; "every body are strangers to me that makes it worse."[34]

Having weighed the risks from Paris's 97,000 prostitutes against savings in shipping and the convenience of having its men closer at hand, the British opened the French capital as a leave centre in 1917.[35] Canadians found it a popular alternative to London. The Army & Navy Leave Club and the YMCA each offered rooms for five francs (a dollar) a night, and a large hall for dances, with dancing pumps for rent and English girls as partners, "most of them very pretty."[36] The "Corner of Blighty" in the Place Vendôme offered free tea, and the *Daily Mail* provided a free map. British ladies in Paris arranged sightseeing tours. A stern lecture on VD and twenty-four-hour prophylactic centres provided protection from other welcoming ladies. So did strict police regulations unknown in England until 1918. For many Canadians, the best feature of Paris was the absence of "officers only" signs: one small manifestation of republican spirit was that French colonels and *poilus* drank, ate, and danced in the same places.[37]

Like their men, Canadian families had not anticipated the length of the war or the strain of coping amidst anxiety. In 1914, marriage ties were permanent, divorce was a costly rarity, and deserting one's wife and family a largely hidden and unmeasured crime. Those who brought their families to England left them to the strains of living in a strange country, often far from emotional and financial support. When the soldier's wife was English, and could guarantee that she would not become a public charge, the Canadian Patriotic Fund provided passage money: it could not guarantee her happiness in her "Old Country."

Between the Patriotic Fund and separation allowance, Ottawa complacently assumed that it had relieved soldiers of family worries, but primitive bureaucracies never caught up with the complexity of the human condition. Separation allowance, for example, might have seemed straightforward to its designers, but it produced a variety of headaches. Of more than 200,000 files in Ottawa, about 40,000 were in limbo by 1917 as investigators tracked down allegations of fraud. Married men insisted they were single, wives claimed to be deserted, and widowed mothers complained when their sons married and they lost their allowance. In October 1916, an order-in-council on "unmarried wives" directed that a woman supported at the time of enlistment would be favoured over an earlier and often legal wife in England.[38] In 1917, a board of review was appointed to provide an avenue for appeals.[39] The complex marital relations of members of the CEF would make a useful basis for studying Canadian family life.

Considering their predominantly British roots, surprisingly few CEF members married in England. Soldiers needed their commanding officer's permission to marry and, unlike what happened during the Second World War, most Canadians spent most of the war in France or Flanders. Official policy reflected Major-General Carson's fear that popularizing the $20-a-month separation allowance would bankrupt the country: "There is no doubt at all," he warned, "but that we are being 'soaked' with many men that are getting married."[40] Private William Kerr was one of the exceptions: he found his future wife in a Wesleyan chapel canteen at Bramshott and discovered that his stutter and her shyness made them a compatible couple.

In 1917, as the German U-boat blockade squeezed Britain's food supplies, the Overseas Ministry attempted to reverse the flow of families to England. OMFC officials persuaded 15,000 Canadians wives and children to accept transportation back to Canada.

Anxiety about families back home in Canada could prey on a soldier's mind. A battered photograph and a few creased letters in a soldier's haversack were a poor excuse for family life. A soldier wondered if his baby would recognize him when he returned, and, perhaps spurred by his own guilty conscience, worried about whether his wife had remained faithful. At home, wives waged a lonely struggle to keep children under control without a husband's heavy hand.

In theory, the Patriotic Fund existed to solve family problems, meet financial need, and, with its "Third Responsibility," supply the wisdom, frugality, and moral rectitude that the absent male might ideally have provided. That was not necessarily the image of "The Patriotic" in the eyes of wives (or their husbands). Frank Bell recalled that the CPF in Montreal was "run by a group of rich men's wives and if they found out that a wife was running around, if she was living beyond her means (they thought) or something, they would cut her off."[41] Even renting a telephone seemed an extravagance for a private's wife.

Proud of their self-reliance, men resented that the army had made them dependents on charity, however patriotic. When his wife in Regina claimed to be starving, Private M.C. Lewis appealed directly to the prime minister: "I am no beggar, sir, and all I ask for is that my wife and children are looked after while I am away and my house and bit of land protected."[42] "Don't be a bit backward about going after the Patriotic & get all you can," Ernest Hamilton urged his wife, Sara.[43] The wife of another man in his hut also had two children and, Hamilton had been told, she got more.

In theory, CEF regulations allowed officers and men to apply for special leave to sort out urgent problems at home, but the privilege was chiefly enjoyed by senior officers who could easily be replaced. Only a few hundred of the third of a million Canadian other ranks ever qualified to return to Canada. Bombardier John Miller reported that his hired man had quit and he stood to lose his farm. Gunner Saul, sole support of an invalid wife and three children, had an $800 mortgage coming due and no means to pay it off. Sergeant Broadbent's mother died intestate, leaving two younger children alone in the world. All had served more than a year in France; all were denied special leave.

The Post Office did its best to bridge the gap between soldiers and families, sending enough staff to provide a railhead office for each division and suboffices where soldiers bought stamps and money orders. Canadian mail reached London, was bagged by the

British post office for units in the field, and reached them by the usual daily ration train. The chief delay was censorship: soldiers were not allowed to discuss troop movements, armaments, or morale, or to offer "criticism of operations, other branches, allies and superiors." Part of a soldier's humiliation was the knowledge that his officers read every word of his personal letters and, as mess waiters knew, sometimes joked about them with brother officers. Soldiers could ask for one "green" envelope a week for specifically private and personal matters, to be censored only at the base, but often these were unavailable. Those who broke censorship rules faced court martial, and the 10th Brigade lost the right to green envelopes for a time because of security breaches. Censors preferred soldiers to use the renowned Field Service Post Card, with its fill-in-the-blanks approach to communication and its plaintive final sentence: "I have received no letter from you lately—— / for a long time——."

Canadians wanted news from home. Newspapers and magazines took weeks to arrive, and London newspapers seldom had anything worth reading about Canada or, for that matter, about the war. In 1916, Hughes authorized a fifty-word daily news cable to the Corps. To help soldiers come to the right conclusions before the 1917 election, the Canadian-born London newspaper magnate Lord Beaverbrook created the a handsomely produced little tabloid the *Canadian Daily Record*, which mixed a little wire-service copy from Canada, enthusiastic reports about the war, and official photos from his other wartime enterprise, the Canadian War Records Office. Most soldiers knew propaganda when they saw it, but apart from letters from home and crudely reproduced trench newspapers, there was no real alternative. Along with the British *Wipers Times*, scores of cheaply cyclostyled unit newspapers, such as the 4th Battalion's *Dead Horse Corner Gazette* or the 14th Battalion's *Growler*, appeared intermittently—always "approved by the commanding officers." The *Daily Record* continued to the end of the war.

Forcibly separated from home and family, men shaped their own

lives, often in ways polite society would not have preferred patriots
to behave. Gambling was a soldier's chief pastime, whether with a
greasy, broken-cornered pack of cards or with an illicit Crown-
and-Anchor board operated by some wily entrepreneur. What else
could fill hours of utter boredom and, if a soldier's life was at risk,
why not chance the few shillings or francs that separated him from
the next payday?

Drunkenness was a serious problem in the CEF, made worse by
the hypocrisy engendered by the contemporary prohibition campaign in Canada.[44] Rum fuelled soldiers before attacks and
through the brutal winters. Officers had limitless access to liquor,
and mess life revolved around the bar. Soldiers in France spent
their spare hours in *estaminets*, the tiny taverns that occupied the
front rooms of countless farms. The chief attraction was weak beer
at a cent a glass and thin red wine at 1.74 francs a bottle. Men supplemented their unappetizing rations with eggs and chips at an
average of one franc (20 cents) per meal.

Though they lived among French and Flemish civilians, soldiers insisted in their memoirs as well as their letters home that the
local women were unattractive. For most, language remained a
barrier. French women, claimed Archie Surfleet, were too old and
tired. Apart from the men of the French-speaking 22nd Battalion,
few soldiers acquired more than a handful of mispronounced
phrases, and inhabitants responded, sometimes in innocence, with
the raw profanities learned from their English-speaking visitors.
Teaching such words to French or Belgian women was one of a soldier's cruder pleasures.

Troops billeted with civilians learned to make themselves at
home, enjoying the domesticity of eggs chuckling in a frying pan
or the initially alarming sight of a woman slicing a loaf clutched
tightly against her stomach. Some local customs were unexpected.
One man recalled how he wrote letters and chatted about Canada
while his elderly hostess, with no undue modesty at all, stripped
and climbed into her laundry tub for a bath. Then her daughter
came home from a job in a mine, removed her clothes, and calmly
joined her. "She was as slim as her mother was fat, and I made a lot

of mistakes in my writing." Finally, the father returned, "stood in the tub and was scrubbed by Madame."[45]

Despite the hundreds of thousands of young Canadians who spent years in France, only a few hundred marriages resulted. Seventy-five per cent of the heavy incidence of VD resulted from contacts in England. Most Canadians found the long line-ups and brisk efficiency of French *maisons tolerées* unappealing. Understandably, surviving letters and memoirs insisted that Canadians were too gentlemanly to take advantage of women, though court-martial records and a few memoirs give a harsher view. Tom Dinesen found his Canadian friends kind, decent, and tactful to each other, but not with women: "With the girls you may use any trick however mean and shabby—the only thing is to get what you want from them and then beat it."[46] Fred Noyes and his fellow ambulance men roared with delight when a corporal tipped "a broad-hipped Flemish girl" into the swill-tub she had come to collect: "She was quite a sight, what with her broad expanse of red drawers, her violently kicking legs and her waving sabots—and more of a sight when she extricated herself." When her vengeful father appeared, waving a sickle, the soldiers assured him that the perpetrator had already been shot.[47] When Elise Jerome refused "money for immoral purposes," a drunken Canadian struck her and her friend, knocked over her sewing machine, and smashed her furniture. A court martial gave him fifty-six days of F.P. No. 1. The staff of the First Army denounced the trivial punishment: "a worse case of assault could hardly be imagined."[48]

If few soldiers had the opportunity or the inclination to make friends with women, the institution of "pal-ship" or the "buddy system" was almost universal. Most veterans remembered a close friendship, often established in training and preserved until an all-too-early death. In the chill of a barrack hut or a dugout at the front, men slept together for warmth, shared parcels from home, and swore to see the other to safety if wounded, or properly buried if dead. Once broken by death, wounding, or transfer, the first friendship was seldom fully renewed. The implication of homosexuality is more apparent now than it may have been to men in 1917.

Ernest Hamilton complained to his wife that his bunk-mate "slept too close for a man."[49]

Several officers charged with sodomy were acquitted, essentially on the grounds of fine character and the fact that their accusers were men in the ranks and there were no corroborating witnesses. One of them, an Anglican chaplain, had gone through more bat-men than any other officer, according to his adjutant, but the court accepted that, as he was a respected clergyman and former Boy Scout commissioner, his word could be trusted. His accusers, the court ruled, were "base, despicable and uncorroborated." One officer who was convicted of using his authority to assault his men had notably lacked friends and a war record. He was cashiered.[50]

Gradually and reluctantly, the CEF took responsibility for the morale and morals of its soldiers. Officially, this was a primary role for regimental officers, though the inherent fatuity of expecting a soldier to treat a callow subaltern as a father-figure reached its limits in wartime.

Most units planned long in advance for a special celebration at Christmas, a time of year that inspired soldiers with memories of home and family. Army custom dictated a special commitment of regimental funds to provide a traditional feast. In Saturnalian style, officers served dinner to their men and endured a certain amount of teasing. Kilted battalions ignored Christmas and celebrated Hogmanay instead. Colonel Leckie's 16th Canadian Scottish welcomed 1916 with "Soup Puree a la French Maid, Roast Turkey and Roast Beef, Tatties mashed and Green Peas shelled, Plum Pudding and Respirator sauce, Stewed Apples, Trench mortar Jelly, Cafe, Cigars and Toasts."[51] Private Albert Smith's Christmas a year later was celebrated with turkey, peas, corn, fancy biscuits, a handful of raisins and grapes, and a plum pudding doubtless supplied from the Army Christmas Pudding Fund, backed by two London daily newspapers.

Not everyone could celebrate Christmas. Fraternization between British and German troops during the famous "Christmas truce" in 1914 had led to courts martial and annual warnings. Division headquarters ordered double sentries and warned that the Hun was capable of any fiendish trick. In 1916, with ammunition plentiful, a light barrage was ordered for Christmas Day. Many front-line soldiers spent at least one Christmas in the line, contemplating rain, snow, and another bully-beef dinner.

With few exceptions, Canadian soldiers acknowledge a Christian denomination on their enlistment papers, though some denominations alleged that men who were vague on the subject were automatically ascribed to the Church of England. This was more than a jealous sneer. Denominational entitlement to chaplains depended on the religious affiliations stated by soldiers on enlistment. Anglicans predominated; Presbyterians followed; and Methodists, to their indignant fury, lagged even behind Catholics.

While Protestants were considered at least somewhat interchangeable, Catholics were not. Language was a further complication since Catholic chaplains had to serve virtually all the French-speaking soldiers, though the great majority of their flock was English-speaking. A bitter wrangle over the overwork and underrepresentation of Catholic chaplains in France was one of the many issues inherited and at least partially resolved by the Overseas Ministry when it emerged at the end of 1916.

Chaplains preserved the values of an army filled with conventional and sometimes devout Christians. Most soldiers resented church parades and patriotic sermons, but, as Tom Dinesen discovered, they found his open atheism disconcerting. Most soldiers believed that men were free to seek salvation any way they could, but there simply had to be a God, if only to keep order, reward the good, and punish the wicked. It was not always clear in soldiers' minds whether chaplains were wicked or good. A handful, led by the 1st Division's venerable Canon Frederick Scott, acquired impressive reputations among soldiers of all faiths. The tall, white-haired, and unassuming Scott wandered among his vast flock, sharing dugouts, huts, and rations with soldiers, and braving their dangers until he was wounded at Cambrai in the last month of fighting.[52] Catholic padres were rumoured to risk their lives more readily than Protestants, and Father W.T. Workman, an English Benedictine and the chief Catholic chaplain with the Corps, ranked, in his more austere way, with Scott. Military authorities preferred chaplains to remain at hospitals and casualty clearing stations, comforting the wounded, but the Corps's chief chaplain, Colonel J.M. Almond believed the view that chaplains' prestige was enhanced by sharing front-line dangers—and prestige was a vital commodity if chaplains were to lead the Christian revival Almond expected in the aftermath of war.

However, with their ranks and aloofness, all army chaplains clearly belonged to the species called officers. It was not much easier for a private to share fears and doubts with them than with any other captain or major. Shocked by swearing, Major-General David Watson of the 4th Division gave his patronage to the spread of the Holy Name Society. The 1st Division's Sir Archibald Macdonell preferred to denounce swearing in a personal message to "The Old Red Patch," warning officers in particular that bad language would damage their prospects. Some colonels and brigadiers supported their chaplains; others regarded them as a nuisance.[53]

More important than any chaplain in most soldiers' lives—and a bitter rival to the Chaplains' Service—was the Young Men's Christian Association (YMCA). Beginning with an authorized strength of six YMCA officers per division, by the end of the war the "Y" had 140 officers and 745 other ranks. It ran canteens, cinemas, and coffee bars and used the profits to buy sports equipment. The YMCA organized baseball leagues and sports tournaments and managed the huge Dominion Day celebration at Tincques in 1918, the apotheosis of the increasingly nationalistic Canadian Corps. YMCA officers helped inspire the ambitious adult-education program entitled "the University of Vimy Ridge." The YMCA's Captain Al Plunkett assembled the singers, musicians, and the brilliant female impersonators who made up the 3rd Division's famous Dumbbells.[54] Others helped create the 4th Division's Maple Leaves, and most other amateur entertainment in the Corps. Soldiers appreciated YMCA huts with their coffee bars, writing paper, and reading rooms and the chance to buy such homemade products as Lowney's chocolate bars, Imperial Mixture, and Old Chum tobacco, but they never forgot that the "Y" expected payment. Freezing and famished after a two-day train journey to Boulogne, John Sutton found that the YMCA hut would not sell him a meal until 6:00 p.m. The same regulation applied to the Salvation Army canteen, but its staff gave him a free meal and hoped for payment when he had the chance. Sutton acquired a further complaint when he paid a dollar for a pair of socks at a YMCA hut only to find a note inside from the Winnipeg girl who had donated them: "Since then I have felt kindly towards the Salvation Army and otherwise to the YMCA."[55]

Welfare in the field included "comforts." When Sam Hughes gave commissioned rank to the two women members of the Canadian Field Comforts Commission, he was unaware that Canadians in England, spurred on by the acting high commissioner and his wife, had created the Canadian War Contingent Association with much the same goal: delivering homemade socks, mitts, handkerchiefs, shirts, towels, cigarettes, and ultimately mouth-organs, pipes, boxing gloves, tooth brushes, and 21 tons of maple sugar to men in the field. From the outset, the two organizations were rivals: thanks to Sir George and Lady Perley, the association was better placed to prevail.

Long before 1918, most Canadian soldiers had lost any enthusiasm for the war, but they had not changed their minds that it must be won. Like the Australians and Scots, Canadians regarded the Germans as efficient, dangerous, and relentless enemies. In the Canadian Corps, there was little of the spirit of "live and let live" Tony Ashworth discovered among English divisions. Unlike the Australians, though, Canadians were content to fill their ranks with conscripted "slackers" if it brought victory closer and improved their own chances of survival. Twice Australian Imperial Force (AIF) voters helped defeat conscription to avoid polluting their ranks. The CEF voted overwhelmingly in 1917 for the Union government and the Military Service Act.

In the summer of 1917, the Imperial Order Daughters of the

Empire (IODE) had taken up the cause of home leave for the "Old Originals." Sir Arthur Currie approved, but only if the men were replaced from Canada. By October, discovering something the soldiers wanted suddenly acquired political importance. The Military Voters Act of 1917 enfranchised all soldiers and nursing sisters, regardless of age or prior residence in Canada.[56] Voting for the Union Government and the Military Service Act would send conscripts to the front and allow "Old Originals" and Second Contingent men to see Canada again. The promise of three months of home leave won Maheux's vote for Sir Robert Borden's candidate: "if he don't keep his promise we will cut his xxx when all the old boys goes back home."[57]

Maheux would be disappointed. In all, only 838 "Old Originals" came home on furlough. Men from the 1st Division destined for home leave shared a sermon from Canon Scott, a stirring address from a staff officer on pride in "The Old Red Patch," and a "right hearty" rendition of "God Save the King." They got away before the German March offensive killed the furlough policy. Most of the beneficiaries managed to stay in Canada for the rest of the war.

Armies exist to fight, not to improve their soldiers' character or to provide employment or recreation. Most generals had little understanding of what made their men fight. Largely immune from the terror and squalour of the trenches, remote in their comfortable châteaux, buffered by their staff officers, they remembered campaigning against Pathan tribesmen or Boer farmers. A majority of the Canadian generals had served in South Africa, some of them in the ranks, but their experience had little relevance to the drawn-out misery and recurrent terror their men faced in the trenches and during periodic "pushes."

The Canadian Corps commander seems to have been particularly well buffered from contact with his men's state of mind. Admirable in his tactical skills, his organizational sense, and his admirable preference for wasting shells, not lives, Sir Arthur Currie was anything but a charismatic leader. Frank Baxter recalled a couple of recruits marvelling at Currie's substantial shape: "Who'd want to be 'three-to-a-loaf' with that bugger?"[58] Currie's closest contact with most of his men occurred at ceremonial inspections. Unschooled in higher military etiquette, he often behaved like a sergeant-major, pouncing on dirty rifles and checking haversacks for the requisite clean towel.

Currie also had a taste for grandiloquence. On March 17, 1918, at the time of the German offensive, an evil genius persuaded him to issue an "Order of the Day": "You will not die but step into immortality. Your mothers will not lament your fate but will be proud to have borne such sons. Your names will be revered forever and ever by your grateful country and God will take you unto Himself." Despite lavish praise for the message from *The Times* and Sir Douglas Haig, Currie's men saw a pompous general telling them how to die. At least one brigadier had the sense to scrap the message.[59] Other soldiers nursed the memory of the pompous prose to their graves.

Beyond orotund orders of the day, generals had a few incentives to offer gallant soldiers and some brutal penalties for the others. Traditionalists had protested that, since all soldiers were expected to be gallant, any distinction would be invidious, but the French example proved contagious, particularly when they were allies in the Crimean War. The first British army decorations for gallantry began in 1854 with the promise of a medal for "distinguished conduct," and in 1856 with the institution of the soon-coveted Victoria Cross.

Decorations and medals should not be confused. *Medals*, such as the 1914–15 Star, the British War Medal, and the Allied Victory Medal, were issued to all serving men and women who participated in a campaign. Any CEF member who served overseas earned the last two, while "Old Originals" and any soldier who reached France by December 31, 1915, qualified for the first.[60]

Decorations were awarded to individuals as a special distinction. In the First World War, as Andrew Munro insisted, the Victoria Cross, or VC, was "the only one worth having now-a-days."[61] Private Thomas Dinesen won his on August 13, 1918, as the steam went out of the Canadian attack. He persuaded fellow Black

Watch privates near Parvillers to follow him until he had taken two miles of trenches.

There were other respectable decorations. Any effective unit commander could expect the white enamelled cross of the Distinguished Service Order (DSO). Gallantry in a junior officer earned the purple and white ribbon of the Military Cross (MC). Other ranks qualified for the Military Medal (MM) or, more exceptionally, for the Distinguished Conduct Medal (DCM). A second award of the same decoration brought a silver bar on the medal and a small silver rosette on the ribbon.

Usually soldiers disparaged decorations, insisting, like Fraser, that they were "sprinkled around like water, the vast majority of the recipients doing absolutely nothing out of the common to earn these awards."[62] Certainly there was a large measure of luck— notably, being observed by an officer who survived to write a recommendation. That benefited runners, signallers, and others who worked under an officer's eye and overlooked men whose heroism was remote from scrutiny. Still, other ranks' decorations, despite occasional dismissive comments, "did not come up with the rations."[63]

The army's ultimate resource for making men fight, especially as the long war ground on, was discipline. A soldier who learned instinctive obedience to the repetitive and even absurd orders on the drill square or in the barrack room would presumably obey on the battlefield, even if his life was forfeit. Canadian Corps orders, echoed through divisions, brigades, and battalions, insisted that there could be no let-up. "Discipline is strengthened by insisting at all times on the thorough performance of all duties, by demanding smartness in appearance, tidiness in camp, punctuality, care in saluting and attention to all the minutiae associated with the soldier's daily life."[64] Burt Woods, a sergeant from western Canada, learned his lesson to any general's satisfaction and passed it on: "One thing I always learned to my men who was under me: obey your orders whether your officer or sergeant is giving you the wrong order; you obey whether it is right or wrong. That's one thing I used to drill in. Your superior was never wrong. If he did something he shouldn't have done, you didn't go against it.... You always obeyed orders as they were given to you by the command, because your superior was always ahead of you, and superior to you."[65]

Veterans would have recognized Woods's dictum without necessarily endorsing it. Discipline helped terrified men behave well when they faced mortal peril. Men who knew their weapons well used them better than the half-trained recruits who always formed a substantial portion of any battalion in action. Their example, in turn, steadied the newcomers. Yet, for some soldiers, discipline alone failed. Even the best front-line soldiers had their breaking-points. Over time, perhaps too late for the war, the observant recognized that courage was a finite human resource.

In *The Anatomy of Courage*, Lord Moran observed, "Men wear out in battle like their clothes."[66] A regimental medical officer in the 1914–18 war and later better known as Winston Churchill's doctor, Moran used the analogy of a bank account which a soldier drew on daily. Another veteran British medical officer, Frank Richardson, compared courage to a car battery that can be recharged but, over time, holds the charge for shorter periods, and eventually not at all.[67]

Front-line soldiers felt fear in all its symptoms, from the fiercely pounding "soldier's heart," uncontrollable trembling, and cold sweat, to the final, humiliating loss of bowel control. Courage drained faster when men sat immobile and helpless under an artillery bombardment or waiting for an attack. The myth of shell shock allowed men who had been buried alive to claim evacuation even if they were physically unharmed. Fighting back, even the near-futile gesture of shooting a rifle at aircraft, helped sustain a soldier. Ernest Davis and his brother recalled "a sort of fierce enjoyment—usually productive of much violently abusive language addressed to the enemy, if one was so inclined—and we both were."[68] External appearances were no predictor of courage. At Courcelette, waiting for his battalion to attack, Fraser saw an officer, "a little middle-aged man, badly shell shocked, his mouth quivering like a child crying," led out by a private holding his hand.

He also remembered a big, blustering captain from the 50th Battalion as "without exception the windiest and biggest funk of an officer I ever came across."[69] Another "very fussy, effeminate" officer who had to have his tea just so, turned out to be absolutely fearless under fire.[70]

A soldier whose courage failed faced a few desperate options. He could run, hide, or even give himself the "Blighty" for which so many soldiers yearned. More soldiers dropped on the battlefield than were ever knocked over by enemy shells or bullets, but a defender's artillery and machine-guns swept no man's land, and there was little added safety in falling behind the line of attack. Men who fled had to slip through crowded support and reserve trenches, and past the cordon of stragglers' posts established by the military police. Few could survive for long in the French or Flemish countryside or escape across the English Channel.

Some soldiers deliberately made themselves sick. George Bell remembered a man scrounging rotten meat from an incinerator: "to eat it meant ptomaine poisoning but he was willing to take a chance....His nerves could stand it no longer."[71] The army watched closely for evidence of self-inflicted wounds (SIWs). By 1917, trench foot was *prima facie* evidence; by 1918, so was the lack of a respirator during a gas attack. E.W. Russell recalled a former NWMP sergeant who dug a hole, planted his foot and a grenade, and blew his leg off to escape service. CEF records include 582 cases of SIW in France, among them 4 officers. One of them was summoned back from Canada where he had been promoted to lieutenant-colonel to command a new CEF battalion. He was court-martialled and cashiered.[72] Humbler suspects were sent to special SIW hospitals, convicted by standing courts martial, and given sentences that ranged from a few days of field punishment to two years' imprisonment with hard labour. Private Michael Norman was typical: wounded at Hill 70 and a survivor of Passchendaele, Norman got twenty-eight days of F.P. No. 1 after he shot himself while cleaning his rifle.

Traditionally, officers who "lost their nerve" had been invalided home to avoid disgrace. Only those who had few friends in a new battalion faced the shame of a court martial and cashiering. Ex-lieutenant F.M. Leader, a Saskatoon accountant condemned to ten years in Maidstone Prison, insisted that the 72nd Battalion had never wanted him. Nor had the 46th Battalion ever welcomed Lieutenant Morley Anderson, whose terror in the trenches was clearly associated by members of his court martial with his self-confessed habit of masturbation.

Good units spotted officers and men who were breaking under the strain and tried to send them on leave before their turn or arrange a course or a few weeks at one of the rest camps established behind the lines. Currie finally managed to spell off his weary brigadiers, giving them turns commanding training camps in England. After Passchendaele, Brigadier-General Griesbach told company commanders that they could ease the problems created by desertion and cowardice by getting to know their men: "Where a man is known to be a coward he ought to be got rid of. If he is a young, weak or nervous man, his failing should be suspected or foreseen and he should be disposed of in some other way before commission of the offence."[73] Fraser recalled that, when one terrified member of his company was not reformed by threats or ridicule, he joined "Canada's large army of misfits" down the line.[74]

The army's ultimate disciplinary weapon was the same fate that war itself threatened: death. Cowardice and desertion in the face of the enemy ranked with betraying a post and striking a superior officer as capital offences under the Army Act. Between 1870 and 1914, the British army had shot 3 of its men; in four years of war, it executed 346.

True to character, Sir Douglas Haig took a hard line: "I am of the opinion that it is necessary to make an example to prevent cowardice in the face of the enemy as far as possible."[75] Australians refused to allow their men to be shot and suffered in Haig's estimation; Canadians and New Zealanders conformed. In all, twenty-five Canadians were shot by firing squad, twenty-two for desertion, one (a previously decorated NCO) for misbehaviour in the face of the enemy, and two for murder. On review, most death sentences, including several on officers, were reduced to imprisonment. In most cases, men got another chance. For men in a state of terror, it was not much of a mercy. Two of those shot had been reprieved before. Others, as memoirs reveal, were carried by reluctant comrades out of pity for the fate that awaited them.[76]

Death by firing squad was bitterly controversial. As Voltaire had written of the execution of Admiral Byng, the death penalty was intended "pour encourager les autres." When Lieutenant-Colonel Thomas Tremblay returned to his 22nd Battalion, he found that the devastating casualties of the Somme had been replaced by the tramps and ne'er-do-wells recruited by other French-speaking CEF battalions. To restore his unit, he insisted on five successive executions. Fifteen other cases were commuted, many of them over Tremblay's objections. The 22nd Battalion's most recent historian, Jean-Pierre Gagnon, upheld Tremblay's tough attitude: "son bataillon representait la nationalité canadienne-française. Pour lui, l'indiscipline et l'absence illégale devait donc être mâtées. Autrement, elles risquaient de mettre en péril la réputation chèrement acquise de son bataillon, et aussi de discréditer la nationalité qu'il représentait sur le champ de bataille."[77]

Whenever possible, the soldiers of a condemned man's battalion were marched to whatever lonely site had been chosen for the execution, and the firing-squad was selected from his platoon. Executions occurred in the cold light of dawn, with the prisoner, escort, and attending chaplain all visible. "En passant près de nous," Arthur Lapointe recalled, "il nous jette un regard si triste que je me sens ému jusqu'aux larmes."[78] Guards strapped the man to a post behind a canvas screen, blindfolded him, and placed an aiming mark. The firing-squad, save for one man with a blank round, did its best; an assistant provost marshal waited to deliver a *coup de grâce*. Then the troops marched past the dead body.

Whatever their contempt for cowards, slackers, and "bomb-proofs," veterans who witnessed executions recalled long after their anguish, pity, and then fury at a military system that took a man beyond the limits of his endurance and then shot him. "That shuffling figure is one of us," George Bell of the 3rd Battalion recorded in his diary. "He has fought with us, slept with us, eaten with us. He comes from Canada where most of our homes are."[79] "To say that we were all dumbfounded & angry is to put it mildly," recalled D.E. Pearson, describing the same execution. "Some thought the Colonel was responsible & threatened to shoot him the next time we were in action. The feeling was that we were all volunteers...and that no volunteer deserved the death sentence if he was unable to face the enemy in battle."[80]

Posterity might agree, but there were many things posterity would find hard to understand about the First World War.

CHAPTER ELEVEN

RETURNED MEN

COMING HOME AGAIN

Unknown to most Canadians, a few officials offered Canada some rational, tough-minded, and pioneering policies for coping with returned soldiers. They offered "a minimum of sentimentality and a maximum of practical common sense." In the end, Canadians did what everyone else did and suffered the usual consequences.

A S EARLY as September 1914, at Valcartier, men who had gone off to war were sent home again. In January 1915, the first wounded members of Princess Patricia's regiment returned to Canada. With an insensitivity notable even by army standards, they were shipped from England with a draft of alcoholics, thieves, and other "King's Hard Bargains." At Halifax, they were stripped of their uniforms and shipped home to their relatives in clothes fit for tramps. When Sam Hughes finally acknowledged the problem, his harried staff proposed to put returning wounded under canvas at Valcartier and to ask the Red Cross or St. John's Ambulance to escort the men home. The more patriotic of the wealthy offered their summer mansions as convalescent homes. In Winnipeg, the Imperial Order Daughters of the Empire (IODE) offered a rest home with "a little bit of a motherly touch."[1] The Calgary Brewing & Malting Co. handed over an unprofitable hotel. An MP offered his unmarried daughter.

Sensing an impending scandal, Sir Robert Borden recognized that charity would not do for veterans.[2] In June 1915, he created the new Military Hospitals Commission (MHC), directed by prominent businessmen, to meet the needs of sick and wounded soldiers once they returned to Canada. At its head was Sir James Lougheed, a Calgary lawyer, government leader in the Senate, and minister without portfolio.

Canada had a lot to learn about veterans. The militia pension regulations in 1914 had been hurriedly improvised for the 1885 Rebellion and differed only in detail from arrangements made for the War of 1812. Captain John French, who perished heroically at Batoche, left his widow a pension of $514 a year; the widow and daughter of Gunner Ryan, who died unheroically in his bed, could count on $83. As for Private Neely's widow and orphans, they got nothing, for Toronto's police chief claimed that Maria Neely was "a loose, profligate woman."[3] A widow received a pension only if she were in need, remained unmarried, and "proved worthy of it."

Canada's military pensions followed the example of a British army recruited from the urban slums and the rural unemployed. The British had attempted to compensate for miserable pensions—and the frequent sight of legless, bemedalled beggars in the streets—with a profusion of military charities, ranging from the Royal Patriotic Fund for widows and orphans to the Corps of Commissionaires for steady old soldiers. The Soldiers' and Sailors' Family Association subsidized mothers and children left penniless by soldier-fathers. The Soldiers' Help Society taught handicrafts to the disabled. Retired officers and their ladies found power and occupation in managing such associations. Meanwhile the Royal Hospital, Chelsea, with its apple-cheeked pensioners in scarlet coats, partially camouflaged a thoroughly British example of amateurism, class distinction, and inefficiency.

Canada's counterpart was the Patriotic Fund, an all-purpose charity begun in 1812 and revived for the Crimean and Boer wars. Its managers enjoyed the freedom of a private charity, ignoring the undeserving and pleasing its wealthy patrons by responding to their sentiments. After the Boer War, for example, it financed an Oxford education for Lorne Mulloy, a former Queen's University student who had become famous as "the blinded trooper."[4] When the emergency 1914 session of Canada's Parliament re-established the CPF, Herbert Ames insisted that it could do no more than support the families of serving soldiers. Widows, orphans, and the disabled must be someone else's concern.

If wounded veterans were not to be left to charity, there was always the U.S. model. In a short list of democratic excesses in the neighbouring republic, the "pension evil" ranked with lynch law and elected judges. Ten years after the Civil War, with plenty of evidence that disabled veterans had been shamefully treated, the Grand Army of the Republic (GAR) was organized to represent crippled comrades and their widows. Allied with the Republicans, the GAR soon grew into an impressive lobby, with claims agents and pension attorneys as its outriders. Its priority soon switched from the widows and the disabled to all who had served in the war and who still had votes. Surely every one of them deserved something from the nation they had served—even for ninety days in a safe place. Narrowing its focus to only the most deserving would have robbed the GAR of its political strength. Democratic voters are not altruists. When Benjamin Harrison squeezed into the White House in 1888, the GAR took the credit. "God save the surplus," his pension commissioner, "Corporal" James Tanner cried, and pledged to drive a six-mule team through the Treasury.[5] Spending on veterans devoured a fifth of U.S. national revenue, and the flow increased at a rate that at least Canada's more affluent citizens found appalling.

Canada would have to find her own way between the American Scylla and the British Charybdis. Her agent would be the shrewd and perceptive Ernest Scammell, the able, if deferential, secretary the MHC borrowed from the Canadian Peace Centenary Association.[6] The son of an English Baptist minister who had worked hard for war veterans, Scammell set to work on a blueprint for MHC operations that put Canada well ahead of its co-belligerents. Scammell's views dominated a brief and amicable federal-provincial conference on October 18, 1915.

Scammell's priority was employment—understandable in a country still in the grip of a pre-war depression. Patriotic employers would take back their former workers; other veterans must be found work at suitable wages. "With regard to the disabled," warned Scammell, "their care is an obligation which should fall primarily on the state, and this liability cannot be considered as being extinguished by the award of a pension from public funds."[7]

A French expert, Dr. Maurice Bourillon, had insisted that each disabled soldier could be found suitable work, and many, with training, could even improve their earning capacity. Ina Matthews, sister-in-law of the Montreal multi-millionaire J.K.L. Ross, had offered a training scheme to Dr. Fred Sexton, principal of the Nova Scotia Technical College. Word of the scheme spread to Ottawa. Even with vocational training in its infancy in Canada, nothing is so powerful as an untested idea.

After a year of pointless, garrulous meetings, the MHC gradually yielded to the influence of the professional staff Lougheed and Scammell created. Scores of buildings were acquired, adapted, and equipped as hospitals, TB sanatoria, and lunatic asylums. Samuel Armstrong, who had developed the Guelph Reformatory and the Whitby Hospital, took over as MHC director. Using the latest "quick-build" methods, the MHC created new institutions across the country, from Halifax's Camp Hill Hospital to the TB sanatorium at Tranquille, B.C. After discovering that free-enterprise limb makers possessed limited skill and patents and unlimited appetites for profit, the MHC decided to manufacture prostheses in its own Toronto factory. Within a few years, the commission could supply artificial legs, boots, glass eyes, and face masks for the hideously scarred. Its arms were uncomfortable and ineffective, but no one else's were much better. After struggling with straps, hooks, and pulleys, most frustrated arm amputees tried to get what use they could from their stump. Canadian war blind were lucky if they benefited from St. Dunstan's, a hostel established by a British philanthropist, Sir Arthur Pearson, in London's Regent's Park. Canadian blind charities, eager to use blinded soldiers to improve their public image, protested and persuaded some of the homesick blind that they would be better friends to them than the government. The MHC responded by creating a special section for the blind under the charge of Captain E.A. Baker, a St. Dunstan's graduate who had been blinded as a young Canadian engineer officer in France. The St. Dunstan's philosophy and methods, plus Baker's energy, led to the Canadian National Institute for the Blind.[8]

The commission's staff soon realized that the disabled defied stereotypes. Out of 138,000 Canadian wounded, fewer than 70 had been blinded and 3,802 had lost limbs.[9] Most of the disabled had been sick, not wounded. Many should never have been enlisted in the first place. Coping with the Militia Department's recruiting mistakes kept the commission busy for a year, treating tuberculosis and heart-disease cases before large numbers of invalids flooded back from England. Even by the war's end, most of the MHC's 7,000 hospital cases had come from training camps in Canada and not from overseas. Tuberculosis, which affected 8,571 of the 590,572 members of the CEF, required a major commitment of capital and care. By 1917, the MHC had taken over fourteen sanatoria across Canada, transforming them from "glorified summer camps to hospital-like institutions."[10] Euclid Hall at Toronto became home to the commission's "incurables." The mentally ill were consigned to provincial asylums, though "shell shock" cases were hospitalized at Cobourg and subjected, by the MHC's testimony, to "every imaginable treatment," from warm baths to shock therapy. Playing golf allegedly restored one former bank accountant to his stool.[11]

The war brought part of the country's enormous burden of ill health into the army. If postwar Canada was not to stagger under the load and become unattractive to immigrants and foreign capital, Scammell warned, "there must be a minimum of sentiment and a maximum of hard business sense concerning the future of the returned soldier to civil life."[12] Independently, a Canadian army doctor in England had come to a similar conclusion. J.L. Todd, professor of parasitology at McGill, had earned an international reputation for his work in tropical medicine. Independent means, research expertise, and a short temper made him an uncomfortable member of the wartime CAMC, and he was dumped on the overseas branch of the Militia Department's Pensions and

Claims Board. Surprisingly, he stuck with the chore because, as he explained to his wife in 1915, "the biggest thing in Canada at the present time is the whole Pensions question. If it is not removed from politics and put into the hands of a small commission of about three men...we will have pensions trouble in Canada that, for our size, will make that of the USA's look like a beginner."[13] Todd designed his message for powerful friends, including a prime minister who was always eager to take such traditional log-rolling issues as tariffs, railways, and now pensions "out of politics."

Unlike Scammell, Todd could visit France and see for himself whether Bourillon was right. He admired the hard rationality of French pension practice and criticized the untidiness of the thousands of philanthropic societies that helped French soldiers find new skills. French pensions were mean and hard to get, but no matter how much a veteran earned, his pension was not cut. British pensions were reduced as earnings grew, an obvious disincentive to work. The disabled, Todd concluded, could work. "Everyone must understand," he proclaimed, "that armless, legless men *can* become self-supporting."[14] From Chelsea, Todd borrowed the basis for assessing disability: since a soldier brought nothing to the army but a healthy body, the market for healthy bodies was "the general market for untrained labour." The French assessed that body by a chart that ruled the loss of both arms, legs, or eyes as 100 per cent disability, a single eye or a lower leg as 40 per cent, and varicose veins as 10 per cent. A burst of Gallic sentiment valued reproductive organs at 60 per cent.

Todd's ideas led to creation of the Canadian Board of Pension Commissioners (BPC) in June 1916. Ten-year terms and good salaries were intended to insulate the three members from political pressures: Jack Ross, the Montreal millionaire-yachtsman; Colonel R.H. Labatt, a Hamilton offshoot of the brewing family; and Todd himself. The key officials would be medical advisers: doctors who would read the files; examine the diagnoses made by local boards; scan the disability table; and make an objective, emotion-free rating of each applicant. Parliament went a step farther, giving Canadians the most generous pension rates in the world. After all,

Todd's pension system made generosity cheap. Fewer than 5 per cent of Canada's war disabled got the top rate; the vast majority got 25 per cent or less. One reason was "attributability": how much of a disability was due to service? A gunshot wound or a battlefield amputation was easy—though one suppurating head wound was attributed to a pre-war mastoid operation. Was syphilitic paresis really attributable to contact with a toilet seat at Camp Hughes? No. Could Lieutenant John Diefenbaker, painfully injured during training in England, seek a pension? Yes, said the Pension commissioners, but only if his subsequent discomfort affected his prospects in the market for unskilled labour. Could a soldier knocked down by a bus in the London blackout, as Lieutenant Lester Pearson claimed to have been late in 1917, make a claim?[15] No, said Todd; pensions were not insurance.

This was all easier to argue because pensions were not supposed to be an important part of a disabled soldier's earnings. By restoring a soldier's will and ability to work, real wages would soon outpace any pension income. To Todd's delight, Scammell and the MHC had already been persuaded. By 1916, the commission had begun to improvise some forms of vocational training—albeit elementary and uncertain in its early stages. Teachers preferred their more familiar classrooms to learning on the job. Doctors condemned anything that complicated their routines. Convalescents proved unenthusiastic. "Most of the men come back with sluggish mental action," explained an MHC pamphlet. "They have been under military discipline so long, clothed, fed and ordered about that they have lost independence."[16] After long months in hospital, complained Colonel Alex Primrose of the CAMC, invalids "have become accustomed to having everything done for them, they lose all ambition and have no desire to help themselves."[17]

Matters improved when the MHC hired Walter Segsworth, a Toronto engineer with a brisk, practical approach. No one ever learned a trade in a hospital, he realized. Invalids should be taught to be busy. Young women hired as "ward aides" at $60 to $75 a month would coax and prod the men into working on crafts. Once

ambulatory, they would move into "curative workshops" to practise wood-working, motor mechanics, or shoemaking, and to
revive factory disciplines and old skills. Serious retraining began at
discharge, ideally on the job. Training boards firmly guided a man
to his new occupation—preferably close to his old job. A one-
legged carpenter could become a cabinet-maker; a crippled train-
man could be a station agent or telegrapher. Teams of ex-salesmen
set out to find job opportunities and look after placement and follow-up. When absenteeism became a problem, an inspector was
sent to offer a trainee "sound advice as to his future line of conduct, and emphasis is laid that he is there for the purpose of applying himself diligently to the learning of his new trade."[18]
Social-service workers helped families adjust to a disabled bread-
winner and his income. Returned Soldiers' Insurance in 1920 provided cheap life insurance coverage that commercial firms refused
to provide. Ottawa covered any added cost from workers' compen-
sation.

This was a revolution in theory and, like most revolutionary
theories, it ran into practical problems. Most courses were too
ambitious and, at a few months' duration, too brief for men
adjusting to disabilities and a long way from their classroom days.
Training allowances, calculated like the pension to give "decent
comfort," could give a couple with three children as much as $110 a
month—rather more than an employer was likely to offer a disabled worker. In Ontario, the Department of Education did its best
to sabotage training after Segsworth refused to use only its teachers. The University of Toronto, an important centre for the MHC's
rehabilitation programs, backed out after its president, Sir Robert
Falconer, felt pressure from politicians and officials at Queen's
Park, resentful that Ottawa would invade their jurisdiction over
education.[19] The University of New Brunswick pledged a fully
equipped machine shop and provided some old rusty tools in a
basement "unfit for a root cellar." "Most of these [offers] start out
with a blare of trumpets," admitted one of Segsworth's assistants,
"and end up with very little."[20]

Still, Canada led the way. When the United States entered the war, Todd, Scammell, and other Canadians found that Americans welcomed their advice. Canadian rehabilitation policy was publicized in pamphlets, posters, and magic-lantern shows. Canadians, too, needed to understand and appreciate what was being done for their men. The most widespread pamphlet was "A Little Chat with Private Pat" or, in the French version, "Poil-aux-Pattes." "I'll be a real returned soldier," claimed Pat, "when I've got back to work." Providing for his family was a bigger challenge to him than his missing leg. "From the way my old father writes and my wife too, they seem to think there's nothing for me to do but some kid's job like peddling pins or bobbing up and down with an elevator." That was not for Pat. Nor was "scratching paper for my living." Instead, in through a back-to-the-land theme that was Sir James Lougheed's main contribution to reconstruction planning, Pat would be a farmer: "The country life's the life for me, with a cow and a hen and a honey bee."[21]

Like other propaganda, the "Private Pat" pamphlet misled its readers a little. Amputees numbered a minority of the disabled. If "Pat" expected help from the Soldier Settlement Act, adopted in 1917 and greatly extended in 1918, he would be disappointed. Soldier Settlement was intended for serious, physically fit farmers. Loan committees consciously excluded nursing sisters and the disabled from those eligible. However the stereotype showed the government's determination to instil economic independence in its war veterans.

In their prescience, Todd and Scammell had anticipated that what was easy in wartime would be much more difficult when peace returned and the veterans' sacrifices were forgotten. When politicians promised "full re-establishment" during the 1917 election campaign, they really meant that veterans would resume at once the responsibilities as well as the pleasures of civil life by becoming wholly self-sufficient. The introduction of conscription in 1918 ended the succession of annual increases in pension rates, just as the country's inflation rate soared.

Still, the Hospitals Commission accomplished much. From hard experience, the MHC learned how to coax and even bully the bedridden into old work disciplines. "Ward occupations" taught by women specially trained at the University of Toronto's Hart House busied men's fingers and minds with handicrafts. "Curative workshops" in hospital basements and sheds moved the disabled closer to their old working skills. Once discharged, ex-soldiers learned new trades, while the commission persuaded employers that the disabled could be valuable workers. D.J. McDougall, blinded during service with the PPCLI, learned the skills of a masseur at St. Dunstan's in London and passed them on at Hart House in the first stage of a teaching career that ended in the university's history department. The CAMC's only female amputee, a nurse injured in a hospital bombing, found a job as a social worker among tubercular veterans, while the CEF's sole quadrilateral amputee, Private Curly Christian, was found a job as a billiard marker.

As it grew to its full wartime strength, the CAMC resented the civilian commission that had supplanted it in Canada. Colonel Frederick Marlow, a Toronto gynaecologist, had led a parallel investigation to Colonel Bruce's into the CAMC in Canada. His target turned out to be the MHC, publicizing its problems and assuring a parliamentary committee that putting invalid soldiers under civilian control broke the Geneva Convention. "Patronage first, economy second and efficiency third" claimed the headlines announcing Marlow's angry resignation.[22] Certainly the commission was not strong medically: most of its homes and hospitals were served by militia doctors who had preferred to protect their civilian practices. The medical director, Lieutenant-Colonel A.T. Thompson, was better known as MP for the Yukon and a businessman than as a doctor.

   The public furore only delayed efforts to convert the commission's hospitals to CAMC control until February 1918. The commission gave up 51 hospitals and 12,369 beds to the Militia Department and soon transferred its staff and the remaining 5,575 beds for incurables, the insane, tuberculars, and anyone else the CAMC did not want to a new Department of Soldiers' Civil Re-establishment

(DSCR).[23] It was a token victory. As the end of the war approached, the ablest medical officers thought only of their return to civil practice. When the 1918 influenza epidemic proved unexpectedly fatal to scores of young men in CAMC hospitals, the army took the blame. Running hospitals close to unfettered public opinion was awkward: "The grumbler, the malingerer and the neurotic," complained Macphail, "never failed to find an audience equally neurotic."[24] The CAMC rejoinder that it had cut costs and so prevented needless hospital expansion, while true, somehow failed to appease public indignation.

In any case, as the war ended, the wisdom of military authorities suffered a deep discount. "The sooner we in Canada get away from military titles and everything connected with the war," declared Colonel Clarence Starr to waiting Toronto reporters, "the better it will be for the country and the average citizen."[25] To some, "militarization" almost ranked as a disability itself. "When a civilian entered the army," explained Walter Segsworth, "everything was done to make him a small unit in a large organization. He was taught to obey rather than to think; he was for the most part relieved of the care of his dependents; clothing, food and a place to sleep were provided for him. If he was guilty of a misdemeanour he was punished, but he was not deprived of the necessities of life, whereas in civil life he would have been discharged. Thus the whole system, for the time being, tended to reduce the action of his own will and relieve him of all sense of responsibility."[26]

The robustly civilian Department of Soldiers' Civil Re-establishment under Lougheed, created in 1918 from the MHC, and shaken by its defeat at the hands of the military, had a cure for militarization. Returned men must face cold economic reality, not handouts. Only the disabled would be trained, and the courses for them must be short. Although they might have evaded danger by their mental condition, shell-shock cases must not be encouraged by pensions to evade personal and family responsibilities.

"The returned soldier," intoned Lord Atholstan, proprietor of the Montreal *Star*, "must not be allowed to consider himself an unlimited creditor of the State, to be supported in idleness."[27] The government entirely agreed. The Repatriation Committee, headed by H.J. Daly, manager of the soon-to-be-bankrupt Home Bank, limited its services to providing a cheerful welcome. The new DSCR offered the returning Ulysses, if physically fit, little more than help in finding work. To do more might have crippled the men psychologically.

Veterans were expected to work hard and be grateful. They had no part in planning their own re-establishment. It was experts who set pensions, selected appropriate retraining programs and approved Soldier Settlement loans. In practice, returned men had their own ideas and their influence grew. By the end of 1916, hundreds of Ypres veterans returned every week, and the flow steadily increased. By 1917, most communities had a veterans' association. In Toronto, Mayor Tommy Church worked hard to bring them into his municipal Tory machine. In Montreal, the civic reformer W.D. Lighthall sent for the constitution of the Grand Army of the Republic to help local veterans get organized. In Winnipeg, veterans rejected a citizen-run Returned Soldiers' Association and formed their own. Winnipeggers hosted the meeting on April 10–13 when delegates from other provinces gathered to form the Great War Veterans' Association (GWVA). It was the same week that the United States joined the war and the Canadian Corps took Vimy Ridge. A year later, also at Winnipeg, a pre-war club of largely British veterans was reorganized as the Army and Navy Veterans (ANV) with a descendant of Sir Charles Tupper as president. The GWVA was clearly fated to be the dominant organization.

Veterans were not unique. Many Canadian civilians were poor, physically and mentally disabled, and wracked with pain. But if veterans were poor, it was a conscious result of public policy. Ottawa had set CEF pay scales and held them steady throughout the war while other wages and prices soared. The government had also decided that disabled veterans and their families would remain poor by basing pensions on the wage rates of unskilled labour. The awkwardness of a missing limb, the shame of disfigurement, or the pain of a lung or heart condition would be joined to the humiliation of poverty.

Yet the veterans' claim was for fulfilment of their contract, not charity. For the first time a group of largely poor men approached the Canadian government on the basis of moral entitlement, not sympathy. Returned soldiers were seldom socialists; almost everywhere veterans' organizations veered to the political right. Their members had a special stake in the societies they had helped defend. Nevertheless, veterans' conservatism had an egalitarian, radical edge. Ex-soldiers remembered their resentment at the barriers of rank and the unearned privileges of the officer class. In Britain, the National Federation of Ex-Servicemen barred officers unless they had risen from the ranks. The American Legion forbade the use of army ranks. In the GWVA, members addressed each other as "comrade." Generous pensions for officers rankled: "That an officer with an arm off should get twice as much pension as a private with an arm off," raged Harris Turner, a blinded Saskatchewan veteran, "is unfair, unjust, unsound, undemocratic, unreasonable, unBritish, unacceptable, outrageous and rotten."[28]

Such tones came easily from the new GWVA. Its officers, notably C. Grant MacNeil, an ex–machine-gunner who became secretary-treasurer in early 1919, established themselves as guides and counsel to parliamentary committees and ministers.[29] By insisting that veterans have preference in government hiring and by persuading Parliament to raise pensions for all other ranks to the rate for a lieutenant, and by mobilizing his organization as a voice for widows and the disabled, MacNeil rivalled Scammell and Todd in setting veterans' policy.

The GWVA insisted that, until the Armistice, it was only the vanguard for a huge returning army. In fact the association remained primarily an organization of the disabled and out of touch with most of the 350,000 soldiers who, on November 11, 1918, suddenly felt free to come home if Ottawa could find the means to bring them.

The war ended in a seemingly inconclusive way. An armistice, after all, only interrupted the fighting. If the Allied forces dissolved, might the Germans resume fighting? At Nivelles, units of the 7th

Canadian Brigade mutinied on December 17 when they were ordered to march in helmets and full pack. If the war was over, why should they bother? When, after a day, the units marched, military police grabbed ringleaders and stragglers.[30] The 1st and 2nd Canadian Divisions set out on a long, weary march through Belgium and Germany to occupy bridgeheads at Bonn and Cologne. It became part of an Allied army of occupation. The rest of the Corps waited out the winter in Belgium, only slightly distracted by programs of adult education managed by the YMCA's "University of Vimy Ridge."

Elaborate demobilization plans, based on British schemes, had proposed releasing "demobilizers" and "pivotal men" to get the economy running fast enough to absorb the rest of the army smoothly. The GWVA itself appealed to Ottawa to keep the troops overseas during the winter, when jobs were always scarce. In fact, it would be hard enough simply to get the Canadians home. Not only was shipping scarce and in high demand, railway connections with the winter ports of Halifax and Saint John were so worn from wartime traffic that their maximum capacity for troop trains was 20,000–30,000 men a month. Halifax had not yet recovered from the devastating 1917 explosion in its harbour.

In Europe, Sir Arthur Currie believed that Canadians should see the splendid army they had produced. CEF units should return under their own officers to a proper civic welcome. Otherwise, he warned his superiors, he could not be held responsible for any breakdown in discipline. The Canadians must also have a chance to visit friends and relatives in England before they went home. Even in 1918 half the Corps was British-born.

Ottawa and the British authorities glumly accepted Currie's demands. In mid-January, Canadian occupying troops began moving out of Germany. Currie's arrangements meant that the 3rd Division, its ranks filled by MSA men, was the first Canadian formation to pass through England to Liverpool and home.

Soldiers endured medical examinations, briefings on "civil reestablishment" and soldier settlement, and the usual documentation in quadruplicate before boarding ship for Halifax. Soldiers with wives and families in England joined them at Buxton and travelled on "family ships" to Saint John. The wounded and sick crossed by hospital ship through Portland, Maine, to Montreal. "Venereals" waited in England until they were pronounced cured. Their names would be sent to provincial health authorities, to be used to control any further infection.

The steamer *Northland* compounded the repatriation problems. When the old German liner docked at Halifax on Boxing Day, waiting reporters eagerly scribbled down the soldiers' complaints about bad accommodation, rotten food, thieving stewards, and other staples of wartime troopship travel. The ensuing editorial storm led to a royal commission, which, in turn, urged the Canadian authorities in Britain to insist on better shipping for their men.[31] That meant more delays.

Stuck in England, suffering from epidemic influenza, miners' strikes, and the coldest winter in years, Canadian troops lost patience. At Kinmel, a dreary, rain-sodden repatriation camp in North Wales, 20,000 soldiers heard a rumour that MSA men were heading home before longer-serving soldiers. Next came news that the next ship to take them home had fallen short of the new post-*Northland* standards and been rejected as unsatisfactory. Thousands of Canadian soldiers boiled over into a rampage.[32] On the night of March 5 and all next day, rioters ransacked Kinmel's canteens, wrecked the ramshackle stores in the nearby "Tin-Town," emptied guardrooms, and fought each other until 5 men were dead and 23 wounded. At other camps, smaller riots exploded periodically through the spring. At Epsom on June 24, an elderly British police sergeant died of a heart attack when Canadian convalescents attacked his station. Even King George V reacted with shock. By the summer, almost all the Canadian troops were home—much sooner than the experts had predicted.[33]

Once in Canada, soldiers travelled by train to the military district where they had joined or where they requested a discharge. If they accompanied a unit, a last parade through welcoming crowds and a final "Dismiss" at the city hall or the armouries released them to civilian life. Next day, the men turned in their steel helmets and equipment and collected railway tickets, an allowance for civilian clothes, and a modest War Service Gratuity. They were civilians again.

On average, Canadian soldiers who went overseas spent about two years in England and France before they returned.[34] Veterans came back to a country far removed from the ideals they had remembered from a distance.

Relatives harped on the deprivations they had faced, of "Meatless Fridays" or "Fuelless Mondays," but to men who had seen wartime France or England, Canadians had obviously done well out of the war. Inflation had effectively doubled most prices, but wages on the whole had kept pace—but not for soldiers or their families. The Patriotic Fund stopped raising its allowances in 1917 for fear that community and private generosity was drying up, and the government increased its $20 a month separation allowance to $30 only at the end of the war. It seemed easy to identify war profiteers. An automobile cost more than most soldiers earned during the entire war, but the number of cars on the road more than tripled between 1915 and 1919.[35]

Men accustomed to English mores found that war had not loosened the grip of Canadian sabbatarians or moral reformers on society. In English-speaking communities, anything more entertaining than church was still banned on Sundays. To make Canada fit for heroes and to appeal to newly enfranchised women voters, temperance enthusiasts had persuaded Borden's government to impose an absolute coast-to-coast prohibition on the consumption of liquor. Soldiers, of course, had not been consulted on the matter.[36]

For veterans, 1919 was the year of disillusionment. For tens of thousands the Armistice had restored a prize they might otherwise have lost—their lives. Now, as with all prizes, the problem arose of how to use it. Men came home with wounds to minds and bodies, and some with drug and alcohol addictions, to say nothing of the minor vices of swearing, gambling, and athlete's foot. They found broken marriages, children who had forgotten them, and families who had already heard more than enough about the war.

Scammell and others who had tried to anticipate the veterans' needs had overlooked the ex-soldiers' restlessness. It was as much a part of war as a wooden leg, claimed the veteran and journalist George Pearson. "It is that terrible restlessness which possesses us like an evil spirit; the indefinite expression of a vague discontent, the restlessness of dying men, little children and old soldiers."[37] "There had been a thunderstorm and the atmosphere had failed to clear," wrote Pierre van Paassen. "It was the same petty, monotonous, joyless, suffocating world of three years before, only now I was more intensely aware of it."[38]

Turmoil was everywhere in 1919. French veterans rioted against back taxes they were expected to pay. British veterans demonstrated for the "homes fit for heroes" Lloyd George, their prime minister, had promised them. In Canada, restless mobs of veterans attacked labour organizers, Chinese laundries, and price-gouging restaurants. Canada experienced its worst year ever for strikes, with Winnipeg's general strike in May and June as only the centrepiece. Veterans participated on both sides of the struggle. Some resented the "slackers" and unionists who had benefited from the war. Others contrasted wealthy wartime profiteers with their own threadbare families.

In the general cacophony, returned men found their own issue: the "Calgary Resolution." Adopted on a frigid Sunday in January at Calgary's Allen Theatre, the resolution demanded a $2,000 bonus for each veteran as compensation for the income soldiers had lost during their service. Applause-seekers everywhere, from feminists to the national Liberal leadership convention in August, offered prompt support. So did Mayor Tommy Church and his fellow Toronto Tories, as part of their search for ex-soldier supporters. The bonus issue drew returned men to the GWVA, sending membership soaring from 20,000 to 200,000 in a year. As a bonus crusader, J. Harry Flynn, a flamboyant American who had served in the CAMC, seized control of the veterans' organization in Toronto. When GWVA leaders, anxious lest it cost them their moral high ground as defenders of widows and the disabled, proved cool to the bonus demand, Flynn organized a Toronto-based breakaway group, the Grand Army of United Veterans (GAUV).[39]

In Ottawa, the Borden government portrayed the bonus as a $2-billion grab and stood firm against it. Once the Liberals' convention fever subsided, Liberal MPs forgot their support for the bonus. By November 1919, the sole member of Parliament to back it was Simcoe County's Colonel J.A. Currie, last encountered at Ypres. The Bonus campaign helped bring veterans flooding into their new organizations, but when the campaign failed and their own gratuities were spent, they flooded out again.

Painfully, veterans recognized what Ernest Scammell had foreseen in 1915; they would have to make their own way in a world that had little time for their stories and even less for their problems. Flynn's career as a veterans' leader ended with rumours that a young man was his bosom companion.[40] *The Veteran*, organ of the GWVA, was almost out of business by 1923.[41]

Medical associations toyed briefly with the notion of public health insurance as a way of finding employment for returning colleagues whose practices had vanished. The urge was frail and soon forgotten until the 1930s when, once again, too few could afford a doctor's services. Governments ordered married women dismissed from civil-service jobs and put veterans in their place. As any cynic might have predicted, the public soon concluded that veterans were loafers whom only the post office or public-works departments would hire. Returned men learned to remove their discharge pins and forget what they had been doing between 1914 and 1918 if they wanted a chance to work.

The separate fates of half a million veterans defy generalization. Some were "Old Originals" from 1914; others were MSA men with a few months' service. Half the members of the CEF never got beyond England. Veterans included cooks, orderlies, staff officers, and front-line infantry privates. Most had lived fast and furiously in the present; few had devised clear idea about how to cope with the future. Some fled to British Columbia or California. Perhaps they had had all the damp cold they needed for a lifetime. Many who stayed in England, waiving their rights to repatriation, fulfilled Perley's gloomy expectations by demanding paid passage back to Canada.

Soldier Settlement, a colonization scheme for veterans, had looked like a huge bonus. Five-per-cent loans and record farm prices promised easy prosperity. Instead, settlers bought farms, livestock, and equipment at equally high prices and struggled to repay their loans as returns on crops and livestock plummeted. By 1930, almost half the 24,709 soldier-settlers had abandoned their dreams.[42] The prices of 1919 would not return until another world war a generation later.

Men whose jobs had been held open often resumed them only to quit after a few days or weeks. Employers felt aggrieved; men themselves wondered why they should still be office boys or apprentices when stay-at-homes had risen in seniority and salary. Only fellow veterans seemed to understand their grievance. Disabled veterans found that their carefully arranged jobs vanished in the 1921 depression. Employing them had turned out to be more patriotic than profitable.

Veterans found work where they could. Duncan McIntyre, who had risen from organizing brilliant raids for the 27th Battalion to a top staff job in the 3rd Division, resigned himself to selling furniture in the Ottawa valley. E.W. Russell stayed in England, became a municipal surveyor, and enjoyed the fact that former colonels and majors worked for him. Frank Maheux built forest-ranger towers. Claude Craig went back to his job as a railway telegrapher, married, had children, and died in 1923, paralyzed by a stroke. Roy Macfie and his wounded brother Arthur went back to the farm in McKellar. John, the youngest and biggest of the brothers, had been killed by a sniper at Fresnoy. In May 1919, Arthur died instantly in the explosion of a box of detonators he was using to blow up stumps. Family members wondered whether the constant pain from his disabled arm had been a factor.

Most veterans eventually settled down. Some never did. Always there was a part of their lives deep within them, that no one else could share. In 1928 they showed it. Few rank-and-file Canucks had a good word to say about their cold, pompous corps commander and they might have cheered when a Port Hope editor and ex–Liberal organizer known as "Hug the Machine" Preston alleged that Currie had deliberately slaughtered his men for the glory of capturing Mons on Armistice Day. The ensuing libel trial in Cobourg destroyed Currie's health and left him with huge legal bills and derisory damages, but it rallied his men. Soldiers might have their own opinions about Currie, but they would defend even an unloved general from mere civilians.[43]

By 1924, American Legionnaires had partially won their bonus battle. Canadian veterans would never win theirs. Grant MacNeil and other veterans' leaders believed that the Americans had sacrificed their obligation to widows and disabled comrades. The GWVA executive tried to keep veterans working together for those who could not help themselves. Like veterans' leaders elsewhere, they failed. By the 1930s, separate organizations for the disabled had emerged in many countries. In France, the *mutilés de guerre* kept their distance from other veterans; elsewhere, the British Limbless Ex-Servicemen's Association (BLESMA) in Britain and the Disabled American Veterans (DAV) in the United States represented the disabled; in Canada, the Amputations Association (or "Fragments from France"), the Tuberculous Veterans Association, and the Sir Arthur Pearson Club for the war-blind. MacNeil fought the trend, rallying the smaller organizations to fight for fairer pension legislation and practice. Revenues from a shrinking membership paid for an adjustment bureau, whose staff helped widows and veterans present cases to increasingly hard-faced officials, committed to a new policy of "tightening up."[44]

Like the Bonus Drive, the GWVA pension campaign faced opposition. Pension Act amendments were annually blessed by the House of Commons, gutted by the Senate, and subverted by the Board of Pension Commissioners. Colonel John Thompson, the son of a former prime minister and an arid but ingenious lawyer, used the board's tangle of rules to protect the Treasury and sustain Todd's original tight-fisted principles. The 1922 "attributability" argument was typical. Parliament, MacNeil insisted, had promised to give returned men "the benefit of the doubt." Thompson politely agreed, but, he added, he never had any doubts.

The new Liberal government, elected at the end of 1921, gave MacNeil a chance to reopen his battle. Choosing deliberately provocative language, the GWVA secretary-treasurer charged the Pension Board with "a contemptible and cold-blooded conspiracy to deprive ex-Servicemen of rights previously guaranteed by Parliament."[45] MacNeil's reward was a royal commission to investigate pensions and civil re-establishment, headed by respected Nova Scotia Liberal Lieutenant-Colonel J.L. Ralston, the former commanding officer of the 85th Battalion. Within weeks, Ralston decided that MacNeil's specific charge was unfounded: the Pension Commissioners had exploited a minor amendment to the Pension Act with scrupulous rigour. The fact that Thompson had provided the precise words to his Senate allies was irrelevant.

To his credit, Ralston persisted beyond the narrow point of law. For three years he and his colleagues prodded and probed the state of soldiers' civil re-establishment, from soldier settlement to care for the insane. MacNeil himself was sent to interview witnesses and gather testimony. The result was an inquest into what Canada had really done for her soldiers. It was sadly little.

In all, 40,000 disabled veterans had been retrained and 64 per cent had been placed in skill-related jobs. Then, to save money, training, placement, and follow-up were dissolved. By the end of the 1921 depression, one-fifth of all returned men and most of the disabled were jobless, and there were no plans for more help. Employers now openly favoured the able-bodied. Too many had chosen overvalued or unproductive land in the Soldier Settlement plan. By 1939, barely a third of the original soldier settlers remained on the land, and half the government's $100 million investment had blown away.

Because settlement and retraining failed, pension policy mattered more than Scammell and Todd had ever imagined. MacNeil paraded his "human documents" before Ralston as evidence of how arbitrary and unfair BPC rulings had become. Ralston was sufficiently impressed to propose a federal appeal board, complete with "soldier advisers," paid by the government, to help veterans prepare their cases. The grounds for a veteran's pension grew. In 1930, a woman unwise enough to marry a man after he was disabled finally won a guarantee of support. The fear of "pension widows" was overcome.[46]

Amendments that year created an even more judicial procedure, with the Pension Tribunal to review BPC decisions and the Pension Appeal Court to review and often reverse tribunal rulings. The predictable result by 1933 was a huge backlog. In a few days, R.B. Bennett smashed and rebuilt the system, creating a single Canadian Pension Commission with an Appeals Division that survives, essentially, to this day.

Veterans' organizations also changed. In 1925, after a number of attempts, most rival veterans' organizations came together again in Winnipeg, as they had in 1917, but this time under the leadership of senior officers and the inspiration of their wartime British commander, Earl Haig. The result was the Canadian Legion of the British Empire Service League (BESL). Except for the Army and Navy Veterans—too conservative to join—and some of the disabled organizations, most Canadian veterans accepted the new organization as their own. The Legion took credit for the 1930 Pension Act reforms and the drastic 1933 reorganization. It won recognition of "burn-out" among aged veterans as the basis for a War Veteran's Allowance, and mobilized enough sympathy for veterans that Bennett, with all his Depression-bred cuts, felt no temptation to reduce pensions, as did Franklin Delano Roosevelt's 1933 Economy Bill in the United States. On the other hand, no one could seriously call Canada's pensions extravagant. In 1932, a quarter of a million men, women, and children shared about $40 million a year. Almost all collected an individual pittance. That pittance was enough for municipalities to deny relief.

The depression hit veterans especially hard. Farms, professional practices, and businesses nursed into a fragile prosperity through the 1920s collapsed when no one had money, and the banks called their loans. Major-General Andrew McNaughton, the wartime

YOUR NUMBER'S UP

4-A (above) A soldier in the 15th Battalion has his wound dressed in the trenches near Neuve Chapelle, March, 1915. His biggest danger was not from a German shell fragment or bullets, but from the anaerobic bacteria in the soil that led to gas gangrene and forced surgeons to cut away large amounts of living flesh as a preventative. (J.A. Currie collection, Erindale College)

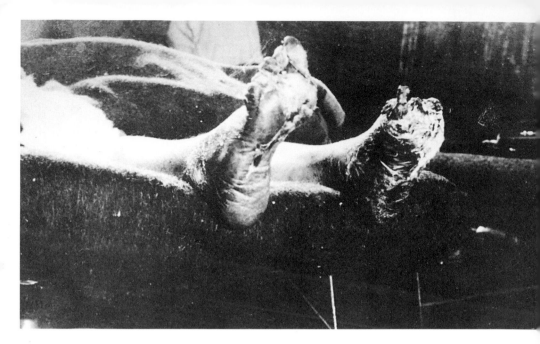

4-B (above) A severe case of trench foot, probably Canadian, from photographs taken by Dr. W.L. Kidd in France, 1917. The result of long exposure to freezing water, trench foot was often crippling and occasionally fatal. Military authorities insisted it could be prevented by clean socks and regular inspections and punished both sufferers and their superiors. (National Archives, PA 149311)

4-C (below) Another Kidd photograph of a soldier with a compound fracture and shrapnel wounds. Treatment would include radical debridement and drainage with Carrel-Dakin solution to prevent fatal infection. The patient, according to Kidd, recovered. (National Archives, PA 149312)

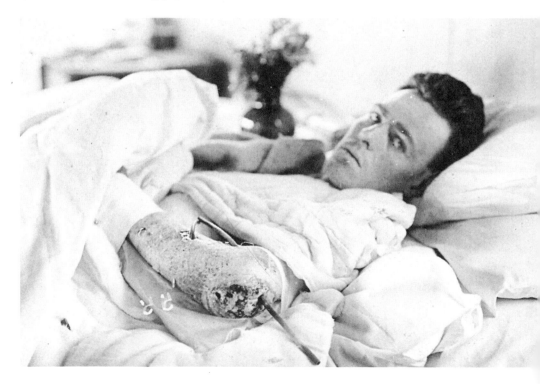

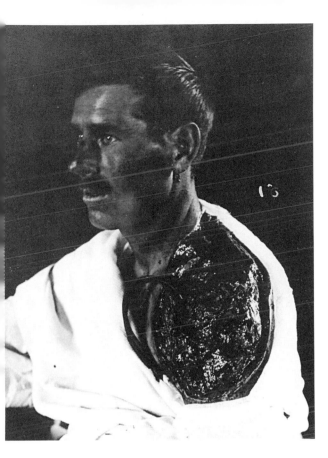

4-D (left) Few doctors were prepared for the devastating extent of wounds from shell fragments. Kidd reported that this soldier's left arm had been blown off at the shoulder. His fate was not recorded.

4-E (below) Another flesh wound under the arm. While medical science had developed antiseptics and was experimenting with blood transfusions, anti-biotics would have to wait for a later world war. (National Archives, PA 149310)

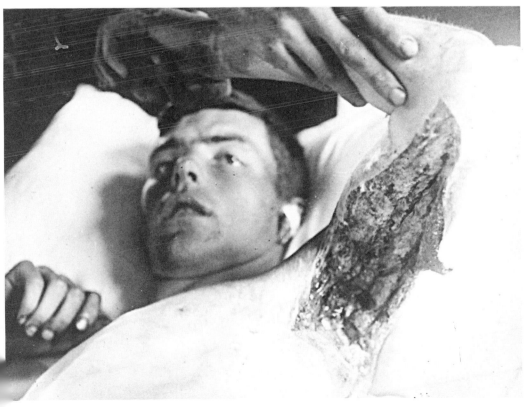

4-F (above) The admissions area of No. 2 Canadian General Hospital at Le Tréport. Here the process of *triage* or sorting determined a wounded man's fate. Surgeons gave first priority to those

they could help. A lucky soldier got his "Blighty" when casualties were few and doctors had more time to treat him. Mass casualties meant long waits in tents like this. (National Archives, PA 149309)

4-G (left) As in most other aspects of army life, officers were different. A dentist and his colonel read a request for an appointment dropped from the air by a passing pilot. (National Archives, PA 1963)

4-H (below) Other ranks wait in line to have their oral health checked by an army dentist. Free dental care was not a blessing most veterans remembered with fondness. The army allowed only enough treatment to allow a soldier to "masticate his rations." On the other hand, many soldiers had probably never seen a dentist before they enlisted. (National Archives, PA 2787)

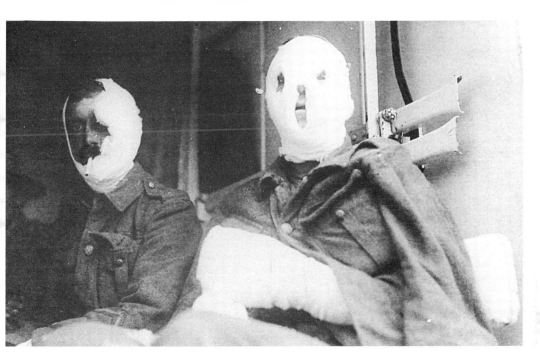

4-J (above) Mustard gas casualties in an ambulance, waiting for evacuation. Externally, mustard was painful and disfiguring but most victims recovered; taken into the lungs, it brought an agonizing death. (Ontario Archives, acc 11595-2-7, 2836)

4-K (below) Patients at the Duchess of Connaught's Canadian Red Cross Hospital at Taplow enjoy their 1917 Christmas dinner. Patients wear a mixture of uniform and cotton "hospital blues." The tin plates, tin mugs and tin-topped tables are reminders, despite the efforts at decoration, that the soldiers are a long way from home. (National Archives, PA 5063)

4-L (above) The grave of Lieutenant F.G. Scott, one of many gunners killed when the artillery had to move over Vimy Ridge and into the plain beyond. Units were normally responsible for burials but the arrangements broke down and the forebear of the Commonwealth War Graves Commission was born. (National Archives, PA 1612)

4-M (below) Fly-covered, bloated German corpses. Death in war had no glamour. Soldiers faced it with a gambler's fatalism, persuaded that they were safe until they were hit by the bullet or shell with "their name on it." Many remembered comrades predicting, before a battle, that "their number was up." (National Archives, PA 868)

gunner and postwar chief of the general staff, persuaded the government to open relief camps, staff them with veteran officers and
NCOs from the CEF, and put unemployed youth to work at a wage
of 20 cents a day. The relief campers dubbed themselves "the Royal
Twenty Centers"; critics denounced the camps as the Prussian militarism they had fought a war to defeat.

Some of the young men and even a few of the sergeants went to
Spain to start the next war early. Many veterans in the 1930s tried to
forget their troubles by commemoration. The decade saw the rise
of battalion and battery associations and, in 1934, the creation of a
Canadian Corps Association. The Legion turned its energies to
organizing a Vimy Pilgrimage to unveil the bold Canadian monument on Hill 145, whose capture had cost the 4th Division so many
lives. Only months before another war, King George VI and Queen
Elizabeth would finally unveil the national war memorial in
Ottawa's Confederation Square. In a decade with few good experiences, the past was a refuge.

All biography has a funereal close. The history of Canada's First
World War veterans must end sadly in disappointment, sickness,
and death. Still, Canadians have reason for immense pride in the
tough, weather-beaten men of the Canadian Corps and all that
they accomplished in war and in peace. Like Moses, it was not
given to them to pass into the promised land their children and
grandchildren would enjoy. It was given to few men of the CEF to
find much comfort from the land they had volunteered to defend.
It was their children and the children of men who had stayed home
and prospered who would be the beneficiaries. That is, perhaps,
the rule of human affairs.

APPENDIX

A STATISTICAL PROFILE OF THE CEF

L ONG BEFORE the age of Cliometrics, Canada's official historian, Colonel A.F. Duguid, set members of his staff to work processing data with Hollerith cards, needle sorting devices, and other advanced information technology of the time. The input came from 619,636 sets of attestation papers filled out by members of the CEF.

Like all collections of data, it was subject to error. How much did clerks lose or "repair"? Had the British term "Wesleyan" deterred good Methodists from claiming their correct denomination? At least 21,097 men admitted to having served earlier in the CEF. They are double-counted. How many others had concealed their past? So many men lied about their age that the expression "thirty-niner" was invented for those men who darkened their hair. A Young Soldiers' Battalion held youthful deceivers until they reached the age of nineteen. Did men also mislead authorities about their occupation, birthplace, and marital status? Like other evidence, statistics can be twisted to reveal lies or to conceal the truth. Or they can be used—cautiously—to test a few familiar hypotheses.

Two seductive images of Canadian soldiers in the Great War persist: the tortured aesthete and the rugged frontiersman. It is easy for historians to see all soldiers as replicas of the relative handful of articulate diarists, letter writers, and memoirists whose phrases illuminate these pages. Whatever common sense tells us, we trust our own tribe, particularly when they reinforce our own admirable ideas. However right writers might have been, they are untypical. In an army whose members had seldom advanced beyond Grade 6, most diarists were university or at least high-school graduates. Will Bird was a highly literate exception; Frank Maheux reminds us that eloquence can transcend run-on sentences and a complete absence of punctuation.

A more common image, seized by the British when the First Contingent first arrived and never relinquished, was that "Canadoos" were robust, free-spirited pioneers. In his moving account of the CEF, Pierre Berton renewed the stereotype for 1917: "to a very large extent the men who fought at Vimy had worked on farms or lived on the edge of the wilderness."[1] Perhaps they had, since all the settled parts of Canada were within a day's train journey of the rough mining frontier, but of the 263,111 men who had enlisted by March 1, 1916—the men of Vimy—6.5 per cent were farmers or ranchers, 18.5 per cent came from clerical occupations, and 64.8 per cent had been manual workers. By the war's end, with help from the MSA, farmers, hunters, fishermen, and lumbermen formed 22.4 per cent of the CEF, while 36.4 per cent listed their occupations as "industrial." Even the 126,387 white-collar workers outnumbered the 123,060 farmers.

The "frontiersman" stereotype struggled with the fact that 70 per cent of the First Contingent were British-born and -bred.[2] An immigrant people, Canadians wisely put more stock in commitment than in birthplace. As one of our first great national institutions, the CEF was dominated by the foreign-born. Only the MSA allowed the Canadian-born to become a 51.2 per cent majority by November 1918.[3]

Of 470,224 soldiers who served overseas during the war, 47.0 per cent were Canadian-born; of the 194,869 who never left Canada, 61.1 per cent were native-born. (In Canada as a whole, the native-born were a 77 per cent majority in the 1911 census.) The other main birthplace was the British Isles (36.8 per cent), with England dominant (25.3 per cent) over Scotland (7.7 per cent) and Ireland (3.1 per cent). American-born volunteers contributed 1 per cent of the CEF overseas.

Religion mattered in 1914–18, perhaps intrinsically, and certainly for the allocation of chaplaincies. Anglicans predominated (30.9 per cent); Catholics followed (22.9 per cent); and the Methodists (13.6 per cent) fell far behind their Presbyterian rivals (21.1 per cent). As already noted, army lore suggests that the undecided automatically became Anglicans on their attestation forms unless they had joined a kilted battalion, for which the faith of John Knox seemed more appropriate. A small minority of 56 officers, a nursing sister, and 2,655 other ranks professed themselves to be Jews.

The Patriotic Fund could be grateful that, overwhelmingly, the CEF was single (79.6 per cent), though the MSA guaranteed that there would be more bachelors in the whole CEF than in the overseas part of the CEF (78.3 per cent). Officers were much less likely to be single (64.7 per cent) than their men, while nursing sisters were almost obliged to be more so (98.4 per cent).

However celibate, the CEF was a little older than its common image. The average age at enlistment was 26.3 years. Most soldiers —61.7 per cent—were in their twenties, with 10 per cent younger and 28.3 per cent older. The oldest recorded member was 80; the youngest, 10.

For a professedly unmilitary people, more than a third of those who joined the CEF reported previous military experience, although 152,865 could claim service only in the militia. No group was more influential than the 18,959 ex–British regulars, barely 3.1 per cent of the total but conspicuous in almost every unit history and memoir.

NOTES

I: BUSINESS AS USUAL

1 Nicholson, *C.E.F.*, 5–6; Wilson, *Ontario*, xvii–xix.

2 Morton, *Military History of Canada*, 129; Morton, "The Cadet Movement in the Moment of Canadian Militarism," *Journal of Canadian Studies* 13/2 (1978), p. 66; Toronto *Globe*, Dec. 12, 1913.

3 W.D. Woods, "Reminiscences of a Private Soldier," in the author's possession, p. 1.

4 On the Canadian peace movement, pre-1914, see Socknat, *Witness Against War*, pp. 28–48.

5 Nicholson, *C.E.F.*, 4-5.

6 Winter, *Hon. Sir Sam Hughes*, pp. 132 34.

7 On Hughes and the militia, see Haycock, *Sam Hughes*, and Winter, *Hon. Sir Sam Hughes*.

8 Morton, *The Canadian General*, p. 309.

9 *Canadian Annual Review*, 1912, p. 287; Morton, *The Canadian General*, pp. 309–10; see also Woodman Leonard papers, University of Western Ontario.

10 See James L. Hughes, "Drill in Schools," *The Canadian School Journal* 1/5 (1877) and 1/7 (1877), p. 112, and Morton, "The Cadet Movement."

11 *Report of the Department of Militia and Defence*, 1913; *The Militia List*, 1914.

12 See Morton, *Ministers and Generals*. Though a Canadian, Brigadier-General W.D. Otter, took the senior military post, Chief of the General Staff, in 1908, it was promptly subordinated to the Inspector General, a British officer. When the Canadian, in turn, became Inspector General, the British officer who became Chief of the General Staff once again was senior. Not until 1919 did a Canadian become the senior officer in the Department of Militia and Defence. See Morton, *The Canadian General*, pp. 292–93.

13 See, for example, Denison, *Soldiering in Canada*, pp. 283–84; Morton (*The*

Last War Drum, pp. 142–43, 153–54) bluntly disagrees and insists that Middleton's good sense and professionalism shortened the campaign and saved soldiers' lives. Praise for a British general is uncommon in Canada.

14 Morton, *The Canadian General*, pp. 242–43.

15 Gwatkin's predecessor had been fired after resisting Hughes's desire to expand "provisional" courses for would-be officers. See NAC RG 7 G 21, no. 265, Memorandum re General, June 1913; PRO CO 537.498, "Resignation of Major-General Mackenzie," encl. B; Mackenzie to Borden, Apr. 19, 1912; Harris, *Canadian Brass*, pp. 297–98.

16 See Morton, *Military History of Canada*, pp. 96–97.

17 *Canadian Annual Review*, 1914, 201.

18 When Robert Borden formed his cabinet in 1911, his cousin Fred had been one of Hughes's warmest supporters for the militia portfolio. In turn, Sir Fred was the Borden commemorated when Hughes opened the big new camp on the Angus Plains in central Ontario. See Brown, *Borden*, vol. 1, pp. 202–4; Borden, *Memoirs*, vol. 1, p. 33.

19 On reforms under Borden, see Carman Miller, "Sir Frederick William Borden and Military Reform, 1896–1911," *Canadian Historical Review*, 1969.

20 Ontario had three divisions, based in London, Toronto, and Kingston; Quebec had two, centred on Montreal and Quebec City. The 6th Division, with headquarters at Halifax, covered the Maritimes. In the West, the old military districts continued. Military District (MD) 10 covered Manitoba and northwestern Ontario; MD 11 was British Columbia; Saskatchewan was MD 12; and Alberta, MD 13. In 1916, the "divisions" were renamed Military Districts. Nova Scotia became MD 6, and New Brunswick and P.E.I., MD 7. Since there were now seven districts in the East, not nine, there were no MDS 8 and 9.

21 On the American threat, see Harris, *Canadian Brass*, pp. 83–85 and *passim*.

22 The label is, of course, borrowed from Carl Berger, *The Sense of Power*, exp. ch. X.

23 Harris, *Canadian Brass*, pp. 82 ff; Preston, *Canada and "Imperial Defence,"* pp. 344–461 *passim*.

24 Brereton, *The British Soldier*.

25 Haycock, *Sam Hughes*, pp. 180–81; Harris, *Canadian Brass*, pp. 92–95; Nicholson, *C.E.F.*, pp. 14–15.

26 Canada, House of Commons, *Debates*, Jan. 26, 1916.

27 *Ottawa Citizen*, July 31, 1914.

28 Canada, House of Commons, *Debates*, Aug. 22, 1914, p. 95.

29 Duguid, *Official History*, appx. 44, p. 37.

30 Morris, *But This Is Our War*, pp. 26–27.

31 Macfie, *Letters Home*, pp. xiv–xv.

32 *Canada Year Book*, 1915; Thompson, *Harvests of War*, pp. 46–47.

33 Duguid, *Official History*, pp. 25–34, appxs. 51–66.

34 Morton and Wright, *Winning the Second Battle*, pp. 5–6; Morris, *Canadian Patriotic Fund*, pp. 9–16, 21–26.

35 IWM, 90/7/1 Garnet Durham, "My Experiences in the War, 1914–1918," Durham to R.J. Archibald Steuart, Sep. 14, 1914, pp. 3–4.

36 Anderson, *I, That's Me*, pp. 17–18.

37 Port Credit *Review*, Aug. 22, 1914.

38 Erindale, Sinclair Diary, August.

39 Fetherstonhaugh, *Royal Montreal Regiment*, pp. 5–7.

40 Duguid, *Official History*, appx. 133; Williams, *Princess Patricia's*, pp. 6–10.

41 Erindale, Mackenzie Papers, A.C. Mackenzie to brother, Aug. 21, 1914.

42 Duguid, *Official History*, pp. 89–90.

43 Greenhous, *Dragoon*, pp. 173–86; Haycock, *Sam Hughes*, pp. 182–83. Hughes was accused of choosing Price because he was a Conservative and of choosing Valcartier because it gave substantial business to the railway promoters Sir William Mackenzie and Sir Donald Mann. The charges seem groundless.

44 On the Army Service Corps, see Warren, *Wait for the Waggon*, pp. 68–70; on the Medical Corps, see Macphail, *Medical Services*, pp. 20–24.

45 Interview, J.A. Stoddart. Pay rates are reported in Duguid, *Official History*, pp. 56–57, appx. 91.

46 Macfie, *Letters Home*, p. 6.

47 This effectively robbed Militia Headquarters of one of its most senior staff officers, but Williams was a Conservative and biddable. Harris, *Canadian Brass*, pp. 95–96.

48 Among those who encountered him on their arrival were Sinclair (Diary) and Anderson (*I, That's Me*, pp. 21–23.)

49 Nicholson, *C.E.F.*, pp. 14-15.

50 Erindale, Sinclair Diary, p. 5.

51 Canada in 1914 was a self-governing colony in which British law prevailed when Canadian law was silent. Canada's Militia Act made no provision for an overseas expeditionary force, beyond section 79, a provision obviously designed to allow troops to cross the U.S. frontier in event of a replay of the War of 1812.

52 Duguid, *Official History*, pp. 54–57.

53 The divisional artillery in 1914 consisted of three brigades, each of three bat-

teries, and an ammunition column to collect and deliver munitions. Each battery initially had six 18-pounder field guns. In addition, a division had a battery of 60-pounder heavy guns with its own ammunition column. Because British factories had not delivered their orders, Canada could not provide the battery of 4.5-inch howitzers that formed part of a normal British division's artillery. Those of Canada's 200 modern guns not assigned to the division were shipped to England as a patriotic gift to the mother country, leaving little to train later contingents.

54 Duguid, *Official History*, pp. 62–65; Haycock, *Sam Hughes*, pp. 184–85; Hyatt, *Sir Arthur Currie*, pp. 4–14.

55 Macphail, *Medical Services*, pp. 11–14.

56 Frank Yates, 3rd Battalion, a British veteran, recalled whispering advice to his officer when Hughes had suddenly appeared to demand that they form a square to receive cavalry (Interview).

57 Duguid (*Official History*, pp. 89–90) claimed that all men fired at least 50 shots from the 100- and 200-yard range, and some fired at 300 yards.

58 British army tacticians believed that rushing the enemy with "cold steel" was the best way of moving soldiers across the last 300 to 400 yards of fire-swept ground. The alternative—moving from one fire position to another—took too long and, they feared, gave a frightened soldier too many opportunities to duck out of the battle. Bayonet fighting might seem silly in retrospect, but it had a logical, if sacrificial, purpose.

59 IWM, 81/9/1, W.S. Lighthall Memoirs, pp. 1–2, in Mathieson, *Grandfather's War*. Veterans will note that later drill books reduced the angle between the feet.

60 IWM, P 443, S.V. Brittain, "The First World War Papers of Lieutenant S.V. Brittain," Diary of Stanley Victor Brittain, Sep. 17, 1914, p. 3. (The title of the collection refers to "Stanley" but a biographical note supplied by the family refers to "Sidney.") Loomis survived his men's censure, distinguished himself in battle, and ended the war in command of the 3rd Canadian Division.

61 Macfie, *Letters Home*, p. 3.

62 Later generations might find the word *imperial* confusing. Under the Army Act, "Imperial troops" were those raised in directly ruled colonies like Jamaica and Malaya. Canadians (and Australians, New Zealanders, and South Africans) were called "Imperials" by their British hosts, while *they* applied the term to the British troops. The Australian equivalent to CEF was "Australian Imperial Force," or AIF. Confusing, eh?

63 Macfie, *Letters Home*, p. 3.

64 The clothing issue is detailed in Duguid, *Official History*, appx. 106, pp. 70–73.

65 Morton, *Ministers and Generals*, p. 121; Morton, *The Canadian General*, pp. 157, 148, 203.

66 IWM, 79/31/3, John E. Sutton memoirs (compiled by Miss V.W. Sullivan, niece), pp. 8–9.

67 By the Second World War, the claim might even be true, as the Colt had evolved into the Browning, a machine-gun used in British fighters and by the U.S. Army. Unfortunately, the evolution still had a long way to go in 1914.

68 Duguid, *Official History*, pp. 72–73, 84.

69 Macfie, *Letters Home*, p. 3. See also IWM, Stanley Brittain papers.

70 IWM, Lighthall Memoirs, p. 4.

71 IWM, Garnet Durham diary, p. 5.

72 Ibid., p. 4.

73 Brown, *Borden*, vol. 2, p. 15.

74 A.J. Gorrie to Price, Oct. 6, 1914, in Duguid, *Official History*, appx. 130.

75 Duguid, *Official History*, p. 100.

76 Cited fully by Duguid, ibid., appx. 140.

77 Ibid., p. 104; Erindale, Sinclair diary, p. 8.

II: THE OLD ORIGINALS

1 The exceptions included men in ships where there were too many horses to be cared for properly and others where feeding arrangements were bad. See Nicholson, *C.E.F.*, pp. 30–31; Dancocks, *Welcome to Flanders Fields*, p. 54.

2 Anderson, *I, That's Me*, p. 27.

3 IWM, Brittain memoirs, pp. 10–14.

4 NAC, Lou Elliott Papers, Elliott to Askew, Oct. 13, 1914. See also W.S. Lighthall, 4.

5 Duguid, *Official History*, pp. 105–9.

6 NAC, MG 30 E 8, Creelman Papers, diary, Oct. 18, 1914.

7 IWM, Bombardier John Sutton, Oct. 13, 1915.

8 Macfie, *Letters Home*, p. 9.

9 Trythall, *Boney Fuller*, p. 33. Garnet Durham, who had trained in the Territorials, agreed Canada had sent "a fine army"—"but badly officered," he insisted. IWM, Garnet Durham diary, pp. 6–7.

10 Trythall, *Boney Fuller*, p. 34.

11 Nicholson, *C.E.F.*, p. 32.

12 Ibid., pp. 28–29; Morton, *Peculiar Politics*, pp. 21–23.

13 Thanks to Duguid's credulity (*Official History*, pp. 126–27), the myth persists. In fact, the British had asked for and received an infantry division. As we shall see, Canadians would be broken up for training at the front and then would take over a quiet sector. The British did not break up Territorials or any colonial contingents (see ibid., appx. 119).

14 Haycock, *Sam Hughes*, pp. 186–88.

15 Ibid., pp. 188–89.

16 On Carson, see Morton, *Peculiar Politics*, pp. 31–33; Duguid, *Official History*, pp. 127–28, appx. 188.

17 Dancocks, *Gallant Canadians*, p. 10; Dancocks, *Welcome to Flanders Fields*, pp. 65–66; based on interview with Victor Lewis on "In Flanders Field," CBC transcript, program 3, 1964.

18 IWM, Garnet Durham diary, p. 10.

19 Macphail, *Medical Services*, p. 29, and below.

20 The issue arose in 1916 over the question of which wife in a bigamous relationship received a soldier's pension. Ottawa decided that the wife in Canada, even if "unmarried," had priority. Morton and Wright, *The Second Battle*, p. 6 and n. 18.

21 NAC, MG 30 E 11, E.W.B. Morrison diary, Oct. 21, 1914. Duguid, *Official History*, p. 138, appx. 189; Dancocks, *Welcome to Flanders Fields*, pp. 66–67. Colonel Creelman noted the immediate improvement in order and discipline. See NAC, Creelman diary, Dec. 19, 1914.

22 Greenhous, *Dragoon*, p. 177; on weather, see Duguid, *Official History*, pp. 135–36.

23 Comment by Sinclair, Diary, Nov. 4, 1914.

24 In Mathieson, *Grandfather's War*, p. 34, and cited by Dancocks in *Welcome to Flanders Fields*, pp. 61–62.

25 Mathieson, *Grandfather's War*, p. 35.

26 Swettenham, *McNaughton*, vol. 1, p. 37; RG 24, C5 vol. 1832, GAQ 8-15-0.

27 Morton, *Peculiar Politics*, pp. 45 ff.

28 Cited by Dancocks in *Welcome to Flanders Fields*, p. 63; see also NAC, MG 30 E 505, Curtis Papers, Curtis to mother, Dec. 6, 1914.

29 Macphail, *Medical Services*, pp. 157–58; Macfie, *Letters Home*, pp. 9–10, 27 Oct. and Nov. 10, 1914.

30 Tuchman, *The Guns of August*; MacDonald, *1914*; Corbett-Smith, *Retreat from Mons*.

31 On 1st Ypres, see MacDonald, 1914; Giles, *The Ypres Salient*; Farrar-Hockley, *Death of an Army*, p. 181; Owen, *Glory Departing*, pp. 113–14.

32 Bidwell and Graham, *Fire-Power*.

33 Of 131 officers and 1,013 other ranks lost to the Contingent during its months in England, 91 officers and 460 other ranks were in various categories of misfit. Five officers and 63 other ranks died during the time on Salisbury Plain (Duguid, *Official History*, pp. 140–41).

34 NAC, MG 30 E 1, Alldritt Papers, letters of Jan.-Feb. 1915.

35 Worthington, *Amid the Guns*, pp. 16–17.

36 On the Ross, see ibid., appx. III. The British army's school of musketry had recommended a semi-automatic rifle such as the one the Mexican army had already adopted. Budget and military conservatism meant that British soldiers had to wait until 1949 for the .280-mm rifle under study before 1914 (Bidwell and Graham, *Fire-Power*, p. 27).

37 Erindale, Sinclair Diary, p. 37.

38 Ottawa sent 40,000 pairs of overshoes to make up for the fact that the boots leaked and even dissolved in the wet (Duguid, *Official History*, appxs. 204 and 205). A parliamentary committee repudiated the claim from the field that cardboard had been used in the soles ("Report of the Special Parliamentary Committee on the Boot Inquiry," Canada, House of Commons, *Journals*, 51, appx., part III; Duguid, *Official History*, appx. 205.

39 Duguid, *Official History*, appxs. 209, 227; RG 9 III, vol. 20, 4-10-4, Alderson to Carson, Mar. 28, 1915.

40 Duguid, *Official History*, appxs. 203 and 214, and, on Hughes's response, 221; Greenhous, *Dragoon*, p.178.

41 Duguid, *Official History*, appxs. 210-12.

42 Kerry and McDill, *Royal Canadian Engineers*, vol. 1, p. 80, citing Duguid, *Official History*, vol. 1, appx. 227.

43 Duguid, *Official History*, pp. 143–44.

44 On the shovels, OC 2302, Sep. 4, 1914; RG 9 III, vol. 69, 10-4-12, McRae to Perley, May 15, 1917.

45 Duguid, *Official History*, appx. 227.

46 Battalions of the British army in Britain had changed from eight to four companies on January 1, 1914, partly to reflect European organization, chiefly to conceal their skeletal condition after sending drafts to Imperial garrisons. Some infantry reformers saw the benefit in smaller fire-units—platoons with four 10-man sections under a corporal rather than two half-companies, each with 25-man sections under a sergeant. Unfortunately, the state of training of raw British or Canadian battalions almost precluded any real tactical units smaller than the 200-man company under a captain or major (Bidwell and

Graham, *Fire-Power*; John A. English, *On Infantry*, pp. 4, 8; Duguid, *Official History*, pp. 147–50).

47 Currie fought in vain to preserve Edmonton's 11th Battalion for his brigade but lost to the 10th Battalion, with its contingents from Calgary and Winnipeg (Dancocks, *Welcome to Flanders Fields*, p. 74).

48 iwm, Garnet Durham diary, p. 13; Anderson, *I, That's Me*, pp. 17 ff.

49 Cavalry brigades had three regiments and a couple of batteries of horse artillery, provided in this case by the permanent force's Royal Canadian Horse Artillery. King Edward's Horse was formed from "colonials" who happened to be living and working in London.

50 In 1914, Britain's Liberal government approved Home Rule for Ireland. Ulster Protestants threatened civil war. The loyalty of army officers, many of them Irish Protestants, was in doubt. When Seely attempted to find out whether he could count on the Irish garrisons to put down resistance in Ulster, officers of a cavalry brigade at the Curragh, headed by Brigadier-General Hubert Gough, resigned. The "Curragh Mutiny" led to the resignations of Seely and the military chief of staff, Sir John French. The outbreak of war in August was a blessed relief. Home Rule was postponed for "the duration," and officers patched up (though they did not forget) their differences, but Seely, as a "politician," remained *persona non grata*. Handing him to the Canadians must have seemed a shrewd move. See Morton, *Peculiar Politics*, pp. 35–36; Seely, *Adventure*, p. 217.

51 nac, Perley Papers, vol. 2: Borden to Perley, Feb. 6, 1915.

52 Dancocks, *Welcome to Flanders Fields*, p. 75; Mathieson, *My Grandfather's Way*, pp. 37–38.

53 Erindale, Sinclair diary, Feb. 9, 1915.

54 Ibid.

55 iwm, Brittain diary, Feb. 9, 1915.

56 Ibid., Feb. 13, 1915.

57 Ibid., Feb. 15, 1915. Also Sinclair diary, Feb. 11–14, 1915.

58 Johnson letters, Feb. 26, 1915.

59 Duguid, *Official History*, p. 173.

60 Ibid., 60.22, p. 175.

61 Ibid., pp. 189–94; Nicholson, *C.E.F.*, pp. 50–53.

62 Duguid (*Official History*, p. 195) reports 1 officer and 67 other ranks killed and 10 officers and 200 wounded on the first 24-day tour in the front lines.

63 Morton, *Canadian General*, pp. 184 ff.

64 Duguid, *Official History*, pp. 200–1; Nicholson, *C.E.F.*, p. 56.

65 Nicholson, *C.E.F.*, pp. 56–57; Dancocks, *Welcome to Flanders Fields*, p. 101.

66   Dancocks, *Welcome to Flanders Fields*, p. 102.

67   Nicholson, *C.E.F.*, p. 56.

68   NAC, MG 30 E 505, Curtis Papers, letter to his mother, Apr. 16, 1915.

69   Duguid, *Official History*, appx. 339.

70   Nicholson, *C.E.F.*, pp. 58–61.

71   On the use of the gas, see Haber, *The Poisonous Cloud*, pp. 30–32.

72   Nicholson, *C.E.F.*, p. 64.

73   RG 24, G.S. Diary, 1st Canadian Division, "Report on Operations, 22 April–4 May 1915"; Nicholson, *C.E.F.*, p. 62.

74   Nicholson, *C.E.F.*, p. 63.

75   Ibid., p. 66; Dancocks, *Welcome to Flanders Fields*, pp. 122–31.

76   Dancocks, *Welcome to Flanders Fields*, pp. 131, 140–43.

77   Ontario Archives, MV 2060, Sgt. William Miller, letter, n.d.

78   Pte. Tom Drummond in RG 24, C5, vol. 1832, GAQ 8-15-0.

79   Nicholson, *C.E.F.*, pp. 71–74; Dancocks, *Welcome to Flanders Fields*, pp. 162–64.

80   Cited in McWiliams and Steel, *Gas!*, p. 119.

81   Nicholson, *C.E.F.*, pp. 76–77.

82   Ibid., p. 77.

83   Dancocks, *Welcome to Flanders Fields*, pp. 192–93. The episode would be remembered as both truth and rumour since the British official historian, Brigadier-General J.E. Edmonds, had been Snow's staff officer. The episode and its interpretation is treated in Travers, *The Killing Ground*, p. 204 n. 2. See also NAC, MG 30 E 75, Urquhart Papers, E.F. Lyon to Urquhart, Jun. 22, 1935.

84   Nicholson, *C.E.F.*, pp. 77–88.

85   Ibid., pp. 88–90; Williams, *P.P.C.L.I.*, vol. 1, pp. 30–34.

86   NAC, MG 30 E 8, Creelman diary, Jul. 30, 1915, p. 42; Dancocks, *Welcome to Flanders Fields*, 177n.

87   Harold Peat, *Private Peat*, 22.

III: DOING YOUR BIT

1   Montreal *Star*, Oct. 8, 1914, cited also in *Canadian Annual Review*, 1914, p. 217.

2   *Canadian Annual Review*, 1915, p. 188, from Canada, House of Commons, *Debates*, Feb. 24, 1915.

3 The "Yellow Peril" helped persuade Australia and New Zealand to adopt versions of universal military training. That helped the two countries to send a combined two divisions as the famous Australian and New Zealand Army Corps (ANZAC) when Canada, with a larger population, sent only one.

4 Speech to the Canadian Club, Halifax, Dec. 18, 1914, cited by Brown, *Borden*, vol. 2, p. 22.

5 Cited in *Canadian Annual Review*, 1915, p. 186.

6 Gagnon, *Le 22e bataillon*, p. 57.

7 NAC, MG 30 E 277, Francis-Xavier Maheux papers, Folder, Aug.-Dec. 1914, to his wife [Oct. 1914].

8 Macdonell Papers (private collection), letter to his father, [1915.]

9 NAC, MG 30 D 150, Macphail Papers, diary, Oct. 28, 1915.

10 IWM, 76/169/1, M.M. Hood, "The First World War Memoirs of M. McIntyre-Hood," Part 1, p. 8.

11 Roy, *Journal of Private Fraser*, pp. 11–14; Roy, *For Most Conspicuous Bravery*, p. 28.

12 IWM, 88/46/1, Lieutenant A.G. May, "Personal Experiences of the War Years, 1915–1917," p. 1.

13 NAC, MG 30 E 393, Edward Foster, narrative, p. 1 (Foster joined the 159th Battalion on June 26, 1916).

14 "Recollections of Edgar Harold" (unpublished manuscript by Donald A. Smith for the Paris *Star Transcript*, contributed by the author), p. 331.

15 IWM, 79/17/1, F.H. Underhill interview by R.D. Francis, pp. 124–26.

16 IWM, Garnet Durham letters, May 15, 1915, p. 30.

17 Haycock, *Hughes*, pp. 199 ff.

18 See J.M. Bliss, "The Methodist Church and World War I," in Berger, *Conscription*, pp. 43-44. Hughes's casual suggestion of a battalion of clergy was taken seriously by R.M. Dickey of the Reading Camp Association, forerunner of Frontier College. Major General Gwatkin, with his customary irony, observed: "I would not group these godly men into a battalion, I would distribute them among the different units of the CEF so that the lump may be leavened." NAC, RG 24, vol. 1998, HQ 593-6-2 vol. 10.

19 NAC, RG 24, vol. 6993.

20 See Nicholson, *C.E.F.*, p. 221. The Chief Recruiting Officer for Canada and the person appointed in Toronto were also Methodist ministers named Williams. The Québécois press, claimed Nicholson, "indiscriminately confused the records of the three officers of the same name, thereby aggravating a largely imaginary grievance."

21 The colonels of CEF battalions are listed in the *Canadian Annual Review*, 1916, p. 304.

22 Dempsey, "The Indians and World War One."

23 NAC, RG 24, vol. 1401, HQ 593-6-2, vol. 18, Daigle to GOC, 1st Brigade, Aug. 29, 1916.

24 On recruiting, see *Canadian Annual Review*, 1916, pp. 306 ff; NAC, RG 24, vol. 1399 ff. On events in Berlin, see Chadwick, *The Battle for Berlin, Ontario*, esp. chs. II and III.

25 See Walker, "Race and Recruitment in World War I," pp. 9–21 and *passim*.

26 Ibid., pp. 16–17. Of 194 Japanese Canadians identified in the CEF, 31 were killed; 41 were wounded, of whom 11 died; and 4 won the Military Medal. See Canada, House of Commons, *Debates*, Apr. 29, 1920, p. 1812.

27 *Canadian Annual Review*, 1916, p. 423.

28 Van Paassen, *Days of Our Years*, pp. 64–65.

29 Desmond Morton, "What Did Peel Do in the Great War?" *History and Social Science Teacher*, 23, 1987, p. 28.

30 *Toronto Daily Star*, Apr. 22, 1916.

31 Morton and Wright, *Winning the Second Battle*, pp. 25–26.

32 The colonel of the 41st was incompetent; the chaplain was a drunk; and the assistant adjutant was convicted of murder, escaping the gallows when a petition by prominent Quebeckers explained that he had always been known as an imbecile. See Morton, "The Short, Unhappy History of the 41st Battalion," pp. 76–78; NAC, MG 30 E 351, Claude Craig diary, 1915. See also Gagnon, *Le 22e bataillon*, pp. 48–52.

33 Morton, "French Canadian Officers and the First World War," p. 93.

34 NAC, RG 24, vol. 4509, f.50-1-49, vol. 9; Colonel Fages to the Adjutant General.

35 See Frost, *Fighting Men*, pp. 88–94. The future Ontario premier blamed the generals, not his hero, Sam Hughes. Of 258 CEF battalions formed form volunteers, only two with a number higher than 90 served as infantry with the Corps, the 102nd and the 116th. The Royal Canadian Regiment, the PPCLI, four battalions created from CMR regiments, and four CEF battalions were collected in France in early 1916 to form the 3rd Canadian Division. In the spring of 1916, the 4th Division was formed in England from twelve more CEF battalions. The 123rd and 124th from Toronto, with Campbell's 107th, went to France as Pioneers—essentially labour battalions. Thirteen battalions were held for the 5th Division. The rest were converted into reinforcement holding units, or broken up after they reached England.

36 NAC, RG 24, vol. 4256 f. 10-27-1-10, vol. 1, Proceedings of COS conference, London, Ontario, Feb. 12, 1917.

37 Ibid., vol. 1402, HQ 593-6-2, vol. 22, Adjutant General memorandum, Jan. 9, 1917.

38 Canada, House of Commons, *Debates*, May 18, 1918, also cited in Borden, *Memoirs*, vol. 2, pp. 698–99.

39 See Canada, House of Commons, *Debates*, Aug. 20, 1917, p. 4721.

40 Cited by Granatstein and Hitsman, *Broken Promises*, pp. 85–86.

41 On administration and statistics associated with the Military Service Act, see ibid., pp. 83-88 and *passim*; Nicholson, *C.E.F.*, pp. 347–53, 551.

42 NAC, MG 26 H, R.L. Borden Papers, OC 516, Borden to Kemp, Apr. 11, 1918; ibid., Sefton to Borden, Mar. 26, 1918, f 58539, cited in Granatstein and Hitsman, *Broken Promises*, p. 89.

43 Erindale, Hamilton Papers, Ernest Hamilton to Sara, Jun. 14, 1917.

44 Erindale, Captain C.V. Williams Papers, Feb. 1, 1918.

45 Socknat (*Witness Against War*, pp. 81-88) describes these and other coercive incidents.

46 War Diary of the 2nd Depot Battalion, EOR, MD no. 3, Ottawa, Feb. 15, 1919.

47 As Corps commander, Sir Arthur Currie strongly objected to creating French-speaking units larger than a platoon. The sad memory of the 41st Battalion and the difficulties experienced by the 22nd Battalion with the men available from bad Quebec battalions may have influenced him. In fact, the break-up of the 5th Division and its French-speaking battalion restored the 22nd to its valiant and sacrificial role at Cherisy in 1918.

48 Cited in Nicholson, *C.E.F.*, p. 552, Appendix E.

IV: SOLDIERING

1 Captain Norman Rawson, cited in Canadian Military Institute, *Selected Papers*, 1926, p. 48.

2 Worthington, "*Worthy*," p. 52.

3 Will Bird, who enlisted in 1916, claimed that his doctor was paid $2. Regulations set the fee in 1916, as the daily pay of a captain, with a ceiling of $3.

4 Ernest Davies Papers, letter, Feb. 25, 1916.

5 RG 9 III, vol. 3750, Major G.S. Strathy War Diary, pp. 1, 3, 5.

6 Dinesen, *Merry Hell*, p.32.

7 Erindale, Hamilton Papers, Ernest Hamilton to Sara, Jun. 7, 1917.

8 IWM, Lighthall Papers, pp. 9-10.

9 NAC, MG 30 E 65, Harold Baldwin to family, Jul. 30, 1928.

10 IWM, C.S. Munro Papers, A.M. Munro to his father, H.G. Munro, Jan. 16, 1916, pp. 4–5.

11 IWM, E.W. Russell Papers, memoirs.

12 Macfie, *Letters Home*, to Jessie, Dec. 19, 1914, p. 15.

13 IWM, Garnet Durham letters, Dec. 13, 1915, p. 44.

14 Erindale, Youell Papers, Youell to his mother, Feb. 1, 1916.

15 NAC, MG 30 E 8, Creelman diary, Mar. 22, 1915. See also Winter, *Death's Men*, ch. III.

16 IWM, A.G. May Papers, memoirs, p. 2.

17 Noyes, *Stretcher Bearers on the Double*, p. 75.

18 NAC, MG 30 E 277, Maheux to his wife, Dec. 22, 1917.

19 NAC, MG 30 E 427, Macfie papers, Roy to Muriel, Feb. 2, 1918.

20 Morton, "French Canada and War," p. 84.

21 See Dempsey, "Indians in World War One," p. 83.

22 Wilson, *Ontario and the First World War*, pp. xlix–l. For a personal account of the heat and the consequences, NAC, MG 30 E 393, W. Foster memoir, July 1916. The 125th Battalion made equipment out of string and men insisted on using it to carry their water bottles, despite orders from their officers. One of their comrades collapsed from heat and was discharged (W.B. Woods to the author, Aug. 29, 1992).

23 Cited by Brereton, *The British Soldier*, p. 114.

24 See Howard Graham, *Citizen and Soldier*, pp. 24–25.

25 NAC, MG 30 E 351, Claude C. Craig memoirs.

26 A simplified drill thereafter limited saluting to the right arm.

27 British army regulations for field punishment:

Where an offender is sentenced to field punishment No. 1, he may, during the continuance of his sentence, unless the court-martial or the commanding officer otherwise directs, be punished as follows:

(a) He may be kept in irons, i.e. in fetters or handcuffs, or both fetters and handcuffs; and may be secured so as to prevent his escape.

(b) When in irons he may be attached for a period of periods not exceeding two hours in any one day to a fixed object, but he must not be so attached during more than three out of any four consecutive days, nor during more than twenty-one days in all.

(c) Straps or ropes may be used for the purpose of these rules in lieu of irons.

(d) He may be subjected to the like labour, employment, and restraint and dealt with in like manner as if he were under a sentence of imprisonment with hard labour.

28 NAC, MG 30 E 8, Creelman diary, Aug. 13, 1916, 70.

29 Bird, *Ghosts Have Warm Hands*, p. 5.

30 Erindale, Youell Papers, Lieutenant L.L. Youell to his mother, Mar. 3, 1916.

31 NAC, MG 30 E 459, Albert Nelson Papers, letter, Oct. 16, 1915.

32 Erindale, Angus Mowat Papers, Mowat to his parents, Apr. 25, 1915.

33 Erindale, Hamilton Papers, E.W. Hamilton to Sara, Apr. 28, 1917.

34 Noyes, *Stretcher Bearers on the Double*, p. 17.

35 IWM, A.G. May memoirs (approximately Jun. 24, 1915), p. 2.

36 NAC, MG 30 E 277, Maheux to his wife, May 16, 1915.

37 MG 30 E 170, Hazlewood to his mother, Dec. 1, 1916.

38 Noyes, *Stretcher Bearers on the Double*, p. 25.

39 IWM, Garnet Durham, Dec. 29, 1915, p. 51.

40 NAC, MG 30 E 277, Maheux to his wife, Aug. 1, 1915.

41 NAC, MG 30 E 459, Nelson Papers, Nov. 1916.

42 NAC, MG 30 E 351, Claude Craig, Dec. 1915.

43 IWM, A.G. May memoirs, p. 2.

44 Erindale, Hamilton Papers, Hamilton to Sara, May 19, 1917.

45 In *The Fiddlers*, a popular children's writer named Arthur Mee condemned the British liquor traffic for debauching innocent young Canadians when they had come to give their all for the Empire. To the indignation of temperance enthusiasts, censors suppressed the pamphlet on both sides of the Atlantic. See R.L. Borden Papers, OC 387. See also ibid., RLB 2343 on Mee's *The Parasites*, an outspoken anti-vice pamphlet by a prominent children's writer.

46 IWM, A.M. Munro letters, Jan. 16, 1916, p. 8.

47 Russenholt, *Six Thousand Canadian Men*, p. 16.

48 Duguid, *Official History*, appx. 111, pp. 97–99.

49 Worthington, "*Worthy*," p. 60.

50 Erindale, Captain C.V. Williams to his mother, Feb. 1, 1918.

51 MG 30 E 459, Dec. 5, 1916.

52 Erindale, Correll Papers, Correll to Will Correll, Jul. 12, 1916.

53 NAC, MG 30 E 8, Creelman diary, Nov. 19, 1916, p. 78.

54 Dinesen, *Merry Hell*, p. 149.

55 Ibid., p. 87.

56 Erindale, Claude V. Williams, to his mother, Oct. 7, 1916, pp. 26–27.

V: OFFICERS AND GENTLEMEN

1 From the commission of Lieutenant E.H. Pope, Canadian Engineers, 1916 (author's possession).

2 Morton, *A Military History of Canada*, p. 96.

3 Among Hughes's innumerable decisions was a small feminist "first." Unlike the CAMC's nursing sisters, who held non-combatant commissions like those of medical officers and chaplains, Lieutenants Joan Arnoldi and Mary Plummer of the Canadian Field Comforts Commission had the same commissions as male CEF officers, making them unique in all the warring armies.

4 See Harris, *Canadian Brass*, p. 100.

5 NAC, MG 30 II F 9, Harold M. Daly Papers, memoirs.

6 Professor R.C. Brown performed the original analysis of inspection reports though he is not responsible for this interpretation of it.

7 NAC, RG 9 III B 5, vol. 5, Lessard to Adjutant General [1915].

8 NAC, RG 24, vol. 1402, Lieutenant-Colonel G.S. Cantlie to GOC, 7th Infantry Brigade, Sep. 25, 1916.

9 See Smythe, *If You Can't Beat 'Em in the Alley*, pp. 54–55; Cohen won a Military Cross at Vimy; at Passchendaele he and his men took Graf House and he died defending it. His colonel recommended him for the Victoria Cross and a small Mogen David is part of the Black Watch memorial window in a Montreal Presbyterian church. See Topp, *The 42nd Battalion*, pp. 162–63, 165.

10 *Regulations and Orders for the Militia of Canada*, s. 541, Dec. 13, 1915.

11 "Officers' Ps & Qs: List of subjects which a young officer must know of or have some knowledge of before he can be selected for service in the field." Erindale Collection, Pope Papers.

12 Erindale Collection, Donald McKinnon Papers, letter to his family, Jul. 15, 1915.

13 *Canadian Military Gazette*, Feb. 9, 1915, cited in Warren, *Wait for the Waggon*, p. 73.

14 NAC, RG 24 v. 2043, HQC 2043, Hughes to Gwatkin n.d. [1916].

15 Ibid., Helmer to Gwatkin, Jan. 14, 1917.

16   Erindale, Youell Papers, Youell to his mother, Nov. 15, 1915.

17   Ibid., Nov. 19, 1915. Raymond Massey, a future actor, recalled of Ringwood that "he did give us young subalterns who knew nothing of the army an example of what an officer should be." Ringwood, a PF officer, finally escaped at the end of 1916, commanding the 60th Battery from Regina and endowing it with its formidable reputation for efficiency. While he was reconnoitering an advanced position during the battle of Amiens on August 10, 1918, a shell splinter killed him (Nicholson, *The Gunners of Canada*, vol. 2, p. 345).

18   Erindale, Youell Papers, Youell to his father, Dec. 6, 1915.

19   Ibid., Youell to his mother, Feb. 1, 1916.

20   Donald McKinnon Papers (author's possession). Canada's small peacetime Signals Corps provided units for the 1st Division but other units followed the British model and belonged to the Corps of Canadian Engineers. In 1915, when McKinnon joined, their depot was in Ottawa, but it later moved to Valcartier and then St. Jean.

21   Erindale, Donald McKinnon to his parents, Oct. 14, 1915.

22   McKinnon rose rapidly to sergeant in the unit that became the signal company for Canadian Corps Headquarters. Claiming to his parents that he wanted to make a more direct contribution to victory, he again dropped his rank and transferred to the field artillery in 1917, only to be killed by a shell splinter in his abdomen six months later.

23   Erindale, Sinclair Papers, Sinclair to Deborah, Apr. 30, 1915.

24   NAC, MG 30 E 545, D'Arcy Leonard to Blanid, Nov. 5, 1915.

25   Erindale, Mowat Papers, Angus Mowat to his father, Nov. 27, 1915.

26   Ward, ed., *The Memoirs of Chubby Power*, p. 44.

27   NAC, RG 24, vol. 1810, GAQ 1-7, p. 7.

28   NAC, MG 30 E 46, R.E.W. Turner Papers, pp. 7–39; Hunter to Mewburn, Nov. 5, 1917, p. 5334. Cited in Morton, *Peculiar Kind of Politics*, p. 151.

29   *Report of the OMFC*, 1918, p. 15.

30   UWO, Leonard Papers, D'Arcy Leonard to Jack Leonard, Feb. 29, 1916.

31   Erindale, Joseph Clark Papers, J.W.G. Clark to father, Aug. 19, 1916, p. 45.

32   Leonard Papers, D'Arcy Leonard to Jack Leonard, Feb. 29, 1916.

33   An analysis based on *Statistics of the Military Effort of the British Empire During the Great War, 1914–1920* (London, 1922), pp. 667 ff.

34   At Aldershot, Company Sergeant-Major William Bains, Royal Engineers, claimed that Lieutenant Charles Watt had knocked him off his bicycle by sticking his cane through the spokes and then punched him. A military policeman corroborated the story. Watt insisted that he had simply called out to the NCO for failing to salute and an officer with him agreed. So did the

member of the court martial (NAC T-8694, case 558-23-16).

35 Harris, *Canadian Brass*, p. 120; *Platoon Training, 1918* (March 1918).

36 See above, chapter II; Harris, *Canadian Brass*, pp. 98 ff.

37 NAC, MG 26 H, R.L. Borden Papers, OC 223-235(1), Alderson to Connaught, Dec. 4, 1914, 22857.

38 RG 9 III, v. 4024, fld. 4, f. 8, Macdonell to 1st Canadian Division, Jul. 27, 1918.

39 Greenhous, *Dragoon*, p. 237.

40 Court Martials, T 8695, 3828-1, Captain F.M. Perry.

41 NAC, MG 30 E 351, Claude Craig diary, Sept. 16, 1916.

42 NAC, MG 30 E 170, Frank Hazlewood diary, Aug. 24, 1917.

43 Erindale, Correll Papers, Correll to Lil, Sep. 19, 1916.

44 Noyes, *Stretcher Bearers on the Double*, p. 39.

45 *Streetsville Review*, Sep. 16, 1915.

46 Roy, ed., *Journal of Private Fraser*, p. 241.

47 Russenholt, *Six Thousand Men*, p. 132.

48 Ibid., p. 31.

49 Noyes, *Stretcher Bearers on the Double*, p. 160.

50 IWM, A.M. Munro Papers, Munro to his father, Feb. 4, 1917, p. 40.

51 Ibid., Nov. 27, 1918.

52 NAC, MG 30 E 417, Baxter Papers, memoirs, p. 13.

53 Dinesen, *Merry Hell*, p. 206.

54 IWM, Garnet Durham Papers, letter, June 1916, pp. 83–84.

55 Roy, ed., *Journal of Private Fraser*, p. 314.

56 Bird, *And We Go On*, p.143.

57 Ibid., pp. 143–44.

58 If I were fierce and bald and short of breath
   I'd live with scarlet majors at the Base
   And speed glum heroes up the line to death.
   You'd see me with my puffy petulant face,
   Guzzling and gulping in the best hotel,
   Reading the Roll of Honour. "Poor young chap,"
   I'd say, "I used to know his father well;—
   Yes, we've lost heavily in this last scrap."
   And when the war is done and youth stone dead,
   I'd toddle safely home and die—in bed.
   (Cited by Noyes, *Stretcher Bearers*, p. 156.)

59 Burns, *General Mud*, p. 63.

60 To compare the process that produced Canada's generals in the two world wars, see C.P. Stacey, "Canadian Leaders of the Second World War," *Canadian Historical Review* 66/1 (March 1985); Harris, *Canadian Brass*; and particularly John A. English, *The Canadian Army and the Normandy Campaign*.

61 NAC, RG 24, vol. 1504, HQ 683 1-30-5, vol. 1, Brown to MacBrien, n.d.

62 NAC, MG 30 E 8, Creelman Diary, Jan. 29, 1917 and *passim*.

63 Bird, *Ghosts Have Warm Hands*, p. 21.

64 Erindale, Ernest Davies memoirs, p. 33.

VI: UP THE LINE

1   Erindale, Claude V. Williams Papers, letter, n.d.

2   NAC, MG 30 E 351, Craig Papers, Claude Craig to his family, Jul. 17, 1916.

3   Erindale, W.B. Woods memoirs.

4   William Woods recalled that French and Belgian farms were better kept than Canadian, that the manure pits were usually neat and, even in hot weather, there were few flies (Woods to author, Aug. 29, 1992).

5   Bird, *And We Go On*, pp. 21–22.

6   Duguid, *Official History*, appx. 267, p. 193.

7   Dinesen, *Merry Hell*, p. 128.

8   See IWM, Magnus Hood memoirs, Part II, p. 4.

9   William Woods claimed that in his unit, the 1st Battalion, this ritual, like others, was ignored by all but outputs and men in the fire trenches (letter to the author, Aug. 29, 1992).

10 NAC, MG 30 E 731, J.V. Lacasse memoir, p. 51.

11 Rawling, *Surviving Trench Warfare*, pp. 25, 100, and *passim*.

12 Chapman, *A Passionate Prodigality*, p. 41.

13 Rawling, *Surviving Trench Warfare*, pp. 47-48, 71, 86, 88-89, 101-5. Woods, like other veterans, insists that resentment of the raiding policy was also an invitation to officers to fake the extent and vigour of their probes of the German line (letter to the author, Aug. 29, 1992).

14 Ashworth, *The Live and Let Live War*, p. 185.

15 Blunden, *Undertones of War*, pp. 36, 126.

16 Burns, *General Mud*, pp. 40–41. Rawling (*Surviving Trench Warfare*, pp. 128–29) insists that the losses from the raid had no effect on April 9 since the battalions decimated during the March 1 raid either did better than the

unscarred 87th Battalion, which failed to reach its objective or, in the case of the hard-hit 75th Battalion, never left its trenches because of the failure of the 87th.

17 The Colt had 348 parts, some of them defective. It was the forebear of the much-admired Browning machine-gun, used in fighter aircraft and by the U.S. infantry in the Second World War. Until it evolved, Canadians were happy to replace it with the Lewis gun.

18 By April, 1918, some Canadian battalions already had 32 Lewis guns, two per platoon. Each platoon was split in half-platoons, each under a sergeant and each with a Lewis-gun section and a rifle and grenade section (Rawling, *Surviving Trench Warfare*, pp. 174–75).

19 NAC, RG 24, vol. 1504, HQ 683 1-30-5, vol. 1, Anderson to Duguid, Feb. 4, 1937.

20 IWM, Lighthall "Memoirs," pp. 46–47.

21 William Woods to author, Aug. 29, 1992. For the more flattering views of staff officers and for evidence of growing tactical dependence on rifle grenades, see Rawling, *Surviving Trench Warfare*, pp. 83–84, 97–98, 172, and *passim*.

22 Cited in Reid, *Poor Bloody Murder*, p. 19.

23 William Woods, letter to author, Aug. 29, 1992.

24 NAC, MG 30 E 11, G.M. Davis private war diary, May 22, 1915.

25 F.W. Powell, "Soldiering," *The Goat*, 1927, cited by Greenhous in *Dragoon*, p. 192.

26 NAC, MG 30 E 113, George Bell, "Back to Blighty" m.s., p. 80.

27 NAC, MG 30 E 393, Arthur Foster Papers, p. 9.

28 Ibid., pp. 29–30.

29 Roy, ed., *Journal of Private Fraser*, p. 258.

30 Wise, *Canadian Airmen and the First World War*, appx. C.

31 NAC, MG 30 E 297, Maheux to his wife, Sep. 18–19, 1917.

32 Nicholson, *Gunners of Canada*, pp. 235, 333–34.

33 Cited by Captain Walter Moorhouse, Canadian Machine Gun Corps, in Reid, *Poor Bloody Murder*, p. 171. W.B. Woods insisted that he survived several gas attacks by using his respirator and that he remembered no discomfort (letter to the author, Aug. 29, 1992).

34 Cited by Graham, "*Sans Doctrine*"; see also Winter, *Death's Men*, p. 184.

35 NAC, RG 24, vol. 6992.

36 Ibid.

37 NAC, MG 30 E 442, Griffiths Papers, memoirs, p. 4.

38 Gagnon, *Le 22e bataillon*, p. 259.

39 Dinesen, *Merry Hell*, p. 120.

40 Nicholson, *Gunners of Canada*, p. 253. Woods dismissed the rat legends, insisting that he saw only one rat in twenty months at the front and four more months as a brigade runner (letter to the author, Aug. 29, 1992).

41 Erindale, Williams Papers, Williams to his mother, Dec. 9, 1916, p. 63.

42 Ibid., Williams to his father, Jan. 2, 1917, p. 75.

43 IWM, W.S. Lighthall, "Memoirs," p. 31.

44 Dinesen, *Merry Hell*, pp. 127-28. W.B. Woods passionately agreed: "Why do some people tell such lies, they give themselves away as they tell their story," he says of Dinesen (letter to the author, Aug. 29, 1992).

45 Cited in D. Read and others, *The Great War and Canadian Society*, 144. W.B. Woods recalled no abnormal discomfort in 1917. He kept his feet warm by rhythmically kicking his heels together (letter to the author, Aug. 29, 1992).

46 F.W. Powell, "Soldiering," *The Goat*, cited by Greenhous in *Dragoon*, p. 192.

47 NAC, MG 30 E 84, R.G.E. Leckie papers, Jan. 1, 1916.

48 Gagnon, *Le 22e bataillon*, p. 234.

49 NAC, MG 30 E 442, Griffiths memoirs, p. 4.

50 As usual, official intentions were not always apparent to ordinary soldiers. W.B. Woods remembered cold sentry duty but no hot drinks (letter to the author, Aug. 29, 1992).

51 Erindale, Beatty Papers, p. 7.

52 Erindale, Williams Papers, Williams to his mother, Nov. 18, 1916, p. 53.

53 Corneloup, *L'épopée du vingt-deuxième*, p. 30.

54 Bird, *Ghosts Have Warm Hands*, p. 112.

55 NAC, MG 30 E 442, Griffiths memoirs, p. 5; Black, *I Want One Volunteer*, p. 11.

56 W.B. Woods letter to the author, Aug. 29, 1992.

57 *Official History of the Medical Services: Hygiene*, vol. 2, p. 43.

58 IWM, John E. Sutton, "Memoirs," p. 56.

59 Roy, ed., *Journal of Private Fraser*, pp. 78–80.

60 NAC, MG 30 E 442, Griffiths memoirs, pp. 2–3.

61 Roy, ed., *Journal of Private Fraser*, p. 252.

62 Winter, *Death's Men*, pp. 147–48.

63 Noyes, *Stretcher Bearers*, p. 60.

64 NAC, MG 30 E 1, Bell memoirs, p. 38.

65 Ibid., p. 103.

66 Lapointe, *Souvenirs et impressions*, cited by Gagnon in *Le 22e bataillon*, pp. 261–62.

67 Boots had to be cleaned and blackened, and troops got skilful in scraping

gobs of mud from their uniforms or beating out the dirt if it had dried (Woods to the author, Aug. 29, 1992).

68 IWM, A.M. Munro to his father, Dec. 30, 1916, p. 37.

69 IWM, Garnet Durham to R.J. Archibald Steuart, Dec. 23, 1915, p. 109.

70 See below, chapter IX.

71 *Notes for Infantry Officers on Trench Warfare Compiled by the General Staff* (London, March 1916), p. 5.

VII: OVER THE TOP

1 See Morton, *Last War Drum*, pp. 65, 82, 105; Morton, *The Canadian General*, pp. 188–89.

2 Bidwell and Graham, *Fire-Power*, p. 51.

3 Cited by J.A. English, *On Infantry*, p. 13.

4 From the French "dégommer" or "to unglue."

5 Howard, "Men Against Fire," p. 522.

6 RG 24, vol. 1504, HQ 683-1-30-5, vol. 4, Odlum to Duguid, Feb. 16, 1937.

7 A few readers of this chapter may recognize some ideas which, distorted or misunderstood, sprang from their own heads. Among them may be Colonel John English, whose *On Infantry* is as incisive a work of applied history as any Canadian has written, and my own friend and former student, Bill Rawling, whose own work on tactics and technology in the Canadian Corps, *Surviving Trench Warfare: Technology and the Canadian Corps*, paralleled and inspired my own.

8 See Nicholson, *C.E.F.*, p. 170.

9 Goodspeed, "Prelude to the Somme," pp. 156–59.

10 *British Official History*, 1916, vol. 1, p. 436; Nicholson, *Fighting Newfoundlanders*, pp. 264–77; Cave, *Corporal Pittman*, pp. 100–23.

11 See, for example, Macdonald, *Somme*; Martin Middlebrook, *The First Day at the Somme*; and for a detailed look at the battlefield, Stowe and Woods, *Fields of Death*.

12 The 5th Division, still in England, wore maroon. Battalions were identified by a shape in a brigade colour, green for the 1st, 4th, 7th, and 10th; red for the 2nd, 5th, 8th, and 11th; and blue for the 3rd, 6th, 9th, and 12th. In each brigade, the first battalion wore a circle (one side), the second a semi-circle, the third a triangle, and the fourth a square. See Nicholson, *C.E.F.*, appx. G, facing page 556.

13 IWM, A.M. Munro letters, Jun. 14, 1917, p. 46.

14 NAC, MG 30 E 297, Maheux to his wife, Sep. 20, 1916.

15 Russenholt, *Six Thousand Canadian Men*, p. 44.

16 RG 24, vol. 1402, G.S. file 1, folder 44, "Lessons to be derived from Operations on the Somme," Dec. 23, 1916.

17 After the Somme, in November 1916, Turner agreed to assume the military command under Perley at the Overseas Ministry in London, and command of his division passed to Currie's able gunner, Harry Burstall.

18 *Instructions for the Training of a Division for the Attack* (London: War Office, December 1916), p. 58.

19 Ibid.

20 Ibid.

21 RG 9 III, vol. 1803, 1 C.I.B., Griesbach memorandum, Mar. 3, 1917.

22 Rawling, *Surviving Trench Warfare*, pp. 91–92.

23 W.B. Woods remembered only an afternoon of training for Vimy, "wandering around in a wood where there were supposed to be tapes." Nine 2x4s represented nine elm trees along a road. He was prepared for a useful landmark (letter to the author, Aug. 29, 1992).

24 Swettenham, *McNaughton*, vol. 1, pp. 67–74.

25 MacDonald, *Gun Fire*, p. 73, cited by Nicholson in *Gunners of Canada*, I, p. 275.

26 Burns, *General Mud*, p. 43.

27 W.B. Woods, who actually moved down a slope in his part of taking Vimy Ridge, recalled encountering a single machine-gun that held up his 1st Battalion for twenty minutes. He would have welcomed some of the artillery fire lavished on the first German line. He also remembered a troop of the Canadian Light Horse sent into a hopeless attack (letter to the author, Aug. 29, 1992).

28 RG 9 III vol. 2526 52/7, Report of 1st Division.

29 Roy, ed., *Journal of Private Fraser*, p. 261.

30 Haig's explanation for continuing the battle, never crystal clear, was not so much the French army mutinies or the alleged need to close Belgian ports to German U-boats. Rather, Haig's concern was to counter the growth of a peace party in Britain headed by a former governor general of Canada, Lord Lansdowne, by delivering a clear victory. Paradoxically, nothing fed war-weariness in the army as much as the dreadful Passchendaele struggle.

31 RG 9 III, vol. 4393, Training Directive, 2nd Division, December 1917.

32 NAC, MG 30 E 393, Foster memoirs, p. 34.

33 Five large divisions had sixty infantry battalions; six smaller ones would require only fifty-four battalions. An additional divisional artillery would have had to be organized, as well as an extra divisional and three brigade headquarters, not to mention a second corps headquarters and a small army headquarters. The resulting opportunities for promotion were boundless.

34 Kerry and McDill, *History of the Royal Canadian Engineers*, p. 162.

35 Nicholson, *C.E.F.*, p. 389.

36 Topp, *The 42nd Battalion*, p. 282.

37 NAC, MG 30 E 32, Corporal Albert West diary, Sep. 9, 1918.

38 Currie diary, Nov. 1, 1918, cited by Nicholson in *C.E.F.*, p. 475.

39 Nicholson, *C.E.F.*, pp. 405, 420.

40 Dancocks, *Spearhead to Victory*, pp. 115–17, 129–130.

41 Correspondence with the author, 1988–1992.

VIII: A BLIGHTY

1 In 1939–45, despite major improvements in blood transfusion and the first antibiotics, John Ellis argues, in *The Sharp End*, that mobile warfare over greater distances often meant a longer interval between the infliction of a wound and medical treatment.

2 Macphail, *Official History: Medical Services*, p. 235; Dancocks, *Welcome to Flanders Fields*, pp. 112, 114.

3 Macphail, *Official History: Medical Services*, pp. 250–1.

4 Adami, *War Story of the CAMC*, p. 34.

5 Among the Matron-in-Chief's problems was the sister of a member of Parliament who, whatever her devotion to her patients, tangled with a succession of matrons whom she regarded as her social inferiors. When the woman failed to get a promotion, she appealed for justice to her brother and the Overseas Minister, Sir Edward Kemp: "Now do you think it is fair that a common R.C. woman like Miss MacDonald should out of personal spite be able to keep on giving me kicks and get away with it?" The minister, at least, was unmoved.

6 *Report of the Overseas Ministry*, 1918, pp. 403–7.

7 On Kelly, Neiley, and the operations of the CADC, see RG 9, II B 2, vol. 3747.

8 *Report of the Overseas Ministry*, 1918, p. 408.

9 On Pearson's experience in the CAMC, see John English, *Shadow of Heaven: The Life of Lester Pearson*, vol. 1: *1897–1948* (Toronto: Lester & Orpen Dennys,

1989), pp. 29–38. On Power, see Ward, ed., *A Party Politician*, pp. 43–45.

10　NAC, MG 30 D 150, Macphail diary. (Jones was the son of a former Liberal minister of militia and lieutenant governor of Nova Scotia, Alfred Gilpin Jones.)

11　On "clearing the battlefield," see report by Captain Hall, 27th Battalion, in RG 9 II B, vol. 3746.

12　*Instructions for the Training of Divisions*, 1916.

13　Erindale, Correll Papers, Correll to Lil, Sep. 11, 1916.

14　NAC, MG 30 E 475, Gosford memoir, pp. 10–11.

15　NAC, MG 30 E 442, Griffiths memoir, pp. 13–14. Later, as a brigadier, H.M. Dyer commanded the 7th Brigade.

16　Raymond LeBrun, cited in Macdonald, *They Called it Passchendaele*, p. 219.

17　NAC, MG 30 E 393, Foster memoirs, pp. 29–30.

18　RG 9 II B 2, vol. 3746, Strathy report, Nov. 1, 1917.

19　Noyes, *Stretcher Bearers*, p. 124.

20　Ellis, *The Sharp End of War*, pp. 169–70.

21　Lieutenant-Colonel W.L. Watt, cited by Adami in *War Story of the CAMC*, pp. 118–19.

22　Ellis, *The Sharp End of War*, pp. 170–72.

23　*Toronto Daily Star*, Mar. 27, 1917.

24　While "hospital blues" might be more comfortable than khaki serge uniforms, the wearers were banned from being served drinks in any otherwise friendly pub.

25　RG 9 II B 2, box 3746, "Convalescent Depots."

26　Ellis, *The Sharp End of War*, p. 169.

27　NAC, MG 30 E 446, Papers of Brigadier-General A.E. Ross, Memoirs.

28　Nicholson, *Canada's Nursing Sisters*, p. 84.

29　Ibid., pp. 365–77.

30　Elizabeth T. Paynter diary, September 1916 (lent by family).

31　IWM, Garnet Durham letters, May 15, 1915, pp. 28, 29.

32　NAC, MG 30 E 1, George Bell diary, p. 113.

33　NAC, MG 30 E 297, Maheux to his wife, n.d. [July 1916].

34　R.J. Manion, a surgeon from Port Arthur, encountered similar problems in the French army. See *A Surgeon in Arms*, pp. 163–64.

35　See Major E.H. Young, "The Care of Military Mental Patients," pp. 896 and *passim*. On Cobourg and Canadian attitudes, see Morton and Wright, *Winning the Second Battle*, pp. 27, 39.

36 See Macphail, *Official History: Medical Services*, p. 278, also pp. 276–79. For a modern review, see Brown, "Shell Shock in the Canadian Expeditionary Force, 1914–1918." See also Major Norman Q. Brill, "War Neuroses," *Journal of Laboratory and Clinical Medicine* 28, 1943, pp. 484 ff.

37 Lewis R. Yealland, *Hysterical Disorders of Warfare* (London, 1918), pp. 3, 8–23, and *passim*.

38 Lieutenant-Colonel C.K. Russell, "The Nature of War Neuroses," 61, p. 550 for citation. See also Russell, "Psychogenetic Conditions in Soldiers," pp. 227–37.

39 Erindale, Claude V. Williams Papers, Williams to mother, Dec. 28, 1916, p. 71.

40 On venereal disease and the CEF, see Cassell, *Secret Plague*, and Macphail, *Official History: Medical Services*, pp. 292–93.

41 See RG 9, II B 2, vol. 3746, War Diary and History of the Canadian Special Hospital, Etchinghill.

42 Ibid., War Diary, Witley Special Hospital, n.p.

43 Cassell, *Secret Plague*, pp. 127–29; RG 9 II B 2, vol. 3746, War Diary and History.

44 Macphail, *Official History: Medical Services*, p. 179.

45 RG 9 II B 2, vol. 3747, *History of the CADC*.

46 Colonel H.A. Bruce, "Report on the Canadian Army Medical Corps," cited in Bruce, *Politics and the CAMC*.

47 Morton, *Peculiar Kind of Politics*, p. 93; on medical problems and solutions, see pp. 94–95.

48 Cited in Carman, *Return of the Troops*, p. 99.

49 Adami, "Medicine and the War," p. 82.

50 Bernard Langdon Wyatt, "Industrial Medicine," *Canadian Medical Association Journal* 13, 1923, p. 114. See ibid., "Industrial Medicine: Its Motives and Merits," *Canadian Medical Association Journal* 13, 1923, pp. 662 and *passim*.

IX: FANNIGANS

1 Wise, *Canadian Airmen in the First World War*, pp. 647–48.

2 On the suspected deserter, see RG 24, vol. 6992; also John Cooke in McDougall, *Further Report*, 56.

3 Ussher's account of the circumstances of his capture is in NAC, MG 30 E 376.

4 McDougall, *Report of the Reparations Commissioner*, vol. 1, *Maltreatment*, p. 291. For an eyewitness, see NAC, MG 30 E 426, D.S. O'Brien memoir.

5   RG 9 II, vol. 4737, folder 152, Interrogation Report, Private F.J. Hamilton, 26th Battalion.

6   Philipson, *International Law and the Great War*, p. 252. Technically, since Bulgaria and Turkey had yet to ratify the 1907 convention, the belligerents were bound only by the 1898 agreement, but both sides tacitly accepted the later and slightly more comprehensive agreement. See Morton, *Silent Battle*, p. 10.

7   Hauptstadtarchiv Stuttgart, M1/11/Bn 800 Copy of remarks made in the course of conversation of the Canadian Brigadier-General Victor Williams by Captain Tettenborn, Grenadier Regiment Queen Olga, Jun. 26, 1916 (trans., Stephen Brown). Williams's evidence for Canadian attitudes was based, he claimed, on the preference for referring to the German enemy as "Fritz" rather than "Huns" or "Boche." An attendant German intelligence officer gravely confirmed that these were the words they found in Canadian letters. Having no artillery of its own in June 1916, the 3rd Division depended on the artillery of a former Indian Army formation, the Lahore Division. The Allied offensive began on July 1 at the Somme, the juncture between the British and French armies and well to the south of Ypres.

8   Major T.V. Scudamore, "Lighter Episodes in the Life of a Prisoner of War," *Canadian Defence Quarterly* 7/3 (April 1930), p. 397.

9   Pearson, *The Escape of a Princess Pat*, p. 81.

10 McCarthy, *The Prisoner of War in Germany*, pp. 54–55.

11 The best general accounts of camp conditions are in McCarthy, *The Prisoner of War in Germany*, and Jackson, *The Prisoners, 1914–18*.

12 McPherson, Horrocks, and Beveridge, *Official History: Medical Services: Hygiene*, pp. 148-49; NAC, MG 26 H, R.L. Borden Papers, RLB 1081, High Commissioner to P.E. Blondin, Jan. 15, 1917.

13 Anderson, *I, That's Me*, pp. 89–90.

14 McDougall, *Maltreatment*, pp. 139–40.

15 Canadian Bank of Commerce, *Letters from the Front*, vol. 1, p. 322.

16 James Brown Scott, *The Hague Conventions and Declarations of 1899 and 1907 Accompanied by Tables of Signatures, Ratifications and Adhesions of the Various Powers and Texts of Reservations*, 3d ed. (New York: Oxford University Press, 1918), p. 109. See also James Gerard, *My Four Years in Germany* (New York: George Doran, 1917).

17 McCarthy, *The Prisoner of War in Germany*, p. 178; Richard Speed, *Prisoners, Diplomats and the Great War: A Study in the Diplomacy of Captivity* (New York: Greenwood [1990]), p. 77.

18 McDougall, *Final Report of the Reparations Commissioner, 1932*, pp. 154–55.

19 See MG 30 E 204, Harry Howland, "March With Me" (unpublished ms.), pp. 183–97; RG 9, III, vol. 1124, statement of Private Langlois.

20 McDougall, *Maltreatment*, p. 275.

21 Ibid., p. 301.

22 McDougall, *Final Report*, p. 102.

23 McDougall, *Maltreatment*, pp. 212–13.

24 Robert Younger, *Report on the Employment in Coal and Salt Mines of British Prisoners of War in Germany*, Comd. 958 (London: HMSO, 1918), p. 2.

25 Ibid., p. 282.

26 RG 9 III, vol. 4757, folder 150, file 1, Statement by Lance Corporal Haley-Jones, 15th Battalion.

27 RG 9 III, vol. 4737, folder 150, file 1A. Alldritt was regarded by his friends in Winnipeg's élite as a man of character and integrity. The YMCA took him back after the war, but his back injury and failing eyesight left him increasingly disabled. He died at the age of fifty-two. NAC, MG 26 J, R.B. Bennett Papers, 383511-26.

28 CWRO, "Statement of Lance Corporal Haley-Jones," folder 152, f. 2. See also McDougall, *Final Report*, p. 57.

29 McDougall, *Maltreatment*, pp. 39–40. Lickers was a powerfully built man of twenty-six when he enlisted. He was a semi-paralyzed physical wreck when McDougall saw him in 1931. On other cases, see ibid., pp. 150, 182, and for others, *passim*.

30 RG 9 III D 1, vol. 4738, folder 154, 36-1-T, Private J.C. Thompson.

31 NAC, MG 30 E 33, Wilken, "Short Record."

32 RG 9 II B 2, vol. 3746, Adami file, Statement of Captain F.S. Park.

33 RG 9 III D 1, vol. 4737, folder 150, 36-1-B, statement of Private Claude Allan Beesley.

34 RG 9 III D 1, vol. 4738, file 154, 36-1-C, Private Arthur Corker; McDougall, *Maltreatment*, p. 251.

35 McClung, *Three Times and Out*, pp. 165–66. Obviously, allowances must be made for colourful prose but, apart from Germany's critical wartime food shortage, controlled starvation appears to have been a deliberate aspect of penal policy. Since it applied to German soldiers as well as war prisoners, German authorities complied with the Hague Convention.

36 On the policy for exchanges, see RG 9 III, Carson file, vol. 32, file 8-1-80.

37 RG 9 III, vol. 2922, P-254-33, report of Lieutenant-Colonel Claude G. Bryan to Colonel C.A. Hodgetts, Dec. 15, 1917.

38 Based on experience with Henri Beland, a former postmaster general interned for much of the war in Berlin despite efforts to have him repatriated, the government reminded those who sent such requests that direct intervention on behalf of a specific individual seemed to make the Germans

treat him more severely. True or not, it was a shrewd rebuttal to pestering relatives. RG 9 III, vol. 94, file 10-12-59x, Kemp to Ferguson, Mar. 14, 1918. See also ibid., J. Pitblado to Kemp, Jan. 25, 1918. See also NAC, Borden Papers, OC 261(1) Clarence J. McCuaig to Borden, Sep. 8, 1916, 29062 and *passim*.

39 RG 9 III, vol. 94, OMFC 1012–59; Lieutenant-Colonel Gerald Birks to Kemp, Oct. 29, 1918.

40 London *Daily Express*, Jan. 4, 1919.

41 As Sir Robert Borden explained to Kemp after meeting Currie in Paris: "he could never obtain the slightest evidence to lead him the belief that such an incident had occurred and he did not believe that it ever did occur" (NAC, MG 26 G I, OC 414, Borden to Kemp, Feb. 17, 1919, 55804). A typical story, reported by an American civilian who had shared a lengthy train journey with a Canadian soldier, insisted that the victim, discovered by Sergeant G. Lyons and forty-two others, was a Sergeant Brant of the 16th Battalion. Only the soldier, Lyons, and one other had allegedly survived the war. Currie personally interviewed Lyons, a former business associate in Vancouver, and discovered the story was groundless.

42 On the statue, see Tippett, *Art at the Service of War*, pp. 65, 81-87; RG 24 V 817, HQ 54-21-8-48, H.W. Brown A/DM-Director, National Gallery of Canada, May 13, 1930.

43 Mullins, *The Leipzig Trials*, pp. 205 and *passim*.

44 McDougall, *Maltreatment*, p. 262; MG 30 E 204, Howland, "March With Me," pp. 337–38.

45 McDougall, *Maltreatment*, pp. 34–35.

X: SOLDIER'S HEART

1 IWM, A.M. Munro to his father, Jun. 14, 1917, 146 overleaf.

2 Erindale, J.W.G. Clark Papers, Clark to sister, Oct. 20, 1916.

3 Ibid., Clark to father, Dec. 12, 1916.

4 Burns, *General Mud*, p. 26.

5 NAC, MG 30 E 393, Foster memoir, p. 28.

6 NAC, MG 30 E 297, Maheux to his wife, Apr. 12, 1916.

7 Erindale, Clark Papers, Clark to father, Aug. 27, 1916.

8 NAC, MG 30 E 297, Maheux to wife, Nov. 4, 1915.

9 Erindale, Correll Papers, Correll to Lil, Jul. 14, 1916.

10 NAC, MG 30 E 417, Frank Baxter memoir, pp. 12–13.

11 NAC, MG 30 E 1, George V. Bell memoir, pp. 134–35.

12 Roy, ed., *Journal of Private Fraser*, pp. 144–45. Fraser was badly wounded at Passchendaele when his officer led him and other members of an ammunition party through a German barrage. His right arm, almost torn off by shrapnel, never regained its strength (ibid., pp. 17, 313–16).

13 Ibid., p. 177.

14 NAC, MG 30 E 8, Creelman diary, Dec. 4, 1915.

15 IWM, 76/170/1, E.W. Russell, "A Private Soldier's Views on the Great War, 1914–1918," p. 22.

16 Defined in chapter III (from the French "*il n'y en a plus*").

17 Frederick Manning, *Her Privates We* (London: Peter Davies, 1930), p. 12.

18 NAC, MG 30 E 84, Bishop P.K. Fyson to Leckie, May 21, 1915.

19 Bank of Commerce, *Letters from the Front*, p. 337.

20 Raymond LeBrun, cited in Macdonald, *They Called it Passchendaele*, p. 229.

21 Noyes, *Stretcher Bearers*, p. 122.

22 RG 9 III, vol. 4364, folder 2 f S 1, 1st Division to Divisional Engineers, Nov. 11, 1916.

23 Percy Bowes Picken, Nov. 12, 1917 (letter made available by family).

24 Roy, ed., *Journal of Private Fraser*, p. 71.

25 It took the few survivors several days under fire to recover and bury the dead of their battalion. See Nicholson, *Fighting Newfoundlanders*, pp. 175-76.

26 See NAC, MG 26 H 1 a, R.L. Borden Papers, OC 325, and Wood, *Silent Witness*.

27 See RG 24, vol. 6993.

28 Erindale, Donald McKinnon Papers, Lieutenant J.C. Hannington to Mrs. McKinnon, Sep. 15, 1917.

29 Eridnale, Correll Papers, Eva Plewman to Mrs. Correll, Sep. 1916.

30 IWM, Joshua Strong Papers.

31 NAC, MG 30 E 1, George Bell, p. 103.

32 Ibid., fall, 1915, p. 68.

33 IWM, A.M. Munro to father, Dec. 4, 1916.

34 NAC, MG 30 E 297, Maheux to wife, Oct. 17, 1916.

35 RG 9 II, vol. 4939, AA & QMG 1 Division, "Report of the Canadian Staff Officers on Leave."

36 Ibid.

37 Noyes, *Stretcher Bearers*, pp. 164–66.

310

38 PC 2615, Oct. 28, 1916; Morton and Wright, *Winning the Second Battle*, pp. 159–60.

39 PC 447, Feb. 16, 1917. On administration, see NAC, Borden Papers, OC 33, "Memo No. 3 Respecting Work of the Department of Militia and Defence, February 1, 1916 to December 31, 1916," pp. 56–58; ibid., Memo No. 4, January 1, 1917, to December 31, 1917, pp. 24–25.

40 RG 9 III, vol. 178, 6-M-377, Carson to Hughes, Jun. 8, 1916.

41 Frank Bell, cited in Read, ed., *The Great War and Canadian Society*, p. 189.

42 NAC, Borden Papers, OC 267, M.C. Lewis to prime minister, Jun. 18, 1916. (Philip Morris of the CPF reported that the allowance had been cut off pending investigation of a report that Mrs. Lewis was receiving pay from her husband's former employer.)

43 Erindale, Hamilton Papers, Hamilton to Sara, Oct. 30, 1917.

44 For popular histories of Canada's anti-liquor campaign, see James H. Gray, *Booze: The Impact of Whiskey on the Prairie West* (Toronto: Macmillan, 1972), and Gerald A. Hallowell, *Prohibition in Ontario* (Toronto: Ontario Historical Society, 1972).

45 Erindale, Corey Papers, Bert Corey to Alf, May 17, 1917.

46 Dinesen, *Merry Hell*, p. 186.

47 Noyes, *Stretcher Bearers*, pp. 104–5.

48 NAC, Records of Courts Martial, 649-x-15470, Private Wm. Connolly.

49 Erindale, Hamilton Papers, Hamilton to Sara, Nov. 18, 1917.

50 See Records of Courts Martial, T-8694, 341-10-10; 602-12-6; see also T-8696, 694-H-4384.

51 NAC, MG 30 E 84, R.G.E. Leckie, Jan. 1, 1916.

52 See Noyes, *Stretcher Bearers*, pp. 166–68, and F.G. Scott, *The Great War as I Saw It* (Toronto: F.D. Goodchild, 1922). W.B. Woods recalled Scott as running needless dangers and causing needless apprehensions among troops he visited (letter to the author, Aug. 29, 1992).

53 On Canadian chaplains, see Duff Crerar, "Padres in No-Man's Land: Chaplains of the Canadian Expeditionary Force and the Great War" (unpublished ms., 1992).

54 See RG 9 III, vol. 4554, folder 1, f 66, 10th Canadian Field Ambulance.

55 IWM, John Sutton memoirs, p. 73.

56 See Morton, "Polling the Soldier Vote," *passim*. Soldiers who had no constituency could choose one, and Unionist agents persuaded men to switch to ridings where their votes were most likely to defeat anti-conscription Liberals. This generated such an outcry that few noticed that such votes had been

disallowed, at least outside England, by the chief election official, W.F. O'Connor.

57 NAC, MG 30 E 297, Maheux to his wife, Dec. 22, 1917.

58 NAC, MG 30 E 417, Frank Baxter memoirs, p. 10.

59 On the text, circumstances, and reactions, see Dancocks, *Sir Arthur Currie*, pp. 132–34, and W.D.B. Kerr, *Arms and the Maple Leaf.*

60 See L.L. Gordon and Edward C. Joslin, *British Battles and Medals*, 4th ed. (London, 1971), pp. 310–13.

61 IWM, Andrew M. Munro.

62 Roy, ed., *Journal of Private Fraser*, p. 84.

63 Some units devised their own distinctions. When the 5th and 7th battalions were mentioned in Haig's first dispatch for their successful raid, they adopted a coloured stripe, sewn on the cloth covers of their steel helmets. The battalions involved in the attack on Kitchener's Wood on April 24, 1915, adopted an oak-leaf design for their brass shoulder titles, still worn by the Calgary Highlanders. Wounds earned their sufferers a vertical gold stripe, worn above the left cuff.

64 RG 9 III, vol. 5307, 2nd Division training instructions, 1918.

65 Erindale, Woods Papers, Burt Woods memoirs, n.p.

66 Moran, *Anatomy of Courage*, p. 70.

67 Richardson, *Fighting Spirit.*

68 Erindale, Ernest Davies memoir.

69 Roy, ed., *Journal of Private Fraser*, p. 213.

70 Ibid., p. 81.

71 NAC, MG 30 E 1, George Bell, p. 114.

72 Records of Courts Martial, T-8965, 3093-1 Captain W.H. Allen, 15th Battalion. Allen's accuser, a sergeant, had been promoted to lieutenant and could therefore testify with an officer's status. Resentment against an officer promoted in Canada did not help Allen, though the evidence was also strong against him.

73 RG 9 III, vol. 3042, folder 216, vol. 7, Griesbach training circular, 1918.

74 Roy, ed., *Journal of Private Fraser*, p. 94.

75 Babington, *For the Sake of Example*, p. 7; see also Putkowski and Sykes, *Shot at Dawn.*

76 On the subject, see Morton, "The Supreme Penalty," pp. 346–51.

77 Gagnon, *Le 22e bataillon*, pp. 379–80.

78 Arthur Lapointe, cited by Gagnon in *Le 22e bataillon*, p. 264.

79 NAC, MG 30 E 1, George Bell, pp. 83–84.

80 Letter to the author from D.E. Pearson, n.d. [June 1983].

XI: RETURNED MEN

1 On facilities, see *Report of the Military Hospitals Commission*, pp. 17–32.

2 The British agreed, but it took two years of aristocratic trench warfare before their charities were displaced. See Wooton, *The Politics of Influence*, ch. 1.

3 On the Neely case, see RG 9 II A 1, vol. 185, A 3744. See also NAC, Caron Papers, vol. 98 f. 56380, Lieutenant-Colonel Grasett to Sir Adolphe Caron, Apr. 17, 1888 and *passim*.

4 On Mulloy, see RG 38, vol. 69, f 175; RG 7 G 21, vol. 365, f. 2425, and Special Committee, 1920, p. 210. Not everyone approved of the generosity: one man threatened to shoot someone if Mulloy got any more money! See Morton and Wright, *Winning the Second Battle*, pp. 11–12.

5 See Dearing, *Veterans in Politics*, for a modest view of the GAR's alleged depredations.

6 RG 38, vol. 225, f 8-62, *Minutes of the Interprovincial Conference*, Oct. 18–19, 1915.

7 Scammell, *Provision of Employment*, p. 5.

8 On Baker, see Campbell, *No Compromise*. See also *The Soldiers' Return*, pp. 24–25.

9 The Royal Commission on Pensions (Ralston Commission) reported 2,659 leg amputees and 1,143 men with a missing arm. See *Final Report*, Canada Sessional Papers, 203a, 1925, p. 51.

10 McCuaig, "From Social Reform to Social Service" 61/4, p. 486.

11 *The Soldiers' Return*, p. 44.

12 Ibid., p. 9.

13 Todd to Marjory Todd, Oct. 3, 1915, cited in Fialkowski, ed., *Todd*, p. 309.

14 Todd diary, Mar. 17, 1916, cited in ibid., p. 324.

15 English, *Shadow of Heaven*, p. 44–5 raises doubts about Pearson's memoirs, see Pearson, *Mike*, vol. I, p. 35.

16 Invalided Soldiers' Commission, *Occupational Therapy and Curative Workshops*.

17 Colonel A. Primrose, "Presidential Address," *Canadian Medical Association Journal* 9/1 (January 1919), pp. 8–9.

18 *Department of Soldiers' Civil Re-establishment*, p. 22.

19 See Morton and Wright, *Winning the Second Battle*, p. 95; RG 38, vol. 232, f 2310, Lougheed to Falconer, Nov. 4, 1918.

20 RG 38, vol. 225, f. 18-02 NB, Norman Parkinson to W.R. Caldwell, n.d. [September 1919].

21 See *The Soldiers' Return; A Cheerful Chat with Private Pat*; and *Le Soldat revient: Une causerie avec Poil-aux-Pattes* (Ottawa, 1917).

22 On Marlow's report and resignation, see *Report of the Special Committee on Returned Soldiers, 1917*, pp. 166–80, 182–130, 805–7; Morton and Wright, *Winning the Second Battle*, pp. 85–86.

23 Morton, "Noblest and Best," p. 81.

24 Macphail, *Official History: Medical Services*, p. 322.

25 *Toronto Daily Star*, Mar. 3, 1919.

26 Segsworth, *Retraining Canada's Disabled Soldiers*, p. 67. See also Todd, "The Meaning of Rehabilitation," p. 6.

27 NAC, MG 30 D 150, Macphail Papers, vol. XI, "Conversation with Lord Atholstan, 17 December 1917."

28 *Harris Turner's Weekly* 2 (January 1919).

29 In 1935, MacNeil was elected as a CCF member of Parliament. Defeated in 1940, he spent much of the rest of his life as a union and CCF organizer.

30 Some were involved in another mutiny at the notorious Calais prison, and at least one Canadian was sentenced to death. He was reprieved and eventually released after pressure from his father's Orange lodge. Sir Edward Kemp, a pillar of the order, understood his fraternal duty. See MG 27 II D 9, Kemp Papers, vol. 155, on Charles MacDonell. On the Nivelles mutiny, see RG 9 III, vol. 2232 D-6-29 and RG 9 III, vol. 93, f 10-12-50, vol. I.

31 Royal Commission to Inquire into…the Treatment of the men of the Canadian Expeditionary Force while on Board the Transport *Northland*…, *Report* (Ottawa, 1919).

32 Sir Arthur Currie's insistence that CEF battalions return as units under their own officers meant that the MSA men who had filled the ranks at the end of the war went home before veterans who had recovered from wounds and were still in the reinforcement stream. Another cause of the Kinmel riot was cancellation of two troopships that were condemned, in the light of the *Northland* enquiry, as inadequate for Canadian troops.

33 See Morton, "Kicking and Complaining: Demobilization Riots in the Canadian Expeditionary Force, 1918–19," pp. 334–60.

34 Maheux's hope that the promised furlough for Old Originals would be extended to his contingent was not fulfilled. Because he went to Murmansk,

his return to Canada occurred only in June 1919. See above.

35   In 1915, there were 60,688 passenger cars on Canadian roads; by 1919, there were 196,347. (*Historical Statistics of Canada*, 2d ed., series T-148).

36   See Gerald A. Hallowell, *Prohibition in Ontario* (Ottawa: Ontario Historical Society, publication no. 2, 1972), pp. 82–83, n 14.

37   Pearson, "Fitting in the Returned Men," *Maclean's Magazine* 32 (March 1919), pp. 27–28.

38   Van Paassen, *Days of Our Years*, p. 66.

39   On the bonus campaign, see Morton and Wright, "The Bonus Campaign, 1919–21: Veterans and the Campaign for Re-establishment," pp. 148–61.

40   See Morton and Wright, *Winning the Second Battle*, p. 183, n 32.

41   It vanished so fast that no complete run of the magazine, once the largest-circulation monthly in Canada, exists outside the Library of Congress.

42   Morton and Wright, *Winning the Second Battle*, pp. 208–9.

43   On the trial, see Sharpe, *The Last Day, The Last Hour*.

44   Morton and Wright, *Winning the Second Battle*, pp. 160–64.

45   Cited in Royal Commission on Pensions, *First Report* (Ottawa, 1923), p. 5. See also *The Veteran*, Jun. 24, and Sep. 9, 1923.

46   One aspect of the American "pension evil" was the practice of marrying young women to aged pensioners to guarantee them an income for the rest of their lives. The last "widow" of the War of 1812 died during the Korean War.

APPENDIX:
A STATISTICAL PROFILE OF THE CEF

1   Berton, *Vimy*, p. 21.

2   In *The Myth of the Digger*, Jane Ross reports that the Australians were different. In the first contingent of the Australian Imperial Force, 73 per cent were Australian born and, by the end of the war, the proportion was 82 per cent. At the time, 84.3 per cent of Australian males aged fifteen to sixty-four were Australian born.

3   As of October 31, 1917, as conscripts began to enrol, the CEF reported it had enlisted 438,806 men, of whom 194,473 were Canadian born, 215,769 were British born, and 26,564 claimed other birthplaces.

BIBLIOGRAPHY

1. DOCUMENTS AND PERSONAL PAPERS

a) National Archives of Canada

Records of the Department of Militia and Defence

Records of the Department of National Defence
(including Ministry of the Overseas Military Forces of Canada).

Personal Papers:

William J. Alldritt (MG 30 E 1)
Sir William Babtie (MG 30 E 3)
Harold Baldwin (MG 30 E 65)
John Bassett (MG 30 E 302)
Frank Baxter (MG 30 E 417)
George V. Bell (MG 30 E 113)
Richard Bedford Bennett (MG 26 K)
Sir Robert Laird Borden (MG 26 H)
Nicholas Garland Bradley (MG 30 E 341)
Louis Edward Breault (MG 30 E 532)
Henry Burdett-Burgess (MG 30 E 416)
Brooke Claxton (MG 32 B 5)
Claude C. Craig (MG 30 E 351)

John J. Creelman (MG 30 E 8)

Alan Fairfax Crosman (MG 30 E 36)

Felix J. Cullen (MG 30 E 45)

Sir Arthur Currie (MG 30 E 100)

William Curtis (MG 30 E 505)

Harold M. Daly (MG 27 II F 9)

G.M. Davis (MG 30 E 11)

Kenneth L. Duggan (MG 30 E 304)

Lou Elliott (MG 30 E 246)

R.K. Findlayson (MG 30 E 143)

Arthur James Foster (MG 30 E 393)

Sam Gagnon (MG 30 E 277)

Thomas Gosford (MG 30 E 475)

Aubrey Griffiths (MG 30 E 442)

Sir Willoughby Gwatkin (MG 30 E 51)

Frank Hazlewood (MG 30 E 170)

Edward Hilliam (MG 30 E 229)

Sophie Hoerner (MG 30 E 290)

Gordon Holder (MG 30 E 203)

Charles A. Hounsome (MG 30 E 476)

Harry Howland (MG 30 E 204)

Elmer Watson Jones (MG 30 E 50)

Sir Albert Edward Kemp (MG 27 II D 9)

J.V. Lacasse (MG 30 E 731)

R.G.E. Leckie (MG 30 E 84)

John Macfie (MG 30 E 427)

Roy Macfie (MG 30 E 427)

Frank Macfie (MG 30 E 427)

Duncan E. MacIntyre (MG 30 E 241)

Ian A. Mackenzie (MG 27 III B 5)

John P. McNab (G 30 E 42)

Sir Andrew Macphail (MG 30 D 150)

Francis Xavier Maheux (G 30 E 277)

Ernest Nelson (MG 30 E 459)

F.W. Newberry (MG 30 E 525)

David Stephen O'Brien (MG 30 E 426)

M.H.S. Penhale (MG 31 GG 21)

Sir George Perley (MG 27 II D 12)

James Roy Pond (MG 30 E 325)

Charles Gavan Power (MG 27 III B 19)

Ernest F. Pullen (MG 30 E 219)

Hugh Clapp Pullen (MG 30 E 353)

William Quinton (MG 30 E 162)

A.E. Ross (MG 30 E 446)

George Scott (MG 30 E 28)

Ernest Jasper Spillett (MG 30 E 209)

David Sobey Tamblyn (MG 30 E 451)

Russell C. Tubman (MG 30 E 285)

Sir Richard Turner (MG 30 E 46)

Hugh McIntyre Urquhart (MG 30 E 75)

John Ussher (MG 30 E 376)

Albert C. West (MG 30 E 32)

The Rev. Gillies Wilken (MG 30 E 33)

b) Imperial War Museum, London

Stanley Brittain

Garnet W. Durham

Magnus Hood

John Keddie

William Kerr

W.S. Lighthall

A.G. May

Andrew M. Munro

E.W. Russell

Joshua Strong

John E. Sutton

N.E. Tyndale-Syscoe

Frank H. Underhill

c) Erindale College, University of Toronto, Mississauga

Peter F. Anderson

Kenneth Austin

J. Gordon Beatty

Adelbert F. Brayne

A.J. Chadwick

Joseph W.G. Clark

William Commins

Albert Corey

Robert Correll

Stanley Cribb

Carroll Cudlipp

N.F. Davidson

Ernest Davies

E.N. Edmonds

Alvin Ferguson

J.A. Gagnier

Adair Gibson

Ernest W. Hamilton

Allan A. Hawkes

Roy E. Henley

A.M. Jackson

C.L. Kirby

G.S. McCulloch

Alex C. Mackenzie

Donald C. McKinnon

Hector McKinnon

William Miller

Angus Mowat

A.H. Paull

D.E. Pearson

E.J. Pope

M.C. Purvis

Norman Rawson

E.C. Rowland

Ian Sinclair

Albert Smith

Robert P. Somerville

W. Gordon Stepler

William E. Taylor

A.F. Telfer

S.T. Thompson

Marion Wallwyn

William Wallwyn

Walter Ward

Claude V. Williams

Frederick J. Williams

William B. Woods

G.C. Wright

Lawrence L. Youell

d) University of Western Ontario

D'Arcy Leonard

Harold Leonard

e) Ontario Archives

William Miller (MV 2260)

2. PRINTED BOOKS AND MANUSCRIPTS

Adami, J.G. *The War Story of the CAMC.* Vol. 1: *The First Contingent, 1914–1915.* London, n.d.

Anderson, Lt.-Col. Peter. *I, That's Me: Escape from German Prison Camp and Other Adventures.* Ottawa: Bradburn Printers, n.d.

Armstrong, Elizabeth. *The Crisis of Quebec, 1914–1918*. New York: AMS, 1967; Toronto: McClelland & Stewart, 1974.

Army and Navy Veterans. *Proceedings of the First Convention of the Army and Navy Veterans in Canada*. Winnipeg, 1918.

Ashworth, Tony. *Trench Warfare, 1914–1918: The Live and Let Live System*. London: Macmillan, 1980.

Babington, Anthony. *For the Sake of Example: Capital Courts Martial, 1914–1920*. London: Leo Cooper, 1983.

Bayonet Training 1916. Ottawa: Government Publishing Office, 1916.

Beckett, Ian F.W., and Keith Simpson, eds. *A Nation in Arms: A Social Study of the British Army in the First World War*. Manchester: University of Manchester Press, [1985].

Berger, Carl. *The Sense of Power: Studies in the Ideas of Canadian Imperialism, 1867–1914*. Toronto: University of Toronto Press, 1970.

———. ed. *Conscription, 1917*. Toronto: University of Toronto Press, 1969.

Bernhardi, Friedrich von. *On War of Today*, 2 vols. London: Rees, 1912.

Berton, Pierre. *Vimy*. Toronto: McClelland & Stewart, 1986.

Bidwell, Shelford, and Dominick Graham. *Fire-Power: British Army Weapons and Theories of War, 1904–1945*. London: Allen and Unwin, 1982.

Bird, W.R. *And We Go On*. Toronto: Hunter Rose, 1930.

———. *Ghosts Have Warm Hands*. Toronto: Clarke, Irwin, 1960.

Bishop, C.W. *The Canadian YMCA in the Great War*. Toronto: YMCA, 1924.

Bishop, W.A. *Winged Warfare*. New York: George Doran, [1918].

Black, Ernest Garson. *I Want One Volunteer*. Toronto: Ryerson [1965].

Blake, Robert, ed. *The Private Papers of Douglas Haig, 1914–1919*. London: Eyre & Spottiswoode, 1952.

Blunden, Edmund. *Undertones of War*. Harmondsworth: Penguin Books, 1982.

Borden, Henry, ed. *Letters to Limbo*. Toronto: University of Toronto Press, 1971.

Borden, R.L. *Memoirs*, 2 vols. Toronto: Macmillan, 1938.

Boyd, Captain F.F. *Strategy in a Nutshell*. Aldershot: Gale & Polden, 1915.

Brereton. J.M. *The British Soldier: A Social History from 1661 to the Present Day*. London: Bodley Head, 1986.

Brittain, Vera. *Testament of Youth*. New York: Seaview Books, 1980.

Brown, R.C. *Robert Laird Borden: A Biography*, 2 vols. Toronto: Macmillan, 1980.

Brown, R.C., and G.R. Cook. *Canada, 1896–1921: A Nation Transformed*. Toronto: McClelland & Stewart, 1974.

Bruce, Herbert A. *Politics and the Canadian Army Medical Corps.* Toronto: Wm. Briggs, 1919.

———. *Varied Operations.* Toronto: Clarke Irwin, 1958.

Burns, E.L.M. *General Mud.* Toronto: Clarke Irwin, 1970.

Cairns, Alex, and A.H. Yetman. *The History of the Veteran Movement, 1916 to 1925, and of the Canadian Legion, 1926 to 1935,* 2 vols. Winnipeg: Manitoba Veteran, [1961].

Campbell, Marjorie Wilkins. *No Compromise: The Story of Colonel Baker and the* CNIB. Toronto: McClelland & Stewart, 1965.

Canadian Bank of Commerce. *Letters from the Front, 1914–1919.* Toronto: Canadian Bank of Commerce, 1919.

Carman, Francis. *The Return of the Troops: A Plain Account of the Demobilization of the Canadian Expeditionary Force.* Ottawa: King's Printer, 1920.

Carnegie, David. *The History of Munitions Supply in Canada.* London: Longmans, 1925.

Carter, David J. *Behind Barbed Wire: Alien and German Prisoner of War Camps in Canada, 1914–1946.* Calgary: Tumbleweed Press, 1980.

Cassar, George. *Beyond Courage.* Ottawa: Oberon Press, 1985.

Cassel, Jay. *The Secret Plague: Venereal Disease in Canada, 1839–1939.* Toronto: University of Toronto Press, 1987.

Chaballe, Joseph-Henri. *L'Épopée du vingt deuxième.* Montreal: Les Éditions Chantecler, 1961.

Chadwick, W.R. *The Battle for Berlin, Ontario: An Historical Drama.* Waterloo: Wilfrid Laurier University Press, 1992.

Chapman, Guy. *A Passionate Prodigality: Fragments of Autobiography.* New York: Holt, Rinehart & Winston, 1966.

Charlton, Peter. *Pozières, 1916: Australians on the Somme.* London: Leo Cooper, 1986.

Coppard, George. *With a Machine Gun to Cambrai.* London: HMSO, 1969.

Corbett, E.A. *Henry Marshall Tory: Beloved Canadian.* Toronto: Ryerson Press, 1954.

Corbett-Smith, E.A. *The Retreat from Mons.* London: Cassell, 1916.

Corneloup, Claude. *La Coccinelle du 22e: Roman canadien.* Montreal: Beauchemin [1934].

———. *L'Épopée du vingt-deuxième.* Montreal: La Presse, 1919.

Craig, Grace Morris. *But It Is Our War.* Toronto: University of Toronto Press, 1981.

Cruttwell, C.R.M.F. *A History of the Great War, 1914–1918*, 2d ed. Oxford: Clarendon Press, 1936.

Dancocks, Daniel G. *Sir Arthur Currie: A Biography*. Toronto: McClelland & Stewart, 1985.

———. *Legacy of Valour: The Canadians at Passchendaele*. Edmonton: Hurtig, 1986.

———. *Spearhead to Victory: Canada and the Great War*. Edmonton: Hurtig, 1987.

———. *Welcome to Flanders Fields: The First Canadian Battle of the Great War: Ypres, 1915*. Toronto: McClelland & Stewart, 1988.

———. *Gallant Canadians: The Story of the Tenth Canadian Infantry Battalion, 1914–1919*. Calgary: Calgary Highlanders Regimental Fund Trust, 1990.

Dark, Stanley. *The Life of Sir Arthur Pearson*. London: Hodder & Stoughton, [1922].

Dearing, Mary R. *Veterans in Politics: The Story of the Grand Army of the Republic*. Westport, Conn.: Greenwood Press, 1974.

Diltz, Bert. *Stranger Than Fiction*. Toronto: McClelland & Stewart, 1969.

Dinesen, Thomas. *Merry Hell: A Dane with the Canadians*. London: Jarrolds, [1930].

Dornbusch, C.E. *The Canadian Army, 1855–1965: Lineages and Regimental Histories*. Cornwallville, N.Y.: Hope Farm Press, 1966.

Douglas, J.H. *Captured: Sixteen Months as a Prisoner of War*. Toronto: McClelland, Goodchild & Stewart, 1918.

Duguid, A.F. *Official History of the Canadian Forces in the Great War, 1914–19, General Series*. Vol. 1: *Chronicle, August 1914–September, 1915*. Ottawa: King's Printer, 1938.

Du Picq, Charles-Arden. *Etudes sur le combat: Combats antiques et modernes*. Paris, 1942.

Durkin, Douglas. *The Magpie*. Toronto: University of Toronto Press, 1974.

Durnford, H.G. *The Tunnellers of Holzminden with a Side Issue*. Cambridge: Cambridge University Press, 1920.

Eayrs, James. *In Defence of Canada*. Vol. 1: *From the Great War to the Great Depression*. Toronto: University of Toronto Press, 1964.

Ellis, John. *Eye-Deep in Hell: The Western Front, 1914–1918*. London: Croom Helm, 1975.

———. *The Social History of the Machine Gun*. London: Croom Helm, 1975.

———. *The Sharp End of War: The Fighting Man in World War II*. New York: Scribner's, 1980.

English, John. *The Decline of Politics: The Conservatives and the Party System,*

1901-20. Toronto: University of Toronto Press, 1977.

English, John A. *On Infantry.* New York: Praeger, 1981.

————. *The Canadian Army and the Normandy Campaign: A Study of Failure in High Command.* New York: Praeger, 1991.

England, Robert. *Discharged: A Commentary on Civil Re-establishment of Veterans in Canada.* Toronto: Macmillan, 1943.

————. *Living, Learning, Remembering: Memoirs of Robert England.* Vancouver: University of British Columbia Centre for Continuing Education, 1980.

Farrar-Hockley, Anthony. *Death of an Army.* London: Barker, [1967].

Farwell, Byron. *Mr. Kipling's Army.* New York: Norton, 1981.

Fetherstonhaugh, R.C. *The 13th Battalion, Royal Highlanders of Canada, 1914–1919.* Montreal: 13th Battalion, R.H.C., 1925.

————. *The Royal Montreal Regiment, 14th Battalion, C.E.F., 1914–1925.* Montreal: The Gazette, 1927.

————. *The 24th Battalion, C.E.F. Victoria Rifles of Canada.* Montreal: The Gazette, 1930.

————. *The Royal Canadian Regiment, 1883–1933.* Fredericton: Centennial Print, 1936.

Fialkowski, Bridget, ed. *John L. Todd, 1876–1949: Letters.* Senneville, PQ: Quebec, privately published, 1977.

Francis, R.D. *Frank A. Underhill: Intellectual Provocateur.* Toronto: University of Toronto Press, 1986.

Frost, Leslie M. *Fighting Men.* Toronto: Clarke Irwin, 1967.

Fussell, Paul. *The Great War and Modern Memory.* New York: Oxford University Press, 1975.

Gaffen, Fred. *Forgotten Soldiers.* Penticton, B.C.: Theytus Books, 1985.

Gagnon, Jean-Pierre. *Le 22e bataillon (canadien-français), 1914-1919: Une étude socio-militaire.* Québec: Presses de l'université Laval, 1986.

Gammage, Bill. *The Broken Years: Australian Soldiers in the Great War.* Canberra: Australian National University Press, 1974.

Gibbons, Arthur. *A Guest of the Kaiser: The Plain Story of a Lucky Soldier.* Toronto: J.M. Dent, 1919.

Gibbs, Philip. *Now It Can Be Told.* New York: Harper & Bros., 1920.

Giles, John. *The Ypres Salient.* London: Leo Cooper, 1970.

Godley, Hugh, ed. *The Manual of Military Law,* 6th ed. London: HMSO, 1914.

Goodspeed, D.J. *The Road Past Vimy: The Canadian Corps, 1914-1918.* Toronto: Macmillan, 1969.

Gordon, C.W. *Postscript to Adventure: The Autobiography of Ralph Connor.*

Toronto: Ryerson, 1975.

Graham, Howard. *Citizen and Soldier: The Memoirs of Lieutenant-General Howard Graham.* Toronto: McClelland & Stewart, 1987.

Granatstein, J.L., and J.M. Hitsman. *Broken Promises: A History of Conscription in Canada.* Toronto: Oxford, 1977; Toronto: Copp-Clark Pitman, 1985.

Graves, Robert. *Goodbye to All That.* London: Cassell, 1957.

Great War Veterans' Association. *Report of the First Convention, Winnipeg, Manitoba.* Winnipeg, 1917.

Greenhous, Brereton. *Dragoon: The Centennial History of the Royal Canadian Dragoons, 1883–1983.* Belleville: n.p., 1983.

Griesbach, William Antrobus. *I Remember.* Toronto: Ryerson, [1946].

Gudmundsson, Bruce I. *Stormtroop Tactics: Innovation in the German Army, 1914-1918.* New York: Praeger, 1988.

Haber, L.F. *The Poisonous Cloud: Chemical Weapons in the First World War.* Oxford, Clarendon Press, 1986.

Harris, Garrard. *The Redemption of the Disabled: A Study of Programmes of Rehabilitation for the Disabled of War and Industry.* Toronto: McClelland & Stewart, 1919.

Harris, Stephen J. *Canadian Brass: The Making of a Professional Army, 1860–1939.* Toronto: University of Toronto Press, 1988.

Harrison, Charles Yale. *Generals Die in Bed.* New York: Morrow, 1930.

Haycock, Ronald. *Sam Hughes: The Public Career of a Controversial Canadian, 1885–1916.* Waterloo: Wilfrid Laurier University Press, 1986.

Hayes, Joseph. *The Eighty-Fifth in France and Flanders.* Halifax: Regal Printers, 1920.

Hopkins, J. Castell. *The Province of Ontario in the War.* Toronto: Warwick Bros. & Rutter, 1919.

Hunt, M. Stuart. *Nova Scotia's Part in the Great War.* Halifax: Nova Scotia Veteran Publishing Co., 1920.

Hyatt, A.M.J. *General Sir Arthur Currie: A Military Biography.* Toronto: University of Toronto Press, 1987.

Instructions on Bombing. Part 2: Training and Employment of Bombers. London: HMSO, November 1917.

Instructions for the Training of Divisions for Offensive Action. London: War Office, 1916.

Jackson, Robert. *The Prisoners, 1914–18.* London: Routledge, 1989.

Johnson, Paul B. *Land Fit for Heroes: The Planning of British Reconstruction, 19160–1919.* Chicago: University of Chicago Press, 1968.

Jones, Richard Seelye. *A History of the American Legion*. Indianapolis: Bobbs-Merrill, 1946.

Kerr, Wilfred Brenton. *Shrieks and Crashes, Being Memoirs of Canada's Corps, 1917*. Toronto: Hunter Rose, 1929.

———. *Arms and the Maple Leaf: Memories of Canada's Corps, 1918*. Seaforth: Huron Expositor, 1943.

Kerry, A.J., and W.A. McDill. *The History of the Corps of Royal Canadian Engineers*, vol. 1. Ottawa: Military Engineers' Association, 1962.

Laffin, John. *Tommy Atkins: The Story of the English Soldier*. London: Cassell, 1966.

Lamb, David. *Mutinies, 1917-1920*. Oxford and Cambridge, n.p., n.d.

Lang, W.R. *The Organization, Administration and Equipment of His Majesty's Land Forces in Peace and War*. Toronto: Copp Clark, 1916.

Lapointe, Arthur. *Soldier of Quebec 1916–1919*. Montreal: Garnad, 1931.

Leed, Eric. *No Man's Land: Combat and Identity in World War I*. Cambridge, 1979.

Legion, Canadian [Jane Dewar, ed.] *True Canadian War Stories: From Legion Magazine*. Toronto: Lester & Orpen Dennys, 1986.

Lucas, Sir Charles, ed. *The Empire at War*. Vol. 2: *Canada* (by F.H. Underhill). London, Oxford: Clarendon Press, 1923.

Luciuk, Lubomyr. *A Time for Atonement: Canada's First National Internment Operations and the Ukrainian-Canadians, 1914–1920*. Ottawa: Ukrainian National Committee [1988].

Macdonald, Lyn. *They Called it Passchendaele: The Story of the Third Battle of Ypres and the Men Who Fought in It*. London: Michael Joseph, 1978.

———. *Somme*. London: Michael Joseph, 1981.

———. *1914*. London: Michael Joseph, 1987.

Macfie, John. *Letters Home* [letters from Macfie brothers]. Meaford: Oliver Graphics, 1990.

MacLaren, Roy. *Canadians in Russia, 1918–1919*. Toronto: Macmillan, 1976.

MacLeod, J.N. *A Pictorial Record and Original Muster Roll of the 29th Battalion, C.E.F.*. Vancouver: R.P. Latta, 1919. [account by Capt. H.J. Biggs]

Macphail, Sir Andrew. *Official History of the Canadian Forces in the Great War, 1914–1919: Medical Services*. Ottawa: King's Printer: 1925.

McCarthy, Daniel J. *The Prisoner of War in Germany: The Care and Treatment of the Prisoner of War with a History of the Development of the Practice of Neutral Inspectorate*. New York: Moffatt, Yard & Co., 1918.

McClung, Nellie. *Three Times and Out as Told by Private M.C. Simmons*. Toronto: Thomas Allen, 1918.

McDonald, F.B., and John J. Gardner. *The Twenty-Fifth Battalion, Canadian Expeditionary Force: Nova Scotia's Famous Regiment in World War One*. Sydney: City Printers, 1983.

McDougall, Errol M. *Report of the Royal Commission for the Investigation of Illegal Warfare Claims and for the Return of Sequestered Property in Necessitous Cases: Interim Report*. Ottawa: King's Printer, 1931; *Supplementary Report*. Ottawa: King's Printer, 1931; *Special Report upon Armenian Claims*. Ottawa: King's Printer, 1931; *Report of the Commission on Reparations: Maltreatment of Prisoners of War*. Ottawa: King's Printer, 1932; *Reparations, 1932: Further Report*. Ottawa: King's Printer, 1933; *Reparations, 1932: Final Report*. Ottawa: King's Printer, 1933.

McLennan, J.S. *What the Military Hospitals Commission Is Doing*. Ottawa: King's Printer, 1918.

McMullen, Fred, and Jack Evans. *Out of the Jaws of Hunland: The Stories of Corporal Fred McMullen, Sniper, and Private Jack Evans, Bomber, Canadian Soldiers Three Times Captured and Finally Escaped from German Prison Camps*. Toronto: William Briggs, 1918.

McMurtrie, Douglas C. *The Disabled Soldier*. New York: Macmillan, 1919.

McPherson, W.G., W.H. Horrocks, and W.W.O. Beveridge. *History of the Great War Based on Official Documents: Medical Services: Hygiene of the Great War*, vol 2. London: HMSO, 1923.

McWilliams, J.L., and J.R. Steel. *The Suicide Battalion*. Edmonton: Hurtig, 1978.

———. *Gas!* St. Catharines: Vanwell Publishing, 1985.

Manion R.J. *Life Is an Adventure*. Toronto: Ryerson Press, 1936.

———. *A Surgeon in Arms*. New York: Doran, 1918.

Manning, Frederick. *The Middle Parts of Fortune: Somme & Ancre, 1916*. London: Peter Davies, 1929.

Manual of Military Cooking and Dietary: Mobilization, 1915. London: HMSO, 1915.

Mathieson, William B. *My Grandfather's War: Canadians Remember the First World War*. Toronto: Macmillan, 1977.

Mearsheimer, John. *Liddell Hart and the Weight of History*. Ithaca, N.Y.: Cornell University Press, 1988.

Memorandum for Camps of Instruction, 1914. Ottawa: Department of Militia and Defence, 1914.

Middlebrook, Martin. *The First Day at the Somme: 1 July 1916*. New York: W.W. Norton, [1972].

Mitchell, T.J., and G.M. Smith. *History of the Great War Based on Official Documents: Medical Services: Casualties and Medical Statistics of the Great War*. London: HMSO, 1931.

Moore, Mary M. *The Maple Leaf's Red Cross: The War Story of the Canadian Red Cross Overseas*. London: Skeffington & Son, 1919.

Moore, William. *The Thin Yellow Line*. London: Leo Cooper, 1974.

Moran, Charles McMoran. *The Anatomy of Courage*. London: Constable, 1945.

Morris, Philip. *The Canadian Patriotic Fund: A Record of Its Activities from 1914 to 1919*. Toronto: n.p., n.d.

Morton, Desmond. *Ministers and Generals: Politics and the Canadian Militia, 1868–1904*. Toronto: University of Toronto Press, 1970.

———. *The Last War Drum: The North-West Campaign of 1885*. Toronto: Hakkert, 1972.

———. *The Canadian General: Sir William Otter*. Toronto: Hakkert, 1974.

Morton, Desmond. *A Peculiar Kind of Politics: Canada's Overseas Ministry in the First World War*. Toronto: University of Toronto Press, 1982.

———. *A Military History of Canada: From Champlain to the Gulf War*, 3d ed. Toronto: McClelland & Stewart, 1992.

———. *Silent Battle: Canadian Prisoners of War in Germany, 1914–1919*. Toronto: Lester Publishing, 1992.

Morton, Desmond, and J.L. Granatstein. *Marching to Armageddon: Canadians and the Great War, 1914–1919*. Toronto: Lester & Orpen Dennys, 1989.

Morton, Desmond, and Glenn Wright. *Winning the Second Battle: Canadian Veterans and the Return to Civilian Life, 1915–1930*. Toronto: University of Toronto Press, 1987.

Moynihan, Michael. *Black Bread and Barbed Wire: Prisons in the First World War*. London: Leo Cooper, 1978.

Mullins, Claud. *The Leipzig Trials: An Account of the War Criminals' Trials and a Study of German Mentality*. London: H.F. and G. Witherby, 1921.

Murray, W.W. *The History of the 2nd Canadian Battalion (East Ontario Regiment), CEF in the Great War, 1914–1919*. Ottawa: n.p., 1947.

Nicholson, G.W.L. *Official History of the Canadian Army in the First World War: Canadian Expeditionary Force, 1914–1919*. Ottawa: Queen's Printer, 1962.

———. *The Fighting Newfoundlanders: A History of the Royal Newfoundland Regiment*. St. John's: Government of Newfoundland, [1964].

———. *The Gunners of Canada: The History of the Royal Regiment of Canadian Artillery*, vol. 1. Toronto: McClelland & Stewart, 1967.

———. *Canada's Nursing Sisters*. Toronto: Samuel, Stevens & Hakkert, 1976.

———. *Seventy Years of Service: A History of the Royal Canadian Army Medical Corps*. Ottawa: Borealis Press, 1977.

Notes for Infantry Officers on Trench Warfare. London: HMSO, March 1916.

Notes on Gunnery. General Staff, May 1918.

Noyes, Frederick W. *Stretcher Bearers on the Double…The History of the Fifth Canadian Field Ambulance.* Toronto: Hunter Rose, [1937].

Organization of Shell-Hole Defences. General Staff, December 1917.

Overseas Military Forces of Canada. *Report, 1918.* London: n.p., 1919.

Owen, Edward. *1914: Glory Departing.* London: Buchan & Enright, 1986.

Pearson, George. *The Escape of a Princess Pat: Being the Full Account of the Capture and Fifteen Months Imprisonment of Corporal Edwards of the Princess Patricia's Canadian Light Infantry and His Final Escape from Germany into Holland.* New York: George Doran, 1918.

Pearson, L.B. *Mike: The Memoirs of the Right Honourable Lester B. Pearson, PC, CC, OM, OBE, MA, LLD,* vol. 1. Toronto: University of Toronto Press, 1972.

Peat, Harold. *Private Peat.* Indianapolis: Bobbs-Merrill, 1918.

Pedley, J.H. *Only This: A War Retrospect.* Ottawa: Graphic Publishers, [1927].

Pettigrew, Eileen. *The Silent Enemy: Canada and the Deadly Flu of 1918.* Saskatoon: Western Producer Prairie Books, 1981.

Phillipson, Coleman. *International Law and the Great War.* London: Unwin, [1915].

Platoon Organization. London: War Office, January 1917.

Pope, Maurice. *Soldiers and Politicians: The Memoirs of Lieutenant-General Maurice A. Pope.* Toronto: University of Toronto Press, 1962.

Pottle, Frederick A. *Stretchers: The Story of a Hospital Unit on the Western Front.* New Haven: Yale University Press, 1929.

Preston, R.A. *Canada and "Imperial Defense": A Study of the Origins of the British Commonwealth Defense Organization, 1867–1919.* Toronto: University of Toronto Press, 1967.

———. *Canada's R.M.C.: A History of the Royal Military College.* Toronto: University of Toronto Press, 1969.

Prost, Antoine. *Les anciens combattants et la societe française: 1914–1939.* Paris: Presses de la Fondation nationale des sciences politiques, [1987].

Provencher, Jean. *Québec sous la loi des mésures de guerre, 1918.* Trois-Rivières: Boréal-Express, 1971.

Putkowski, Julian. *The Kinmel Park Camp Riots, 1919.* Clwyd: Flintshire Historical Society, 1989.

Putkowski, Julian, and Julian Sykes. *Shot at Dawn.* Barnsley: Wharncliffe Publishing, 1989.

Rawling, Bill. *Surviving Trench Warfare: Technology and the Canadian Corps.* Toronto: University of Toronto Press, 1992.

Rawlinson, James H. *Through St. Dunstan's to Light.* Toronto: Thos. Allen, 1919.

Read, Daphne, et al. *The Great War and Canadian Society: An Oral History.* Toronto: New Hogtown Press, 1975.

Reid, Gordon, ed. *Poor Bloody Murder: Personal Memoirs of the First World War.* Oakville: Mosaic Press, 1980.

Regulations for the Use of the Provost Marshal's Branch, British Armies in France. London: HMSO, 1917.

Richardson, Frank. *Fighting Spirit: A Study of Psychological Factors in War.* London: Leo Cooper, 1978.

Robinson, Catherine Beverly. *Soldier Citizens.* Toronto, 1918.

Rodney, William. *Joe Boyle, King of the Klondike.* Toronto: McGraw-Hill Ryerson, 1974.

Ross, Jane. *The Myth of the Digger: The Australian Soldier in Two World Wars.* Sydney: Hale & Iremonger, 1985.

Roy, R.H., ed. *The Journal of Private Fraser, 1914–1918, Canadian Expeditionary Force.* Victoria: Sono Nis Press, 1985.

———. *For Most Conspicuous Bravery: A Biography of Major General George R. Pearkes V.C., Through Two World Wars.* Vancouver: University of British Columbia Press, 1977.

Russenholt, E.S. *Six Thousand Canadian Men: Being the History of the 44th Battalion, Canadian Infantry, 1914–1919.* Winnipeg: De Montfort Press, 1932.

Scammell, Ernest. *The Provision of Employment for Members of the Canadian Expeditionary Force on Their Return to Canada and the Re-education of Those Who Are Unlikely to Follow Their Previous Occupations Because of Disability.* Ottawa: King's Printer, 1916.

Scudamore, Major T.M. *Lighter Episodes in the Life of a Prisoner of War.* Aldershot: Gale & Polden, 1933.

Seely, J.E.B. *Adventure.* London: Heinemann, 1930.

Segsworth, Walter. *Retraining Canada's Disabled Soldiers.* Ottawa: King's Printer, 1920.

Serle, Geoffrey. *John Monash: A Biography.* Melbourne: Melbourne University Press, 1982.

Sharpe, Robert. *The Last Day, the Last Hour: The Currie Libel Trial.* Toronto: The Osgoode Society, 1988.

Singer, H.C. *History of the 31st Canadian Infantry Battalion, C.E.F.* n.d., n.p. [1938].

Slowe, Peter, and Richard Woods. *Fields of Death: Battle Scenes of the First World War.* London: Robert Hale, 1986.

Smithers, A.J. *A New Excalibur: The Development of the Tank, 1909–1939*. London: Grafton Books, 1988.

Smythe, Conn. *If You Can't Beat 'Em in the Alley*. Toronto: McClelland & Stewart, 1981.

Socknat, Thomas. *Witness Against War: Pacifism in Canada, 1900–1945*. Toronto: University of Toronto Press, 1987.

The Soldier's Return: A Cheerful Chat with Private Pat/Le Soldat revient: Une Causerie avec Poil-aux-Pattes. Ottawa: King's Printer, 1919.

The Soldiers' Return: How the Canadian Soldier Is Being Refitted for Industry. Ottawa: King's Printer, 1919.

Statistics of the Military Effort of the British Empire. London: HMSO, 1922.

Steinhart, Allan L. *Civil Censorship in Canada during World War I*. Toronto: Unitrade Press, 1986.

Strachan, Tony, ed. *In the Clutch of Circumstances: Reminiscences of Members of the Canadian National Prisoners' of War Association*. Victoria: Cappis Press, 1985.

Swettenham, J.A. *To Seize the Victory: The Canadian Corps in World War I*. Toronto: Ryerson, 1965.

———. *Allied Intervention in Russia, 1918–1919, and the Part Played by Canada*. Toronto: Ryerson Press, 1967.

———. *McNaughton*, vol. 1. Toronto: Ryerson Press, 1969.

———. *Valiant Men: Canadian Victoria Cross and George Cross Winners*. Toronto: Hakkert, 1973.

Swyripa, Frances, and John Herd Thompson, eds. *Loyalties in Conflict: Ukrainians in Canada During the Great War*. Edmonton: University of Alberta Press, 1983.

Terraine, John. *Douglas Haig: The Educated Soldier*. London: Hutchison, 1963.

———. *General Jack's Diary, 1914–1918*. London: Eyre & Spottiswoode, 1964.

———. *Impacts of War: 1914 and 1916*. London: Hutchison, 1970.

———. *The Road to Passchendaele: The Flanders Offensive of 1917: A Study in Inevitability*. London: Sidgewick & Jackson, 1977.

———. *To Win a War: 1918: The Year of Victory*. London: Sidgewick & Jackson, 1978.

———. *The Smoke and the Fire: Myths and Anti-Myths of War, 1861–1945*. London: Sidgewick & Jackson, 1980.

———. *White Heat: The New Warfare, 1914-1918*. London: Sidgewick & Jackson, 1982.

Thompson, John H. *The Harvests of War: The Prairie West, 1914–1918*. Toronto: McClelland & Stewart, 1978.

Thorn, J.C. *Three Years a Prisoner in Germany: The Story of Major J.C. Thorn, A First Canadian Contingent Officer who was Captured by the Germans at Ypres on April 24th, 1915, Relating His Many Attempts to Escape (Once Disguised as a Widow) and Life in Various Camps and Fortresses, with Illustrations.* Vancouver: Cowan and Brookhouse, 1919.

Tippett, Maria. *Art at the Service of War: Canada, Art and the Great War.* Toronto: University of Toronto Press, 1984.

Topp, C. Beresford. *The 42nd Battalion, C.E.F., Royal Highlanders of Canada in the Great War.* Montreal: The Gazette [1931].

Training and Employment of Divisions. London: War Office, January 1918.

Travers, T.H.E. *The Killing Ground: The British Army, The Western Front and the Emergence of Modern Warfare, 1900–1918.* Boston and London: Allen and Unwin, 1987.

Trythall, A.J. *Boney Fuller: The Intellectual General, 1878–1966.* London: Cassell, 1971.

Tuchman, Barbara. *The Guns of August.* New York: Macmillan, 1952.

Urquhart, H.M. *The History of the 16th Battalion (The Canadian Scottish) Canadian Expeditionary Force, in the Great War, 1914–1919.* Toronto: Macmillan, 1932.

———. *Arthur Currie: The Biography of a Great Canadian.* Toronto: Macmillan, 1950.

Van Paassen, Pierre. *Days of Our Years.* New York: Dial Press, 1946.

Voight, Thomas. *Combed Out.* London: Jonathan Cape, 1920.

Ward, Norman, ed. *A Party Politician: The Memoirs of Chubby Power.* Toronto: Macmillan, 1966.

Warren, Arnold. *Wait for the Waggon: The History of the Royal Canadian Army Service Corps.* Toronto: McClelland & Stewart, 1961.

Wecter, Dixon. *When Johnny Comes Marching Home.* Boston: Houghton Mifflin, 1944.

Whalen, Robert W. *Bitter Wounds: German Victims of the Great War, 1914–1918.* Ithaca, N.Y.: Cornell University Press, 1984.

Williams, Jeffrey. *Byng of Vimy: General and Governor-General.* Toronto: University of Toronto Press, 1992.

Williams, Ralph Hodder. *Princess Patricia's Canadian Light Infantry, 1914–1919.* London: Hodder & Stoughton, 1923.

Wilson, Barbara. *Ontario and the First World War, 1914–1918.* Toronto: University of Toronto Press, 1977.

Wilson, Trevor. *The Myriad Faces of War: Britain and the Great War, 1914–1918.* Cambridge: Polity Press, 1986.

Winter, C.F. *The Hon. Sir Sam Hughes: Canada's War Minister, 1911–1916*. Toronto: Macmillan, 1931.

Winter, Denis. *Death's Men*. Harmondsworth: Allen Lane, 1975.

———. *The First of the Few*. Harmondsworth: Allen Lane, 1979.

———. *Haig's Command: A Reassessment*. New York: Viking, 1991.

Wise, S.F. *Canadian Airmen and the First World War: The Official History of the Royal Canadian Air Force*, vol. 1. Toronto: University of Toronto Press, 1980.

Wood, H.F. *Vimy*. Toronto: Macmillan, 1967.

———. *Silent Witness*. Toronto: Hakkert, 1974.

Woods, Walter F. *Rehabilitation: A Combined Operation*. Ottawa: Queen's Printer, 1953.

Wooton, Graham. *The Politics of Influence: British Ex-Servicemen, Cabinet Decisions and Cultural Change (1917–1957)*. London: Routledge & Kegan Paul, 1963.

Worthington, Clara. *"Worthy": A Biography of Major-General F.F. Worthington*. Toronto: Macmillan, 1961.

Worthington, Larry. *Amid the Guns Below: The Story of the Canadian Corps (1914–1918)*. Toronto: McClelland & Stewart, 1965.

3. ARTICLES

Adami, Colonel George. "Medicine and the War." *Canadian Medical Association Journal* 9, 1919.

Archibald, Edward. "A Brief Survey of Some Experiences in the Surgery of the Present War." *Canadian Medical Association Journal* 6, 1916.

Armstrong, George E. "The Influence of the War on Surgery, Civil or Military." *Canadian Medical Association Journal* 9, 1919.

Bélanger, Réal. "Albert Sévigny et la participation des Canadiens-français à la grande guerre (1919–1918)." In *Canada as a Military Power*, ed. by W.A.B. Douglas and Desmond Morton. Ottawa: RIHM, 1982.

Bell, F. McKelvey. "Effects of Wet and Cold: Trench Foot." *Canadian Medical Association Journal* 6, 1916.

Bishop, W.A. "Soldiering." *The Goat*, February 1927.

Bliss, J.M. "The Methodist Church and World War I." *Canadian Historical Review* 49/3, September 1968.

———. "War Business as Usual: Canadian Munitions Production, 1914–1918." In

Mobilization for Total War: The Canadian, American and British Experience, 1914–1918, 1939–1945, ed. by N.F. Dreisziger. Waterloo: Wilfrid Laurier University Press, 1981.

Boudreau, J.A. "Western Canada's 'Enemy Aliens' in World War One." *Alberta Historical Review* 12/1, Winter 1964.

Bray, R.M. "Fighting as an Ally: The English-Canadian Patriotic Response to the Great War." *Canadian Historical Review* 61/2, June 1980.

———. "A Conflict of Nationalities: The Win the War and National Unity Convention, 1917." *Journal of Canadian Studies* 15/4, Winter 1981.

Brown, R.C. "Whither are we being shoved?: Political Leadership in Canada During World War I." In *War and Society in North America,* ed. by J.L. Granatstein and R.D. Cuff. Toronto: Nelson, 1971.

———. "Sir Robert Borden, The Great War and Anglo-Canadian Relations." In *Character and Circumstance: Essays in Honour of Donald Grant Creighton,* ed. by J.S. Moir. Toronto: Macmillan, 1974.

Brown, R.C., and Donald Loveridge. "Unrequited Faith: Recruiting the C.E.F., 1914–1918." *Revue Internationale d'Histoire Militaire* 51, 1982.

Brown, R.C., and Desmond Morton. "The Embarrassing Apotheosis of a 'Great Canadian': Sir Arthur Currie's Personal Crisis in 1917." *Canadian Historical Review* 60/1, March 1979.

Brown, Thomas E. "Shell Shock in the Canadian Expeditionary Force, 1914–1918: Canadian Psychiatry in the Great War." In *Health, Disease and Medicine: Essays in Canadian History,* ed. by C.G. Roland. Hamilton: Hannah Foundation, 1984.

Bruce, Herbert A. "Surgical Efficiency in an Army Medical Service." *Canadian Medical Association Journal* 9, 1919.

Buckley, Suzann, and Janice Dickin McGiniss. "Venereal Disease and Public Health Reform in Canada." *Canadian Historical Review* 63, 1982.

Cuff, Robert. "Organizing for War: Canada and the United States During World War I." *Historical Papers,* 1969.

Dempsey, James. "The Indians and World War One." *Alberta History,* Summer 1983.

Dionne, Raoul. "Journal d'un aumônier de la guerre 1914." *Les Cahiers de la Société historique acadienne* 17/2, avril-juin 1986.

Durocher, René. "Henri Bourassa, les évêques et la guerre de 1914–1918." *Historical Papers,* 1971.

English, John. "The 'Riddle of the Trenches.'" *Canadian Defence Quarterly* 15/2, Autumn 1985.

Gauvreau, Michael. "War, Culture and the Problem of Religious Certainty:

Methodist and Presbyterian Church Colleges, 1914-1933." *Journal of the Canadian Church Historical Society* 29, April 1987.

Girard. Camil. "Le *Times* de Londres et la conscription militaire au Canada." *Etudes canadiennes/Canadian Studies* 22, 1987.

Goodspeed, D.J. "Prelude to the Somme: Mont Sorrel, June, 1916." In *Policy by Other Means*, ed. by Michael Cross and Robert Bothwell. Toronto: Clarke, Irwin, 1972.

Graham, Dominick. "*Sans Doctrine*: British Army Tactics in the First World War." In *Men at War: Politics, Technology and Innovation in the Twentieth Century*, ed. by Tim Travers and Christon Archer. Chicago: Precedent, 1982.

Greenhous, Brereton. "…'The position was desperate, if not fatal': The Canadian Cavalry Brigade at Moreuil Wood, 30 March 1918." *Canadian Defence Quarterly* 17/4, Spring 1988.

———. "'It Was Chiefly a Canadian Battle': The Decision at Amiens, 8–11 August 1918." *Canadian Defence Quarterly* 18/2, Autumn 1988.

Harris, Stephen. "From Subordinate to Ally: The Canadian Corps and National Autonomy, 1914–1918." In *Canada as a Military Power*, ed. by W.A.B. Douglas and Desmond Morton. Ottawa: RIHM, 1982.

Howard, Michael. "'Men Against Fire': The Doctrine of the Offensive in 1914." In *Makers of Modern Strategy: From Macchiavelli to the Nuclear Age*, ed. by Peter Paret, Gordon A. Craig, and Felix Gilbert. Princeton: Princeton University Press, 1986.

Hughes, S.H.S. "Sir Sam Hughes and the Problem of Imperialism." *Historical Papers*, 1956.

Hyatt, A.M.J. "Official History in Canada." *Military History* 30/3, Summer 1966.

———. "Sir Arthur Currie and Conscription: A Soldier's View." *Canadian Historical Review* 50/3, September 1969.

———. "Canadian Generals in the First World War and the Popular View of Military Leadership." *Social History* 12/24, November 1979.

Kay, Z. "A Note on Canada and the Formation of the Jewish Legion." *Jewish Social Studies* 29, July 1967.

Kearney, Kathryn. "Canadian Women and the First World War." *Women's Studies/Cahiers de la femme* 3/1, 1981.

Kerr, W.B. "Historical Literature on Canada's Participation in the Great War." *Canadian Historical Review* 15/4, December 1933; 16/1, March 1934.

Knox, F.A. "Canadian War Finance and the Balance of Payments, 1914–1918." *Canadian Journal of Economics and Political Science* 7/2, May 1940.

———. "Ukrainians and Internment Operations in Ontario during the First World War." *Polyphony* 10, 1988.

Macfie, John. "Letters Home." *The Beaver* 69/5, October-November 1989.

McCuaig, Katherine. "From Social Reform to Social Science: The Changing Role of Volunteers: The Anti-Tuberculosis Campaign, 1900–1930." *Canadian Historical Review* 61/4, December 1980.

McGinnis, Janice Dickin. "From Salvarsan to Penicillin: Venereal Disease Control in Canada, 1919–1965." *Historical Papers*, 1979.

Morton, Desmond. "French Canada and War: The Military Background to the Conscription Crisis of 1917." In *War and Society in North America*, ed. by J.L. Granatstein and R.D. Cuff. Toronto: Nelson, 1971.

———. "The Supreme Penalty: Canadian Deaths by Firing Squad in the First World War." *Queen's Quarterly* 79/3, Winter 1972.

———. "Sir William Otter and Internment Operations in Canada during the First World War." *Canadian Historical Review* 55/1, March 1974.

———. "The Short, Unhappy Life of the 41st Battalion, c.e.f." *Queen's Quarterly* 81/1, Spring 1974.

———. "Polling the Soldier Vote: The Overseas Campaign in the 1917 General Election." *Journal of Canadian Studies* 10/4, November 1975.

———. "Junior but Sovereign Allies: The Transformation of the Canadian Expeditionary Force, 1914–1918." In *The First British Commonwealth: Essays in Honour of Nicholas Mansergh*, ed. by Norman Hillmer and Philip Wigley. London: Frank Cass, 1980.

———. "Kicking and Complaining: Demobilization Riots in the Canadian Expeditionary Force, 1918–1919." *Canadian Historical Review* 61/3, September 1980.

———. "The Limits of Loyalty: French Canadian Officers and the First World War." In *The Limits of Loyalty*, ed. by Edgar Denton iii. Waterloo: Wilfrid Laurier University Press, 1980.

———. "Noblest and Best: Retraining Canada's War Disabled." *Journal of Canadian Studies* 16, 1981.

———. "Resisting the Pension Evil: Bureaucracy, Democracy and Canada's Board of Pension Commissioners, 1916–1933." *Canadian Historical Review* 68/2, June 1987.

Morton, Desmond, with Glenn Wright. "The Bonus Campaign, 1919–21: Veterans and the Campaign for Reestablishment." *Canadian Historical Review* 64/2, June 1983.

Patch, F.S. "The Military Aspect of the Venereal Disease Problem in Canada." *Canadian Journal of Public Health* 8, 1917.

Robin, Martin. "Registration, Conscription and Independent Labour Politics, 1916–1917." *Canadian Historical Review* 47/2, June 1966.

Roy, Reginald H. "The Battle for Courcelette, September, 1916: A Soldier's View." *Journal of Canadian Studies* 16/3-4, Autumn-Winter 1981–82.

――――. "Vimy Ridge—A View from the Ranks." *Canadian Defence Quarterly* 13/2, Autumn 1983.

Russell, C.K. "Study of Certain Psychogenetic Casualties Among Soldiers." *Canadian Medical Association Journal* 7, 1917.

――――. "Psychogenetic Conditions in Soldiers: Their Aetiology, Treatment and Final Disposal." *Canadian Medical Week*, Toronto, 1918.

――――. "The Nature of War Neuroses." *Canadian Medical Association Journal* 61, 1939.

St. Louis, E. "Memorandum on Canadian Indians in the Two World Wars." *Report of the Department of Indian Affairs*, Ottawa, 1950.

Scammell, Ernest. "Canadian practice in Dealing with Crippled Soldiers." *American Journal of Care for Cripples* 5, 1917.

"A Sergeant"; "A Year in German Military Hospitals." *Saturday Westminster Gazette*, January 6, 1917.

Sharpe, Christopher A. "The 'Race of Honour': An Analysis of Enlistments and Casualties in the Armed Forces of Newfoundland: 1914–1918." *Newfoundland Studies* 4/1, Spring 1988.

Strakhovsky, L.H. "The Canadian Artillery Brigade in North Russia, 1918–1919." *Canadian Historical Review* 39/2, June 1958.

Thompson, John H. "The Beginning of Our Regeneration: The Great War and Western Canadian Reform Movements." *Historical Papers*, 1972.

Todd, John L. "The Meaning of Rehabilitation." *Annals of the American Academy of Political and Social Science* 80, November 1918.

Travers, Timothy E. "Allies in Conflict: The British and Canadian Official Historians and the Real Story of Second Ypres (1915)." *Journal of Contemporary History* 24/2, April 1989.

Vince, D.M.A.R. "The Acting Overseas Sub-Militia Council and the Resignation of Sir Sam Hughes." *Canadian Historical Review* 31/1, March 1950.

――――. "Development of the Legal Status of the Canadian Military Forces, 1914-19, as related to Dominion Status." *Canadian Journal of Economics and Political Science* 20/3, August 1954.

Walker, James St. G. "Race and Recruitment in World War I: Enlistment of Visible Minorities in the Canadian Expeditionary Force." *Canadian Historical Review* 70/1, March 1989.

Wallace, John F. "The First Armoured Cars; A Very Canadian Story." *Canadian Defence Quarterly* 11/3, Winter 1981.

Willms, A.M. "Conscription, 1917: A Brief for the Defence." *Canadian Historical*

Review 37/4, December 1956.

Wise, S.F. "The Borden Government and the Formation of a Canadian Flying Corps, 1911–1916." In *Policy by Other Means*, ed. by Michael Cross and Robert Bothwell. Toronto: Clarke, Irwin, 1972.

Wright, H.P. "Suggestions for a Further Classification of Cases of So-called Shell Shock." *Canadian Medical Association Journal* 7, 1917.

Wrong, G.M. "Canada and the Imperial War Cabinet." *Canadian Historical Review* 1/1, March 1920.

Young, Major E.H. "The Care of Military Mental Patients." *Canadian Medical Association Journal* 9, 1919.

Young, W.R. "Conscription, Rural Depopulation and the Farms of Ontario, 1917–1919." *Canadian Historical Review* 53/3, September 1972.

INDEX